MAKING LAW WORK

MAKING LAW WORK
Chinese Laws in Context

EDITORS
MATTIAS BURELL
MARINA SVENSSON

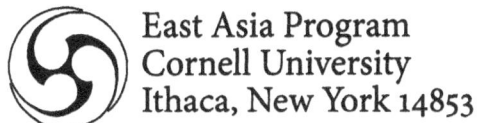

East Asia Program
Cornell University
Ithaca, New York 14853

The Cornell East Asia Series is published by the Cornell University East Asia Program (distinct from Cornell University Press). We publish books on a variety of scholarly topics relating to East Asia as a service to the academic community and the general public. Standing Orders, which provide for automatic notification and invoicing of each title in the series upon publication are accepted.

If after review by internal and external readers a manuscript is accepted for publication, it is published on the basis of camera-ready copy provided by the author who is responsible for any copyediting and manuscript formatting. Alternative arrangements should be made with approval of the Series. Address submission inquiries to CEAS Editorial Board, East Asia Program, Cornell University, 140 Uris Hall, Ithaca, New York 14853-7601.

Number 154 in the Cornell East Asia Series
Copyright ©2011 by Mattias Burell and Marina Svensson. All rights reserved.
ISSN: 1050-2955
ISBN: 978-1-933947-24-2 hardcover
ISBN: 978-1-933947-54-9 paperback
Library of Congress Control Number: 2011920465

25 24 23 22 21 20 19 18 17 16 15 14 13 12 11   9 8 7 6 5 4 3 2 1

CAUTION: Except for brief quotations in a review, no part of this book may be reproduced or utilized in any form without permission in writing from the author. Please address all inquiries to Mattias Burell and Marina Svensson in care of the East Asia Program, Cornell University, 140 Uris Hall, Ithaca, NY 14853-7601.

*We dedicate this book to Cai Dingjian,
a great mentor and friend to all of us working
in the field of China law studies*

Contents

Acknowledgments   ix

Theoretical Frameworks

1. Making Law Work in China   1
   Marina Svensson

2. Assessing Implementation of Law in China: What Is the Standard?   33
   Randall Peerenboom

3. Putting Law in Context: Some Remarks on the Implementation of Law in China   69
   Håkan Hydén

Institutions and Actors in Implementation Work

4. Chinese Courts in Law Implementation   103
   Jonas Grimheden

5. People's Congresses Involvement in Law Implementation: The Case of Environmental Protection Laws   143
   Oscar Almén

6. From Nothing to Something: Development of a Legal Aid System in China   187
   Hatla Thelle

Norms, Politics, and the Law

7 Cultural Heritage Protection in the People's Republic of China: Preservation Policies, Institutions, Laws, and Enforcement in Zhejiang 225
   Marina Svensson

8 The Legitimacy of Law in China: The Case of "Black Internet Cafés" 267
   Johan Lagerkvist

9 Twists and Turns: Anticorruption Law in Beijing 297
   Flora Sapio

Distributive and Regulative Policies and Laws

10 Policy Dilution and Equity Problems: Implementing Housing Policy in China 335
   Mattias Burell

11 Regulating Land and Pollution at Lake Dianchi: Compliance and Enforcement in a Chinese and Comparative Perspective 367
   Benjamin van Rooij

Contributors 405

Index 409

Acknowledgments

We would like to acknowledge the financial support generously provided by the Swedish Research Council and the Swedish International Development Agency that made our research possible during the period 2004–2007. These two organizations also provided support for an international conference on law implementation that we organized in Beijing in 2006, The Swedish Research Council in addition provided essential support for subsequent work on this book. The support provided by the Centre for East and Southeast Asian Studies, Lund University is greatly appreciated. The Centre sponsored a workshop on Chinese law and society in 2005, housed several other meetings, as well as financed Flora Sapio's postdoctoral fellowship during 2004–2006. Our thanks to the Swedish School of Advanced Asia Pacific Studies that sponsored the visit of Professor He Bing at the Centre in 2005. We would like to further thank the Danish Centre for Human Rights and Hatla Thelle for organizing a workshop discussing this project in 2005 as well as a meeting discussing the book in 2007.

Marina Svensson would like to acknowledge support from the Swedish Collegium for Advanced Study for her research stay in Uppsala in the fall of 2004. Mattias Burell would like to thank the Sociology Department at Wuhan University for successful cooperation with the household survey that was carried out in 2006. Hatla Thelle would like to thank the Danish Council for Independent Research/Social Sciences for a research grant received during 2005–2007. Jonas Grimheden would like to thank participants in the Asia Law Colloquium at Cornell Law School for feedback on earlier drafts of this text. Grimheden has also benefited greatly from discussions with Robert S. Summers. Vreni Hockenjos and Kathy Wimsatt. In addition to the overall funding for this project, Grimheden benefited from an individual grant from the Söderberg Foundations. Benjamin van Rooij's chapter is an adapted version of the introduction and conclusion of his Ph.D. dissertation, *Regulating Land and Pollution in China, Lawmaking, Compliance, and Enforcement; Theory and Cases* (Leiden: Leiden University Press, 2006). It is based on research made possible by generous grants from the Dutch Ministry of Education, Culture and Sciences and the Leiden University Fund. The author would also like to thank members of his committee, including Jan Michiel Otto, Jianfu Chen, Peter Ho, Robert A. Kagan, Wim Huisman, Wim Voermans, and Adriaan Bedner, for comments on earlier versions of his paper.

Many individuals have been supportive of our project and participated in different meetings, workshops, and the final conference. We are particularly grateful for constructive discussions and input from Børge Bakken, Jean-Pierre Cabestan, Cai Dingjian, Chen Jianfu, He Bing, Stanley Lubman, Jan Michiel Otto, and Michael Palmer.

Theoretical Frameworks

1
Making Law Work in China

MARINA SVENSSON

Law Implementation as a Research Field: Empirical and Multidisciplinary Studies of Law-In-Action

There is a scholarly consensus that whereas China in the past thirty years has made impressive progress when it comes to lawmaking and the adoption of new laws, there is a huge gap between laws on paper and the actual implementation of these laws and regulations.[1] But is China really doing so poorly when it comes to law implementation as is generally assumed? What is the evidence for such an assertion and how can one measure the level of implementation? The aim of this book is to provide some in-depth studies of the situation for law implementation in various policy areas and legal fields

---

[1] See for example Jianfu Chen, "Implementation of Law in China—An Introduction," in *Implementation of Law in the People's Republic of China*, eds. Jianfu Chen, Li Yuwen, and Jan-Michiel Otto (The Hague: Kluwer Law International, 2002); *Chinese Law: Context and Transformation* (Leiden/Boston: Martinus Nijhoff Publishers, 2008); Stanley Lubman, "Looking for law in China," *Columbia Journal of Asian Law*, vol. 20 (Fall 2006); *Bird in a Cage: Legal Reform in China after Mao* (Stanford: Stanford University Press, 1999); Randall Peerenboom, *China's Long March Toward Rule of Law* (New York: Cambridge University Press, 2002); and Donald C. Clarke, ed., *China's Legal System: New Developments, New Challenges*, (Cambridge: Cambridge University Press, 2008).

in China. The book thus tries to identify the underlying problems and analyze why, how, and when implementation succeeds or fails. The focus is both on institutional, political, as well as economic factors, and the interactions between these factors.

Since the legal reforms took off in China in the early 1980s, Western scholars have in increasing numbers turned their attention to the study of the Chinese legal system. This scholarly attention has undergone important shifts over time that reflect the increasing complexity of the Chinese legal system and changes in Chinese society, as well as more diverse theoretical and disciplinary perspectives among the scholars themselves.[2] Earlier studies predominantly consisted of documentary-based and descriptive analyses of different laws and legal institutions, including the lawmaking activities of the National People's Congress.[3] These works focused more on the macro level and were somewhat removed from the daily workings of the legal system. They therefore did not tell us much about law-in-action and how laws were implemented at the local level. Many works have focused on the broader issues related to legal reforms, including the development of new institutions and areas of law, and the prospects for the rule of law in an authoritarian context.[4] In the

---

2 For an overview of the development of American research on the Chinese legal system, see Stanley Lubman, "The Study of Chinese Law in the United States: Reflections on the Past and Concerns about the Future," *Washington University Global Studies Law Review* 2, no. 1 (2003): 1–35.

3 Representative works in the latter category include Kevin O'Brien, *Reform Without Liberalization, China's National People's Congress and the Politics of Institutional Change* (New York: Cambridge University Press, 1990); Murray Scot Tanner, *The Politics of Lawmaking in China: Institutions, Processes, and Democratic Prospects* (Oxford: Clarendon Press, 1999); and Jan Michael Otto et al., *Law-Making in the People's Republic of China* (The Hague: Kluwer Law International, 2000).

4 For two recent works discussing the implications of the legal reforms in the current political system, see Suisheng Zhao (ed.), *Debating Political Reform in China: Rule of Law vs. Democratization* (Armonk: M.E. Sharpe, 2006) and Randall Peerenboom, *China Modernizes: Threat to the West or Model for the Rest?* (New York: Oxford University Press, 2007).

1970s and 1980s, many Western studies focused on criminal law, but with the deepening of the economic reforms, studies on commercial and financial law have become more commonplace. In recent years, studies on administrative law, environmental law, gender and law, labor law, international law, human rights, and so forth have mushroomed as these fields have seen significant developments in China and come to permeate people's everyday lives.[5] With the maturing of the legal system and the growth of the legal professions, several scholars have also turned their attention to a study of lawyers, the police, and judges.[6]

The edited volume by Chen, Li, and Otto (2002) was the first concerted effort to address the issue of law implementation in a more comprehensive way. They mainly focused on the institutional framework, including court reforms, the role of the National People's Congress, judicial efforts of legal enforcement, and improvements of the Chinese legal profession. Several recent works have

---

5 Examples include Ching Kwan Lee, *Against the Law: Labor Protests in China's Rustbelt and Sunbelt* (Berkley: University of California Press, 2007) and Hong Lu, *China's Death Penalty: History, Law and Contemporary Practices* (London: Routledge, 2009), which show the dynamic and widening scope of Chinese law studies.

6 Although it has sometimes been difficult to get access to some of these legal professions and their institutions there are, however, some excellent examples of recent empirical and fieldwork-based research on lawyers, legal aid centers, and the courts. On lawyers see, Ethan Michelson, "The Practice of Law as an Obstacle to Justice: Chinese Lawyers at Work," *Law & Society Review* 40 (1): 1–38, and "Lawyers, Political Embeddedness, and Institutional Continuity in China's Transition from Socialism," *American Journal of Sociology* 113 (2): 352–414; Wu Peng, "The good, the bad and the legal: Lawyering in China's wild west," *Columbia Journal of Asian Law*, Vol. 21 (2008); and Hualing Fu and Richard Cullen, "Weiquan (Rights Protection) Lawyering in an Authoritarian State: Building a Culture of Public Interest Lawyering," *China Journal* 59 (2008): 111–127. For works on the courts, see Susan Trevaskes, *Courts and Criminal Justice in Contemporary China* (Lanham: Lexington Press, 2007), and Margaret Y. K. Woo and Yaxin Wang, "Civil Justice in China: An Empirical Study of Courts in Three Provinces," *American Journal of Comparative Law* 53 (2005). See also Thelle and Grimheden in this book and their discussion of the work of others in the field.

provided more ethnographic accounts of law implementation at the local level.⁷

Legal scholars have dominated much of the study of the Chinese legal system but sociologists have addressed issues related to deviancy, crime, and social control.⁸ As laws and legal processes now penetrate more areas of Chinese society and people's lives, scholars increasingly focus on law-in-action. The greater importance of law in all aspects of Chinese society has furthermore led to a sociopolitical turn in the study of Chinese law, and a growing interest from disciplines besides law, such as sociology and political science, which enrich our understanding of law implementation issues. The sociopolitical turn has produced new insights into how laws are implemented, used, abused, and resisted by both state actors and individual citizens. It has also yielded important insights into how legal awareness is embedded in, and informs, individual behavior and institutional performance.

This deeper understanding of how law works in China is in no small part a result of the fact that sociologists and political scientists ask different questions than legal scholars, and analyze the functioning of the legal system within a sociopolitical context. Political scientists for example bring to the field a longstanding interest in issues related to state capacity and bureaucratic and institutional fragmentation that are useful for a study of law implementation.⁹

---

7 See, for example, Benjamin van Rooij, *Regulation of Land and Pollution in China: Lawmaking, Compliance, and Enforcement; Theory and Cases* (Leiden: Leiden University Press, 2006).

8 For a recent edited volume in this field, see Børge Bakken (ed.), *Crime, Punishment, and Policing in China* (Lanham: Rowman & Littlefield, 2005).

9 Some early important works by political scientists deserve special mentioning as they focused on issues of policy implementation of high relevance for studies on law implementation. See David Lampton, *Policy Implementation in Post-Mao China* (Berkeley and Los Angeles: University of California Press, 1987), and Kenneth Lieberthal and David Lampton, *Bureaucracy, Politics and Decision Making in Post-Mao China* (Berkeley and Los Angeles: University of California

Sociologists are interested in issues related to institutional culture, legal and social norms, and social movements, and provide important conceptual tools for understanding discrepancies between law on paper and in reality. For their part, China scholars bring to the field an understanding of the historical and cultural environment that underpins the current legal system.[10] In addition, social scientists bring new methods to the study of law, such as the use of interviews and surveys, which complement analyses of law texts traditionally undertaken by legal scholars.[11]

One example of this new sociopolitical turn in legal studies is the volume edited by Diamant, Lubman, and O'Brien (2005). The book addresses the relationship between law and society, and the place of law in Chinese society, asking questions such as how, when, and to whom the law matters, and for what purposes it is used.[12] The volume includes chapters on, among other things, administrative litigation on the countryside and labor disputes.

Like the contributors in the Diamant, Lubman, and O'Brien volume, the authors in this volume represent different disciplines, such as political science, sociology of law, China studies, as well as legal studies. The attempt has been to encourage a multidisciplinary approach and draw upon insights from both sociology of law and

---

Press, 1992), and Kevin J. O'Brien and Li Lianjiang, "Selective Policy Implementation in Rural China," *Comparative Politics*, vol. 31, no. 2 (January 1999): 167–186.

10 See Klaus Muhlhahn, *Criminal Justice in China: A History* (Boston: Harvard University Press, 2009).

11 For an article addressing and discussing various methods and problems while conducting fieldwork on legal issues in China, see Bin Liang and Hong Lu, "Conducting Fieldwork in China: Observations on Collecting Primary Data Regarding Crime, Law, and the Criminal Justice System," *Journal of Contemporary Criminal Justice* 22, no. 2 (2006): 157–172.

12 See the various contributions in Neil J. Diamant, Stanley B. Lubman, and Kevin J. O'Brien (eds.), *Engaging the Law in China* (Stanford, California: Stanford University Press, 2005).

political science when studying legal institutions and law implementation processes. A multidisciplinary approach is called for since the process of implementing laws is influenced by many different factors, including the political system, levels of economic development, and the social structure and cultural tradition of Chinese society. As legal scholar Otto puts it: "To what extent and how law is implemented can only be established by sociolegal and multidisciplinary research, including the sociology and anthropology of law, political science, public administration, economics, and, last but not least, history."[13]

Whereas the Chen, Li, and Otto volume took a more top-down approach and focused on state actors and institutions, and the Diamant, Lubman and O'Brien volume, in contrast, favored a bottom-up approach that focused on how Chinese citizens engage with the law, the present book tries to position itself somewhere in between. Although we realize that different state institutions are of central importance in the law implementation process, we also want to bring in a bottom-up approach that takes into account the input of local institutions as well as acknowledges the role of nonstate actors, including the role of the media. The distinctive features of each law and policy area, as well as issues of access and possibilities for fieldwork, however, meant that some of the case studies pay more attention to state institutions and top-down processes, whereas others focus more on and emphasize bottom-up actors and forces. Since successful implementation of laws depends on the legitimacy of political and legal institutions, and on the existence of underpinning social norms, the book pays particular attention to the development and relation between changing norms and laws (see Hydén in this volume).

---

[13] Jan Michiel Otto, "Toward an Analytical Framework: Real Legal Certainty and Its Explanatory Factors," in Chen, Li, and Otto, *Implementation of Law in the People's Republic of China*, p. 28.

Overview of Policy Areas: Questions of Selection and Representativity

The majority of the contributors study law implementation processes in selected policy and legal areas. The different areas that have been chosen for study are anticorruption policies, cultural heritage preservation, environmental protection, housing reform polices, Internet cafe regulations, and legal aid. The choice of policy and legal areas was in most cases a result of the different scholars' research interests. When the original Swedish research group applied for research funding for a joint project on law implementation, we had an idea of trying to cover as diverse a field as possible and include dynamic policy areas of social and economic importance. We consciously decided to exclude civil and criminal law from our study and rather focus on the social and economic field. This choice reflects the fact that societal and economic relations are becoming increasingly law-based and contested. We also attempted to include both areas characterized by contestations (such as environmental issues, cultural heritage preservation, and Internet cafe regulations) as well as areas that are more "normal" and less openly contested (such as regulations concerning housing funds).

Early on in the project two other scholars joined the original research group, namely Thelle, working on the fairly recently adopted regulations concerning legal aid, and Sapio, working on the longstanding and highly politicized issue of anticorruption regulations. When soliciting additional contributions to the present book after an international conference held in Beijing in December 2006, we were also able to add a study that provides further comparative and local perspectives on the issue of environmental protection (van Rooij).

Apart from the case studies focusing on special policy and legal areas, one of the chapters discusses the court system (Grimheden). Although much has been written on the courts, there is a need for more research on the implications of court reform for law implementation and the legal system more generally. Two chapters, by Hydén and Peerenboom, respectively, provide more theoretical and comparative outlooks on the state of law implementation in China.

Methodology and Fieldwork

All contributors have made a conscious attempt to anchor and ground their studies in empirical investigations. Most of us have also attempted to penetrate beneath the national level and see what happens when national laws meet local realities. It is our hope that the volume will contribute to the already occurring shift from a focus on law-in-the-books to law-in-action. The researchers have used a whole range of different data collection methods, including interviews with officials in state agencies, representatives of various organizations, individual experts and journalists, as well as readings of official documents and laws, academic work in the field, and reports in the media. Most authors have spent considerable time in China doing fieldwork. It should be acknowledged that conducting fieldwork in China is not an easy task. Although the situation has improved significantly during the reform period, many problems still persist with respect to access to data and interviewees with particular difficulties in some policy and legal areas.[14]

Despite the growth and proliferation of more statistics in the legal field, there are, as Peerenboom and several other authors in this volume also point out, still problems with regard to obtaining reliable and comprehensive data. Furthermore, as discussed by Liang and Hong (2006), most empirical legal research to date has been in

---

14 For difficulties in doing fieldwork on legal issues in China, see Liang and Hong, "Conducting Fieldwork in China," and Donald C. Clarke, "Empirical Research into the Chinese Judicial System," in Erik G. Jensen and Thomas C. Heller (eds.), *Beyond Common Knowledge: Empirical Approaches to the Rule of Law* (Stanford: Stanford University Press, 2003), 164–192. For a more general work on fieldwork in China, see Maria Heimer and Stig Thøgersen (eds.), *Doing Fieldwork in China* (Copenhagen: NIAS Press, 2006).

the form of small convenience samples rather than random probability samples. Our studies are no exception to this rule. The researchers involved in this project have also made case studies rather than conducted surveys, but in one instance (Burell) the case study was supplemented with recently collected survey data.[15]

Like Liang and Hong and many others before them, we faced problems getting access and found that personal contacts, institutional networks, and previous research contacts were crucial for getting access to individual informants and legal and other institutions.[16] It is much easier to get access to individual Chinese scholars and certain groups, such as lawyers and journalists, than to officials, which may give rise to a certain bias when identifying and analyzing problems of law implementation. To the extent that we were able to interview and get access to officials, it very rarely led to possibilities to conduct participatory observations or follow the daily implementation work. In some fields more than others, authors had to rely almost exclusively on official documents and available statistics, whereas in other fields academic works and media reports were more plentiful and a useful source of information.[17]

Needless to say, the selection of our case studies can hardly be said to be either representative or comprehensive in scope. Furthermore, given the size of China and its huge economic and social dif-

---

15 Surveys in China require official approval, and foreign scholars encounter many problems in this field. For an example of one of the few surveys on the legal system by foreign scholars in collaboration with Chinese scholars, see Ethan Michelson and Benjamin L. Read, "Popular Perceptions of the Legal System: What Do Surveys Say About Differences Between Chicago and China?" 2007, unpublished conference paper accessed at http://www.indiana.edu/~emsoc/projects.htm.

16 Burell, Chen, Grimheden, Thelle, and van Rooij have benefited from earlier institutional contacts and cooperation projects that have facilitated their contacts with officials.

17 Due to the sensitive nature of the topic, Sapio has thus almost exclusively had to rely on documentary sources, supplemented with interviews with scholars. For Almén, Lagerkvist, and Svensson, media reports have been an important source of information.

ferences, our studies provide but a glimpse of the situation in some selected parts of the country. The contributors have carried out fieldwork and engaged in case studies in Beijing, Tianjin, Shanghai, Zhejiang, Shaanxi, Guangdong, Jiangxi, and Yunnan. Apart from Yunnan, Jiangxi, and Shaanxi, these areas are all well developed, which creates another bias in our study.

An Analytical Framework for Studying Law Implementation

The field of implementation studies has undergone many changes since the early 1970s, and today there exists a wealth of works that use different approaches and advocate different theories.[18] We should bear in mind that there is no coherent theory but a range of divergent views and approaches when we proceed to discuss law implementation in China.[19] The following only briefly discusses how previous works have informed the analytical framework employed in this book. The two chapters by Hydén and Peerenboom provide a more detailed discussion on some of the general aspects of law implementation as well as a comparative perspective on the issue, whereas individual chapters in some cases further discuss their respective theoretical models (see in particular Grimheden).

First of all, it bears remembering that implementation is not only a task for judicial authorities but that administrative organs and bodies at central and local levels are deeply involved in the im-

---

18 For an overview of the theoretical field, see Peter deLeon, "The Missing Link Revisited: Contemporary Implementation Research," *Policy Studies Review* 16, nos. 3–4 (Fall/Winter 1999): 311–338.

19 For a thorough discussion of implementation studies more generally and with respect to China, see Chen, "Implementation of Law in China." For a useful early discussion on policy implementation on the Chinese countryside that builds on some of the central works in the implementation literature, see O'Brien and Li, "Selective Policy Implementation in Rural China."

plementation of laws and regulations. This is an important feature that will be borne out in the following chapters, where the focus is more on the work of different institutions and public agencies, including environmental protection bureaus, cultural heritage bureaus, construction bureaus, and people's congresses, than on the courts. Like many others working on implementation issues, we also pay particular attention to the surrounding policy environment as it is crucial for the implementation process itself.

Drawing on the existing literature in political science, public administration, and sociology of law, we understand implementation as the actions taking place after policy formulation and law adoption. This presupposes a legislative process—at national and/or local levels—producing "policies" enshrined in laws, regulations, or executive directives. Although policymakers generally are aiming for concrete results, lawmaking can also be a form of symbolic politics or event making (see chapters by van Rooij and Grimheden). The symbolic function of lawmaking and law implementation is quite obvious in the Chinese context.[20] Laws can be ambiguous, due to political compromises, and they are often seen as a "method of social change," as was the case, for example, with the 1950 marriage law.[21] They very often also give rise to conflicts that makes implementation quite difficult. In this context Matland's attempt to address the significance and interplay of ambiguity and conflicts for policy and law implementation is a useful analytical tool.[22] A policy or law with high levels of both ambiguity and conflict will be difficult to implement. In China many laws are characterized by high

---

20 But compare examples from Western countries in van Rooij, *Regulation of Land and Pollution in China*.

21 See Neil J. Diamant, "Making Love 'Legible' in China: Politics and Society during the Enforcement of Civil Marriage Registration, 1950–66," *Politics & Society*, vol. 29 no. 3 (September 2001): 447–480.

22 Richard E. Matland, "Synthesizing the Implementation Literature: The Ambiguity-Conflict Model of Policy Implementation," *Journal of Public Administration Research & Theory* 5, no. 2 (1995): 145–174.

ambiguity/high conflict, although it seems that since the revision of many laws in the 1990s the level of ambiguity is falling. However, given the rapid changes in Chinese society and the existence of widely different interests, the level of conflict remains very high. We thus end up with a situation in many fields where implementation outcomes are decided by the relative powers of the actors involved in the process (for a further discussion of Matland's model see Grimheden).

An important question when it comes to law implementation is what we are measuring and against which standards. We will assume that law implementation is an ongoing process with measurable outputs and social outcomes that can match or diverge from the policymakers' intentions. It is therefore important to analyze any deviation between laws on paper and laws in reality. We should also note that enforcement standards of existing regulations may be intentionally lowered because state agencies find it too difficult to achieve full policy coverage, a process that may be called "policy dilution" (on this topic, see Burell). Such compromises mean that the same regulations will not apply or be implemented in all regions or situations. Implementation then becomes an ongoing learning process where problems and experience with implementation are fed back into legislative work, helping to improve the laws, and helping the implementing agencies at different levels to perfect their work (compare, for example, Svensson on implementation of the Cultural Heritage Law, Burell on housing reform policy, and van Rooij on environmental laws).

An important task in this context is to try to identify and account for failures across policy areas, and to compare the role of different actors in this process. Variation in implementation success in different localities also needs to be addressed, as do the reasons behind such variations. The existence of different types of variables, including ad hoc events, however, makes comparisons between law implementation in different policy areas extremely difficult. Unpredictable and uncontrollable events also take place that can produce either a "policy fiasco" or unpredicted successes.[23] While some implementation scholars have used more quantitative methods, listing and weighing different variables and testing them in different policy areas, our study is more modest and qualitative in character.[24] A qualitative case study can better capture a more complex picture and take into account processes and contextual conditions. It also draws more attention to the process of implementation, rather than the product of implementation. Our reason for choosing case studies was also simply because we did not have the resources and ability to carry out large quantitative studies. Although the different case studies are framed in different ways, we have attempted to address at least some of the same issues related to both internal and external factors, such as clarity of the laws, actors involved in the implementation process, institutional culture and norms, institutional capacity and level of professionalism, impact of the socioeconomic environment, and changes over time.

The Political and Institutional Framework

The combination of market reforms and one-party Communist rule creates significant constraints on law implementation in China. The problems are thus in part related to the political structure. In the past, many observers focused almost exclusively on the Chinese Communist Party and its influence on the legal system. This study wants to downplay the role of the party and highlight the complex and fragmented nature of the political and legal system and the implementation process. Political scientists have long called attention to the fragmented nature of the Chinese state.[25] The lines of political

---

23 Mark Bovens and Paul t'Hart, *Understanding Policy Fiascos* (London: Transactions, 1996).
24 Compare deLeon, "Missing Link Revisited."
25 See Kenneth Lieberthal, "The Fragmented Authoritarianism Model and

authority in China crisscross at many levels of the state administration. This fragmentation of authority is particularly detrimental when agents at the local level must carry out national policies and neither has the will nor the financial and institutional capacity to do so. A general problem in law implementation in China seems to originate in the difficulties different organizations have in cooperating and coordinating their work, something that many of the studies in the present volume also show. Poor law implementation is thus very much related to the problem of overlapping or conflicting powers of authority. It is therefore apt to understand law implementation as a field of "politico-legal battles," to borrow Jianfu Chen's words, within and between different departments, levels of governments, companies, and individuals.[26]

A related problem is that of weak institutions. Many departments neither have the staff nor the funding necessary to carry out their work (compare Sapio, Svensson, and Thelle). Depending on policy priorities at national and local levels, state agencies may be more or less endowed with financial and personnel resources (compare Burell). However, we detect an increasing professionalism, including higher levels of education, in many institutions, although the situation varies between different cities and regions, which is positive for implementation. The phenomenon of local protectionism is widespread and systemic and constitutes a formidable obstacle for uniform and fair law implementation. The courts, for example, depend upon local governments for funding and other resources and are subject to pressure and interference from local authorities (see Grimheden). Many other institutions and bureaucracies also face local protectionism and experience that local governments' concern for economic growth makes implementation of

---

Its Limitations," in *Bureaucracy, Politics and Decision Making in Post-Mao China*, Kenneth Lieberthal and David Lampton (eds.) (Berkeley and Los Angeles: University of California Press, 1992), 1–30.

26 See Jianfu Chen, "Implementation of Law as a Politico-Legal Battle in China," *China Perspectives*, no. 43 (September-October 2002): 26–39.

certain national and local laws difficult if not impossible (particularly obvious in the environmental field, see Almén and van Rooij). Finally, the widespread and endemic corruption in both public agencies and society is an important obstacle for law implementation as various institutions, companies, and individuals use their power and influence to affect the administration of justice (see Sapio).

Actors in the Implementation Chain: Top-Down and Bottom-Up Processes

The different case studies in this volume aim to identify and analyze how different state and nonstate actors affect the process and outcome of law implementation in various policy areas. The most crucial institutions in law implementation have traditionally been considered to be the courts at various levels. But in China the legislatures, i.e., the National People's Congress and the local people's congresses, have an unusually strong supervisory power over both the administration and the judiciary that affects implementation work (see Almén).[27] A striking feature of the Chinese system is that administrative authorities, such as ministries and bureaus, are actively involved in the administration of law and also exercise substantial judicial powers.[28] In recent years there has been a strong

---

27 For some recent works, see Cai Dingjian, "Functions of the People's Congress in the Process of Implementation of Law," in Chen, Li, and Otto, *Implementation of Law in the People's Republic of China*; Young Nam Cho, "From 'Rubber Stamps' to 'Iron Stamps': The Emergence of Chinese Local People's Congresses as Supervisory Powerhouses," *China Quarterly* (September 2002): 724–740; Young Nam Cho, "Symbiotic Neighbour or Extra-Court Judge? The Supervision over Courts by Chinese Local People's Congresses," *The China Quarterly*, no. 176 (2003): 1068–1083; and Young Nam Cho, "The Politics of Law-Making in Chinese Local People's Congresses," *The China Quarterly*, no. 187 (2006): 592–609.

28 For a recent work on the labor law and different agencies involved in implementing and enforcing the law, see Sean Cooney, "Making Chinese Labor Law

emphasis on governance and administration according to law (*yifa xingzheng*), and many organizations have been given more administrative power to enforce laws in an effort to reform and strengthen the administrative law regime. A number of laws and regulations have also been adopted in this field, including the Administrative Compulsory Enforcement Law adopted in 2005. The unique features of the Chinese legal and political system discussed above are in many cases due to a lack of a clear separation of powers, which makes for some special challenges when it comes to law implementation.

In implementation studies, different scholars have taken different stands on the top-down versus bottom-up approach.[29] The more traditional understanding of law implementation focuses on top-down processes and the work of legislative bodies and policymakers at the central level. But in the late 1970s some scholars in the West began to take a more bottom-up approach, focusing on "street level bureaucrats" and local organizations, which are the ones to implement the policies and laws at the local level.[30] This means that not only are the administrative skills and knowledge of laws and policies of these actors put in focus but also the broader sociopolitical environment in which laws and policies are implemented. This opens up for interesting discussions on whether, and to what extent and how, local conditions hinder or facilitate implementation, which also necessitates the study of the strategies local actors use to implement or avoid complying with different policies and laws. Later scholars tried to combine the two approaches and

---

Work: The Prospects for Regulatory Innovation in the People's Republic of China," *Fordham International Law Journal* 30 (2007), available at SSRN, http://ssrn.com/abstract=1030105.

29 For an overview of this debate, see deLeon, "The Missing Link Revisited," and Matland, "Synthesizing the Implementation Literature."

30 See Michael Lipsky, *Street-level Bureaucracy: Dilemmas of the Individual in Public Services* (New York: Russel Sage Foundation, 1980).

focused both on the macro and micro level and the interactions between them. One of these scholars is Sabatier, who has developed a more dynamic view of the implementation process.[31] He emphasizes the policy learning process through which implementing agencies learn and adapt. Furthermore, he also discusses and acknowledges the role of different advocacy coalitions that may influence both policymaking and lawmaking and the actual implementation process.

While not ignoring the activities and designs at the macro level, several chapters call attention to these more bottom-up processes, which we understand to include not only the work of so-called street-level bureaucrats and local bodies but also actors such as the media, nonstate organizations, and ordinary citizens. Their supervision, critique, and engagement with the actual implementation bodies can play a crucial role in the implementation process, which we noticed, in particular, in the field of environmental protection and cultural heritage protection among our case studies (see Almén, Svensson, and van Rooij).

Our case studies show that some institutional actors are more crucial for successful implementation than others, but also highlight the complex and changing power relations among them. While the judiciary and the people's congresses continue to play a powerful role in many areas, it is obvious that Chinese society is becoming increasingly complex and pluralistic with different institutions and actors vying for power and challenging each other's authority. Table 1 illustrates which institutions and actors each of our case studies focuses on, and thereby also the extent to which we take a top-top, bottom-up, or a combination of these two approaches.

---

31 See Paul Sabatier, "Top-Down and Bottom-Up Approaches to Implementation Research: A Critical Analysis and Suggested Synthesis," *Journal of Public Policy* 6, no. 1 (1986): 21–48.

Table 1. Policy Areas and Institutions/Actors

Policy areas: Institutions:	Anti-corruption	Housing funds	Cultural heritage	Legal aid	Internet cafes	Environmental protection
The judiciary (JG)	FS		MS	HT		OA
People's congresses		MB	MS	HT	JL	OA
Bureaus and ministries	FS	MB	MS	HT	JL	OA, BR
Media			MS		JL	OA
Nonstate organizations and citizens		MB	MS	HT	JL	OA, BR
Work units and village committees		MB	MS			OA, BR
Communist Party	FS		MS		JL	OA, BR

Abbreviations: Oscar Almén (OA), Mattias Burell (MB), Johan Lagerkvist (JL), Flora Sapio (FS), Marina Svensson (MS), Hatla Thelle (HT), and Benjamin van Rooij (BR).

The Central versus Local Division: Obstructions at the Local Level

Law implementation in China is marked by a considerable degree of local discretion, and it is common that laws are not implemented uniformly across the country. A political saying tellingly illustrates the problem of carrying out national policies and laws at local levels: "The center has policies, local authorities have counterpolicies (*shangmian you zhengce, xiamian you duice*)." In view of this situation, several of the studies look at how Chinese law is implemented at the local level, i.e., at the municipal, township, and county levels.

Successful implementation of central policies is decided by the priority of a particular policy at the local level.[32] National laws are often compromised or diverted by local stakeholders. It is not so

---

32 For an early work that discusses the reasons behind this selective implementation, see O'Brien and Li, "Selective Policy Implementation in Rural China."

much the case that local state agents do not understand or are incapable of carrying out the laws, but whether they actually want to do so. It should also be pointed out that local actors are often very divided and have different interests. There may thus exist differences within the local community, and between local officials, who are held responsible and accountable for policy failures, and local companies and individual citizens. Several case studies in this volume analyze these local efforts to resist or modify national laws (see Almén, Burell, Sapio, Svensson, van Rooij).

The Impact of Economic Development and Geographical Differences

The success of law implementation is dependent on the socioeconomic context in which the laws are to be applied. As Hydén points out in his contribution, in China we find a combination of market reforms and one-party Communist rule that significantly differs from the mixed welfare economy found in the West. This socioeconomic structure creates constraints on law implementation in China and gives the implementation processes a specific character (compare the case of Housing Provident Funds discussed by Burell). Economic factors and considerations as well as uneven development explain both successful implementation as well as violations (see in particular Almén, Svensson, and van Rooij). Lack of economic resources can make implementation very difficult, if not impossible, for poor regions and institutions.

It is a well-known fact that there are huge differences between courts in the more developed coastal provinces and in the poorer inland provinces (see Grimheden). Their situation differs with respect to both finances and staffing, including the number of judges and their level of education, which has a serious impact on the courts' ability to carry out their work and enforce judgments. Similar regional differences and discrepancies are found in the case of other legal departments and professions.[33] The number of lawyers and legal aid centers, for example, differs between rural and urban areas in the country (see Thelle). There also exist huge regional differences when it comes to law schools and legal education more generally, the number of laws adopted and their quality, and the number of cases handled by the courts.

Whereas the level of economic development no doubt matters, we cannot simply assume that problems with law implementation are by definition more severe in poorer regions (for discussions and examples, see Almén, Burell, Sapio, Svensson, Thelle, and van Rooij). Other factors, such as political will and leadership and institutional culture also matter and may be more important in some policy areas and legal fields. In the case of corruption, for instance, Sapio's study shows that the problem may be more acute and difficult to curb in more developed areas, despite the fact that anticorruption institutions in these areas are better staffed and have more resources to fight corruption.

Law implementation may run into difficulties because of corruption within the departments in charge of or supervising law implementation, or become hostage to interest groups that have a stake in the issues at hand. Many organizations and actors, including government departments, are motivated by economic interests when deciding whether to comply, implement, or violate a certain law or regulation. In this context we need to take into account that laws can be more or less difficult to implement depending on whether they are distributive, redistributive, or regulatory in nature. Laws entailing a redistribution of resources can be threatening as they upset vested interests and provoke opposition. In a similar manner, policies involving large amounts of money tend to trigger conflicts among state and nonstate actors and are often difficult to

---

33 A wealth of data and indicators that show the huge geographical discrepancies in China are found in Zhu Jingwen (ed.), *Zhongguo falü fazhan baogao: Shujuku he zhibiao tixi* [Report on China Law Development: Database and Indicators] (Beijing: Zhongguo renmin daxue chubanshe, 2007), 51–52.

implement. Economic conflicts are particularly obvious in some of the case studies in this book, such as environmental protection, cultural heritage preservation, and anticorruption work. Laws need to be in the interest of major actors if they are to be implemented, and sanctions need to outweigh any possible benefits of violations (see, for example, van Rooij).

We also need to realize that law implementation is much more difficult in volatile or rapidly changing societies. It should thus come as no surprise that laws are much harder to implement in a rapidly changing society such as China than in a more static and stable society such as Sweden. Many of the individual case studies analyzed in this book prove this point. In the case of anticorruption policies, in themselves a highly politicized task, the rapidly changing economic development provides new opportunities and possibilities to engage in corrupt activities. This makes enforcement very difficult as it becomes difficult for implementing and controlling agencies to keep step with presumptive violators (see Sapio). The quickly changing economic landscape, with new firms being established each day, has also made it difficult to enforce Housing Provident Fund collections (see Burell). Likewise, in the case of both environmental and cultural heritage protection, strong economic interests and rapid city-redevelopments make for a challenging task.

Social and Cultural Norms and the Implementation of Law

It is important to consider the social context in which laws are enforced. Deeply held social norms underpin people's views on issues related to justice and legitimacy and inform their social and political behavior. The legal system and existing laws need to be in conformity with the prevalent social norms in society in order for laws to be upheld and enjoy legitimacy (for a fuller discussion on norms and laws, see Hydén). In the Chinese context we find a confluence of traditional, customary and socialist norms that are being challenged by, or coexist with, new norms that develop in the rapidly changing Chinese society and under the impact of market reforms and globalization. Dramatic social, economic, and political changes influence people's everyday lives and how they interact with each other as well as with the state (compare Burell's discussion of how housing reform policy has affected people's norms and expectations regarding house ownership). The alleged widespread lack of knowledge of laws and legal procedures within both the legal departments and among other actors has often been cited as an underlying problem for law implementation in China. But the situation is rapidly improving as the Chinese state has made huge efforts to publish and popularize laws and provide legal education for different groups in society. These efforts have resulted in a growing legal knowledge and awareness among broad groups of the Chinese population.

New ideas of rights-based justice are thus circulated and slowly getting embedded in Chinese society, and underpin and strengthen the legal system. The rise of rights consciousness and strengthened legal awareness have led to vocal demands on the Chinese state to implement laws and deliver justice.[34] Poor implementation and open violations and abuse of laws have far-reaching social and political implications and risk undermining the Communist Party's legitimacy. If norms are violated and the legal system cannot deliver, the result may be resentment and open protests. This being said, and referring back to the earlier discussion, different norms coexist in China today, which also poses a problem for law implementation. As Lagerkvist shows in his study on Internet cafe regulations, some norms are stronger than others and enjoy a broader support, which influences both lawmaking and law implementation.

---

34 For some recent works discussing the growing rights consciousness, see Mary E. Gallagher, "Mobilizing the Law in China: 'Informed Disenchantment' and the Development of Legal Consciousness," *Law & Society Review* 40, no. 4 (2006): 783-816, and Kevin J. O'Brien and Li Lianjiang, *Rightful Resistance in Rural China* (Cambridge: Cambridge University Press, 2006).

Making Law Work: Our Contribution and Future Research Agenda

What is it, we may ask, that makes law work? A tentative conclusion based on ours and others' studies would be that successful implementation requires the fulfillment of some preconditions, such as political will, legal knowledge among officials and other actors, effective enforcement mechanisms, popular trust, and favorable socioeconomic factors. The actual importance of and relationship between these different factors may vary in different policy areas and between different geographical regions.

In his influential work on governance and political institutions in Italy, Putnam argued that social capital, trust, and the existence of civic engagement are crucial factors for making democracy work.[35] Putnam's study sensitizes us to the fact that norms of reciprocity and trust and networks of civic engagement influence institutional performance, including, we could argue, law implementation.[36] Although Putnam's study focused on Italy and on political institutions, the insights and questions to which it gives rise to may also be useful for a discussion on policy and law implementation in China and what makes law work.[37]

---

35 Robert D. Putnam with Robert Leonardi and Raffaella Y. Nanetti, *Making Democracy Work: Civic Traditions in Modern Italy* (Princeton: Princeton University Press, 1992). See also Robert D. Putnam, "Bowling Alone: America's Declining Social Capital," *Journal of Democracy* 6, no. 1 (1995): 65–78.

36 For a critique of Putnam that among other things questions his tendency to equate institutional performance with democracy, see Sidney Tarrow, "Making Social Science Work Across Space and Time: A Critical Reflection on Robert Putnam's 'Making Democracy Work,'" *The American Political Science Review* 90, no. 2 (June 1996): 389–397. Tarrow also cautions us about drawing too sweeping conclusions of differences in political culture and institutional capacity between regions.

37 Lily Tsai has showed that public goods provision in rural China rather than being dependent on economic development or well-implemented village elections, more is a result of the local leadership being well embedded in the local community through, for example, strong lineage associations or temple associa-

In order for laws to be upheld and enjoy legitimacy, it is necessary that existing laws be in conformity with the prevalent social norms in society. It is obvious that thirty years of legal reforms have radically changed social norms and ideas of justice, as well as individual behavior and institutional practices, and turned China into a more law-based society. We would therefore expect law implementation to improve over time as laws become more institutionalized and conform with existing norms. But, on the other hand, the fact that dramatic and wide-ranging changes have taken place in a very short time-span also creates problems as some individuals and institutions are not able to keep up with the rapid changes and live up to or conform to a more law-based behavior, or understand what is reasonable to expect from the legal system.[38] Surveys and studies of Chinese citizens' trust in the regime and its institutions show rather complex patterns and trends. We find a surprisingly high level of trust in central authorities but much lower trust in local authorities, which are the ones that often defy national laws and policies.[39]

One of Putnam's key findings is the importance of social cooperation and citizen participation for institutional performance. In this context it could be argued that since trust is low, social capital is weak, and civic organizations few in China, the incentives for co-

---

tions. There thus existed both trust in and moral pressure on the local leadership. See Lily L. Tsai, *Accountability without Democracy: Solidary Groups and Public Goods Provision in Rural China* (Cambridge: Cambridge University Press, 2007).

38 Some surveys show that Chinese people do not distinguish between distributive justice (satisfaction with the outcome) and procedural justice (satisfaction with the fairness of the process) and have low tolerance for outcomes that go against them despite the fact that they are the result of fair procedures. This shows that legal awareness still is rather rudimentary and superficial. See Michelson and Read, "Popular Perceptions of the Legal System," 27–28.

39 For an overview and discussion of surveys and findings regarding trust in the regime, see Joseph Fewsmith, "Assessing Social Stability on the Eve of the 17th Party Congress," *China Leadership Monitor*, issue 20 (Winter 2007) accessed at http://www.hoover.org/publications/clm/issues/6301112.html, and Wang Zhengxu, "Public Support for Democracy in China," *Journal of Contemporary China* 16, no. 53 (2007): 561–579.

operation and implementation of laws are low, whereas the incentives for free-riding and circumventing laws are quite high. Although China is known for its centralized political system, a crucial feature of the reform era has been decentralization of administrative decision-making and regulative powers, which has resulted in a considerable degree of local discretion. In China institutional fragmentation occurs both horizontally and vertically and explains many implementation failures. It is common that laws are not implemented uniformly across the country. It is often the case that well-intentioned laws drawn up by central authorities do not fit local realities, or that local authorities and institutions due to economic and institutional constraints do not have the ability and power to implement them as they face strong vested interests.

But, on a more positive note, and referring, if only tangibly, to Putnam's proposition that civic organizations are important, the increasing pluralism in Chinese society and the growth of actors in the implementation field have given rise to a system of checks and balances of sorts that may have a positive impact on implementation. We have noticed that the increased number of more diverse and vocal actors and institutions that scrutinize and engage in implementation, whether these are people's congresses at different levels, media organizations, or nongovernmental organizations, has had a positive impact in many fields (see in particular Almén, Svensson, and van Rooij).[40]

As Putnam contends in the case of Italy with respect to governance and democracy, whether regions with a higher density of civic organizations of different kinds, and thus also higher levels of trust and cooperation, also do better when it comes to implementa-

---

40 For an interesting study of what makes the labor law work and the role of various institutions, including the weak role of labor bureaus, see Cooney, "Making Chinese Labor Law Work." In a study on China's wildlife protection, Peter J. Li calls for a bigger role for advocacy groups in policymaking and implementation work, see "Enforcing Wildlife Protection in China: The Legislative and Political Solution," *China Information* XXI, no. 1 (2007): 71–107.

tion of laws and regulations is an open question. Tsai found that community organizations in the Chinese countryside, albeit having a positive effect on public goods provision, led to accountability without democracy. Our studies are certainly not comprehensive or detailed enough to answer these questions, although our findings from Shanghai and Guangzhou (Almén), Zhejiang (Svensson), and Yunnan (van Rooij) hint that the existence of stronger and more diverse institutions and actors is more likely to result in better law implementation. But this is more a question of institutional performance rather than indicative of a move toward rule of law.

Zhang Jianjun has made interesting comparisons between the Sunan region (i.e., southern Jiangsu), which is characterized by strong state institutions and companies, and Wenzhou in southern Zhejiang, where private enterprises and business associations dominate. Zhang argues that the different institutional setups, class structures, types of business organizations, as well as differences with respect to how competitive village elections are between the two regions show that the prospects for effective governance and democracy look much better in the Wenzhou case.[41] Tarrow's caution about Putnam's somewhat simplified dichotomy between northern and southern Italy could serve as a reminder for us not to make too much of the differences between Sunan and Wenzhou. However, it is interesting to note that experiments with deliberative democracy and public hearings have taken place in the Wenzhou area and not in Sunan. One reason for these experiments in Wenzhou, and similar public hearings elsewhere, is the government's need to increase people's sense of participation in order to ensure better compliance with policy decisions and promote trust in the regime and the legal system.[42] Although economic interests and constraints often trump law-abiding behavior, more equal patterns

---

[41] See Zhang Jianjun, "Marketization, Class Structure, and Democracy in China: Contrasting Regional Experiences," *Democratization* 14, no. 3 (June 2007): 425–445.

[42] On deliberative democracy experiments in China, see Ethan J. Leib and

of wealth, existence of bottom-up business associations, and more participatory institutions could serve as countervailing forces. On the basis of studies by Zhang, others', and our own studies, we may venture to speculate that there also may exist significant differences between regions with respect to trust in the legal system and degree of law implementation. Ethan Michelson and Benjamin L. Read found that economic development positively promote the utilization of the legal system, the performance of the legal system, as well as people's assessment of it.[43] It might be more complicated, and economic factors certainly are only one part of the story. More cross-regional comparative studies of law implementation, political institutions, and economic development could be a useful topic for future research.

Making law work in actual practice, and in any society, is a matter of degree. It is obvious that China is moving toward a greater reliance on and respect for laws, and that law implementation in most areas, if not all, is steadily improving. Our case studies show that whereas we do indeed find many cases of failures, we should not overlook either the rapid developments in many areas, or overestimate the situation elsewhere in the world (see Peerenboom).

Bibliography

Bakken, Børge, ed. *Crime, Punishment, and Policing in China*. Lanham: Rowman & Littlefield, 2005.

Bovens, Mark, and Paul t'Hart, *Understanding Policy Fiascos*. London: Transactions, 1996.

Chen, Jianfu, Yuwen Li, and Jan-Michiel Otto, eds. *Implementation of Law in the People's Republic of China*. The Hague: Kluwer Law International, 2002.

Jianfu, Chen. "Implementation of Law as a Politico-Legal Battle in China," China Perspectives no. 43 (September–October 2002): 26–39.

He Baogang (eds.), *The Search for Deliberative Democracy in China* (Palgrave Macmillan, 2006).

43 See Michelson and Read, "Popular Perceptions of the Legal System," 25.

Chen, Jianfu. *Chinese Law: Context and Transformation*. Leiden/Boston: Martinus Nijhoff Publishers, 2008.

Cho, Young Nam. "From 'Rubber Stamps' to 'Iron Stamps': The Emergence of Chinese Local People's Congresses as Supervisory Powerhouses," *The China Quarterly* (September 2002): 724–740.

Cho, Young Nam. "Symbiotic Neighbour or Extra-Court Judge? The Supervision over Courts by Chinese Local People's Congresses," *The China Quarterly*, no. 176 (2003): 1068–1083.

Cho, Young Nam. "The Politics of Law-Making in Chinese Local People's Congresses," *The China Quarterly*, no. 187 (2006): 592–609

Clarke, Donald C. "Empirical Research into the Chinese Judicial System." In *Beyond Common Knowledge: Empirical Approaches to the Rule of Law*, edited by Erik G. Jensen and Thomas C. Heller, Stanford: Stanford University Press, 2003, 164–192.

Clarke, Donald C. ed., *China's Legal System: New Developments, New Challenges*. Cambridge: Cambridge University Press, 2008.

Cooney, Sean. "Making Chinese Labor Law Work: The Prospects for Regulatory Innovation in the People's Republic of China," *Fordham International Law Journal* 30 (2007), http://ssrn.com/abstract=1030105.

deLeon, Peter. "The Missing Link Revisited: Contemporary Implementation Research," *Policy Studies Review* 16, nos. 3–4 (Fall/Winter 1999): 311–338.

Diamant, Neil J. "Making Love 'Legible' in China: Politics and Society during the Enforcement of Civil Marriage Registration, 1950–66," *Politics & Society* 29 no. 3 (September 2001): 447–480.

Diamant, Neil J., Stanley B. Lubman, and Kevin J. O'Brien, eds. *Engaging the Law in China*. Stanford: Stanford University Press, 2005.

Fewsmith, Joseph. "Assessing Social Stability on the Eve of the 17th Party Congress," *China Leadership Monitor*, issue 20 (Winter 2007) http://www.hoover.org/publications/clm/issues/6301112.html

Fu, Hualing, and Richard Cullen, "Weiquan (Rights Protection) Lawyering in an Authoritarian State: Building a Culture of Public Interest Lawyering," *China Journal* 59 (2008): 111–127.

Gallagher, Mary E. "Mobilizing the Law in China: 'Informed Disenchantment' and the Development of Legal Consciousness," *Law & Society Review* 40, no. 4 (2006): 783-816.

Heimer, Maria, and Stig Thøgersen, eds. *Doing Fieldwork in China*. Copenhagen: NIAS Press, 2006.

Lampton, David. *Policy Implementation in Post-Mao China*. Berkeley and Los Angeles: University of California Press, 1987.

Lee, Ching Kwan. *Against the Law: Labor Protests in China's Rustbelt and Sunbelt*. Berkley: University of California Press, 2007.

Leib, Ethan J., and He Baogang, eds. *The Search for Deliberative Democracy in China*. Palgrave Macmillan, 2006.

Li, Peter J. "Enforcing Wildlife Protection in China: The Legislative and Political Solution," *China Information* XXI, no. 1 (2007): 71–107.

Liang, Bin, and Hong Lu, "Conducting Fieldwork in China: Observations on Collecting Primary Data Regarding Crime, Law, and the Criminal Justice System," *Journal of Contemporary Criminal Justice* 22, no. 2 (2006): 157–172.

Lieberthal, Kenneth, and David Lampton. *Bureaucracy, Politics and Decision Making in Post-Mao China*. Berkeley and Los Angeles: University of California Press, 1992.

Lipsky, Michael. *Street-level Bureaucracy: Dilemmas of the Individual in Public Services*. New York: Russell Sage Foundation, 1980.

Lu, Hong, and Terence D. Miethe. *China's Death Penalty: History, Law and Contemporary Practices*. London: Routledge, 2009.

Lubman, Stanley. "The Study of Chinese Law in the United States: Reflections on the Past and Concerns about the Future," *Washington University Global Studies Law Review* 2, no. 1 (2003): 1–35.

Lubman, Stanley. "Looking for law in China," *Columbia Journal of Asian Law*, vol. 20 (Fall 2006).

Lubman, Stanley. *Bird in a Cage: Legal Reform in China after Mao*. Stanford: Stanford University Press, 1999.

Matland, Richard E. "Synthesizing the Implementation Literature: The Ambiguity-Conflict Model of Policy Implementation," *Journal of Public Administration Research & Theory* 5, no. 2 (1995): 145–174.

Michelson, Ethan. "The Practice of Law as an Obstacle to Justice: Chinese Lawyers at Work," *Law & Society Review* 40 (1): 1–38.

Michelson, Ethan. "Lawyers, Political Embeddedness, and Institutional Continuity in China's Transition from Socialism," *American Journal of Sociology* 113 (2): 352–414.

Michelson, Ethan, and Benjamin L. Read, "Popular Perceptions of the Legal System: What Do Surveys Say About Differences Between Chicago and China?" 2007, http://www.indiana.edu/~emsoc/projects.htm.

Muhlhahn, Klaus. *Criminal Justice in China: A History*. Boston: Harvard University Press, 2009.

O'Brien, Kevin. *Reform Without Liberalization, China's National People's Congress and the Politics of Institutional Change*. New York: Cambridge University Press, 1990.

O'Brien, Kevin J., and Li Lianjiang. "Selective Policy Implementation in Rural China," *Comparative Politics* vol. 31, no. 2 (January 1999): 167–186.

O'Brien, Kevin J., and Li Lianjiang, *Rightful Resistance in Rural China*. Cambridge: Cambridge University Press, 2006.

Otto, Jan Michiel et al. *Law-Making in the People's Republic of China*. The Hague: Kluwer Law International, 2000.

Peerenboom, Randall. *China's Long March Toward Rule of Law*. New York: Cambridge University Press, 2002.

Peerenboom, Randall. *China Modernizes: Threat to the West or Model for the Rest?* New York: Oxford University Press, 2007.

Putnam, Robert D., with Robert Leonardi and Raffaella Y. Nanetti, *Making Democracy Work: Civic Traditions in Modern Italy*. Princeton: Princeton University Press, 1992.

Putnam, Robert D. "Bowling Alone: America's Declining Social Capital," *Journal of Democracy* 6, no. 1 (1995): 65–78.

Sabatier, Paul. "Top-Down and Bottom-Up Approaches to Implementation Research: A Critical Analysis and Suggested Synthesis," *Journal of Public Policy* 6, no. 1 (1986): 21–48.

Tanner, Murray Scot. *The Politics of Lawmaking in China: Institutions, Processes, and Democratic Prospects*. Oxford: Clarendon Press, 1999.

Tarrow, Sidney. "Making Social Science Work Across Space and Time: A Critical Reflection on Robert Putnam's 'Making Democracy Work,'" *The American Political Science Review* 90, no. 2 (June 1996): 389–397.

Trevaskes, Susan. Courts and Criminal Justice in Contemporary China. Lanham: Lexington Press, 2007.

Tsai, Lily L. *Accountability without Democracy: Solidary Groups and Public Goods Provision in Rural China*. Cambridge: Cambridge University Press, 2007.

van Rooij, Benjamin. *Regulation of Land and Pollution in China: Lawmaking, Compliance, and Enforcement; Theory and Cases*. Leiden: Leiden University Press, 2006.

Wang, Zhengxu. "Public Support for Democracy in China," *Journal of Contemporary China* 16, no. 53 (2007): 561–579.

Woo, Margaret Y. K., and Yaxin Wang. "Civil Justice in China: An Empirical Study of Courts in Three Provinces," *American Journal of Comparative Law* 53 (2005)

Wu, Peng. "The Good, the Bad and the Legal: Lawyering in China's Wild West," *Columbia Journal of Asian Law* 21 (2008).

Zhang, Jianjun. "Marketization, Class Structure, and Democracy in China: Contrasting Regional Experiences," *Democratization* 14, no. 3 (June 2007): 425–445.

Zhao, Suisheng, ed. *Debating Political Reform in China: Rule of Law vs. Democratization.* Armonk: M.E. Sharpe, 2006.

Zhu, Jingwen, ed. *Zhongguo falü fazhan baogao: Shujuku he zhibiao tixi* [Report on China Law Development: Database and Indicators], Beijing: Zhongguo renmin daxue chubanshe, 2007.

2
Assessing Implementation of Law in China
What Is the Standard?

RANDALL PEERENBOOM

The common perception is that while China has passed laws that are generally consistent with international standards, implementation is a serious problem. There is no doubt some truth to this view, more so in some areas than others. The purpose of this chapter, however, is to critically scrutinize this common perception. I will suggest, first, that we know less about implementation than we think—in particular, we know very little about how implementation in China compares to implementation in other countries at China's level of development. Second, how rigorously laws should be enforced—and in some cases whether they should be enforced at all—is often contested, sometimes for good reasons. Third, even when there should be more rigorous implementation, it is often not clear what can or should be done to ensure it. Fourth, and related to the latter, theories about implementation in China are underdeveloped and conflicting, in part because theories about how to regulate a developing country as large as China are underdeveloped and conflicting.

What We Know and Do Not Know about Law Implementation in China

What support is there for the common perception that "implementation of law" is a serious problem in China, and how strong and reliable is the evidence? Information about enforcement comes from a number of different sources. Among them, government entities are required to provide statistical information and report data that may be directly or indirectly relevant to questions of implementation. There are also academic or official surveys of implementation of particular laws or issues that shed light on how well laws are being enforced. And the media, lawyers, scholars, and participants in the legal system are a source of anecdotal evidence.

Despite all this, we know much less than we think we do about implementation of law in China, in part because these sources frequently suffer from shortcomings that call into question their reliability.

Before turning to specific concerns, however, let us take note of a more fundamental common problem. China is a very large country; as in any reasonably developed state, there are many different areas of law; within any given area of law, there are numerous laws and regulations that vary in terms of their status in the legislative hierarchy, scope, complexity, ease of application, and importance; and these laws are implemented and enforced by a wide variety of actors and institutions, including in some cases impersonal forces such as the market. We should therefore be very skeptical of generalizations about implementation of "the law" in China, or about whole areas of law, or even about particular issues such as the enforcement of court judgments. There is likely to be a considerable variety in implementation patterns that merit noting and parsing.

Much of what we know about implementation of law is based on or derived from official statistics or information provided by government entities as part of their reporting duties. A well-known shortcoming of this source of information is that subordinate government entities have an incentive to overstate their accomplishments and understate their deficiencies. This is all the more the case when the central government makes implementation of a particular law a priority. Thus, a campaign to "strike hard at crime" (*yanda*), stop drug use, enforce judgments, or wipe out corruption may lead to astonishing improvements—so astonishing that they cannot possibly be true.

On the other hand, campaigns are likely to lead to some improvement in implementation rates. However, the improvements may be temporary. While having time series data is always desirable, it is essential when the particular area is subject to campaigns or heightened, albeit passing, central government attention.

Still another problem with official statistics is that they are often not available to scholars or the general public. Looking forward, it is possible that more information will become available now that the central government has put more emphasis on government transparency, the State Council has passed the Regulations on Open Government Information and government entities are being encouraged to put more information on their websites.[1]

Despite potential problems in official data, it would be rash to dismiss all government-sourced data as unreliable or to automatically assume that locally generated data are more credible and reliable than national data.[2] Oftentimes, national data may be checked against local data and confirmed or disconfirmed.[3] Similarly, government-sourced data may be checked against data from nongovernment sources. Needless to say, nongovernment sources may also be biased, adopt faulty methodologies or simply not have adequate access to important sources of information.

Surveys are another important source of information. Yet surveys often suffer from a number of shortcomings. Empirical work is still relatively new, particularly in the legal area. While there are

---

[1] As is often the case, local experiments with freedom of information acts paved the way for national legislation. See Jamie Horslee, "Shanghai Advances the Cause of Open Government Information in China," http://www.law.yale.edu/documents/pdf/Shanghai_Advances.pdf, accessed June 17, 2007.

[2] One anonymous reviewer seemed to hold this extreme position.

[3] For instance, Li Ling has noted an inconsistency in national and provincial level data regarding judicial corruption. See Li Ling, "Corruption in China's Courts," in Randall Peerenboom ed., *Judicial Independence in China: Lessons for Global Rule of Law Promotion* (New York: Cambridge University Press, 2009).

many good studies, it remains the case that legal scholars often lack adequate methodological training in how to design a survey, conduct interviews, analyze and report the data, and so on.[4]

Sociologists and political scientists are generally better trained in methodology, but often lack a firm foundation in law. This may sometimes lead them to frame the issue improperly, misinterpret the results, or simply overlook outcomes that are interesting or unexpected—at least to the legally trained eye. For example, one study on dispute resolution found that administrative disputes were much less likely to lead to a compromise than civil or economic disputes. Those trained in Chinese law would not find this surprising as they would know that mediation was prohibited in administrative cases until recently to avoid government officials putting pressure on plaintiffs to drop the case or settle (although obviously it still occurred despite the prohibition). The study also found that parties to administrative disputes were more likely to lose than in civil and economic disputes, and concluded that challenging the state was difficult. Again, this would surely not come as a surprise to comparative law scholars. Success rates for plaintiffs in administrative law cases are always much lower than in civil and economic cases. In fact, the success rate for plaintiffs in administrative law cases in China (somewhere between 20 and 40 percent, depending on how you interpret the high number of withdrawals) is much higher than in the United States (12 percent) and Taiwan and Japan (around 8 percent, respectively).[5]

---

4 In the U.S., empirical work by legal scholars also faces certain challenges, including an emphasis at elite law schools on more theoretical work, the lack of methodological training and statistical analytic skills on the part of most legal scholars, and the long time to complete and high cost of empirical projects, which require legal scholars to take time it takes to seek outside grants. In recent years, these problems have been alleviated to some extent by the hiring of more faculty with an interdisciplinary background (i.e., with graduate degrees in sociology, economics, politics science, etc., as well as a law degree), and in some cases by setting up empirical research centers within the law faculty.

5 Randall Peerenboom, *China's Long March Toward Rule of Law* (Cambridge: Cambridge University Press, 2002), 400.

Conversely, one study on labor dispute resolution casually mentioned in passing that in a certain percentage of cases, parties took their case directly to court without going through labor arbitration. This *would* surprise most lawyers, and be worth pursuing, because according to PRC law, parties are required to arbitrate first before going to court.[6]

Given the comparative strengths of the different disciplines, ideally social scientists and legally trained scholars should work together on empirical studies of legal issues.[7] At minimum, legal scholars should seek the assistance of social scientists in designing survey questions, training those doing the survey and processing and interpreting the data. Conversely, social scientists should consult with legal scholars regarding the legal issues and the hypotheses to be tested, in selecting proper indicators and designing suitable questions, and in interpreting the results.

One of the biggest problems for all empirical researchers is obtaining a representative sample, particularly at the national level. As noted, China is a large country with considerable regional variation. It is expensive to do fieldwork in different places and to generate sufficiently large datasets to be able to draw statistically relevant conclusions.[8] But an even more serious problem is that many government officials see little point in providing information to re-

---

6 At least this was the case until the Supreme Court's *Interpretation of Several Issues Concerning the Applicable Law for the Trial of Labor Dispute Cases (II)*, issued on August 14, 2006, and entered into force on October 1, 2006, which allows parties to proceed directly to court where the worker has written proof of unpaid wages from the employer and there are no other claims raised.

7 There have also been attempts to facilitate empirical research by legal scholars in China. In one Ford-sponsored project, funding was included for a sociologist to advise on the principles of survey design and to help train local interviewers. The Raoul Wallenberg Institute also held a conference in Beijing in 2006 to examine interdisciplinary empirical research on legal issues. The organizers invited legal scholars as well as scholars from other disciplines in the hope of facilitating collaborative projects that would provide the necessary skill-set to do good empirical work.

8 Researchers can overcome this problem to some extent by relying on available national statistics to complement their own more narrowly focused empiri-

searchers. Thus researchers often choose their sites based on their relationship with key individuals who are willing to cooperate and provide the necessary information.

In some cases, researchers may overcome this problem by collaborating with government officials who sometimes participate in their personal capacity or as members of an academic think tank. However, this leads to its own problems as officials will still generally be sensitive to the interests of their institution. In addition, surveys conducted by the National People's Congress (NPC) or government entities run into the previously discussed problem of lower-level entities providing inaccurate information.

A number of private companies and newspapers also conduct public opinion surveys. Some of the companies are reputable and have the competence and resources to conduct national surveys. However, there have also been reports of newspapers simply making up the numbers.

In other cases, the subject matter may not lend itself to determinate conclusions based on survey work. Take the crucial issue of the enforceability of court judgments and arbitral awards. It is often claimed that enforcement is a major problem in China. We do know from surveys what the rates of enforcement are *when parties seek compulsory enforcement.*[9] However, we do not know how often parties *voluntarily comply* with the judgment or the award. To illustrate the importance of this information, assume that the parties voluntarily complied in ninety-nine out of one hundred cases, and in that one case compulsory enforcement failed to result in enforcement. Parties would have a 99 percent likelihood of collecting on their award or judgment, even though the enforcement rate would be

---

cal work. However, national data may not always be available, may not always be directly on point, and may not always be reliable.

9 Donald Clarke, "Power and Politics in the Chinese Court System: The Enforcement of Civil Judgments," *Columbia Journal of Asian Law* 10 (1996): 43; Randall Peerenboom, "Seek Truth from Facts: An Empirical Study of Enforcement of Arbitral Awards in the PRC," *American Journal of Comparative Law* 49 (2001): 262.

zero. Unfortunately, obtaining information about voluntary compliance with judgments, and even more so arbitral awards, is difficult if not impossible.[10]

Perhaps the most pervasive source of information about implementation and the operation of the legal system more generally is anecdotal evidence from the media, lawyers, and scholars. Indeed, it is quite remarkable how many "truths" about the legal system are based on the flimsiest of foundations, "truths" that must often be seriously qualified or simply abandoned when more systematic empirical evidence is brought to bear on the issue. My favorite example was when foreign lawyers, public commentators, and newspaper reporters were claiming that China might as well have not even bothered to sign the New York Convention for the enforcement of arbitral awards as enforcement was all but impossible. Upon closer examination, most claims were based on problems in a single, highly publicized case—the *Revpower* case. What is astounding is that even when these claims were being made, a publicly available survey by China International Economic and Trade Arbitration Commission (CIETAC) showed that there had been hundreds of cases of enforcement, and that over 70 percent of awards were enforced. A subsequent study found that about half of awards were enforced, with the biggest reason for nonenforcement by far being insolvency.[11]

There are many more examples. We often hear, even in the offi-

---

10 One study based on in-depth interviews with the plaintiffs of sixty-six randomly selected economic contract cases in the Pearl River Delta found that local courts were reasonably successful in enforcing judgments, and that local protectionism and political influence were not significant barriers. As a result of improved enforcement, plaintiffs' satisfaction with the court had improved. The improvements were due to: a changed economic environment in which private entrepreneurs have become important players, the institutional development of the courts, and the professionalism of the staff. He Xin, *Economic Contract Enforcement in China: An Empirical Study from a Basic-Level Court in the Pearl River Delta*, draft on file with author.

11 Peerenboom, "Seek Truth from Facts."

cial press, of difficulties in getting cases accepted by the courts (*li an nan*). Yet, I am aware of no systematic survey that shows what percentage of applications are denied, the rejection rates for different types of cases, what the reasons are for rejecting the applications, whether the reasons are valid or not, and whether acceptance rates vary by level of court or region.[12]

Similarly, while courts are now required to try cases in public, and some fifty million people attended trials in 2004,[13] we still often hear complaints that "many" cases are not open to the public. Yet, we have no systematic evidence about the scope of the problem, the types of cases that are most problematic, and whether the problem is more severe in lower-level courts or particular regions.

We are also told that intervention by party organizations and in particular the political-legal committee undermines judicial independence. And yet, as far as I know, there have been no empirical studies to show how often political-legal committees intervene, in what types of cases, the nature of the intervention, and the results. Furthermore, the surveys that are available about key issues such as outside interference with judicial activities are often from the 1990s or even earlier, and thus seriously out of date and of dubious value given the many institutional changes and the development of judicial norms and practices over the last fifteen to twenty years.

Anecdotes and adjectives are no substitute for quantitative studies and empirical data. No one would want the entire U.S. legal system to be judged based solely on isolated horror stories about abuse or corruption reported in the *New York Times*.[14] This is all the more

---

12 For a discussion of some limitations imposed by courts and the reasons for such restrictions in socio-economic cases, see Fu Yulin and Randall Peerenboom, "A New Analytical Framework for Understanding and Promoting Judicial Independence in China," in *Judicial Independence in China*.

13 *Supreme People's Court's 2005 Work Report*, http://www.court.gov.cn/work/200503180013.htm, last visited June 17, 2007.

14 See "Broken Bench: In Tiny Courts of New York, Abuses of Power and Law," *New York Times*, September 25, 2006, http://www.nytimes.com/2006/09/25/nyregion/25courts.html?ex=1159848000&en=437197e48a0b8a3f&ei=5070&emc

the case given that both the popular media and legal scholars are much more likely to focus on areas where there are problems, rather than spending time investigating nonissues or doing surveys showing that, yes indeed, the system functions as it is supposed to. The eye-catching stories reported in the press or used as examples by legal scholars are just that—eye-catching. They are not a repre-

---

= eta1. The article discusses problems in the 1,250 justice courts in New York and thirty other states, which handle 2.2 million cases a year, including 300,000 criminal cases:
"Some of the courtrooms are not even courtrooms: tiny offices or basement rooms without a judge's bench or jury box. Sometimes the public is not admitted, witnesses are not sworn to tell the truth, and there is no word-for-word record of the proceedings.
Nearly three-quarters of the judges are not lawyers, and many—truck drivers, sewer workers or laborers—have scant grasp of the most basic legal principles. Some never got through high school, and at least one went no further than grade school...
People have been sent to jail without a guilty plea or a trial, or tossed from their homes without a proper proceeding. In violation of the law, defendants have been refused lawyers, or sentenced to weeks in jail because they cannot pay a fine. Frightened women have been denied protection from abuse...
Defendants have been jailed illegally. Others have been subjected to racial and sexual bigotry so explicit it seems to come from some other place and time. People have been denied the right to a trial, an impartial judge and the presumption of innocence...
For the nearly 75 percent of justices who are not lawyers, the only initial training is six days of state-administered classes, followed by a true-or-false test so rudimentary that the official who runs it said only one candidate since 1999 had failed...
Some 1,140 justices have received some sort of reprimand over the last three decades—an average of about 40 a year, either privately warned, publicly rebuked or removed. They are seriously disciplined at a steeper rate than their higher-court colleagues...
Many justices preside in intimidatingly tight quarters, admitting participants one by one. Many have heard testimony, settled claims or ruled in criminal cases without notifying the prosecutor, lawyers or even the people directly involved.
Describing his 13 years on the bench, one judge said: 'I just follow my own common sense... [a]nd the hell with the law.'"

sentative sample. The effect of relying on these nonrepresentative stories is to exaggerate the deficiencies in the PRC legal system, perpetuating myths and stereotypes that often fall by the wayside once the empirical evidence from more systematic quantitative studies is presented.[15]

Perhaps the biggest problem in assessing implementation of law in China, however, is the lack of a comparative context. We are often presented with data showing problems with implementation of law in China or shortcomings in the legal system. The data seem overwhelming, the problems severe. And yet often when we compare the findings in China to the findings in other countries, we discover that similar problems exist elsewhere, casting China's performance in a dramatically different light. Take the much-discussed example of enforcement of court judgments. As Don Clarke has noted, available empirical suggests that enforcement is no more difficult in China than in New Jersey: "[I]t seems abundantly clear that the American public and legal community routinely put up with enforcement rates that the Chinese legal community would consider shockingly low."[16]

Similarly, there is allegedly a serious lack of trust in the PRC judicial system, in no small measure because corruption is often reported to be rampant. Yet, several surveys have found just the opposite. One large survey using general population survey readings to generate a representative sample concluded: "The empirical evidence not only indicates that citizens are active users of courts when they seek to resolve their disputes, but also demonstrates a high degree of popular trust in legal institutions and the widespread belief

---

15 Peerenboom, "Seek Truth from Facts," 262, noting that the rate of enforcement in cases where information was obtained directly from the lawyers involved was twice as high as where information was obtained from accounts in the press and academic journals. Borge Bakken also notes the dangers of relying on media reports about crime in China or elsewhere. See his "Introduction: Crime, Control, and Modernity in China," in *Crime, Punishment and Policing in China*, ed. Borge Bakken (Lanham: Rowman & Littlefield, 2005), 3.

16 Clarke, "Power and Politics in the Chinese Court System," 34.

that courts are more effective and fair than preexisting alternatives, such as mediation."[17] In another study, Margaret Woo found that over half of the parties in civil cases in Beijing thought that the court's judgment was fair.[18]

In still another survey, Ethan Michelson found that Beijing respondents are more trusting of the courts than their Chicago counterparts, and evaluate the performance of the courts more positively. Respondents in Beijing were twice as likely as Chicago residents to agree with the claim that courts are "doing a good job." Moreover, whereas over 40 percent of Chicago residents *disagreed or strongly disagreed* that the courts generally guarantee everyone a fair trial, only 10 percent of Beijing residents and 28 percent of rural residents held similar negative views. And whereas 43 percent of Chicago residents disagreed or strongly disagreed with the statement that judges are basically honest, only 9 percent of Beijing residents and 29 percent of rural residents held similar views.[19]

To put these numbers in a broader comparative context, public distrust of judges and the legal system is often high even in countries with well-established legal systems. Barely half of Belgians believe court decisions are just, while 60 percent lack confidence in the judiciary. Over 40 percent of British citizens have little or no confidence in judges and the courts. In Canada, only 5 percent of people express a great deal of confidence in the criminal justice system.[20] In France, only 38 percent of the public trust the judiciary, with only 21 percent believing judges are independent from eco-

---

17 Pierre Landry et al., "Introduction: Markets, Courts and Leninism," *The China Review* vol. 9, no. 1 (2009), p. 12.

18 Margaret Y. K. Woo, "Law, Development and the Socio-Economic Rights of Chinese Women," *Columbia Asian Law Journal* (2005/2006).

19 Email communication with Professor Ethan Michelson, based on a 2001 survey he conducted with sociologists from Renmin University of 1,300 Beijing residents. The Chicago numbers are from a 1990 survey. See Tom Tyler, *Why People Obey the Law* (New Haven: Yale University Press, 1990).

20 Mike Hough and Julian V. Roberts, "Confidence in Justice: An International Review," Findings 243, http://www.homeoffice.gov.uk/rds/pdfs04/r243.pdf.

nomic circles and only 15 percent believing they are independent from political powers.[21]

It is particularly important to measure China's performance against the performance of other countries at its income level. Wealth is highly correlated with rule of law, good governance, human rights, and other indicators of human well-being like literacy and longevity rates.[22] Simply put, one can expect more problems in a lower-middle-income country such as China than in a high-income country. Nevertheless, on the whole, China outperforms the average in its income class on most of these measures, with the exception of civil and political rights and control of corruption,[23]

---

21 "L'opinion des Français sur la justice: réalisée en 1997 par l'institut CA à la demande de la Mission de recherche Droit et Justice," http://www.vie-publique.fr/dossier_polpublic/presomption_innocence/annexes/sondage1.shtml.

22 Wealth is highly correlated with good governance indicators such as government effectiveness ($r = .77$), rule of law ($r = .82$), control of corruption ($r = .76$), social and economic rights ($r = .92$), women's rights as measured by the Gender Developmental Index ($r = .93$), civil and political rights ($r = .62$), and even physical integrity rights though to a lower degree ($r = -.40$). Randall Peerenboom, *China Modernizes: Threat to the West or Model for the Rest* (Oxford: Oxford University Press, 2007), 41.

23 See Peerenboom, *China Modernizes*. After a discussion of a wide range of reforms, including institutional reforms, to combat corruption, and a survey of various indicators of the incidence of corruption, Dali Yang concludes that corruption peaked around 1999. He also notes that based on Transparency International's Corruption Index, China does substantially better than its nominal per capita gross domestic product (GDP) would predict. As he observes, popular attitudes are likely to lag behind improvements in tackling corruption and overstate the amount of corruption because of the so-called paradox of anticorruption—campaigns against corruption and the arrest of a number of high level officials, widely reported in the media, reinforce the public perception that corruption is rampant. Nonetheless, he suggests that polls based on subjective responses from PRC citizens, which tend to reflect a sense of improvement in the early years of this decade, are more likely to be accurate than polls that rely on the subjective views of foreign business people. Dali Yang, *Remaking the Chinese Leviathan: Market Transition and the Politics of Governance in China* (Stanford: Stanford University Press, 2004), 217–258.

though China appears to have done better in curtailing judicial corruption than corruption more generally.[24]

Some national-level data suggest that judicial corruption is extremely rare, and that a wide range of reforms has led to reduced judicial corruption, although as noted previously the national-level data are difficult to square with provincial-level data.[25] According to the *Supreme People's Court 2002 Work Report*, 995 "judicial personnel" violated laws and rules in 2001. It needs to be emphasized that this number is only a tiny fraction of the total number of judicial personnel, includes both judges and all other court personnel and even police and prison workers in some cases, and includes major as well as minor infractions.[26] Of the 995 cases, the infractions were sufficiently serious to result in criminal prosecutions in only 85 cases. In 2002, only 45 judicial personnel were subject to criminal sanctions. Moreover, according to the *Supreme People's Court 2003 Work Report*, the number of judges who violated the laws or rules decreased from an already low 0.067 percent in 1998 to an even lower 0.02 percent in 2002.[27] Further, even the U.S. State Department report, which is always quick to point out shortcomings in

---

24 Citing the World Bank's *World Business Environment Survey*, Clarke et al. conclude that "China has less legal corruption than countries at similar levels of per capita income." Donald Clarke, Peter Murrell, and Susan Whiting, "The Role of Law in China's Economic Development," 22, http://ssrn.com/abstract = 878672.

25 See Li Ling, *supra*. For a description of the many reforms aimed at reducing corruption, see Yang, *Remaking the Chinese Leviathan*, 217–258; Peerenboom, *China's Long March Toward Rule of Law*, 296–298.

26 See e.g., "Inner Mongolian Procuratorial Authorities Investigate and Dispose of Criminal Cases Involving More than 600 Judicial Personnel Over Five Years," in Chinese, Xinhua News Agency, December 20, 2005, http://news.xinhuanet.com/legal/2005-12/20/content_3946861.htm. Note that the figures include police and prison workers.

27 *Supreme People's Court 2003 Work Report*, http://www.court.gov.cn/work/200303280001.htm. The Supreme People's Court reported that in 2005, 378 judicial personnel were found to abuse power for personal interests, with 66 committing infractions sufficiently serious to constitute crimes. These numbers were,

China's implementation of rule of law and protection of rights, acknowledges that most of the convictions are for matters other than corruption. From January 2002 to October 2003, 80 percent of the cases where "judicial officials" were prosecuted involved alleged incompetence or rights violations, while only 20 percent involved suspected corruption or bribery.[28]

The results of a survey conducted jointly by members of the National People's Congress, Supreme People's Court (SPC), and Supreme People's Procuracy also call into question the popular perception that judicial corruption is widespread and getting worse. One of the many methods adopted to curtail corruption has been to increase external supervision by the legislature and the procuracy. Cases involving corruption are among the most likely to be supervised. Yet, the number of supervised cases resulting in a change of verdict on retrial suggests that only a tiny fraction of cases are incorrectly decided, whether because of local protectionism, judicial incompetence, corruption, or other reasons. Each year the courts handle approximately six million cases. Only a tiny fraction—less than 0.3 percent—result in a changed verdict.[29]

Popular reports of widespread corruption highlight the danger in relying on anecdotes or small nonrepresentative samples. In recent years, there have been several high-profile cases of presidents and vice-presidents of courts, including provincial high courts, being removed from office because of corruption.[30] Given the number of high court presidents (only thirty-one at any given time), the

---

respectively, 18 percent and 44 percent less than in 2004. See "China's Judicial Work in 2005," http://en.chinacourt.org/public/detail.php?id = 4030.

28 U.S. Department of State, *Country Reports on Human Rights Practices 2003: China* (2004), 9, http://www.state.gov/g/drl/rls/hrrpt/2003/27768.htm.

29 Randall Peerenboom, "Judicial Accountability and Judicial Independence: An Empirical Study of Individual Case Supervision," *The China Journal* 55 (2006).

30 For a brief overview of some of these cases, as well as other data on judicial corruption, see Minxin Pei, *China's Trapped Transition: The Limits of Developmental Autocracy* 71 (Harvard: Harvard University Press, 2006).

percentages are much higher than the percentages for judges as a whole. More importantly, however, there are reasons to suspect that corruption might be more prevalent among court presidents and vice-presidents than rank and file judges. Parties seeking to corrupt decision makers may find it more efficient to influence the top leaders of higher-level courts as they may have more say in the final outcome. The higher court will often be the final appellate court. And the president or vice-president may be able to exert influence directly on the collegial panel that hears the case or through their position on the adjudicative committee. The alternative would be to try to influence the presiding judge and perhaps one of the other judges on the collegial panel. However, these judges may not have the final authority to decide a "major" or "important" case. Moreover, judges on the collegial panel would be subject to further review, potentially by the adjudicative committee on appeal and through external supervision. In addition, presidents and vice-presidents may be older and approaching retirement age, at which point some officials look to their retirement and succumb to corruption. Finally, it also is noteworthy that at least some presidents and vice-presidents appear to have been removed from office not for their own corrupt behavior but under SPC rules that punish heads of courts for corruption among judges in their courts. Li Ling also found that heads of court are most likely to be guilty of accepting kickbacks on construction projects to build new courthouses or accepting bribes from judges seeking promotion, rather than attempting to influence the outcome of a particular case.[31]

To sum up this section, assessing the state of law implementation in China requires that the performance of the legal system be located in a comparative context. In doing so, one must also take into account China's huge population and report percentages based on total population rather than simply providing absolute numbers. What may seem like a "large" problem when presented in terms of absolute numbers will often seem decidedly less pressing

---

31 Li Ling, *supra*.

when presented in percentage terms. One must also take into consideration the wide variation by region, level of court, area of law, and type of case, and disaggregate the data to avoid painting with too broad a brush.

While the preceding discussion suggests that we often know less than we think about enforcement in China, it does not, and is not intended to, show that we are always completely at a loss about implementation issues in China.

There have been many useful studies by legal scholars and social scientists that address important issues and provide extremely valuable insights; anecdotal evidence may be illustrative in some cases if used with caution; and general observation does suggest that there are often problems with implementation in some areas. However, knowing that laws are not being fully implemented is the beginning rather than the end of the story. We must still ask why they are not being fully implemented, with the even more fundamental question being whether they should be.

How Much Implementation Should There Be?

Reports pointing out that laws are not always fully implemented generally assume that the goal is 100 percent implementation. However, 100 percent implementation may not be practical or normatively desirable, at least for some groups, particularly given the large variation in China.

Not all laws are meant to be fully implemented. In some cases, laws are passed for symbolic reasons, to reinforce the identity of the community or to demonstrate that a country is becoming part of the international community. This is often the case for international human rights treaties. China, for instance, is now facing the challenge of how to respond to the increasing international and domestic pressure to ratify the International Covenant for Civil and Political Rights (ICCPR). On the one hand, China will continue to be criticized unless it ratifies the treaty. On the other hand, ratification will inevitably lead to greater confrontation with the international rights community by forcing the government to defend more explicitly its interpretation on a whole series of contested rights issues. Some reform-minded Chinese scholars have argued that China could ratify the ICCPR without attaching many reservations or qualifying declarations on the basis that the PRC Constitution and other laws already provide for virtually all of the rights set out in the ICCPR. Apart from deliberately downplaying the gap between formal laws and actual practice in this area, this view ignores the politics of interpretation. The rights in the ICCPR are stated at a fairly high level of abstraction, and thus are subject to a wide range of interpretation. The ICCPR Human Rights Committee is charged with interpreting the ICCPR. The committee's interpretations tend to be decidedly more liberal than the interpretation of the Chinese government. Although the committee's interpretations are nonbinding, they do carry weight in the international community, and can and will be used to "shame" China. Were China to ratify the ICCPR, it would most likely do so with either a blanket reservation that the ICCPR has no domestic effect, as the United States has done, or with a series of reservations and statements that greatly limit the domestic impact of the treaty. Either approach is fraught with risk. The United States has been widely criticized for its reservations. China is sure to be subject to considerably greater criticism. In any event, one thing is certain: there will continue to be imitations on civil and political rights when the exercise of such rights is perceived as threatening social and political stability, regardless of whether those rights are grounded in existing domestic laws or international treaties.[32]

Sometimes laws are passed for domestic political reasons, such as when the government rushes out with a law after a major catastrophe. In the haste to "do something," the government may pass

---

32 For the argument that other successful East Asian states followed a similar path of development, and consideration of whether the restrictions are justified, see Peerenboom, *China Modernizes*.

laws that miss the target. This seems to have been the case when the government issued new rules to regulate Internet cafés after a tragic fire broke out in one café, although the regulations also responded to the somewhat alarmist concerns of parents worried their children were becoming addicted to online games and exposed to pornography, superstition, and the decadent cultural practices and norms of Western countries.[33]

In other cases, lawmakers unable to reach agreement agree to disagree, and settle on language that is subject to different interpretations. Those groups adversely affected by the new law may then use the vagueness in the language to avoid implementation of the law.

More generally, given wide regional variations and different levels of development even within regions, national laws and regulations cannot always be fully implemented. In some cases, local governments lack the capacity. Even central administrative agencies responsible for enforcing the law are often seriously understaffed and lack funding.[34]

Moreover, in a country as large and diverse as China, central laws will inevitably conflict at times with local norms and customs. In response, China has established a complex regime of autonomous zones that obviate to some extent the conflict between central laws and local customs in minority regions. Nevertheless, conflicts still occur. It is not always obvious that the best normative solution is to enforce central laws. In any event, from a practical perspective, attempting to implement laws in the face of fierce local resistance is no easy task.

In some cases, enforcing the national laws would cause consid-

---

[33] See Johan Lagerkvist's chapter in this volume. Yang shows that crises—large and small, real, and perceived—have often served as catalysts for institutional and legislative reforms. Yang, *Remaking the Chinese Leviathan*.

[34] Even within a particular area such as intellectual property, there may be differences in funding, staffing, and institutional status. Protection of copyrights has historically been weaker than for trademarks and patents in part for these reasons. See Andrew Mertha, *The Politics of Piracy: Intellectual Property in Contemporary China* (Ithaca: Cornell University Press, 2005).

erable economic hardship. As is true elsewhere, environmental laws have been set aside when they conflict with the livelihood of a significant membership of the local community.[35] Intellectual property rules have also been difficult to enforce when local communities have relied heavily on counterfeit products as a significant source of revenue. More importantly, developing countries have long challenged the fundamental fairness of the intellectual property rights regime, which is largely the product of developed countries. They complain that intellectual property rules serve the interests of the developed countries at the expense of developing countries.[36] The result is a large transfer of wealth from poor countries to a handful of developed countries. At its most extreme, citizens in poor countries are unable to afford lifesaving medicines given the high cost of patented drugs. Accordingly, the creation of generic substitutes through reverse engineering or other means is seen as morally justified.

Finally, it deserves recalling that achieving full implementation would be costly. In many cases, the benefits from marginal improvements in implementation would not justify the amount spent to achieve them. A lower level of enforcement in developing countries may be justified given their limited resources and other more pressing needs.

Factors That Affect Implementation

Implementation is always imperfect, and affected by a wide range of factors: the nature of the rules (are they reasonable, practical, clear,

---

35 See Benjamin van Rooij, *Land and Pollution Regulation in China: Lawmaking, Compliance, Enforcement; Theory and Cases* (Leiden: Leiden University Press, 2006).

36 United Nations Conference on Trade and Development (UNCTAD), *Trade and Development Report 1999* (Geneva: United Nations, 1999). The United Nations Development Programme (UNDP) reports that 96 percent of patent royalties go to companies in developed countries. UNDP, *Human Development Report 2005*, 35, http://hdr.undp.org/reports/global/2005/pdf/HDR05_complete.pdf.

consistent; are they broad standards or specific requirements); who makes them (is the entity authoritative and legitimate); through what process (is the law or rule-making process open, transparent, fair); how they are enforced and by whom (by administrative agencies, the courts, the political process, the market, nongovernmental organizations, civil society, or the media); the amount of resources devoted to implementation and the costs of enforcement; the difficulty and cost of compliance; and the incentive structure both for enforcing laws and for complying with them, including sanctions (and their severity and likelihood) and rewards. As we have seen, sensational events such as tragic accidents or scandals can also have a great impact on the creation and implementation of laws, particularly when picked up by the media.

First, implementation of laws is more difficult when there are *competing interests*. As China has become an increasingly pluralistic society, interest groups have emerged representing sharply competing agendas. This has resulted in inconsistency within and among laws and regulations, which are then subject to wide variation in implementation depending on the ability of different groups to exert influence at the enforcement stage. For instance, the amendments to the Criminal Law in the mid-1900s reflected a compromise on key issues among the more law-and-order-oriented public security ministry and procuracy, the more rights-oriented defense bar and human rights groups, and the courts. Not surprisingly, the different actors then interpreted the law in different ways. Environmental law is another area where competing interests have undermined implementation, with the need to sustain economic growth clashing with the desire for a cleaner environment.

Competing institutional interests also affect implementation of law. There are countless examples in addition to the Criminal Law. An attempt to pass a law on individual case supervision was abandoned in the face of opposition from the courts, which believed the law would undermine judicial independence. When local people's congresses passed regulations providing for individual case supervision, judges often resisted. To defuse tensions, the Supreme People's Court then issued a notice encouraging judges to cooperate with people's congresses and to promptly reply to their requests for information. Efforts to pass a law to replace the regulations on re-education through labor (*laojiao*) have been stymied by the desire of the courts to subject the process to judicial review and the insistence of the public security ministry that they retain the authority to make the decision. The passage of the Anti-Monopoly Law was also held up by the inability to decide which entity or entities would be responsible for enforcement.

Second, *economic factors* clearly affect implementation. Most fundamentally, wealth matters—both in providing the resources to deal with certain issues, and in affecting institutional strength, as supported by the high correlation between wealth and rule of law and good governance. Many of the areas where enforcement is most difficult or implementation weakest are in reality due to the lack of wealth: mine safety, labor issues, migrant's rights, the improper imposition of education fees, land takings, medical care, and the provision of other welfare benefits, etc. The importance of wealth requires that China's performance be located in a broader comparative context that controls for levels of wealth and other factors. Of course, how the state chooses to allocate resources and how wealth is distributed also matter.[37]

In addition to wealth, other economic factors play a role, including the diversity of the economy. Local protection is less severe in Shanghai than in places dominated by a single major company.[38]

---

37 Economic factors and social change also play an important role in undermining efforts at criminal reform. Industrialization, urbanization, and a transition to a market economy generally lead to rising crime rates, particularly when combined, as they usually are, with increased social and economic inequality. Similarly, in China, market reforms have led to higher crime rates, reflecting the reemergence of criminal activity such as violent crime, organized crime, drug-related crime, prostitution, and gambling. See Peerenboom, *China Modernizes*, 199–204.

38 Veron, Mei-Ying Hung, *Judicial Reform in China: Lessons from Shanghai*,

Environmental laws are harder to pass when their implementation would mean the closure of the main employer in the town.

Differences at the firm level also matter. In general, larger companies tend to have better compliance, although, as just noted, their size and local market power can lead to local protectionism and environmental violations. Large multinational companies also have better compliance records on environmental, labor, and tax issues than some of the smaller foreign companies.[39] Companies may also differ in their cost-benefit assessments, with some taking a long-term view, and others taking a short-term view. East Asian companies are often considered to take a long-term and broader view than U.S. firms, which focus more on short-term profits. More so in the past but also to some extent still today, the lack of protection for private companies in China has resulted in entrepreneurs taking a short-term view. Wary of predatory government officials, private entrepreneurs have tended to hide revenue, invested to gain rapid returns on capital, emphasized liquidity, and spent more on consumption rather than reinvesting and building up their companies.[40]

Third, *political factors* must also be considered. The government's concern for stability has clearly resulted in limits on the exercise of civil and political rights, including freedom of speech and assembly. The degree of freedom varies by region. For instance, Buddhists in Tibet and Gansu and Muslims in Xinjiang and other western provinces are subject to more restraints than their counter-

---

Carnegie Endowment for International Peace, Carnegie Paper No. 58, March 2005, http://www.carnegieendowment.org/files/CP58.Hung.FINAL.pdf.

39 Anita Chan, *China's Workers Under Assault: Exploitation and Abuse in a Globalized Economy* (Armonk: M.E. Sharpe, 2001).

40 Che Jiahua and Yingyi Qian, "Institutional Environment, Community Government, and Corporate Governance: Understanding China's Township-Village Enterprises," *Journal of Law, Economics and Organization* 14 (1998); Justin Tan, "Regulatory Environment and Strategic Orientations in a Transitional Economy: A Study of Chinese Private Enterprise," *Information Access Company* 21 (1996).

parts in other regions where the likelihood of religious-based instability is considered to be lower.

The role of local elections has been varied. In some cases, it has facilitated enforcement of laws and regulations, in large part because citizens that participate in the process of making the rules are more likely to follow them.[41] In addition, it has given voters a chance to remove leaders who violate the law.[42] However, local elections have also sometimes hindered enforcement. Some elections are dominated by interest groups seeking to push their own agenda, which may not be consistent with central laws and regulations. Local voters may also elect leaders who emphasize economic growth, even if at that cost of compliance with central laws. In other cases, elections have had no demonstrable effect.

Fourth, *NGOs and civil society* may also play a role in holding government officials accountable and the lawmaking and implementation processes more generally. The overall trend has been toward more transparency and public participation. The NPC has been soliciting public comment on major laws, in accordance with the Law on Legislation. In general, both the NPC and administrative agencies solicit opinions from academic experts during the law and rule-making processes. The NPC is now drafting an Administrative Procedures Law. As is often the case, local governments have gone ahead and passed their own procedural laws. China's World Trade Organization accession agreement also requires that the public, including foreign companies, be given an opportunity to comment on commercial regulations before they become effective (but unfortunately not before they are promulgated).

Recent years have seen attempts to expand the use of hearings both for NPC laws and administrative rules. There are currently a number of projects and experiments on hearings that seek to ad-

---

41 Tyler, *Why People Obey the Law*.
42 There are other mechanisms for holding government officials accountable, including administrative litigation, administrative reconsideration, administrative supervision, media scrutiny, and party discipline.

dress a range of issues: when hearings should be held, how the public is to be notified, who should be able to attend and speak at such hearings (especially if the number of people wishing to attend the hearing and to speak is very large), how the hearings should be conducted, and how the government should respond to inquiries or recommendations from the public.[43]

Nevertheless, the State Council has acknowledged that considerably more needs to be done in making government more transparent and service-oriented. One report noted that some officials have not attached much importance to efforts to increase openness, that regulations are incomplete or not implemented, and that some departments have only made half-hearted, formalistic efforts at compliance.[44] It called on local governments to pass access to information acts, and to make public through the media, websites, information centers, and public hearings information on government budgets, procurements, and tax revenues; land takings; major investment projects; bankruptcies and the distribution of assets; and license and registration requirements. It also called for sanctions for government officials who falsify progress reports or fail to take action in carrying out the directive.

The government has also experimented with citizen committees to supervise and advise on government work.[45] At the central level, the Development and Reform Commission has established an Ex-

---

43 For an overview of developments in this area—which includes both theoretical and empirical and China-focused and comparative perspectives, see *The Search for Deliberative Democracy in China*, eds. Ethan J. Leib and He Baogang (New York: Palgrave McMillan, 2006). In their chapter, James Fishkin, He Baogang, and Alice Siu describe an interesting experiment that attempted to create a representative sample through random selection of citizens to participate in deliberative discussions.

44 State Council, *Opinion on Further Promoting Openness in Governmental Affairs*, March 24, 2005.

45 See e.g., State Council Office of Legislative Affairs, *Undertaking Administration According to Law: Review and Prognosis*, report prepared for the Asian Development Bank, on file with author.

pert Consultation System. At the provincial level, Shanxi recently established the Government Decision-making Consultation Committee, and invited sixty well-known experts to participate as consultants on key decisions made by the provincial government. Hunan established the Academics and Experts Consultation System, set up the Opinion Poll Center in the Provincial Statistics Bureau, and established the Public Opinion Collection and Analysis Mechanism. Having created the Governor and Expert Symposia and Foreign Consultant Invitation System, Guangdong now holds a symposium every two years where the heads of the top fifty enterprises in the world are invited to advise the governor on every economic development in Guangdong. Hainan has set up a system where regulations and official documents are sent out for review by outside legal counsel before being sent to the governor for signature. Hebei has also established legal expert consultation bodies in eleven city governments and more than half of the county governments.

Even the procuracy, one of the most conservative and least open institutions, has jumped on the bandwagon. Beginning in October 2003, the procuracy established citizen supervision committees in ten provinces. The system is now used by 86 percent of procuratorates nationwide. The committee is charged with conducting independent appraisals of cases the procuracy placed on file for investigation but later decided to withdraw or terminate prosecution. According to the State Council's white paper on political democracy in China: "They can also participate, upon invitation, in other law-enforcement examination activities organized by the people's procuratorates regarding crimes committed by civil servants, and make suggestions and comments on violations of law and discipline discovered. By the end of 2004, a total of 18,962 people's supervisors had been selected, who had supervised the conclusion of 3,341 cases."[46]

There is no doubt that the number of social organizations has

---

46 State Council, *White Paper: Building of Political Democracy in China*, October 19, 2005.

increased rapidly in China and that civil society is exerting a greater influence on the policymaking and implementation processes. Nevertheless, the utility of civil society as a mechanism for input and supervision has been hampered in various official and unofficial ways. First, the regulatory framework makes it difficult for citizens or social groups to organize and be recognized by the government. Approval requirements limit the number of social organizations established in some areas and prevent the establishment of other organizations that are likely to be politically active in promoting the interests of some socially vulnerable groups or in pressing for change in certain politically sensitive areas. Second, citizens and groups seeking to protest must obtain prior permission, which is often not given in practice. Third, and more generally, existing social organizations face limited avenues to influence the political process despite recent reforms to increase public participation. Fourth, there are numerous restrictions on what the press can report. Fifth, government officials as well as owners of businesses and private citizens have used broad defamation laws to attack aggressive media reporters. Sixth, in recent years, some lawyers have been arrested, experienced intimidation, or had their licenses revoked in the process of representing criminal defendants or citizens challenging government decisions to requisition their land for development purposes and the amount of compensation provided, often on what seem to be trumped-up charges.[47] Meanwhile citizens seeking to protect their property rights, uphold environmental regulations, or challenge government actions have been beaten by thugs and gangs often with links to the local government or have been detained for their efforts.[48]

---

[47] See e.g., "China Shutters Prominent Lawyer's Firm," *Washington Post*, November 6, 2005. See also Fu Hualing, "When Lawyers are Prosecuted: The Struggle of a Profession in Transition," May 2006, http://ssrn.com/abstract = 956500.

[48] See e.g., "Five Chinese Nuns Hospitalized After Land Dispute," *Washington Post*, December 1, 2005; "Blind Social Activist, Lawyers Beaten in China," *Radio Free Asia*, http://newsblaze.com/story/20051004141709nnnn.nb/newsblaze/TOPSTORY/Top-Story.html.

Fifth, *institutional capacity* also has a clear impact on implementation. China of course has had to rebuild key institutions such as the courts, procuracy, law schools, the legal profession, administrative agencies, and the civil service, all of which were weakened or destroyed during the Cultural Revolution.

A related issue is institutional culture and the compatibility of reforms with institutional norms and practices. China's civil and criminal law systems were based on an amalgam of civil, socialist, and traditional law. Efforts to introduce elements of a common-law system have challenged the theoretical underpinning and normative assumptions of the existing system, and required judges, prosecutors, and lawyers to adopt different roles. Similarity in legal systems facilitates understanding between external and internal actors, reduces system friction, and decreases the likelihood of unexpected consequences arising. At minimum, reforms are likely to be more effective when relevant actors are familiar with the laws, practices, or institutions being adopted.[49] Fortunately, in this era of mixed legal systems, most of the key actors in China will be aware of the general features of other systems.

Sixth, *social and cultural* factors may play a role in implementation of rule of law and in the adoption and operation of particular institutions or the application of particular rules. One study found that countries that emphasized autonomy and egalitarianism had higher levels of rule of law and accountability and less corruption, whereas countries that emphasized embeddedness and hierarchy had a lower level of rule of law and accountability and far more corruption.[50] In short, English-speaking countries and Western Europe scored significantly higher than other regions. The authors suggest

---

49 Daniel Berkowitz et al., "Economic Development, Legality, and the Transplant Effect," *European Economic Review* 47, no. 1 (2003). Using data from forty-nine countries, the authors argue that countries with developed legal orders and a population familiar with basic principles of the transplanted law were more successful at incorporating the transplanted law than those without, and that differences in legal families were less important.

50 Amir N. Licht et al., "Culture Rules: The Foundations of Rule of Law and

that cultural orientation in East Asia may make it more difficult to implement rule of law, restrict corruption, and increase accountability or that "good governance" in Asia may differ in some respects from "good governance" in Western liberal democracies. Good governance in Asian countries no doubt differs in significant respects from good governance in rich, liberal-democratic Western countries once one examines in more detail the broad variables of rule of law, accountability, and corruption. Nevertheless, Asian states have outperformed other regions in terms of rule of law on the same World Bank good-governance scales used by the authors of the study, suggesting that culture may not be as important at least in Asia as the authors claim.

While culture may not be an absolute bar to implementation of law in China, cultural factors are likely to have an impact in particular areas. For instance, administrative litigation has been infrequently invoked in part because people are still getting used to the idea that citizens may sue officials. Cultural factors are more likely to be important in areas such as criminal and family law, as opposed to areas such as commercial law.

Conclusion: Toward a "Pragmatic Theory" of Implementation—and Regulation

A theory of implementation would take into account and control for the above factors. It would also take into account the related but more general topic of regulation, and incorporate the insights of regulatory theory. Unfortunately, there is no consensus about how to regulate a developing country as large as China.

Debates continue about the relative advantages and disadvantages of top-down (command and control) approaches versus bottom-up or post-Fordist approaches in general, and in develop-

---

Other Norms of Governance," June 9, 2002, http://papers.ssrn.com/sol3/papers.cfm?abstract_id = 314559.

ing countries where institutions are weak and resources lacking in particular.[51]

Some studies have traced a cycle of centralization, decentralization, and recentralization. Dali Yang and others have documented the recentralization of regulation through vertical or semivertical integration of the administrative hierarchy in a number of areas, including tax collection, environmental protection, food and drug administration, workplace safety, and information collection, with the State Statistical Bureau conducting more of its own surveys rather than relying on reporting from local governments.[52]

This pattern is consistent with trends in Asia and more globally. Michael Howlett and M. Ramesh have traced a regulatory cycle of regulation, deregulation, and re-regulation in Asia.[53] Intersecting with this line of research in an interesting if complicated way is the work of Håkan Hydén, who points out that China is undergoing three significant transformations at the same time.[54] Parts of the economy are still based on a guild society; other parts are at different stages in the transition to an industrial society; and there is now beginning to emerge a postindustrial information society. Hydén notes that each of these economic modes has its own form of regulation, which follows a general cycle in the shape of an S-curve, emerging, maturing, and then decaying and giving way to another form. The different phases lead to different types of regulation, which may explain to some extent the regulatory cycles noted by

---

51 World Bank, *Greening Industry, New Roles for Communities, Markets and Governnments* (Oxford: Oxford University Press, 2000). The World Bank advocates a flexible approach that relies on local communities and nonstate informal mechanisms.

52 See e.g., Yang, *Remaking the Chinese Leviathan*; Mertha, *The Politics of Piracy*.

53 Michael Howlett and M. Ramesh, "Preface: The Evolution of De/Reregulation," in *Deregulation and its Discontents: Rewriting the Rules in Asia*, eds. M. Ramesh and Michael Howlett (Cheltenham, UK; Northampton, MA: Edward Elgar, 2006), 1–10.

54 See Hydén's chapter in this volume.

others. The guild sector in China is increasingly more open and less dependent on internal rules binding on its members. Parts of the industrial sector, already heavily regulated, have undergone deregulation, and in some cases re-regulation. Meanwhile, the emerging information society is now giving rise to a host of new laws and regulations as the government grapples with the Internet, the role of foreign investment in key information sectors such as telecommunications, the media, and banking and finance, and the need to set technical standards that will determine the development path of key industries and China's competitiveness in the global economy.

Another fault line in regulatory theory lies along the divide between deterrence-based and cooperative approaches to regulation. Empirical work by John Braithwaite and Toni Makkai, among others, has challenged the assumptions regarding the relationship between compliance and the certainty or severity of sanctioning.[55] On the other hand, they also find that relying on persuasion or a more cooperative approach alone is insufficient. In their view, exclusive reliance on one approach is not as desirable as a flexible approach that combines different strategies.

The flexible regulator's toolbox includes a wide range of tools, both formal and informal, and legal and nonlegal. In addition to privatization, deregulation, centralization, and decentralization, there are corporatist and negotiated rule-making approaches that involve key stakeholders in the lawmaking and implementation processes; self regulation and other informal (non-state or quasi-non-state) approaches, including restorative justice programs; public disclosure and sunshine laws that emphasize transparency and openness; increased participation and supervision by consultative committees, NGOs, and the media; and the list goes on.

While there are vast literatures on these various approaches, there is as yet no overall theory of the optimal approach to regula-

---

55 John Braithwaite and Toni Makkai, "Testing an Expected Utility Model of Corporate Deterrence," *Law & Society Review* 25, no. 1 (1991): 7.

tion. Perhaps there never will be, given the diversity in levels of development, institutional culture, social and cultural practices, and a host of other contingent factors that differentiate countries. Indeed, the quest for a unified theory or optimal approach to regulation may be at odds with the emerging view that what is needed is a pragmatic, flexible, balanced approach that takes into consideration these differentiating contingent factors.[56] Unfortunately, the general advice to policymakers to adopt a pragmatic, flexible, balanced approach does not provide much guidance.

Even in the absence of a general theory of regulation and implementation, however, there are many specific issues that could be clarified through further research and experimentation. One of the issues concerns the rationalization of governance. In China, different entities often have overlapping jurisdiction and responsibility for implementing laws. Citizens also have a variety of channels for seeking redress, including informal channels, a wide range of administrative mechanisms, judicial remedies, and in some cases political channels. There is considerable potential for forum shopping, and for inefficiency and redundancy. Some scholars have found that overlapping jurisdiction leads to lax enforcement as agencies pass the buck back and forth—especially when there are no revenues associated with enforcement or providing the service.[57] Others, however, find competition may increase efficiency and enhance enforcement.[58]

---

56 See generally the chapters by Michael Dowdle, Jerry Mashaw, Michele Ford, and Colin Scott, all of which challenge, to one degree or another, the notion that a system of governance and accountability can be created by design, in *Public Accountability: Designs, Dilemmas and Experiences*, ed. Michael W. Dowdle (Cambridge: Cambridge University Press, 2006).

57 Martin Kostadinov Dimitrov, *Administrative Decentralization, Legal Fragmentation, and the Rule of Law in Transitional Economies: The Enforcement of Intellectual Property Rights (IPR) Laws in China, Russia, Taiwan, and the Czech Republic*, Ph.D. dissertation, Department of Political Science, Stanford University, 2004.

58 Mertha, *The Politics of Piracy*.

Another pressing issue in developing countries is how to govern well with limited resources. Again, there are a number of techniques to cut costs, including contracting out government services to private companies. Fu Hualing and D. W. Choy have examined the controversial case of contracting out police functions.[59] Andrew Mertha has shown how companies have hired private investigation firms to collect evidence to document intellectual property violations and in some cases have even paid the public security a fee to raid the violating companies and confiscate counterfeit goods.[60] Other techniques to achieve good governance cheaply include the use of information networks to enhance enforcement, as in the recent practice of courts publishing the names of companies that do not comply with court judgments or the public blacklisting of construction companies who offered bribes. Further research would be useful to determine the efficacy and sustainability of these approaches.

The fact that rule of law, good governance, and most indicators of human well-being are so highly correlated with wealth suggests that law implementation will be a dynamic process, and a topic that scholars must revisit on a regular basis.[61]

---

59 F. Hualing and D. W. Choy, "Policing for Profit: Fiscal Crisis and Institutionalized Corruption of Chinese Police," in *Police Corruption: Paradigms, Models and Concepts: Challenges for Developing Countries*, Stanley Einstein and Menachem Amir (eds.) (Huntsville: Office of International Criminal Justice, 2003), ch. 21. Murray S. Tanner argues that the reliance on strike hard campaigns, which draw heavily on citizen involvement in reporting crime, is due in no small part to the low ratio of professional police to citizens. While acknowledging traditional aspects to the campaigns, Michael Dutton points out that they reflect a general trend from a political-based to a market/contract-based philosophy found in policing and society more generally during the reform era. See Murray S. Tanner, "Campaign-Style Policing in China and Its Critics," and Michael Dutton, "Toward a Government of the Contract: Policing in the Era of Reform," in Baaken, *Crime, Punishment and Policing in China*.

60 Mertha, *The Politics of Piracy*.

61 For an interesting companion to this volume, compare *Implementation of Law in the People's Republic of China*, eds. Jianfu Chen et al. (The Hague: Kluwer Law International, 2002).

Bibliography

Bakken, Borge. "Introduction: Crime, Control, and Modernity in China." In *Crime, Punishment and Policing in China*, edited by Borge Bakken. Lanham: Rowman & Littlefield, 2005.

Berkowitz, Daniel, et al. "Economic Development, Legality, and the Transplant Effect," *European Economic Review* 47, no. 1 (2003).

Braithwaite, John, and Toni Makkai, "Testing an Expected Utility Model of Corporate Deterrence," *Law & Society Review* 25, no. 1 (1991).

Chan, Anita. *China's Workers Under Assault: Exploitation and Abuse in a Globalized Economy*. Armonk: M.E. Sharpe, 2001.

Che, Jiahua, and Yingyi Qian, "Institutional Environment, Community Government, and Corporate Governance: Understanding China's Township-Village Enterprises," *Journal of Law, Economics and Organization* 14 (1998).

Chen, Jianfu, et al., eds. *Implementation of Law in the People's Republic of China*. The Hague: Kluwer Law International, 2002.

Clarke, Donald. "Power and Politics in the Chinese Court System: The Enforcement of Civil Judgments," *Columbia Journal of Asian Law* 10 (1996).

Clarke, Donald, Peter Murrell, and Susan Whiting. "The Role of Law in China's Economic Development," http://ssrn.com/abstract=878672.

Dimitrov, Martin. *Administrative Decentralization, Legal Fragmentation, and the Rule of Law in Transitional Economies: The Enforcement of Intellectual Property Rights (IPR) Laws in China, Russia, Taiwan, and the Czech Republic*. Ph.D. dissertation, Department of Political Science, Stanford University, 2004.

Dowdle, Michael, ed. *Public Accountability: Designs, Dilemmas and Experiences*. Cambridge: Cambridge University Press, 2006.

Dutton, Michael. "Toward a Government of the Contract: Policing in the Era of Reform." In *Crime, Punishment and Policing in China*, edited by Borge Bakken. Lanham: Rowman & Littlefield, 2005.

Fu, Hualing. "When Lawyers are Prosecuted: The Struggle of a Profession in Transition," May 2006, http://ssrn.com/abstract=956500

Fu, Hualing, and D. W. Choy. "Policing for Profit: Fiscal Crisis and Institutionalized Corruption of Chinese Police." In *Police Corruption: Paradigms, Models and Concepts: Challenges for Developing Countries*, edited by Stanley Einstein and Menachem Amir. Huntsville: Office of International Criminal Justice, 2003.

He, Xin. "Economic Contract Enforcement in China: An Empirical Study from a Basic-Level Court in the Pearl River Delta," *American Journal of Comparative Law*, vol. 59, no. 2 (2009): 419–456.

Horslee, Jamie. "Shanghai Advances the Cause of Open Government Information in China," http://www.law.yale.edu/documents/pdf/Shanghai_Advances.pdf, accessed 17 June 2007.

Hough, Mike, and Julian V. Roberts. "Confidence in Justice: An International Review," *Findings* 243, http://www.homeoffice.gov.uk/rds/pdfs04/r243.pdf.

Howlett, Michael, and M. Ramesh. "Preface: The Evolution of De/Reregulation." In *Deregulation and Its Discontents: Rewriting the Rules in Asia*, edited by. M. Ramesh and Michael Howlett, 1–10. Cheltenham, UK; Northampton, MA: Edward Elgar, 2006.

Hung, Veron Mei-Ying. *Judicial Reform in China: Lessons from Shanghai, Carnegie Endowment for International Peace*. Carnegie Paper No. 58, March 2005, http://www.carnegieendowment.org/files/CP58.Hung.FINAL.pdf.

Landry, Pierre, et al. "Introduction: Markets, Courts and Leninism," *The China Review* 9, no. 1 (2009): 1–17.

Leib, Ethan, and He Baogang, eds. *The Search for Deliberative Democracy in China*. New York: Palgrave McMillan, 2006

Li, Ling. "Corruption in China's Courts." In *Judicial Independence in China: Lessons for Global Rule of Law Promotion*, edited by Randall Peerenboom. New York: Cambridge University Press, 2009.

Licht, Amir, et al. "Culture Rules: The Foundations of Rule of Law and Other Norms of Governance," June 9, 2002, http://papers.ssrn.com/sol3/papers.cfm?abstract_id=314559.

Mertha, Andrew. *The Politics of Piracy: Intellectual Property in Contemporary China*. Ithaca: Cornell University Press, 2005.

Peerenboom, Randall. *China Modernizes: Threat to the West or Model for the Rest*. Oxford: Oxford University Press, 2007.

———. "Judicial Accountability and Judicial Independence: An Empirical Study of Individual Case Supervision," *The China Journal* 55 (2006).

———. *China's Long March toward Rule of Law*. Cambridge: Cambridge University Press, 2002.

———. "Seek Truth from Facts: An Empirical Study of Enforcement of Arbitral Awards in the PRC," *American Journal of Comparative Law* 49 (2001).

Peerenboom, Randall, and Fu Yulin. "A New Analytical Framework for Understanding and Promoting Judicial Independence in China." In *Judicial Independence in China: Lessons for Global Rule of Law Promotion*, edited by Randall Peerenboom. New York: Cambridge University Press, 2010.

Pei, Minxin. *China's Trapped Transition: The Limits of Developmental Autocracy*. Harvard: Harvard University Press, 2006.

Tan, Justin. "Regulatory Environment and Strategic Orientations in a Transitional Economy: A Study of Chinese Private Enterprise," *Information Access Company* 21 (1996).

Tanner, Murray S. "Campaign-Style Policing in China and Its Critics." In *Crime, Punishment and Policing in China*, edited by Borge Bakken. Lanham: Rowman & Littlefield, 2005.

Tyler, Tom. *Why People Obey the Law*. New Haven: Yale University Press, 1990.

United Nations Conference on Trade and Development (UNCTAD). *Trade and Development Report 1999*. Geneva: United Nations, 1999.

UNDP. *Human Development Report 2005*, http://hdr.undp.org/reports/global/2005/pdf/HDR05_complete.pdf.

van Rooij, Benjamin. *Land and Pollution Regulation in China: Law-making, Compliance, Enforcement; Theory and Cases*. Leiden: Leiden University Press, 2006.

Woo, Margaret Y. K. "Law, Development and the Socio-Economic Rights of Chinese Women," *Columbia Asian Law Journal* (2005/2006).

World Bank. *Greening Industry, New Roles for Communities, Markets and Governments*. Oxford: Oxford University Press, 2000.

Yang, Dali. *Remaking the Chinese Leviathan: Market Transition and the Politics of Governance in China*. Stanford: Stanford University Press, 2004.

3

Putting Law in Context

Some Remarks on the Implementation of Law in China

HÅKAN HYDÉN

Short Introduction to Understanding Law and Implementation

Law does not come into being merely by an act of legislation. In itself law is just words on a piece of paper. For law the other systems in society are just noise, as Gunther Teubner puts it.[1] Law tells you how to act in certain situations. But what makes law operational? In order to have any influence on people's behavior, law has either to be followed spontaneously or to be forced upon actors. Sometimes people can be talked into or persuaded to follow the law. This process is said to work by either the carrot-and-stick strategy or as a result of a sermon. The former has to do with actors' self interests, inasmuch as an individual will follow the law when it is in an actor's best interest or when not abiding by the law entails the threat of punishment or sanctions. This way of viewing the implementation of law is mainly related to private and criminal law. In these areas law has the role of setting up borders for acceptable behavior, providing instruments for cooperation. In other words, law does not

---

[1] Gunther Teubner, "The Two Faces of Janus: Rethinking Legal Pluralism," *Cardozo Law Review* 13, no. 5 (1992).

tell us what to do but what not to do, as in criminal cases. It prescribes the limits for what is socially and economically acceptable behavior in society, or in those contexts where actors require instruments for joint activities in social life or in business. Law also provides certain rules for the regulation of economic interaction, for example, how to conclude a contract, how to do business, how to buy a house.

With regard to administrative law, another dynamic comes into play. Here the law communicates a political message to the political/administrative system. In organizations that are large enough to have separate units for decision-making and implementation, norms or rules play a role in the communication of messages between units. In organizational theory a distinction is made between authority and executive power. Law is the tool for conveying decisions taken by the authority to the executive within a state. In this case the authority referred to is a parliament or similar decision-making bodies, such as the National People's Congress in China, while the executive refers to public authorities. As a consequence of this division of duties, public authorities have to carry out certain functions. Something that is politically decided is meant to be implemented.

In political and legal science, when one speaks of implementation, one is referring to the carrying out of public policy and law. Public policy mediated by law is a course of action chosen by public authorities to address a problem. Public policy can be expressed in the body of laws and in the regulations, decisions, and actions of government. Legislators pass laws, which are then carried out by public servants in bureaucratic organizations. This process consists of rule-making, rule-administration, and rule-adjudication. The factors that impact implementation include the legislative intent, the administrative capacity of the bureaucracy, interest group activity and opposition, and executive support. The activities required for putting a political decision into practice are termed the implementation of the law. With regard to administrative law, it is vital to stress that law in itself is nothing. It is, however, the first step in a chain that manifests itself in the decisions and activities of subordinate public authorities.

The aim of this chapter is to put law in context in order to better understand implementation. The ambition is to create a mindmap for issues dealing with implementation. I will try to set up a general framework as a background for understanding law implementation in China. This will be done by identifying the three dimensions of implementation, i.e., a vertical, a horizontal, and a temporal dimension.

In an era characterized by globalization, the highest level is international law, for instance, the text of a convention, the legal design of which automatically becomes the starting point for the process. It is also the determinant for that which follows at other levels of the implementation chain. The core issue is how to secure the expected legal results when the convention is being transformed into the legal and social cultures of different countries. In China, the effects of globalized regulatory norms are confronted by powerful forces of Chinese local culture and the political system.[2] The next level, the national or state level, is where legislation is formed. This means that the convention must gain support from the national legal machinery. Since legal cultures are not the same all over the world, problems of integrating the convention into the national legal system must be expected.[3] The third step of implementation in a vertical perspective covers the phase before the convention reaches society and the population to be affected by it. This is the nonformal, substate world of norms. Legislation never occurs in a social vacuum. On the contrary, there are and always will be existing norms already operating in society, and legal norms have to compete with or complement them. Stanley Lubman and

---

2 Pitman B. Potter, "Legal Reform in China: Institutions, Culture, and Selective Adaptation," *China Quarterly* (2004): 475.

3 Pitman B. Potter, "Globalization and Economic Regulation in China: Selective Adaptation of Globalized Norms and Practices," *Washington University Global Studies Law Review* 97, no. 1 (2003): 119–150.

Randall Peerenboom both remind us of the relationships between law and underlying social norms and practices in China.[4] Since legal regulations are aimed at influencing individuals and society in certain ways, the relation between norms and legal rules in society becomes the final key issue in understanding the destiny of a ratified convention or a law.

The last or the lowest level brings us to the horizontal dimension. It is a common misunderstanding that law can be treated as one uniform entity. However, society is divided into different sectors that follow their own logic and rationality. Therefore, the horizontal dimension of implementation is related to the view that the legal system consists of different types of law. These types represent totally different legal cultures due to the functions they fulfill, which in turn affects the problem of implementation. One can speak of distinct legal cultures in relation to separate branches of the legal system, such as the law regulating the civil society, the market, the political/administrative system, and the so-called society of mixed economy[5]. Therefore, I will explain and treat them separately later on.

Law and thereby implementation of the law is highly dependent on the societal context within which the law is operating. Hence, some kind of understanding of how law differs in relation to society in terms of societal development stages is necessary. The synchronous perspective, from both a vertical and a horizontal point of view, has to be complemented with a diachronic analysis of how law and society develop over time. This is especially important in relation to the study of the implementation of law in China. Both treat-

---

4 Stanley B. Lubman, *Bird in a Cage—Legal Reform in China after Mao* (Stanford, California: Stanford University Press, 1997); Randall P. Peerenboom, *China's Long March toward Rule of Law* (New York: Cambridge University Press, 2002).

5 The concept of mixed economy covers a socio-economic system where the market economy is complemented by interventions from the state. This is the typical trait of the welfare state.

ing the law as one entity and regarding China as one uniform society are equally impossible tasks.

The process from politics to law and the implementation of law is complex. However, from a legal positivistic point of view, this process is often not considered to be particularly complicated. In line with this point of view, new laws are made by parliament in accordance with existing laws. Political goals are transformed into a legal norm. Legal norms are supposed to be applied in a legal systemic context with no political or other nonlegal influences. This process, however, becomes theoretically more complicated when we view it from a legal realist perspective. In so doing, we find that a legal norm gets its content first when applied in an individual case. Taking this one step further, we find it necessary to reformulate the process in a question, i.e., how does the law work as a political tool in a societal context? As the aim of this chapter is to present a theoretical framework to understand empirical studies on the process of lawmaking and implementation of law and public policy, it is appropriate to remind the reader of Jan Michael Otto's remarks: "Discussing implementation of the law requires that we consider law-in-action rather than law-in-books."[6] On this point, I am in agreement with Otto, who further argues that "[we] are not using the term implementation here in the sense of making lower executive regulations.... Studying implementation of the law forces us to cross the bridge from the conventional study of law to the study of socio-legal reality."

The Vertical Dimension of Implementation

Ideally, the legal text of a convention will be translated properly into the legal regulation at the national level, and these rules will influ-

---

6 Jan Michael Otto, "Toward an Analytical Framework: Real Legal Certainty and Its Explanatory Factors," in *Implementation of Law in the People's Republic of China*, eds. Jianfu Chen et al. (Kluwer Law International, 2002), 23.

ence behavior in society according to the content of the convention. This last step is dependent on the relation between norms and rules in the regulated area[7]. Basically, it is understood that problems of distortion occur at each level due to the different forms of intervening factors. In order to understand transitions between levels, we will look a little closer at the three steps of implementation by exploring an overview of the possible distortions that can occur (see Fig. 1):

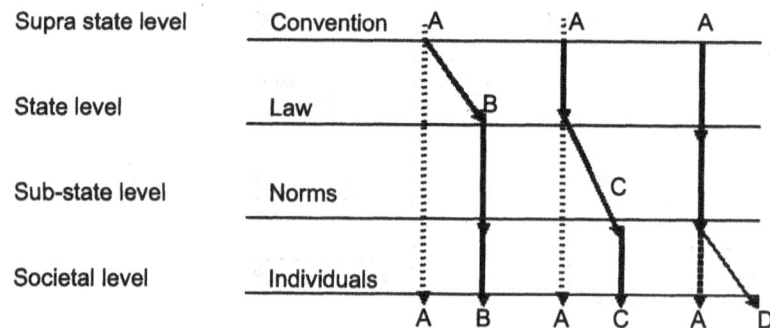

Let us assume that A in Fig. 1 represents a certain provision with a specific content that is expected to be transformed into domestic law, which will then harmonize with existing norms in society in order to be finally implemented. The first possible distortion that can occur can be seen in the relation between the convention itself and domestic law. It is possible that content A may be either misunderstood or implemented in terms of something else, illustrated by B in Fig. 1. In this case, the end result of the implementation process can be expected to be B rather than A. The second problem of implementation has to do with the relation between the law and norms

---

7 See Håkan Hydén, "Implementation of International Conventions—A Socio-Legal Enterprise. Examples from the Convention on the Rights of the Child," in *Human Rights: From Dissemination to Application, Essays in Honour of Göran Melander* (Leiden, The Netherlands: Martinius Nijhoff Publishers, 2006), 375–392.

in society. The legal design of the law must meet the requirements of necessary measurements in order to influence the norms in society in accordance with the content of the convention. Content A in law thereby risks being converted into the norm, as illustrated by C in Figure 1. The final and third step of the implementation chain is related to the norms per se in society. Existing norms function as a filter for legal rules, which otherwise might make them differ from their stated content. Thus, the specific content of the convention, A in the figure, may normatively become D in practice. I will continue by commenting on these potential distortions.

In public international law two strategies are used for implementing an international convention into domestic law. Where countries follow the so-called monistic tradition, public international law is regarded as part of the national legal system. When a country like China ratifies an international convention, the convention automatically becomes valid as domestic law. While China signed the United Nations International Covenant on Civil and Political Rights in 1998, it has so far not ratified the covenant with or without limiting reservations or declarations. It is therefore not yet valid in China, which otherwise would have had an impact on the Chinese criminal justice system.[8] On the other hand, when countries follow a dualistic legal tradition, a ratified convention becomes binding only for the state party but does not become part of the domestic legal system. Sweden belongs to this type of legal tradition. This means that in order to create binding legislation, the convention has to be transferred into domestic law.

A weak point in international law is the lack of sanctions and enforcement mechanisms. Since legal regulation is geared to influencing behavior, it is necessary to take legal design into account. How is the law set up in order to have maximum effect? The wording of any law has no impact as such unless it is backed up by sanctions or if it already corresponds to existing norms in society. In

---

8 Jerome Alan Cohen, "A Slow March to Legal Reform," *Far Eastern Economic Review* (2007).

respect to the latter, it cannot be said that it is the law that sways behavior, as social norms constitute the primary source of influence on human behavior in society. Mostly, law is simply the codification of existing norms. The question arises then as to why the law is at all enacted. The answer is that the function of law is to stabilize and safeguard the norm by relating it to a system of enforcement in order to cope with those who do not freely comply with the norm/legal rule. By upgrading a norm and adopting it as a part of a (legal) system, the argumentative power of the norm is strengthened.

The way law is meant to have an impact on the behavior of people is an important aspect that should not be overlooked. It is only in the case of the incorporation of the convention that a lack of sanctions will occur. However, if the convention is first transformed into domestic law, the existing or new legislation could be backed up by sanctions and a system of enforcement. This brings us to the role of lawmaking. The design of the legislation and the legislative process is crucial for understanding the implementation process. The way this works varies in different parts of the world, depending on legal and political culture. Cai point out that the involvement of the Chinese legislatures in the implementation of law is unprecedented in the West.[9] Sometimes problems of enforceability are built into the law, for example, by making the law too sweeping and soft and thereby dependent upon decisions at lower implementation levels. If this is combined with a decentralization of decision-making power, a gap can arise between political policy on a central level and the reality of implementation on the local level.

The content of law may be detrimental to its implementation. A general understanding is that the more detailed laws are, the less discretion local bureaucrats use in their implementation.[10] Howev-

---

9 Cai Dingjian, "Functions of the People's Congresses in the Process of Implementation of Law," in Jianfu Chen et al., *Implementation of Law*; Chen An, *Restructuring Political Power in China* (Boulder: Lynne Rienner Publishers, 1999).

10 Jessica Korn, "The Legislative Veto and the Limits of Public Choice Analysis," *Political Science Quarterly* 109, no. 5 (Winter 1994-1995): 873–894.

er, local interests might be so strong that even a strict and specific law, like the new environmental protection laws in China, will not work because they are too strict and contrast too strongly with local interest to be enforced.[11]

The norms of a country function as a mirror when viewed from the perspective of an international convention. If one does not recognize oneself in the mirror, it is due to the fact that the norms of the society in question do not reflect the normative content of the international convention or, to put it the other way around, the convention does not correspond to the norms of that society. In either case, the problem of implementation is to understand how norms are constituted and how they can be changed.

The Role of Norms in Society

A law cannot be expected to have any sustainable effect if it does not correspond to the norms already existing in a society. The reason for this is very simple: law comes from above, while norms grow from below.

What is a norm? A simple definition of a norm sufficient for the purpose of this text, is that it is a guide for human actions or behavior. The norm concept, however, consists of three dimensions or three sets of factors. In the first place, norms are an expression of a will. Someone wants to do something and, thus, could be seen in this situation to be following a norm expressing this will. Will is the first basic component, or dimension, of a norm.

It is not, however, enough that a person wants to do something. He or she also has to have the knowledge and competence to carry out his or her purpose. Knowledge together with cognition is, therefore, the second dimension of the norm concept. The way one un-

---

11 Benjamin van Rooij, *Land and Pollution Regulation in China: Lawmaking, Compliance, Enforcement; Theory and Cases*, dissertation (Leiden: Leiden University Press, 2006), 87, 88.

derstands and comprehends the context of a situation is, thus, determinant in terms of the way in which one acts and the normative standpoint that one consequently takes. Differences in opinions, even within legal decision-making, emanate more often from the question of how the situation, a person, or anything else has been understood in cognitive terms than from the judgments made based on pure value standpoints.

The third dimension of a norm is related to the system conditions characterizing the context of the society in which the action and, consequently, the norm occur. It is not enough that an individual wants to do something and has cognitively adequate knowledge on how to go about it. Rather one also has to have actual possibilities to undertake what one wants to do in order for a norm to develop. While the first two dimensions are related to subjective factors among actors, this last, the third set of factors, is related to objective factors, i.e., factors not at the actor's disposal.

The first question will be if we can presuppose that a country that has ratified a convention or enacted a law also agrees with the will component of that specific law. In other words, can we, as a starting point for this analysis, assume that the state party has the will to really implement the convention and the law? Of course this is not necessarily an either-or question, for a state party might agree with some parts of the convention while disagreeing with others without having made any reservations when possible. However, we have reason to believe that some state parties have ratified human rights conventions, such as the Convention on the Rights of the Child (CRC), just to show a "human face" without any intention of paying any real attention to the plight of children.[12]

The will component is related to the political system; therefore, laws are often subject to compromise. It is feasible that a law may lack complete support. There may be many political reasons for

---

12 Patrik Olsson, "Legal Ideals and Normative Realities: A Case Study of Children's Rights and Child Labour Activity in Paraguay," *Lund Studies in Sociology of Law* 19 (2003).

making a law, such as to pacify one's opposition or to show awareness in relation to a specific question, which do not necessarily entail commitment to implementation of the law.[13] Vilhelm Aubert, Torstein Eckhoff, and Knut Sveri showed in a classical study of the controversy in relation to the Norwegian Housemaid Law how a political compromise was set up by giving the law a lot of nice wording without adding necessary enforcement tools.[14] Peerenboom mentions as an example that "sometimes laws are passed for domestic political reasons, such as when the government rushes out with a law after a major catastrophe."[15] In relation to this phenomenon van Rooij has used the expression "law of event," pointing out that law many times comes into being after something more or less dramatic has happened in society.[16]

It is, however, not only the political system that may constitute an obstacle as far as the implementation of a law is concerned; the support of public officials is also important. A lack of support can be a problem for different reasons.[17] Often resistance comes from the surrounding environment in which the law is to be implemented. The normative context in which the law is to be implemented can also enable the legal norm to come into being. A legal norm is merely a social norm or other norm adopted to the legal system and thereby stabilized and formalized. Law is therefore many times in-

---

13 See Randall Peerenboom's chapter in this volume.
14 Vilhelm Aubert, Torstein Eckhoff, and Knut Sveri, *En lov I sökelyset. Socialpsykologisk undersögelse av den norske hushjelpslov* [A law in focus. Social psychological investigation of the Norwegian law about domestic servants] (Oslo: Akademisk forlag, 1952).
15 See Randall Peerenboom's chapter in this volume.
16 van Rooij, Land and Pollution Regulation in China. For another example, see Johan Lagerkvist's chapter in this volume.
17 As shown by Hatla Thelle in her investigation of the legal aid system in China in this volume, the whole system rests on the assumption of the willingness and capability of one professional group—the lawyers—to work for free. As a consequence, the outcome is poor in terms of implementation and the quality of legal aid provided by lawyers quite low.

troduced when certain norms in society are weakened for one reason or another. Through its coupling to a legal machinery of enforcement, the legal norm can be safeguarded in another way than when it belongs to a self-regulated area. But implementation and enforcement has its own price in terms of economic incentives (the carrot), enforcement agencies (the stick), or public authorities (the sermon). In this view, a legal norm can be said to be only as strong as the underlying norm or norms already operating in society.

The knowledge aspect of the norm is something that mainly relates to professional knowledge. In order to implement a certain kind of legislation, professional knowledge within the field is necessary. Regulation of the health sector requires medical knowledge, while pedagogic skills are crucial within the education system and civil engineering skills are necessary for the planning and housing sector. It is not only a question of skill. Norms are formed also by cognitive aspects. The attitude or worldview among those public servants and public authorities in charge of a certain task is fundamental for the understanding of the implementation of that specific law as Svensson shows in her study within this volume regarding the implementation of the Cultural Relics Law.

Turning finally to the possibilities of normative changes in relation to the third dimension of norms, system conditions are the most important intervening factors of all in relation to norm formation and the implementation of law, especially given the fact that political and economic factors and also social structures could become obstacles or possibilities in the implementation process. Among these both the economic system and political ideologies can be mentioned as predominating system conditions.

Implementation of Law in a Horizontal Perspective

The horizontal perspective is about understanding the legal system as consisting of different parts. Law is related to different sectors of society, and it upholds certain functions depending on what role the law plays. One can point out at least four different sectors of society that affect law and give it its special character. These are the civil society, the market, the political/administrative system, and the so-called mixed economy or the welfare state.

Regulation of Civil Society

The regulation of civil society has to do with identity and citizenship. Here not only are there particular rules about immigration, rights of asylum, birth registration, national registration, but also fundamental rules about what is acceptable and what is not acceptable in society. In other words, the regulation of civil society has to do with the question of who belongs to society, complemented by criminal law stipulating what not to do in order to belong to the society. There are also family law and inheritance law as well as rules about legal competence for individuals and organizations. Who is regarded as a competent legal subject in order to conclude a contract, represent an organization, etc.? Within these regulations on personal matters, we also find rules on the relation between spouses in marriage and between parents and their children.

The relevant question in relation to the problem of the implementation of law in this situation is the following: What does the regulation look like? The main problem in these cases is not whether a law is implemented but what the law says about the distribution of personal power in society and whether the law is followed.

Market Regulation

In relation to the market, the law provides instruments for the coordination of business transactions. Peerenboom's conclusion about the potential for the emergence of the rule of law in China draws on his assessment of the interplay between law and economic development.[18] In general the law provides the framework for the rules of the game. Regulation provides possibilities for action without im-

---

18 Peerenboom, China's Long March; cf. Potter, "Legal Reform in China," 467.

posing a certain behavior. But if someone chooses to act on the market, the law prescribes how one is to behave. One is not allowed to go outside the limits of the law. Someone who does will be punished; the rules have the character of prohibition rules. Should someone, by going outside the accepted limits and by not following the rules of the game, inflict damage upon another person, a sanction in terms of tort can be raised in order to restore the situation as it was prior to the event.

Among the basic rules of the game in the market economy, we find rules about property and about contract. These two basic instruments, complemented by economic security rights, form the basis for the operation of a market economy.[19] The invisible hand of the market requires the long arm of the law. A precondition for market economy is the rules of the game. Another aspect of the role of law in these situations is the standardization of business organizations. Contract as a legal instrument can be used in order to set up complex organizations. The concept of juridical person, invented in Germany during the nineteenth century, plays an important role in the possible regulation of the large-scale industrial society geared toward mass production. To stabilize transactions and minimize transaction costs, the legal system has stipulated certain organizational patterns to represent some authorized forms of organizations. A limited liability company follows certain rules and regulations when it comes to the right to represent the company in a competent way, how dividends should be distributed among the shareholders, or how administration of the company should be organized.

Contract is a very flexible legal instrument, which can be used for different purposes and across national borders. In the global economy, contract is the most suitable means for the regulation of transactions between companies from different parts of the world. In this context it is the lawyers, representing large-scale law firms or

---

19 Karl Renner, *The Institutions of Private Law and Their Social Functions* (London: Routledge, 1949).

so-called in-house lawyers within transnational corporations, who articulate the international law emerging from practice. Courts and legislation become subordinated compared to private lawyers and contract as regulators.[20] Thus, contract is a legal instrument whereby private parties, physical and legal persons, can make up their own rules regulating their dealings, and get these rules sanctioned as being on equal footing with law. The key question in relation to the regulation of the (market) economy is not about implementation but rather if the regulation is used, i.e., if it is adequate for the purpose for which it is introduced.[21]

Political/Administrative Regulation

When it comes to the political/administrative system, law plays another role. Here law and politics are brought together. The law constitutes the political system via the constitution, while at the same time the political system passes and promulgates the law. In that sense there is a dualistic relation between politics and law.[22] In order to be able to separate law from politics, the legal system must have some degree of independence. When law is created in the political process, it must be possible to distinguish from politics. The legal system, therefore, has its own institutions, courts, and public authorities, surrounded by public servants, attorneys, the police force, and prosecutors. One of the most important functions of law in this perspective is to set up rules for the division of power in society, between political decision-making, executive, and judicial functions. The autonomy of law and the independence and judicial ac-

---

20 Yves Dezalay, "The Power of the Legal Field," in *An Introduction to Law and Social Theory*, eds. Reza Banakar and Max Travers (Oxford; Portland, Oregon: Hart Publishing, 2002).

21 Stewart Macauley, "Non-Contractual Relations in Business: A Preliminary Study," *American Sociological Review* 28, no. 1 (1963): 55–67.

22 Torstein Eckhoff and Nils Kristian Sundby, *Rettssystemer: systemteoretisk innføring i rettsfilosofien* [Legal systems: System theoretical introduction to legal philosophy], 2nd edition (Oslo: Tano, 1991), 227.

countability of the court system are important indicators of a vital legal system. During the Maoist period, law was an administrative tool consigned largely to the state's exercise of political power and political authority.[23] Even if much has happened in the post-Mao period, law and politics are often blurred.[24] William Alford and Benjamin Liebman refer to the lack of judicial independence as one explanation for the lack of subnational compliance with national laws.[25] They also place blame in part on the National People' Congress' (NPC) "attenuated public mandate" caused by the fact that NPC delegates "are not elected by the public."[26]

The Chinese political and legal system is hugely complex, given its size as well as the specific problems inherent in a one-party state. The plurality of actors and the multilayered hierarchical system of courts and corresponding institutions at each level in China make the coordination and implementation process a highly difficult task. Within a market economy, law plays the role of providing the rules of the game.[27] In such a situation the independence of the court system is vital in order to create credibility for the economic system. In a further transition of the Chinese economic system into a market economy, a growing independence of the courts, therefore, is likely to occur.

Access to justice is a related problem. It places requirements on the courts but also on the regulation of legal aid.[28] If poor people are

---

23 Potter, "Legal Reform in China," 480.

24 When politics in the Western model has been translated into legal matters via law and other legal sources, the politicians have to hand over the handling of the problems to public authorities, while in the case of China, politicians still have a say in the case, as shown, for example, by Oscar Almén in his study in this volume.

25 William P. Alford and Benjamin L. Liebman, "Clean Air, Clear Processes? The Struggle over Air Pollution Law in the People's Republic of China," *Hastings Law Journal* 52 (2000–2001): 703–748, 748.

26 At 741.

27 See Jonas Grimheden in this volume.

28 On legal aid, see Hatla Thelle's contribution in this volume.

to have a chance to use the legal system in order to make their voices heard, they must be helped economically in order to cover court costs.[29] In China basic legal services are provided to poor people via an administrative regulation, i.e., to people without sufficient economic means and to members of the so-called vulnerable groups in society, such as the elderly, minors, women, and people with disabilities.

Besides the constitutive function of the political system, law plays an important role by formalizing and communicating the tasks the political system has decided should be executed by the administrative system. Through the law the parliament gives directives to the government and further along to the public authorities, which are supposed to execute the politics decided upon. In many cases the parliament delegates to the government the exercise of political power and its executing functions. Then the government issues ordinances that complement the law decided upon by the parliament. Even central public authorities might be given competence to issue regulations that concretize the law. In these situations law has another character than it does in the areas of society mentioned earlier, the civil society and the market economy. There is a huge difference between the two systems; in the Western model, law becomes the watershed between law and politics. When politics in the Western model has been translated into legal matters via law and other legal sources, the politicians have to hand over the handling of the problems to public authorities, while in the case of China, politicians still have a say.

The political system fulfills certain functions as a complement to the private sector. These functions can be seen as complementary to the sociocultural and the economic systems which might not be generated by market forces or for which political reasons are set up within the political/administrative system. It is partly a question of rules for protection of the interests of individuals or the collective

---

29 Benjamin L. Liebman, "Legal Aid and Public Interest Law in China," *Texas International Law Journal* 34, no. 2 (1999): 211–286.

group. This part of the law is called the general administrative law, and is primarily procedural in character, i.e., it is about handling cases. An important task for the state is to provide infrastructure in different respects. The regulation of the specific public authorities dealing with this belongs to the specific part of administrative law. We can count up to four complexes of infrastructure having legal implications:

1. The legal infrastructure, whereby the rules of the game of the economic and social life are upheld in the last instance.
2. The physical infrastructure, in the form of transport system, energy and water supply, sewage treatment plant, etc. The role of law in these cases is to distribute tasks.
3. The third complex consists of the social infrastructure, based on rules about care, health and public medical service, in combination with rules about protection of income.
4. The cultural infrastructure, with the regulation of education on different levels, protection of the cultural heritage, and the like.

Furthermore, the political/administrative system is involved in the regulation of the protection of national security, the military force, and public security, the police force, all with their specific laws. In all these areas law conveys the decisions from the political decision-makers to the executive bodies within the administration. Law lays down the guiding principles for the administrative activities and sets up the fundamental organizational forms for the administrative bodies. However, the substantive decisions are taken by different professions depending on which area is to be regulated.

Legal rules within this societal sector have a character different from that of the regulation of the civil society and the market. In administrative law, one does not expect to find prohibition rules.

Law defines the administrative agency. Each public authority is set up by a piece of legislation, an instruction that roughly tells which duties have been assigned to that authority and how the internal organization is structured. If a public authority acts outside its area of competence, as defined in the instruction, the consequence will be that the decision is invalid. This is a strong sanction. The decision taken by the authority is regarded as nonexistent.

Administrative rules and regulations have the character of a decree rather than a prohibition. However, since the administrative law tells the actors, the public authorities, what to do in advance, it has to be general. Otherwise the rules would have to resemble a recipe in a cookbook, and that would not be very suitable. Administrative law is applied *ex ante*, in contrast to private and criminal law, which are applied *ex post*, i.e., after something has happened. Thus, administrative rules do not stipulate "You shall," but set up goals toward which public authority should strive. Furthermore the law points out which means are allowed to be used for the actual purpose, i.e., to achieve a specific end. The rules that belong to the political/administrative system can, therefore, be called means-end rules. The application of rules is meant to be forward looking and precede action. As a consequence, the application of law cannot be said to be rule oriented, but rather result oriented. This is why the concept of implementation fits especially well into this legal context. Law is about carrying out certain tasks. These types of rules are, therefore, purpose oriented and not built as conditional clauses, as is the case within the classical legal tradition related to private and criminal law. Instead of norm-rationality, administrative law is built upon goal-rationality. Hence the implementation of administrative law is in the hands of different professions within certain (expert) authorities. These might constitute medical expertise, as in the system of healthcare and medical service, or civil engineers, as regards road administration. Only after appeal has been made to an administrative court against a decision taken by a local authority do legal considerations come into play.

The Law of the Mixed Economy

The regulation of the so-called mixed economy is characterized by goal-conflicts. Or to put it another way, one wants to have one's cake and eat it too. One can talk about "competing institutional interests" that affect implementation of law. The mixed economy is also a mixture of the private and public law. The background is related to collisions between the different action systems in society, the socio-cultural, the political/administrative system, technical and economic systems, etc., which place incompatible claims on actors. An imperative from one system will be regarded as alien in relation to an imperative from another system, both of which compete as regards influencing behavior in a specific situation. In these situations, what we can call an *intersystem* conflict arises, i.e., a conflict between systems.[30] As a consequence, norm conflicts arise. As long as the different systems coexist, with each of them determining the behavior of actors, no problem will occur. The only expectation is *intrasystem* conflicts, i.e., conflicts that can be handled within one and the same system.

Intersystem conflicts, however, will be severe if they give rise to collisions between systems that have such frequency and strength that they constitute threats on, or at least interfere with, the reproduction of the systems. In these instances a call for political intervention occurs. Then the law becomes an attractive political instrument. The law will relieve the pressure on the political system to solve the problem. It will be the administrative system that has to handle the case. In the Swedish system, politicians are not even allowed to intervene in situations which are regulated by law, according to the separation of power between politicians and public servants, stipulated in the constitution. Thus, by referring to the

---

30 The distinction between inter- and intrasystem conflict is made by the Norwegian peace researcher Johan Galtung, *Fredsforskning* [Peace research], 3rd edition (Stockholm: Prisma, 1970).

constitution, politicians can claim that they are prevented from dealing with political issues that are "taken care of" in law.

Even if the law does not solve the true, underlying problem, the symbolic value of law is used in order to stabilize society when it is exposed to tensions. These kinds of rules can be called intervening rules.[31] These are the distinguishing marks of the welfare state, related to the mixed economy. Intervening rules have both private actors who belong to the civil society or the market and public authorities, as legal addressees in one and the same piece of legislation. Thus, intervening rules are both private and public at the same time. In these cases law recognizes the principles of private production, while at the same time putting restrictions and obligations on private actors, such as employment protection, consumer protection, protection of nature, and requirements in relation to sustainable development. It is up to public authorities to control these pieces of legislation. We cannot expect law to be followed spontaneously in these cases since the law has the character of what the American sociologist James Coleman called "dis-joint norms."[32] This kind of legislation places responsibilities and restrictions on one group in society for the benefit of another group. It might be the employer, as in the case of employment protection for the benefit of employees; or the seller, as in the case of consumer protection; or the company, as in relation to environmental protection.

This part of the legal system consists of what can be called intervening rules since they are an expression of intervention from the political system via law and the administrative system in the social, economic, and natural systems. The first intervening rules introduced in the industrial part of the world had to do with labor protection in relation to the work environment. It happened in the late

---

31 Håkan Hydén, *Rättssociologi som rättsvetenskap* [Sociology of law as legal science] (Lund: Studentlitteratur, 2002).

32 James Coleman, *Foundations of a Social Theory* (Cambridge: Harvard University Press, 1990).

nineteenth century. The background is the so-called labor issue in Europe at that time: how to deal with the rebellious labor class and their political claims. The threat from the new political movement prompted conservative and liberal politicians alike to take this initiative toward labor protection long before the labor movement had obtained political force and power in the form of a trade union or a political party.[33] Gradually similar regulations have emerged in the whole area of labor law, within the social sector, consumer protection of different kinds, environmental issues, promotion of equality between the sexes, to mention some of the most typical examples of intervening regulations.

An intersystem conflict consists in these cases of the collision between the claim for protection of the individual, derived from the social system, on the one hand, and the demand for efficiency from the economic system, on the other hand, as seen, for instance, within the labor and work environment area. It can also be a conflict between different imperatives, stemming from the ecological system in terms of environmental protection and the demand for rationality within the economic system, or between the claim for good and appropriate products from consumers versus the economic interests of profitmaking among producers and salesmen. These are all situations in industrialized societies that have given rise to legitimacy disturbances that have in turn prompted politicians to intervene using law and public administration.

The typical intervening rule—but not all—has the character of a considering or a balancing rule, where the different interests at stake are mentioned and legitimized without telling how the interests involved should be weighed or judged against each other. The main focus of the intervening rules is instead a question of telling who is authorized to form the decision—competence rules—and how, in

---

[33] Håkan Hydén, "Working Environment Legislation in the Nordic Countries," in *The Nordic Labour Relations Model: Labour Law and Trade Unions in the Nordic Countries: Today and Tomorrow*, eds. Niklas Bruun et al. (Aldershot: Dartmouth, 1992).

procedural terms—the decision should be taken, what kind of arrangements should be made in order to form as good a basis for the decision as possible. Thus, a lack of material or substantive rules related to this kind of regulation exists. The phenomenon, when it emerged, inspired legal theorists to label this kind of legislation as responsive law[34] and reflexive law.[35] In a Chinese context Peerenboom gives corresponding examples in his contribution in this volume, such as citizen committees that supervise and advise on government work and the Expert Consultation System and the Government Decision-making Consultation Committee recently set up by the provincial government in Shanxi.

The main function of this kind of regulation is to bring a controversial political issue into the political sphere and bring those with interests at stake together there and let them solve the problem without pointing out ready-made solutions of law in advance. The design of a typical legal body dealing with intervening rules is, therefore, a court or public authority composed of parties representing the interests involved under the chairmanship of a judge. This is the case, for example, in the Labor Court in Sweden, the Market Court, National Board for Consumer Complaints, the Environmental courts, as well as in many of the decision-making boards within central public authorities. Burell brings up a similar example in a Chinese context in his study on the municipal Housing Committees, which have a tripartite composition with representatives from state agencies, local trade unions, and employers' associations.[36] Concurrently with the transition toward a market-oriented economy, we will likely be seeing more and more of this kind of

---

34 Philippe Nonet and Philip Selznick, *Law and Society in Transition. Toward Responsive Law* (New York: Harper and Row, 1978).

35 Gunther Teubner, "Substantive and Reflexive Elements in Modern Law," *Law and Society Review* 17 (1983); Gunther Teubner (ed.), *Autopoietic Law: A New Approach to Law and Society* (Berlin: Walter de Gruyter, 1987).

36 The same system is used in labor arbitration courts in China, see Mattias Burell, "The Rule-governed State: China's Labour Market Policy, 1978–1998," Ph. D. thesis, Department of Political Science, Uppsala University 2001.

legislation in China.³⁷ We have already seen it in the field of environmental protection. Even a small country like Sweden might face problems implementing law due to different interests on the national and the local level. This problem is many times greater in a country as large and complex as China³⁸.

The content of law in these cases is decided in the process of application and in the actual use of law. The problem of implementation of law will, therefore, be an empirical question, something that can be described but not evaluated in relation to politically set up values or goals in law. The ultimate purpose is to reach a compromise built on a model of interest balancing. The rationality of the intervening rules lies in the way it succeeds in solving problems without creating disturbances in the sector of society in which the problems exist. It is also in these terms implementation or lack thereof has to be judged or assessed.³⁹

The Time Dimension of Implementation

In order to put law in a diachronic perspective we need a theory to tell us something about legal and societal development over time. Such theories are developed in economic history,⁴⁰ in history (the

---

37 The introduction of the Housing Provident Funds also represents, as shown by Burell in his contribution in this volume, an indicator of a step away from a political/administrative kind of legislation toward an element of private regulation.

38 Cf Benjamin van Rooij´s study of implementation of environmental legislation in this volume. Another example is the study by Lagerkvist about the implementation of the legislation on Internet cafés in this volume.

39 Eckhoff and Sundby, *Legal Systems*, 108.

40 Lennart Schön, *En modern svensk ekonomisk historia. Tillväxt och omvandling under två sekel* [A modern Swedish economic history: Growth and transformation under two centuries] (Stockholm: SNS förlag, 2000); Rondo Cameron, *A Concise Economic History of the World: From Paleolithic Times to the Present*, 4th edition (New York: Oxford University Press, 2003).

so-called Annelles school),[41] in world system theory,[42] and economics.[43] Due to the scope of this chapter, these theories will not be discussed here. However, their relevance for the cyclical view of societal development with regard to implementation of law in China will briefly be commented upon.

Societies can be said to develop over time as waves or S-curves. They follow the cycle that any system follows. Society is born, grows up, matures, and after a time falls into a process of decay. A new society emerges as a reaction to the existing one. This means that when a society has reached its peak, a new society is already under way. With reference to the common features of societal development, a certain succession can be observed. The societal curve goes through four phases, or rather different parts of society dominate during certain periods of development. The first phase involves a core technology initiating a new societal curve. Each phase is about sixty years, give or take ten years. The second phase is a period of social changes. Society has to adjust to the potential of the new technique, so to say. During the growth of industrial society in Europe in the nineteenth century, a tremendous shift in social life took place. Something similar is going on in many parts of China today. People moved from the countryside into urban areas in order to get work within growing industries. In Sweden, as well as in other parts of Europe, the rate of the population working in the agricultural sector gradually decreased from about 75 to 2–3 percent of the working population in a relatively short period of time. The mechanization of work and the use of fertilizers and

---

41 George G. Iggers, *Historiography in the Twentieth Century: From Scientific Objectivity to the Postmodern Challenge* (Hanover, New Hampshire: Wesleyan University Press, 1997).

42 Immanuel Wallerstein, *World-Systems Analysis: An Introduction* (Durham: Duke University Press, 2004).

43 James B. Shuman and David Rosenau, *The Kondratieff Wave* (New York: Dell Publishing, 1972); Nickolai D. Kondratieff, "The Long Waves of Business Cycles in Economic Life," in *Problems of Economic Fluctuations* (Institute for Business Cycles Research, 1925).

pesticides made it possible to increase productivity with fewer people working in the agricultural sector. This is the same kind of jobless growth we face today, when industrial work is scaled down. In the shift from industrial society to the information society, we can already notice a decrease in employment in the industrial sector from around 55 down to around 20 percent of the working population. This is expected to continue and result in the number of people employed in industries landing at below 10 percent in the coming years. This is a general phenomenon in Sweden today as well as in many other countries in the West, and is also apparent in big cities in China, such as Shanghai and Beijing.

After a new technology has been developed and the societal adjustments have taken place, it is time for the economic boom. This period is characterized by linear economic growth. The new technology makes it possible to produce goods and services in a much more effective manner. When economic growth has accumulated enough societal surplus value, a need for a distribution system arises. In this situation the political system begins to dominate the scene. First, in order to spread the economic wealth among the population, the welfare state will become the natural result. Thus, there is economic pressure for this to occur, which is related to the need to stimulate the demand for mass consumption, in order to uphold the mass production upon which the large-scale industrial society is built. In order to facilitate this economic development, the political system takes on the burden of providing different kinds of infrastructure. This gives rise to the boom of political/administrative regulation of the means-end character mentioned above.[44] At any rate, the welfare state emerges as a natural consequence of societal development reaching its peak. After the peak, when the S-curve turns downward, the role of the political system becomes more concerned with crisis management. In the legal dimension,

---

44 Cf. Michael Dowdle (ed.), *Public Accountability: Designs, Dilemmas and Experiences* (New York: Cambridge University Press, 2006), ch. 13, where he elaborates on different regulatory models of constitutional accountability.

this corresponds with the growth of intervening rules, which was described in the previous section. It was during the 1970s and onward that the intervening rules to a great extent emerged in the industrialized world. Since a characteristic feature of this kind of legislation is the need for control by certain public authorities, in particular different forms of ombudsmen, there is a limit to the growth of intervening rules related to public costs. When this became apparent, a quest for self-regulation occurred in late 1980s and onward.

These factors influence also the legal development trends. The development of law "follows" the S-curves. We can notice that the feudal system in the countryside and the guild system in towns and cities, with its statutes and regulations of who was entitled to get a certificate as master craftsman and carry on craftsmanship, and the mercantile system, with its strong regulation of trade, were both deregulated during the eighteenth century and gradually replaced by a policy of nonrestrictive practices and free-trade policy. In the nineteenth century a new kind of regulatory principles emerged. Through the so-called Code Napoleon in France and Burgerliches Gesetzbuch in Germany, the regulation of the market economy got its features. This applies to the rules regulating property, contract, and economic security rights, which were commented upon above. During the twentieth century the public law system grew. In Europe this took place especially at the time of World War I and World War II, when a large number of public administrative laws were introduced. And when we had reached the peak of the industrial society, a new type of legislation flourished, intervening regulations. Since this time, from 1970 up to the present, society has been covered by an enormous legal superstructure.[45] Therefore a process of deregulation is not only expected, but also to a large extent has already

---

45 The Portuguese sociologist of law Boaventura de Sousa Santos has made use of the metaphor of an overloaded camel being borne down by the load of laws. See Boaventura de Sousa Santos, *Towards a New Common Sense* (New York: Routledge, 1995).

taken place. The first phase of the new information society faces a period of self-regulation and pluralistic efforts to compete over setting the standards for the new development. This is something that could be expected in the economically developed parts of China today.

The economic system will change radically in the aftermath of the introduction of the new information technology. The way of doing business, for instance, by using the Internet in so-called e-business, will change. The system of production and distribution of goods and services will be totally different. The economy will turn from being based on production (plans) to being oriented toward the demands of consumers. Through new digital technique the possibility to communicate consumers' demands will make it possible to take the interests of consumers as a starting point for the economic process, in a way that was unthinkable in the old production system, based on mechanics.

Some Final Remarks

We have in this chapter tried to sort out the most relevant factors when studying implementation of law in general and in China in particular. We have done that by looking at three dimensions, the vertical, the horizontal and the time dimension. In the vertical perspective we touched upon the different steps of implementation that a convention and a law have to go through before reaching its final destination. Implementation of a convention can be called a multilayered governance problem with a high risk of transformations of the content. As has been pointed out, different aspects have to be dealt with at different and separate levels during the implementation process.

Figure 1, representing possible deviations from the original content of the text of the convention, is to be regarded as a mere simplification of the implementation process. The idea presented herein, however, is an attempt to sort out the potential problems occurring at each level, i.e., the international, the state, the substate, and the local level. This does not preclude the fact that deviances in practice can occur at every level in the same case or that distortion at one level can be reinforced at another level. We have in the previous presentation chosen to deal with them one at a time.

The implementation of the political content of the law at a provincial level is a delicate legal issue due to the heterogeneity of legal cultures that intervene in the process. There is a close connection between societal and legal development. The different provinces in China are at different positions on the societal development curve, which affects the legal culture and the legal needs. The design of the legal text and the legal machinery that will give support to the implementation process thus represents a tricky step to be taken in the implementation chain. This sociolegal enterprise requires insight into the specific kind of problems that the law raises. The final battle in the implementation process takes place when the legal ideals of the law meet the normative realities of the particular society where it is to be implemented. It is when the normative content from above and from outside, in terms of transplants,[46] meets the undercurrent of existing norms in the society that the real challenges begin to occur.[47] It is here that tensions are at their highest in the implementation process.

By introducing a norm-model, I have tried to indicate the kind of dimensions that have to be taken into account in an actual study. The norm-model serves as a heuristic device that can help screen potential and relevant factors that can come into play on the normative scene which the convention is meant to influence. The dif-

---

46 Dowdle, Public Accountability.

47 Per Wickenberg, *Normstödjande strukturer. Miljötematiken börjar slå rot i skolan* [Norm supporting structures: The environmental theme begins to take root in schools], doctoral thesis, *Lund Studies in Sociology of Law* 5 (1999).

ferent examples of law implementation in China have to be analyzed with regard to the vertical level where the study takes place. What are the legal regulations about? What superior level of guiding principles, including norms of different kinds, interferes in the process of implementation?

If we look at the horizontal aspect of implementation, we have to locate the specific study in one or the other of the different societal sectors mentioned. Does the study belong to the civil society, the market economy, the planned economy, or to other aspects of the political/administrative system? Or does it fall within the sector of the mixed economy and the welfare state? Depending on the answer, different questions have to be raised and different theoretical and methodological considerations have to be taken. Most of the case studies presented in this volume fall in the categories of either political-administrative or mixed economy.

The role of law within the political/administrative sector represents a difference in relation to a shift in decision-making from politicians—in a one-party state system—to professional groups of different kinds, as in the market-oriented socioeconomic systems. In the one-party system politicians fill the law with content in the implementation processes, while in the market-oriented system this role is filled by professions performing different tasks in accordance with what the goal-oriented law tells them to do. China seems to be in a transition from one to the other of these systems, which is shown in many of the examples put forth in this volume.

We have also to take into consideration the geographical part of China in focus and thereby determine the character of the legal culture in which the problem exists. This brings us finally to the time dimension of implementation. As discussed above there is a difference if the implementation takes place within the agricultural mode or the industrial mode of production. Different geographical areas belong to different socioeconomic stages that influence the conditions for implementation, such as if a province or geographic area finds itself in the initial phase or the large-scale phase of industrialism. Or is the implementation study even related to the phase of a society in transition with its special problem of pluralism and conflicting demands? The answers to these questions will guide us in finding the proper way of understanding what is influencing the implementation process. Sapio's analysis of corruption and anticorruption legislation in this volume shows us the relevance of these distinctions. One can also refer to the uneven development of the legal system in different provinces, which is seen in Zhu Jingwen's report on law and development in China.[48] Here we can see clear evidence of the relation between economic development and the development of law in terms of number of lawyers, legal education, law firms, the court system, and the like.[49]

Bibliography

Alford, William P., and Benjamin L. Liebman. "Clean Air, Clear Processes? The Struggle over Air Pollution Law in the People's Republic of China," *Hastings Law Journal* 52 (2000–2001): 703–748.

Aubert, Vilhelm; Eckhoff, Torstein; and Knut Sveri. *En lov I sökelyset. Socialpsykologisk undersögelse av den norske hushjelpslov. A Law in Focus. Social Psychological Investigation of the Norwegian Law About Domestic Servants.* Oslo: Akademisk forlag, 1952.

Burell, Mattias. "The Rule-Governed State: China's Labour Market Policy, 1978–1998," Ph.D. thesis. Uppsala: Uppsala University 2001.

Cameron, Rondo. *A Concise Economic History of the World: From Paleolithic Times to the Present*, 4th edition. New York: Oxford University Press, 2003.

Chen, An. *Restructuring Political Power in China: Alliances and Opposition, 1978–1998.* Boulder: Lynne Rienner Publishers, 1999.

Cohen, Jerome Alan. "A Slow March to Legal Reform," *Far Eastern Economic Review* (2007).

Coleman, James. *Foundations of a Social Theory.* Cambridge: Harvard University Press, 1990.

---

48 Zhu Jingwen, *The Report on China Law Development: Database and Indicators* (China: Renmin University Press, 2007).

49 This is also reflected in the development of the legal aid system in China, see Hatla Thelle's contribution in this volume.

Dezalay, Yves. "The Power of the Legal Field." In *An Introduction to Law and Social Theory*, edited by Reza Banakar and Max Travers. Oxford: Portland, Oregon: Hart Publishing, 2002.

Dingjian, Cai. "Functions of the People's Congresses in the Process of Implementation of Law." In *Implementation of Law in the People's Republic of China*, edited by Jianfu Chen et al. The Hague: Kluwer Law International, 2002.

Dowdle, Michael, ed. *Public Accountability: Designs, Dilemmas and Experiences*. New York: Cambridge University Press, 2006.

Eckhoff, Torstein, and Sundby, Nils Kristian. *Rettssystemer: systemteoretisk innføring i rettsfilosofien* [Legal systems: System theoretical introduction to legal philosophy], 2nd edition. Oslo: Tano, 1991.

Galtung, Johan. *Fredsforskning* [Peace research], 3rd edition. Stockholm: Prisma, 1970.

Hydén, Håkan. "Working Environment Legislation in the Nordic Countries." In *The Nordic Labour Relations Model: Labour Law and Trade Unions in the Nordic Countries: Today and Tomorrow*, edited by Niklas Bruun et al. Aldershot: Dartmouth, 1992.

———. *Rättssociologi som rättsvetenskap* [Sociology of law as legal science]. Lund: Studentlitteratur, 2002.

———. "Implementation of International Conventions—A Socio-Legal Enterprise. Examples from the Convention on the Rights of the Child." In *Human Rights: From Dissemination to Application, Essays in Honour of Göran Melander*. 375–392. Leiden: Martinius Nijhoff Publishers, 2006.

Iggers, George G. *Historiography in the Twentieth Century: From Scientific Objectivity to the Postmodern Challenge*. Hanover: New Hampshire: Wesleyan University Press, 1997.

Jingwen, Zhu. *The Report on China Law Development: Database and Indicators*. China: Renmin University Press, 2007.

Kondratieff, Nickolai D. "The Long Waves of Business Cycles in Economic Life," *Problems of Economic Fluctuations*. Institute for Business Cycles Research, 1925.

Korn, Jessica. "The Legislative Veto and the Limits of Public Choice Analysis," *Political Science Quarterly* 109, no. 5 (1994–1995): 873–894.

Liebman, Benjamin L. "Legal Aid and Public Interest Law in China," *Texas International Law Journal* 34, no. 2 (1999): 211–286.

Lubman, Stanley B. *Bird in a Cage—Legal Reform in China after Mao*. Stanford, California: Stanford University Press, 1997.

Macauley, Stewart. "Non-Contractual Relations in Business: A Preliminary Study," *American Sociological Review* 28, no. 1 (1963): 55–67.

Nonet, Philippe and Philip Selznick. *Law and Society in Transition: Toward Responsive Law*. New York: Harper and Row, 1978.

Olsson, Patrik. *Legal Ideals and Normative Realities: A Case Study of Children's Rights and Child Labour Activity in Paraguay*. Lund: Lund Studies in Sociology of Law 19, 2003.

Otto, Jan Michael. "Toward an Analytical Framework: Real Legal Certainty and Its Explanatory Factors." In *Implementation of Law in the People's Republic of China*, edited by Jianfu Chen et al. The Hague: Kluwer Law International, 2002.

Peerenboom, Randall P. *China's Long March toward Rule of Law*. New York: Cambridge University Press, 2002.

Potter, Pitman B. "Globalization and Economic Regulation in China: Selective Adaptation of Globalized Norms and Practices," *Washington University Global Studies Law Review* 97, no. 1. (2003): 119–150.

Potter, Pitman B. "Legal Reform in China: Institutions, Culture, and Selective Adaptation," *China Quarterly* (2004): 475.

Renner, Karl. *The Institutions of Private Law and Their Social Functions*. London: Routledge, 1949.

Schön, Lennart. *En modern svensk ekonomisk historia. Tillväxt och omvandling under två sekel* [A modern Swedish economic history: Growth and transformation under two centuries]. Stockholm: SNS förlag, 2000.

Shuman James B., and David Rosenau. *The Kondratieff Wave*. New York: Dell Publishing, 1972.

Sousa Santos, Boaventura de. *Towards a New Common Sense*. New York: Routledge, 1995.

Teubner, Gunther. "Substantive and Reflexive Elements in Modern Law," *Law and Society Review* 17 (1983).

_____, ed. *Autopoietic Law: A New Approach to Law and Society*. Berlin: Walter de Gruyter, 1987.

_____. "The Two Faces of Janus: Rethinking Legal Pluralism," *Cardozo Law Review* 13, no. 5, (1992).

van Rooij, Benjamin. *Land and Pollution Regulation in China: Lawmaking,*

Compliance, Enforcement; Theory and Cases. Leiden: Leiden University Press, 2006.

Wallerstein, Immanuel. *World-Systems Analysis: An Introduction.* Durham: Duke University Press, 2004.

Wickenberg, Per. *Normstödjande strukturer. Miljötematiken börjar slå rot i skolan* [Norm supporting structures: The environmental theme begins to take root in schools]. Lund: Lund Studies in Sociology of Law 5, 1999.

*Institutions and Actors in
Implementation Work*

4

Chinese Courts in Law Implementation

JONAS GRIMHEDEN

Courts' implementation of law beyond the case at hand, formulating principles and precedence, affects implementation very broadly. Courts ultimately, with a sufficient degree of status, independence, and credibility along with their very central function, affect the legal system as a whole and even the political sphere by ideally providing a formal, neutral, and apolitical avenue for justice.[1]

What are the constraining and enabling factors in this regard for courts in China? Issues that will be dealt with in answering this question are in particular the status of courts in the politico-legal system and the reform efforts of and by the judiciary. I proceed by first providing an overview of constraining and enabling features of the Chinese court system and the reform process, discussing in turn restraints, potentials, and restrained potentials. In doing so, I elaborate on the relationships between courts and other actors as well as the relationships within and between courts, potentially affecting the operation negatively as well as positively. I conclude with an analysis of enabling and constraining factors of the Chinese judiciary[2] based on a set of models on law implementation seeking to

---

[1] See generally on courts in this respect, Herbert Jacob, "Courts as Organizations," in *Empirical Theories About Courts*, eds. Keith O. Boyum and Lynn Mathers (New York: Longman, 1983), and Herbert Jacob et al., *Courts, Law, and Politics in Comparative Perspective* (New Haven: Yale University Press, 1996).

[2] Irrespective of the Chinese language connotations, "judicial" or the "judiciary" is here limited to the system of courts, excluding the procuratorate—the special form of prosecutors with a broad supervisory mandate in China.

explain the shortcomings of implementation of law and of judicial reform in China.

Law Implementation

Implementation here is not limited to enforcement of court verdicts, but focuses on the broader issues of how courts implement law by boosting the legal system through being a credible actor of stature. This study moreover does not aim at a particular piece of legislation or a particular area of law but tries to capture the courts' role in law implementation more generally. The area of law certainly affects the efficacy of the courts as implementers. I focus, however, in particular on the judicial reform process, given its larger implications on not only the legal but also the political system. The geographical size of China, its vast population, the huge differences in economic development, and the often great differences between levels of courts in the four-tier hierarchy make a generalized perspective difficult. Case studies of several courts at various locations and levels throughout the country would have been fascinating, but quite different a project.[3]

Methodologically, I am supplementing literature findings with information based on interviews with, in particular, Chinese judges and court officials but also scholars at various locations in China. Over the last few years, I have had possibilities to discuss the many

---

3 See e.g., Margaret Y. K. Woo and Yaxin Wang, "Civil Justice in China: An Empirical Study of Courts in Three Provinces," *American Journal of Comparative Law* 53 (2005): 911; Stéphanie Balme, "The Judicialisation of Politics and the Politicisation of the Judiciary in China (1978–2005)," *Global Jurist Frontiers* 5, issue 1 (2005); Sue Trevaskes, "Courts on the Campaign Path: Criminal Court Work in China's 'Yanda 2001' Anti-Crime Campaign, *Asian Survey* 42, issue 5 (2002); He Xin, "Ideology or Reality? Limited Judicial Independence in Contemporary Rural China," *The Australian Journal of Asian Law* 6, no. 3 (2005); Sida Liu, "Beyond Global Convergence: Conflicts of Legitimacy in a Chinese Lower Court," *Law & Social Inquiry* 31, issue 1 (2006).

problems, solutions, theories, and strategies related to judicial reform and law implementation as part of my efforts to understand the reforms under way.[4] Courts in China have previously been covered from several different angles. This chapter draws on the most important of these studies in assessing the Chinese judiciary, and specifically from a law implementation perspective.[5]

---

4 I have discussed judicial reform with judges at various locations in China such as Beijing, Shanghai, Shandong, and Guizhou; locations that are mainly in the more affluent east but also, such as Guizhou, among the poorer parts of China. Judges have been from all four levels in the court hierarchy. At the various places I have also talked with academics with an interest in judicial reform. At three of the locations, I have conducted repeated informal interviews with the same judges. The results of the discussions have been difficult to integrate in a very systematic way; so they serve here more as exemplifications and for the background as confirmation of written studies.

5 Major studies on courts in China generally include: Susan Finder, "The Supreme People's Court of the People's Republic of China," *Journal of Chinese Law* 7 (1993): 145; Susan Finder, "Court System," in *Doing Business in China*, ed. Bruckhaus Deringer Freshfields (New York: Juris Publishing, 2002); Ronald C. Brown, *Understanding Chinese Courts and Legal Process: Law with Chinese Characteristics* (The Hague: Kluwer Law International, 1997); Xin Chunying, *Chinese Courts: History and Transition* (Beijing: Konrad-Adenauer-Stiftung, 2005); Fu Hualing, "Putting China's Judiciary into Perspective: Is It Independent, Competent, and Fair?" in *Beyond Common Knowledge: Empirical Approaches to the Rule of Law*, eds. Erik G. Jensen and Thomas C. Heller (Stanford: Stanford University Press, 2003); Yuwen Li, "Court Reform in China: Problems, Progress and Prospects," in *Implementation of Law in the People's Republic of China*, eds. Jianfu Chen et al. (The Hague: Kluwer Law International, 2002); Jean-Pierre Cabestan, "The Political and Practical Obstacles to the Reform of the Judiciary and the Establishment of a Rule of Law in China", *Journal of Chinese Political Science* 10 (2005); Randall Peerenboom, "Judicial Independence and Judicial Accountability: An Empirical Study of Individual Case Supervision," *The China Journal* (January 2006); Jonas Grimheden, "The Reform Path of the Chinese Judiciary: Progress or Stand-Still?" *Fordham International Law Journal* 30, no. 4 (2007); Benjamin Liebman, "China's Courts: Restricted Reform," *The China Quarterly* 191 (2007); and Sue Trevaskes, *Courts and Criminal Justice in Contemporary China* (Lanham: Lexington Press, 2007).

Restraining and Enabling Factors

Judicial implementation in China suffers from numerous restraints while also having and developing numerous enabling features that potentially can overcome at least some of the restraints. The explanations for restraining and enabling factors that the implementation models offer are pertinent for China as the following analysis of the Chinese judiciary and the reform process shows.

Restraints

The four-tier, 3,500 courts,[6] 170,000 judges strong Chinese judiciary organized under the leadership of the Supreme People's Court (SPC) is not quite as strong or as centralized as might be assumed. Numerous factors affect its powers, not least at the local level. First, at the central level, the court has to struggle, in a more ordinary way, with other powers: the government and the parliament, but also with the procuratorate—with supervisory powers also over the courts—and the constant, dominant Communist Party.

At the local level, the judiciary lacks power in a more uncommon way for a purportedly centralized system. With funding and allocation of resources coming from the corresponding levels of congress and government, and where the same congresses are approving prospective judges, the horizontal influence on the judiciary is indeed strong.[7] Added to this is the omnipresence of the party—also at the local level—influencing selection and approval of

---

6 If the branch-courts of the basic courts are included, the number increases with more than ten of thousands. Donald C. Clarke, "Puzzling Observations in Chinese Law: When Is a Riddle Just a Mistake?" in *Understanding China's Legal System*, ed. C. Stephen Hsu (New York: New York University Press, 2003), 180, who specifies the number of people's tribunals to 12,000 by the end of 1999, based on data in the Chinese *falü nianjian* [Law Yearbook] (2000).

7 See e.g., Finder, "Court System," 13, 14; Randall Peerenboom, "Judicial Independence in China," draft electronic paper on file with the author, page numbers in the following will be as they appear when printed. See also the chapter by

judges, promotions and work allocation, and at times also directly and indirectly the outcome of specific adjudications.[8] The party is influential on the individual level through most of the judges being party members[9] but also through party organs within courts and through "coordinating" bodies for the legal system and beyond. The latter is done by way of political and legal affairs committees at each level in the government hierarchy composed *inter alia* of the highest representatives of courts, prosecutors, and police, where important issues are addressed and settled.[10] These bodies can prevent courts and judges from acting independently.

Party influence at the local level is not always identical with a central party line, however; it can also be that of or against the local government or other local interests. This influence is not necessarily negative from a narrow law implementation viewpoint, but in a broader perspective it nevertheless is likely to undermine the effectiveness of law implementation.[11]

The role of the procuratorate and the party along with strong local powers with extensive potential influence are core restraining factors. There are, however, numerous other elements limiting the judiciary in its role as a good, credible implementer. Starting from the court and moving outward through the judiciary as a whole and to the political-legal system, I highlight the main restraining features. Within each court, the very traditional bureaucratic system with hierarchies and ranking of seniority affects the operations of the courts. The ranking of the judges in detailed systems that cor-

---

Oscar Almén in this volume, regarding for instance individual case supervision (*ge'an jiandu*).

8 See e.g., Finder, "The Supreme People's Court of the People's Republic of China," 149, and Peerenboom, "Judicial Independence in China," 2 et seq., 13 et seq.

9 Stanley Lubman and Leïla Choukroune estimate the number of judges that are party members at some 90 percent. See their "L'incomplète réforme par le loi," *Esprit* (February 2004).

10 Finder, "Court System," 11.

11 See Peerenboom, "Judicial Independence in China," 2, 3, 32, 33.

responds to power and benefits makes the status of an individual judge fall into a strict hierarchy.[12] Before the adoption of the Judges Law of 1995,[13] the ranking system was identical to the overall state bureaucracy but was then changed even though some equivalents still remain.

Court leaders, heading the administration of court affairs, are also influential in various ways related to the actual outcome of verdicts.[14] Dependent as they are on local resources and cooperation to successfully operate the court and being more susceptible to political pressure for position and promotion, court leaders can influence the outcome of cases also where they are not "on the bench" in that specific case. This is done through reviewing cases but also more indirectly by controlling allocation of various benefits to the employees.

Most criticized among the systems that influence the internal operation of the judiciary is the existence of the adjudicative committee (*shenpan weiyuanhui*).[15] The senior judges, being members of the adjudicative committees, intended to build expertise and to gather experience, remove powers from the individual judges sitting on the actual cases and influence the outcome.[16] The influence of these committees is being reduced in the ongoing reform process, but at the same time the committees are also seen as a guarantor for quality of adjudication and as preventing corruption.

---

12 Finder, "Court System," 16.

13 The Judges Law was adopted February 28, 1995, and revised June 30, 2001.

14 Finder, "Court System," 28.

15 Interview with Judge at the SPC, October 11, 2006; interview with judge at a high people's court (HPC), the second highest level in the hierarchy, October 17, 2006. Interesting to note is also that members of the adjudicative committees, according to the judge, are not required to pass the Unified Judicial Exam. See further on this exam below.

16 The Organizational Law of the Courts (Article 11), adopted July 1, 1979, and revisions became effective September 2, 1983; Peerenboom, "Judicial Independence in China," 13.

The same administrative tendencies existing within courts are also problematic between courts in the hierarchy with various forms of supervision affecting the functioning.[17] Superior courts supervise not only by determining cases on appeal and through more bureaucratic forms, such as independent general inspections but also through initiating review of specific cases.[18] Lower courts can further request instructions in specific cases from higher courts, something that undermines the appeal process.[19]

Restraints are also plentiful outside of the judiciary itself. One aspect of this is the courts themselves being responsible for execution of verdicts (e.g., collection of fines and debts) rather than a specialized agency. In order to secure better implementation—and gain needed respect—the courts depend on cooperation with police and other government agencies.[20] The judiciary's position within the legal system is compromised, as mentioned, by the supervisory role of the procuratorate (the prosecutors). This Soviet heritage fits awkwardly with the prosecutor-judge relationship by subjecting the judiciary to monitoring by the prosecutorial organs they in turn are supposed to be supervising. The problems are not reduced by the procuratorial supervisory powers stretching not only to criminal but also to civil and administrative cases.[21]

Police powers are much less problematic even though the situation of the judiciary is thorny with the representative of the police

---

17 Finder, "Court System," 35.
18 Ibid.
19 Finder, "Court System," 34.
20 Introduced requirements on judges in adjudicative positions to have academic (law) degrees and to have passed the judicial exam has pushed those without to nonadjudicative positions within a court, often serving with the implementation branch, which has lowered the professional status of this part of the courts and further the problems with implementation of verdicts.
21 See generally Fu Hualing, "Procuracy," in *Doing Business in China*, vol. 1, eds. Freshfields et al. (Huntington: Juris Publishing, 2003).

often chairing the political and legal affairs committee.[22] The shortage of practicing lawyers in China worsens the problems of the legal system broadly but also the judiciary specifically by too rarely enabling parties to have access to qualified legal advice. In this way judges are also forced to spend more time "explaining verdicts."[23] The party then finally, as discussed above, restrains the context in which the judiciary operates.

Related to the internal operation of courts are the issues that could be placed under the general label of public confidence. In Chapter 3 of this volume Hydén elaborates on social norms. As social norms, public confidence (in the court system) will take time to develop and this potentially slows down the pace of reform. Public confidence moreover greatly depends on the level of professionalism of the judges and court staff as well as on transparency in court operations and the possibility of preventing corruption within the judiciary.[24] The level of education of judges is increasing and with this the public confidence in the courts.[25] However, economically less well-off provinces, in particular, have tremendous problems getting their well-educated judges to stay and even more so recruiting sufficiently qualified judges. With relatively low wages and slim chances of major career improvements, practicing law as an attorney, for instance, is in that respect far more attractive for most.

Public confidence in the judiciary ought to increase with greater stature and independence.[26] This, however, hinges on increased

---

22 Interview with professor of law in Shanghai, April 11, 2005; see also on related issues, Liebman, "China's Courts," 627, 628.

23 Several judges interviewed stated as a problem that they had to spend lots of time explaining, upon request, verdicts after they were issued.

24 For an in-depth discussion on corruption, see Chapter 9 by Flora Sapio in this volume.

25 In 1995 the percentage of judges with a university degree (likely including junior college degrees, so called *dazhuan*) was reported to be below 10 percent, which ten years later had risen to over 50 percent. All new judges are required to have at least a bachelor's degree. Liebman, "China Courts," 625.

26 Stressed by a former senior judge, turned professor of law, April 11, 2005.

public confidence. In order for the judiciary to gain more independence, many argue that judges have to first become more professional and less corrupt.[27] The problem is somewhat circular. Courts are not given more power because they are not seen as able to handle it. Without more power, however, they are likely not able to handle the many challenges.[28] Certainly, greater independence, although positive for law implementation, is also quite politically sensitive, which further reduces clear moves toward greater independence. This quandary has left many proposals for the judiciary on the drawing table.

Confidence in the quality of the judiciary together with the many other restraining factors, internally and externally, are central obstacles to greater independence of the judiciary and thus for a more efficient judiciary as implementer of law in both the narrow adjudicative sense but also as regards the wider credibility for the legal system as a whole.

Potential

I have briefly described the factors potentially undermining the judiciary in China: undermining its status, independence, credibility, and power to support or even ensure law implementation. Numerous efforts have been made to address the problems, some of which have proven successful, others less so.[29]

Judicial reform has in particular been central during the last decade, formally since the mid-nineties, at that time culminating in the adoption of the new Judges Law (1995). That law introduced

---

Also underscored by a judge at a basic people's court (BPC), the lowest level in the hierarchy of courts, October 17, 2006.

27 E.g., Professor Zhu Jingwen, October 12, 2006.

28 This argument is put forth by e.g. Xin Chunying, "What Kind of Judicial Power Does China Need?" *International Journal of Constitutional Law Online* 1, no. 1 (2003): 78.

29 For an overview, see Peerenboom, "Judicial Independence in China."

foundations for a more specialized, professional judiciary, distinct from the administration, for example, by establishing a salary system separate from the administrative one. The law further recognized the need for a modernized judiciary with more focus on the individual judge rather than the institution. Around the same time specialized laws were also adopted for prosecutors as well as lawyers. All three laws were amended in 2001 to accommodate the new Unified Judicial Exam, setting identical entrance standards for all three professional groups.[30]

The reform of the Judges Law of that year included emphasis on justice (prominently placed in the first article) and professional ethics as well as various reinforced measures aimed at improving qualifications and preventing bias. Later in 2001 the Supreme People's Court also issued a Code of Judicial Ethics for Judges, emphasizing the impartiality of judges.[31] From the adoption of the court's Organizational Law[32] in the late 1970s, to the Judges Law in 1995 and its 2001 revision, to the Code of Judicial Ethics, a clear development can be discerned. The judiciary is gradually separating itself from the bureaucracy. Indicative is the usage starting in 1995 of "judge" (*faguan*) as opposed to "adjudicator" (*shenpanyuan*), which had been used in the Organizational Law. Stricter separation from the state bureaucracy directly relates to independence and the judiciary's credibility in society. The modified formulation on independence in the new Code of Judicial Ethics mirrors revisions of the revised Organizational Law (1983, in line with the 1982 constitu-

---

30 Keyuan Zou, "Reform in China: Recent Developments and Future Prospects," *International Lawyer*, issue 36 (2002): 1051.

31 In 2004 the SPC jointly with the Ministry of Justice issued a code intended to regulate the relationship between judges and lawyers in order to ensure fair trial. The code was issued March 19, 2004, effective immediately. See "New code of conduct on judicial corruption," *South China Morning Post*, March 20, 2004.

32 The Organizational (Organic) Law of the People's Courts of the PRC was adopted in 1979 and revised in 1983; it deals with the general structure and organization of the courts as well as the requirements to become judge and appointments to the senior positions.

tion), the Judges Law and the constitution. The old wording was to "exercise justice independently, in accordance with the provisions of the law, and shall not be subject to interference by any administrative organ, public organization or individual."[33] In the Code of Judicial Ethics, Article 2 specifies that a judge should follow the constitution and law based on "the principle of judicial independence [and] ... with no interference from administrative departments, social organizations or individuals and *no influence other than the influence from the laws.*"[34] A gradual move is clear from the texts: where the Code of Judicial Ethics still avoids specifically mentioning, for example, the Communist Party, it nevertheless more clearly stipulates greater independence of the judiciary. This is just one process indicating the overall development.

In 1999 the SPC adopted the first Five-Year Reform Plan (FYRP) with some forty proposed reform measures.[35] The plan identified restrictions of judicial independence based on four widely recognized problems: local protectionism, low professional and moral standards, the bureaucratic management model, and the lack of resources. For instance, the relationship with the procuratorate or the role of the party in the legal system were, however, not identified as obstacles. Many of the detailed issues listed above were nevertheless addressed to some extent. The first FYRP emphasized selection criteria for judges as well as increased independence of those actually involved in the adjudication of specific cases, thus reducing powers of the court leaders and the adjudicative committees.

---

33 The Organizational Law (Article 4), the Judges Law [Article 8(2)], and the Constitution (Article 126).

34 Emphasis added. Translation used, available at e.g. http://www.accci.com.au/code.

35 The SPC president in the spring of 2000 presented the plan to the National People's Congress, and the Party Central Committee later in the year approved the FYRP. See Shigui Tan, *Zhongguo sifa gaige yanjiu* (Beijing: Falü chubanshe, 2000), 55. For the actual text, see e.g., Xin, Chinese Courts, 295 et seq. or http://www.dffy.com/faguixiazai/xf/200511/20051128111114.htm.

A second Five-Year Reform Plan,[36] released in 2005, stressed reform relating mainly to areas such as the adjudicative committees, furthering the reform initiated in the first FYRP; regularizing or underpinning the use of lay judges; and reform of the "rehearing" (*zaishen*) system, restricting the reopening of final decisions. The second FYRP also emphasizes strengthening enforcement of court decisions; focusing on branch courts,[37] tribunals (*fating*), sorting under the basic courts (*jiceng fayuan*, BPC); and the plans of the Supreme People's Court to take back from the provincial-level high courts (*gaoji fayuan*, HPC) control of the final decision-making powers where the death penalty is within the range of punishment. More detailed reform measures include for example how courts and judges must handle the many facets of a case,[38] and that appeals be made more distinct and the process more transparent from first-level hearings. Another detail was that powers of the adjudicative committees were further reduced from direct case-specific influence.

In the spring of 2009, a third Five-Year Reform Plan was released (2009–2013).[39] Mainly the third plan brings details and reinforcement to earlier reform elements by further clarifying, for example, the relationship between various departments within courts

---

36 Already on March 9, 2005, it was announced in the *SPC Work Report to the NPC* that the second FYRP was soon to be made official. See http://www.chinacourt.org/public/detail.php?id=182741. For the actual text, see e.g., http://www.dffy.com/faguixiazai/xf/200512/20051214221735.htm. A few weeks later it was announced that the second FYRP was official, but it took until October that year before it was actually released.

37 In the first FYRP the number of the tribunals was scheduled to be limited, and it seemed as if their importance was diminishing; in the second FYRP this is not as clear any longer or at least formulated very discretely.

38 "Adopted provisions on judicial behavior lists 93 detailed requirements," http://www.xinhuanet.com, October 27, 2005.

39 For the original text, see www.chinacourt.org/public/detail.php?id=350101 and for the English version, see e.g., Flora Sapio's blog, at http://florasapio.blogspot.com/2009/04/third-five-year-reform-outline-for.html.

as well as between courts, securing of funding, and mechanisms for corruption prevention.

These reform measures address, at least, in part, the shortcomings discussed above that restrain the judiciary. For example, relying on lay judges is a means to increase transparency but also to educate and to better communicate proper court operations and the difficulties with adjudication to the population in efforts to gain stronger support for the institution. Other measures introduced or reinvigorated with the second platform aim broadly at making appeal a completely new assessment, trying to sever the bureaucratic ties that exist between the levels in the court hierarchy. There would certainly be room for further improvements to boost the status and functioning of the courts.[40]

At a more abstract level, the stated goal in the first Five Year Reform Plan was to make the judiciary fair and more efficient.[41] This was reiterated in the second and third FYRPs. The format of the reform, in particular the three plans, is the result of compromise between many interests, such as those of the judiciary, the procuratorate, and the party. The language in the plans suggests possibly contradictory reforms, for example, with a very strong emphasis on supervision and submission to the party while also providing for independence.[42] There is certainly also a fair amount of plain rhetoric in the reform plans. All three FYRPs address central issues apparently aimed at the goals of fairness and efficiency; it is not clear how the means proposed lead to these goals. As overall goals, fairness and efficiency may be appropriate, but they also risk being

---

40 Peerenboom suggests, for example, expanded judicial review to include not only concrete cases and to allow courts to annul inconsistent lower legislation. See "Judicial Independence and Judicial Accountability: Preliminary Thoughts on Our Empirical Study on Individual Case Supervision," *The China Journal* 55 (2006): 11.

41 See e.g., Finder, "Court System," 3.

42 See e.g., Xiao Yang's speech on the second FYRP and the sequence of the party and the state in *2005 Work Report to the NPC*, April 1, 2006.

interpreted very differently by different camps within the various institutions and organizations, and also at the various levels in the hierarchy.[43] This vagueness in the overarching goals may, however, also be a good feature in enabling approval and support of reform measures, and permitting a more progressive development than otherwise would have been possible.

The direct impact of the first two FYRPs seems to be surprisingly low.[44] The second FYRP is seen as more realistic, dealing more with matters within the judiciary than the previous one, and the third one follows this pattern. Some judges were even saying that the second FYRP prescribed reforms that are within the ambit of the law, as opposed to the first one. Yet many express criticism of the reform plans, and the second FYRP is taken to be too simple, unclear, and, like the first one, too insensitive to actual local conditions. The central reform plans are coupled with local reform platforms at the level of high courts at the provincial level, which give further details to the central plans for that particular jurisdiction but remain within the scope of the national platform.[45]

The ultimate appeal process in cases risking the application of

---

43 On goals being too broad and vague, interview with attorney, 2005; another interviewee argued, however, that the goals were in fact quite clear as opposed to the method and more importantly the pace, which is not clear to all since many fail to understand the actual implications of the goals, interview with a former senior judge turned professor of law, April 11, 2005, similarly in interview with an academic with senior adjudication experience, 2005.

44 I am drawing here mainly on discussions with judges in Suzhou, Jinan, and Changsha. Further down, the less informed judges seem to be of the two reform platforms. Typically among the lower level judges it is unheard of. To the extent that the platforms are known, judges indicate that the content is irrelevant until it is transferred to them as law: procedural changes in legislation or interpretations. Judges in research divisions or in leadership positions on the other hand are knowledgeable about the reform platforms. This probably makes good sense since the platforms are not directly linked to the everyday work of most judges but rather provide the directions for reform that the leadership should be aware of.

45 According to a judge at a HPC, October 17, 2006.

the death penalty was taken back to the highest court of the land, giving way to strong symbolic effects. The more routine approval of death sentences by the High People's Courts at the provincial level of the past is now being replaced with a tougher scrutiny, aimed at avoiding irrevocable mistakes that have taken place in the past, and ensuring a centralized trial de novo at the Supreme People's Court.[46]

This recentralization is interesting, not the least for law implementation. Problems related to local protectionism, such as undue influence on courts in the interest of local business with associated job opportunities in a business dispute, are difficult to address given that such local incentives typically are so much stronger and immediate than those more principled, which are related to justice. For the Supreme People's Court to resolve such instances and ensure implementation of law, power would have to be centralized, not only within the judiciary but also local powers of appointment and financing. It would require very strong reasons for the central level to undertake such changes in the face of local powers and interests. The highly publicized cases of apparent injustice that evolved in 2005, however, provided sufficient incentives and support for the Supreme Court to revoke provincial powers of final adjudication in death penalty cases.[47] This is possibly only a limited area where the central level claims jurisdiction, but it may also be a test case for lifting more issues up from local levels to the central level, staying clear of local interests. The vice president of the Supreme Court, former law professor Wan E'xiang, is quoted to have stated that this move is essential for "judicial neutrality."[48]

The method chosen to deal with death penalty cases is also in-

---

46 *Agence France Press*, September 28, 2005, <www.legaldaily.com.cn/bm/2005-09/28/content_200178.htm>, <http://rmfyb.chinacourt.org/public/detail.php?id=106249>.

47 See e.g., Benjamin Liebman and Tim Wu, "China's Network Justice," *Chicago Journal of International Law* 8 (2007): 176 et seq.

48 http://zqb.cyol.com/gb/zqb/2005-09/27/content_70228.htm.

teresting. Not only are the cases settled finally by the Supreme Court, but three regional branches of the Supreme Court are set up to process the cases. Many have suggested, and it has even been tested at local levels, that to separate the court jurisdictions from the administrative entities would do away with many of the problems, not least local protectionism, and would strengthen central powers.[49] The solution opted for in death penalty cases may very well prove to be a model for a wider jurisdiction of a central reach of court hierarchies: a solution of more federal type.

Reforms have also aimed at funding or at least supplementing scarce local resources allocated to courts with funds from higher-level administration, and ultimately from the central level.[50] Given the vast numbers of courts and judges, this is hugely expensive, but even a partial change in funding sources may prove efficient. The poorer areas of China, moreover, depend on increased provision of funds to be able to operate on any level similar to courts in the developed eastern parts of the country. The "Develop Westward Campaign" (*xibu da kaifa*) launched in 2000 has led to the transfer of funds for general development projects. Courts are also benefiting from an increased attention in inland China. Judges and even academics from Beijing and other more developed areas are recruited to serve longer periods as judges in western China, with the maintenance of salaries and promises to return to good positions upon

---

49 Consider e.g., the reform of the Bank of China described in Chunming Guo and Zhigang Liu, "Sifa gongzheng: sifa zhidu gaige de mubiao," *Zhongguo Faxue* 4 (2000), 156. See also further examples in the area of environmental protection, Benjamin van Rooij, "The Politics of Law in China: Enforcement Campaigns in the Post-Mao PRC," (2009).

50 For an interesting argument counter to centralized financing leading to greater independence is proposed by Xin He, "Ideology or Reality? Limited Judicial Independence in Contemporary Rural China," *Australian Journal of Asian Law* 6 (3) (2005). For an equally challenging view on judicial independence more broadly, see Randall Peerenboom, "Judicial Independence in China: Common Myths and Unfounded Assumptions," La Trobe Law School Legal Studies Research Paper No. 2008/11, available at http://ssrn.com/abstract=1283179.

completion.[51] This is yet another measure that is increasing central influence and reducing local power, but also aimed at lessening the widening gap between eastern and western China.

Local initiative at times drives the reform process. A case in point could be the Shanghai High Court. Here nomination of judges is regulated by unified tests (within Shanghai) of both a written and practical nature to ensure that senior judges are of the highest degree of professionalism and competence.[52] This way the courts effectively also restrict other sources of influence in the appointment process. Another example is the so-called *Seeds Case* from 2003 where a single judge in a Henan Province court declared void a provincial law that was in conflict with national law.[53] The judge was initially forced to leave the court as a result of the verdict but was eventually reinstated. The case highlights the strong powers of the local people's congresses, here pushing for the removal of the judge. The case also shows how courts are able to slowly make headway.

Restrained Potentials

The judicial reform done and under way also restrains or does not sufficiently enable effective law implementation. General shortcomings of the reform process include a too narrow reform scope, too much of a centralized process unable to accommodate needed local adaptation, yet lacking in a coherent overall approach and vision.

---

51 Interview with e.g., a professor of law who served as a senior judge in one of the western provinces, April 1, 2005.

52 Interview with a judge at a HPC. After passing the national Unified Judicial Exam, in Shanghai the successful candidate then is to work for a year before being up for possible appointment as assistant judge. Assistant judges may take the local unified test typically held once a year, and only at that stage do they have a chance of being promoted to become full judges.

53 *China Youth Daily*, February 6, 2004; *International Herald Tribune*, November 28, 2005; see also e.g., Liebman, "China's Courts," 632.

An obvious reason for the relatively narrow reform is the political sensitivity of too independent a judiciary.

To start with "labeling," the initially simply labeled "judicial reform" (*sifa gaige*) was developed into "judicial *institutional* reform" (*sifa* tizhi *gaige*) by the Sixteenth Party Congress in 2002, a significant change given the context.[54] This change implies a more extensive overhaul that also would have institutional implications with more far-reaching reforms.[55] A requirement to raise the status of the courts also in the constitution in relation to for example the procuratorate was reportedly also stated by one of the Supreme Court justices.[56] In a recent session of the Central Party Committee, the word "mechanism" was added to "judicial institutional reform" ("judicial institutional mechanism reform," *sifa tizhi jizhi gaige*).[57] Zhu Jingwen concludes that this is a narrowing down of the concept to prevent the judicial reform from going beyond the judicial institution itself.[58] Zhu states that the court reform would be limited to the internal aspects, which he, however, suggests was apparent long before this change in words. The people's congresses, for instance, were not to give up powers of appointment of judges for the benefit of a more centralized judicial system.

Within the overall reform process, the party coordinates. In 2003 the Standing Committee (SC) of the party Politburo appointed a coordination group for judicial institutional reform (*zhongyang sifa tizhi gaige lingdao xiaozu*), under the leadership of the then Po-

---

54 Jiang Zemin's speech as reported by Xinhua, November 17, 2002, http://www.china.org.cn/english/features/49007.htm.

55 Interview with a former senior judge, now professor of law, April 11, 2005. He argued that "institutional" implied that constitutional changes would be required.

56 Interview with a professor of law, April 11, 2005, referring to a talk at Jiaotong University, Shanghai, in February of 2005 by Justice Wan E'Xiang.

57 In October of 2006, at the Sixth Session of the Sixteenth Congress, see the report of the session: http://news.xinhuanet.com/politics/2006-10/11/content_5190605.htm.

58 Discussion in Beijing, October 12, 2006.

litburo (*zhengzhiju*) Standing Committee member Luo Gan.⁵⁹ This Central Reform Group is to coordinate the reform measures between the judiciary, the procuratorate, and other central actors in the legal system. The judiciary is, however, pushing for greater reforms than what the Central Reform Group seems to accept or at least sufficiently support. The reform plans have addressed many of the aspects that are possible to resolve within the judiciary.⁶⁰ It leaves out, however, many of the overarching issues that lie beyond the control of the judiciary that would have to be included in a viable reform plan. The Supreme People's Court former president, Xiao Yang, has stated that the reforms so far have dealt with the present problems, but the future requires larger-scale reform.⁶¹ For the reforms envisaged by the SPC to be successful, more institutionally oriented reforms are needed. It has been argued for instance that as a start the constitution would need revisions, in particular related to inter-institutional relationships.⁶² The judiciary is not operating in a vacuum, and the problems are not solely resolved by change within the judiciary. The relationship with local governments and congresses and with the procuratorate and, of course, the party would need to be addressed.

The SPC is often at the front line of reform but not always in

---

59 See e.g., Sohu.com, January 7, 2004. Luo Gan was also at the time state councilor and secretary of the Central Political and Legal Affairs Committee. On Luo Gan's position, see e.g., the article "Chinese offi-cial warns against independence of courts, *New York Times*, February 3, 2007, <www.nytimes.com/2007/02/03/world/asia/03china.html>, giving a very conservative interpretation of a speech, and the speech at <www.qsjournal.com.cn/qs/20070201/GB/qs%5E448%5E0%5E1.htm>.

60 See e.g., Xiao Yang, "Fayuan, faguan yu sifa gaige," *Faxuejia*, no. 1 (2003), where he discusses constitutional and legal reforms as necessities for further reform.

61 "Xiao Yang: Faguan meiyou sili; kaichuang sifa weimin xin jingjie (dawen)," *Zhongxin Wang*, October 15, 2003.

62 E.g., interview with member of the NPC Law Commission, April 7, 2005, and a senior judge of a BPC, April 7, 2005, and also a former senior judge, now professor of law, April 11, 2005, on SPC conflicts with the procuratorate.

conformity or at pace with—typically being ahead of—the rest of the legal reforms. The reform is a rather slow, step-by-step, wait-and-see process not revealing clear ulterior goals or how far reforms will be able to proceed.[63] A general move toward a more modest reform pace has also developed over the last few years. Maybe, as Zhu Jingwen argues, there is a need for the general development to catch up with the aspirations of the reform movement.[64] Maybe the feared consequences of more extensive reforms in the eyes of the party are too risky.

The reforms actually introduced, moreover, suffer from a design intended for the whole of China. With the vast differences in resources, level of education, type of challenges between the more economically developed areas and the poorer regions, reform schemes indeed have difficulties being relevant and applicable for each and every part of the country.[65] Added to this should of course also be the multilayered system with different problems at the various levels in the court hierarchy. Even though the leadership in Beijing is aware of the many problems in implementation of the reform, it is are not always able to resolve the issues on the ground. Obstacles to providing central funding to local courts is an example of the unwillingness of the provinces to surrender power to a more independent national system of courts, but also an indication of the relatively weak position of the central government.[66]

---

63 Interviews with judge of the SPC, October 9, 2005, and a former senior judge, turned professor of law, April 11, 2005.

64 Discussion October 12, 2006. Interview with judge of a HPC, September 15, 2005.

65 On hierarchies, consensus, and win-win recommendations in law implementation, see Derick W. Brinkerhoff, "Coordination Issues in Policy Implementation Networks: An Illustration from Madagascar's Environmental Action Plan," *World Development* 24, issue 9 (1996): 1498, 1505, 1506.

66 In 2005, subsidies totaling almost CNY 5 billion were allocated from the central budget to finance courts, public security, the procuratorate, and related issues in poor areas, an increase of more than CNY 1.5 billion from the previous year. See the *Report on the Implementation of the Central and Local Budgets for*

While many reform measures are tested on a smaller scale and have proven effective, others are not or are tested in areas vastly different from other parts of the country. Reform measures such as raising educational requirements for local judges at the lower-level courts, in a short-term perspective, may be uncalled for and may even prove counterproductive to the overall legal reform.

At the same time as the reform may need more regional variations, at least in a shorter perspective, a more holistic and farsighted approach is needed for a more efficient legal and comprehensive development process in China.[67] The reason for not revealing a possible existing overall blueprint may be that the reforms within the judiciary (as well as elsewhere) are intended to be in part symbolic, aimed at pleasing central-level politicians and showing that they are taking action—even while exhibiting limited or no effect.[68] Another reason is the uncertainty of how far reforms can be allowed to go without compromising political control within the present political system. A small but very symbolic and telling example of restrained progress may be proposed changes to the court organizational law that the authorities did not receive well. Law professors He Weifang and Fan Chongyi, in their report commissioned by the Supreme People's Court, proposed, among many other things, to remove "people's" in the names of the courts, so that for instance "Supreme Court" would replace "Supreme *People's* Court."[69]

2004 and on the Draft Central and Local Budgets for 2005, submitted to the Third Session of the Tenth National People's Congress on March 5, 2005, <http://english.peopledaily.com.cn/200503/15/eng20050315_176928.html>.

67 Interview with a professor of law who served as a senior judge in one of the western provinces, April 1, 2005. See also Woo and Wang, "Civil Justice in China."

68 Interview with a professor of law who served as a senior judge in one of the western provinces, April 1, 2005.

69 *South China Morning Post*, December 8, 2004. At the same time, one local court in Hainan Province, reportedly already in 2003, removed "people's" from its name, interview with prosecutor, April 11, 2005. Maritime courts are typically also not referred to as "people's" courts.

The congresses, through their standing committees, have also toughened their control over the judiciary in some respects. After twenty years of deliberations, a law was adopted in 2006 that regulates and reinforces the supervisory powers of the people's congresses.[70] It is the activities by the standing committees that are being strengthened by way of, for example, making the traditional work reports by, among others, courts better analyze problems by focusing on topical thematic areas, such as development of rural areas, compulsory education, and compensation for housing demolition, etc. The purpose is said to be deepened understanding of the shortcomings of law and its implementation that can enable the standing committees to amend and draft laws appropriately rather than supervision in a negative, restraining way. The Law on Supervision also requires judicial interpretations by the SPC to be registered for review by the National People's Congress Standing Committee (NPCSC).[71]

These stricter measures by the congresses will likely further restrain the judiciary, but they are not necessarily a negative development for the judiciary. It may very well be that these restraints enhance the stature of the judiciary by improved legislative delimitation and other support.

The judicial reform in China is then restrained in three main ways: by being too narrow in scope, at the same time being too inflexible toward the varying problems in different regions and at different levels, and finally by lacking coherence. Three aspects that are quite intertwined but—or maybe therefore—not easily solved.

More broadly on the judiciary and law implementation, the re-

---

70 The Law on Supervision by Standing Committees of People's Congresses at All Levels of the PRC, adopted by the NPCSC, August 27, 2006. For details see e.g., Anbiao Xu, "A Supervisory Law Intended to Guarantee Exercise of Supervisory Power by Standing Committees of People's Congresses," *China Law* (October 2006): 70-73.

71 Xu, "A Supervisory Law."

form process has nevertheless been supportive, not the least through the raised professional standards. A well-functioning judiciary with stature in society greatly depends on credibility with both government agencies and society at large. The dramatically raised educational standards of judges, from less than 20 percent of judges with at least a junior university degree twenty years ago to 100 percent in 2000,[72] coupled with legal training and developed experience has improved the stature of the judiciary.

Increased efforts and actual action to combat judicial corruption has also had positive effects in this regard. Stricter procedural operations within the courts and efforts to make the appeal process a genuine one are similarly supportive. Responsiveness to congresses' demands for oversight while stressing independence in individual cases have also been important steps to boost the credibility. Reform has also included more visual aspects of the judiciary, introducing a unified dress code and official suites and robes inspired by British tradition (through Hong Kong) and construction of new courthouses that ingrain independence and stature. Overall, the enhanced independence of the judiciary with emphasis on justice and efficiency as guiding principles has also had a likely positive impact on the judiciary's law implementation capacity.

Implementation Models

The complexities of lawmaking in any politico-legal system are great. This is even truer for China with its "particular" model of politics, but also its vast country including enormous differences in the level of development. Basic theories or models that can situate the challenges and solutions in a larger framework are needed, and

---

72 Randall Peerenboom, "The X-Files: Past and Present Portrayals of China's Alien 'Legal System'," *Washington University Global Studies Law Review* 2 (2003): 82.

fortunately an array of models exists that seeks to explain success and failure of law implementation generally.[73] Over the last decades of research, various schools have contended for a comprehensive answer. As often is the case, the answer is likely to lie somewhere between all of these efforts. I have chosen two broad explanatory or problematizing models to develop the discussion in a more concrete way.

The first model deals with ambiguity and conflict, where possible "types of law" are situated in a framework consisting of level of ambiguity on the one hand and level of conflict of the issue concerned in society on the other. The second, an incentive-based approach follows, stresses the need for careful consideration of appropriate incentives and disincentives for both individuals and organizations for successful implementation.

Richard Matland in his now over a decade old effort to provide an overview on the research related to implementation problems of policies defined an "ambiguity-conflict" model.[74] Preceding theories on bottom-up and top-down implementation strategies, both of which had their particular advantages but also drawbacks, were synthesized into spectrums of possibilities situated in a framework of ambiguity and conflict. On a scale between high and low, ambiguity and conflict in terms of both means and goals are placed in a matrix of four boxes (see figure). The box (or rather the phenomenon) with low on both dimensions is labeled "administrative imple-

---

73 Søren C. Winter elaborates on "implementation" as also being termed or studied under the heading of new institutionalism, governance, networks, policy design, instruments, regulatory enforcement, street-level bureaucracy, principle-agent theory, public administration, management, in Søren C. Winter, "Implementation - Introduction," in *Handbook of Public Administration*, eds. B. Guy Peters and Jon Pierre (London: Sage Publications, 2003), 205, 206. For an overview in relation to China, see e.g., Jianfu Chen, "Implementation of Law in China - An Introduction," in Chen et al., Implementation of Law.

74 Richard E. Matland, "Synthesizing the Implementation Literature: The Ambiguity-Conflict Model of Policy Implementation," *Journal of Public Administration Research & Theory* (April 1995).

	Ambiguity	
	Low	High
Conflict Low	Administrative	Experimental
Conflict High	Political	Symbolic

Richard E. Matland (1995)

mentation," where the potential conflict on the issue of implementation is very limited and where the meaning and purpose are clear with a low level of ambiguity. Similarly, the box with high on both dimensions is "symbolic implementation," a situation where a highly controversial issue with a high level of conflict is addressed using a relatively vague legislative solution. In the remaining two boxes: the box with low ambiguity but high level of conflict is labeled "political implementation," while the box with high ambiguity but with low level of conflict is called "experimental implementation."

For the low-low box (administrative), implementation is relatively easy and requires not much more than an administrative structure, while for the high-high box (symbolic) implementation becomes much more challenging if at all possible or even desirable. High ambiguity with a low level of conflict (experimental) includes situations where law may be tested on an issue of relatively low controversy but with a more general legislative solution so that there is room for adaptation and stock-taking. High conflict with a low ambiguity (political) is an instance where the legislative aim is clear but is within a controversial area with widely diverging opinions.

Such parameters require substantial powers to ensure implementation.

The framework of ambiguity-conflict neatly encapsulates much of the potential problems in and also indicates needed redress for, successful lawmaking and implementation. It is, moreover, a model that easily includes the crucial greater context of implementation.[75] In China much law seems to fall within the high-high (symbolic) box and so does much of the judicial reform package.[76] High on ambiguity as well as conflict in this respect could be due to numerous reasons, but the high conflict is largely affected by the rapid pace of reform and the at times radical changes. High ambiguity can be due to the sheer size of the country—that the law has to be relatively general or flexible to fit all parts of the country and accommodate the many diverse interests. As will be discussed, high ambiguity may also be due to realization that a less ambiguous law will undermine the credibility of the central legislative institution by reducing the likelihood of compliance. It is not possible to assemble enough power to ensure a clearer legislative solution in a controversial area (low-high, political), either for financial or political reasons or simply because of lack of sufficient power. Another explanation for not shifting from symbolic to political by reducing the level of ambiguity could be risk aversion, again to either avoid local powers countering or even disregarding an initiative, or to

---

75 See related research on success of mergers and acquisitions (M&A), where the context is essential: what the attitude is toward the M&A in the corporate environment, how well the strategies are communicated before, during, and after the change, the consequences of the process, etc. See e.g., Vassils M. Papadakis, "The Role of Broader Context and the Communication Program in Merger and Acquisition Implementation Success," *Management Decision* 43, issue 2 (2005): 236–255.

76 E.g., interviews with a professor of law, October 9, 2005, and an attorney, September 14, 2005. On unclear goals more generally, see Peter J. May, "Policy Design and Implementation," *Handbook of Public Administration* (London: Sage Publications, 2003), 224, 230, 231.

avoid the uncertain results that change would result in—shifting therefore from political to symbolic. At the same time, in a different political climate, the risk averse would want to see change and thus impact of the legislation and would secure sufficient support for a move toward the political box.

The apparent risk is that legislative efforts end up in the high-high box as symbolic implementation that might satisfy the immediate central political agenda but possess little or no impact on the ground, be it intended or unintended.[77] Matland cautions that a scenario where ambiguity and conflict both are high can cause, in particular, professional groupings to step in and fill the implementation process with their own concerns and their own reform agendas.[78] This form of "mission-creep" may be risky, but as I will return to later in relation to China, it may also in some instances be conducive to a more progressive development.

The ambiguity-conflict model overlaps or covers many other theoretical approaches. To reduce the level of conflict in particular, to move upward from political to administrative especially, incentives and disincentives to comply with a new policy or to turn away from an old practice are central. Reducing the level of ambiguity, sliding leftward from symbolic to political, requires clear goals and a designated implementer with sufficient resources, something that the Chinese courts have not yet been granted. These components are the focus of the theoretical approach discussed next.

---

77 On symbolic and "pastiche" legislation, intended only to please certain demands, see also Margit Cohn, "Fuzzy Legality in Regulation: The Legislative Mandate Revisited," *Law & Policy* 23, issue 4 (2001): 480, 482, and Vilhelm Aubert, *In Search of Law. Sociological Approaches to Law* (Totowa: Barnes & Noble Books, 1983), 162.

78 For argumentation for a relatively balanced approach between "certainty and flexibility," see Benjamin van Rooij, *Law as Event. Lessons about Lawmaking, Compliance and Enforcement, Drawn from the Regulation of Land and Pollution in South-West China* (Leiden: Leiden University Press, 2006), e.g., 54 et seq.

One of the earliest comprehensive studies on implementation is that of Eugene Bardach.[79] With his "implementation game" he discusses, in particular, incentives and disincentives of the many actors in an implementation process and stresses the importance of an appropriate form of inducement for success. The core of Bardach's concept on effective implementation is, however, closely associated with incentives: a clear legislative mandate, allocated budgetary resources, and a designated responsible agency.[80] A clear legislative mandate is formulated as a goal. Given the "strategic interaction among numerous special interests all pursuing their own goals," goals introduced must be very distinct and unambiguous.[81] With the risk of these "special interest goals" that are not necessarily compatible with the overall goal, an agreement on the goal among all major stakeholders is required as well as participation in the early phases of change.[82] The "game" itself Bardach characterizes importantly as being that of "*maneuvering* of a large number of semi-autonomous actors, each of which tries to *gain access* to program elements *not under its own control* while at the same time trying to *extract better terms* from other actors seeking access *to elements that it does control*."[83]

Bardach's "implementation game" includes a variety of different scenarios labeled accordingly. We will limit the discussion here to

---

79 Eugene Bardach, *The Implementation Game: What Happens after a Bill Becomes a Law* (Cambridge, MA: The MIT Press, 1977).

80 See e.g., Eugene Bardach, "Implementation: Political," in *International Encyclopedia of the Social & Behavioral Science*, eds. Neil J. Smelser and Paul B. Baltes (Amsterdam: Elsevier, 2001), 7234–7237.

81 Bardach, *The Implementation Game*, 35, 43.

82 Bardach, *The Implementation Game*, 41 et seq. Bardach, moreover, emphasizes the risk with multiple actors: the more actors involved, the greater the danger of diffusing the goal with the various actors rather acting towards the "organizational interests." He refers to "leaking authority" when orders are sent down the hierarchy without clear purposes.

83 Bardach, *The Implementation Game*, 51 et seq. Bardach also cautions that experience suggests that a protracted implementation process may be harmful to implementation.

the three situations pertinent for the Chinese context, which explain the behavior of actors as well as the outcome of implementation. The first scenario is "social entropy," a tendency toward status quo in an implementation process. For reasons of incompetence owing to, for example, turnover of personnel, variability of the object of implementation, with possibly constantly shifting foci, or poor coordination (for instance, too costly or even impossible to undertake), change is not achieved.[84]

Second, strategies may include tokenism, where actors pretend to be contributing to the common goal but in fact are doing so to a very limited extent. In this way they claim to participate but in actuality only stall the process or play wait-and-see, staying sufficiently in the "game" should it prove successful. Third and related to the second scenario is massive resistance, where actors are withholding critical elements needed for successful implementation. Consequently, the uncertainty of success hinging on other actors may lead to crucial actors withdrawing to avoid the risk of being associated with an unsuccessful project.[85]

The three scenarios, social entropy, tokenism, and massive resistance with their strategies and potential results, represent three fundamental obstacles to law implementation. A structure that does not enable or encourage reform, a system that does not sufficiently encourage actors to participate in implementation, or where even actors avoid participating, accordingly faces tremendous problems for successful law implementation. These three scenarios, individually or combined, are then addressed, according to Bardach, first with clear goals of what is to be accomplished and with an agent responsible and sufficiently mandated to implement change. Second, this must be coupled with sufficiently strong incentives and disincentives to get unwilling actors to cooperate.[86]

---

84 Bardach, *The Implementation Game*, 98 et seq.

85 Bardach, *The Implementation Game*, 133 et seq.; see also e.g., Cohn, "Fuzzy Legality in Regulation ," 474

86 For similar conclusions on incentives, see e.g., Gerald N. Rosenberg, "The

Such risks and proposed solutions relate clearly to the ambiguity-conflict distinction. Unclear goals and a lack of a clear agent of change with sufficient resources risks (or enables) symbolic lawmaking or implementation. Efforts to overcome this risk of ambiguity by way of, for example, clearer goals would shift a project either leftward to political forms or upward to experimental forms of implementation depending on the level of conflict of the issue. Conflict, in turn, would be addressed by incentives and disincentives sufficiently strong to reduce conflict. All these measures would then ideally shift more "symbolic" projects diagonally upward toward an easier "administrative" implementation with lesser levels of ambiguity and conflict.

Matland's ambiguity-conflict matrix and Bardach's emphasis on incentives and clear goals confirm the central concerns for successful law implementation of careful reflection on the level of clarity and the importance of reducing conflict by creating incentives, incentives that are created through the form of law in its drafting as well as its more general adoption mechanisms: both supporting the legitimacy of law and through this strengthening its implementation potential.[87]

Implementation of Constitutional Rights: Insights from Law and Economics," *University of Chicago Law Review* 64 (1997): 1215, 1216 (in relation to constitutional rights in the U.S.). Generally on incentives in lawmaking, see Håkan Hydén, *Normvetenskap* (Lund: Studentlitteratur, 2003), 105 et seq., with references to Niklas Luhmann's work. Note also e.g., Tom Tyler's research suggesting that normative impetus for compliance with law is greater than deterrence. Deterrence, according to Tyler's study, is less important, a costly procedure, and not solely sufficient for law obedience; what matters the most is the normative obligation to follow law. Tom Tyler, *Why People Obey the Law* (New Haven: Yale University Press, 1990), 64, 161. The normative concern of the people is essential to tap for successful law implementation. This in turn requires education and even socialization, which is a very slow process. Similarly e.g., social pressures at times are stronger than sanctions. See Hydén, Normvetenskap, 305.

87 Other supportive theories include: Dan M. Kahan's "the logic of reciprocity," where he argues that actors respond very well to trust. Promoting reciprocal trust and awareness of this is therefore important. Popular participation or coop-

Concluding Discussion

Above I have specifically elaborated on a number of restraints of the court's independence and stature, affecting its potential impact on law implementation. I described from two perspectives restraining factors in China that impede law implementation by the courts and more generally that reduce the legitimacy of the legal system by a less credible judiciary at its core: interaction within and between courts and the interaction between courts and other actors. I also discussed shortcomings in the reform process within and related to the judiciary.

I have described the development and the planned and potential impact of the reform process within the judiciary. There are reasons to be impressed by the development that has taken place and that is taking place given the remarkable "return of the law" in the relatively short time of the last quarter of a century. Still, for the (legal) development to take place, the effectuation of law is a multifaceted and multilayered problem.

In order to determine the relative success of the reforms and law implementation in relation to the judiciary, I will proceed on the basis of the theoretical framework developed above. One lesson that comes out of the initial ambiguity-conflict matrix is the need to seek to reduce both dimensions of "high" so as to move away from "symbolic" reforms toward "administrative" reforms, that is, to enhance the clarity and consensus on what needs to be done. What Chinese judicial reforms so far have done, however, is perhaps a positive form of mission creep. As long as this creep is constructive and takes the development in a progressive direction, "symbolic" may also mean flexible and more easily accepted and adopted. For more general application as well as in the longer term also in relation to judicial reform, that flexibility may not be solely positive. An

---

eration in lawmaking and law implementation in a decentralized way is promoted by Kahan. See e.g., his "The Logic of Reciprocity: Trust, Collective Action, and Law," *Michigan Law Review* 102 (2003).

unclear mandate even with positive results is likely to undermine the credibility of the process as well as the judiciary. A clear vision, how to reach that vision, and what the ultimate goal should be would improve implementation of reform as well as improve the implementation capacity of and through the judiciary.[88]

Related to ambiguity are also incentives. Unclear or inconsistent law or reforms are typically not conducive to well-motivated participation.[89] In China the general incentives for legal modernization and for implementation of, for instance, judicial reform are said to be social stability, reduction of societal conflicts, and promotion of economic development.[90] Other reasons given include globalization, justice, and transformation toward rights protection.[91] One judge argued that the incentives for reform at the central level are not strong enough even though scholars and media are doing a good job of stimulating the process. For the judiciary, however, the incentives are awesome.[92] At the same time, local-level actors try to avoid new legislation or changes more broadly if they are not appropriate with regard to the local agenda.[93] One issue may be local-level participation in the decision-making, and there is also a lack of incentives to take part and to believe in the possibility of a posi-

---

88 See e.g., Xin, "What Kind of Judicial Power Does China Need?" 58.

89 See the chapter by Oscar Almén in this volume regarding a similar discussion, and that of Benjamin van Rooij concerning overly specific laws. On the risk of ambiguity in relation to China, see e.g., Roy Prosterman et al., "Implementation of 30-Year Land Use Rights for Farmers Under China's 1998 Land Management Law: An Analysis and Recommendations Based on a 17 Province Survey," *Pacific Rim Law & Policy Journal* 9 (2000): 557, 558. On selective implementation, see Flora Sapio, "Implementing Anticorruption in the PRC: Patterns of Selectivity," *Working Papers in Contemporary Asian Studies* no. 10 (2005), available at http://www.ace.lu.se.

90 E.g., in interview with vice-president of BPC, April 7, 2005.

91 Interview with prosecutor, April 11, 2005.

92 Interview with SPC judge, October 9, 2005.

93 Interview with attorney, September 14, 2005.

tive development.[94] Lower-levels courts have only the pressure from higher courts to adapt, while imposed reforms may even be counterproductive to the more "personal" goal of processing cases.[95] For the judges, the main incentive for reform is workload, while for the court there are the many societal problems that they are forced to resolve.[96]

Randall Peerenboom argues that one clear advantage with the party and its dominance is the coordinating powers they have, potentially enabling different agendas to merge.[97] These powers are close to what Margit Cohn describes as central for successful implementation: good access to applying and changing rules at the same time as preventing external scrutiny.[98]

With sufficient incentives for the party to lead the reform process, seemingly much headway could be made. In fact, the party is rather taking the backseat, as the discussion above on the Central Reform Group indicates. Again, this could be due to numerous reasons, but likely causes are related to absence of agreement on the pace and reach of reforms, lack of a clear model, and ultimately un-

---

94 Interviews with e.g., a former senior judge, turned professor of law, April 11, 2005; a professor of law who served as a senior judge in one of the western provinces, April 1, 2005; a vice-president of BPC, April 7, 2005, where the latter suggested that consultation now had improved. Local participation in planning was, however, not a problem according to another, an attorney, September 14, 2005.

95 Two separate interviews with judges from two different courts in Shanghai, BPC and HPC, September 15, 2005, concurring but stating that in the more affluent parts of the country, courts are more likely to see incentives even though confused as to what the right direction may be.

96 Interview with a former senior judge, turned professor of law, April 11, 2005.

97 See e.g., Peerenboom, "Judicial Independence in China," 13.

98 Cohn, "Fuzzy Legality in Regulation," 481. This, Cohn concludes, is why regulators and regulated alike prefer "fuzzy," somewhat unclear legislation. Such an ambition is, however, very similar to the "symbolic" implementation discussed earlier.

certainty with regard to the political implications of far-reaching judicial reforms. In the meantime, Chinese implementation actors are playing the games Burdach warned about: social entropy with stagnation due to unclear resources and goals, and tokenism and massive resistance with lack of true commitment until the reforms are proven successful or are officially fully supported or even countering the activities until such a stage is reached. Burdach's crucial elements for successful implementation, clear mandate with budgetary resources and a responsible agency, are also not sufficiently guaranteed. The judiciary has an unclear mandate with very limited budgetary resources explicitly for the reform and is not given powers to be the lead agency other than, at most, within its own structure.[99]

Finally, an additional component is the form of law, something related to the conflict side of the matrix.[100] The form of law for successful law implementation is better understood through, e.g., Robert Summers' requirements for the proper "form of law."[101] Form relates to the coherence and consistency of law: clarity, generality, completeness, conformity with societal norms, and rational definiteness, yet with an appropriate level of flexibility. The form's purposive nature in Summers's more abstract elaboration confirms the earlier discussed need for a reduced level of ambiguity while still recognizing the need to balance this with a certain degree of flexibility. The unambiguous goals of the law in question must also,

---

99 Xin Chunying has proposed a coordinating National Judicial Reform Committee under the Standing Committee of the NPC. Xin, "What Kind of Judicial Power Does China Need?" 72, 73.

100 For an interesting parallel analysis of implementation in the European Communities, see Silvere Lefevre, "Interpretative Communications and the Implementation of Community Law at National Level," *European Law Review* 29, issue 6 (2004).

101 Robert S. Summers has dealt with form of law extensively. See e.g., *Form and Function in a Legal System: A General Study* (Cambridge: Cambridge University Press, 2006); see e.g., also "How Law Is Formal and Why It Matters," *Cornell Law Review* 82 (1997).

argues Summers, be formulated in a coherent and consistent way, drawing on rational and existing norms. This craft or legislative technique is then in Summers's "form" matched with institutional aspects of form: legitimacy of the process of lawmaking, and law implementation.[102]

Improved implementation is based on increased agreement or understanding of reform goals as well as of the role of the judiciary. State institutions seem to lack a sufficient level of authority for effective management of many, societal aspects, even highly challenging ones, including, and even particularly, implementation of law. The "form of law" is faulting, the process and the outcome of the lawmaking, and in this case especially the formulation and implementation of judicial reform. Finally, considering the need for legitimacy and incentives, a balance must be struck between overly rapid changes, reform fatigue with too many and reoccurring reform schemes, and the need for momentum and change.[103]

This elaboration on lessons from implementation models ends up on arguments of legitimacy and incentives for implementation. Here, the judiciary may differ only marginally from general implementation challenges. For the judiciary, however, within the administration of justice, the courts have a special role by their very nature. In China this is compromised by the influence of Soviet le-

---

102 Summers, Form and Function, e.g., 97 et seq., 141 et seq.; for some of these elements, see Cohn, "Fuzzy Legality in Regulation," 486. Tyler's *Why People Obey the Law* also shows how the context in the sense of legitimacy of the leaders and the fairness of the procedures were deemed essential (162–165). The more profound insight here relates to the morality of law, e.g., the natural law tradition stating that immoral laws are not binding, while legal positivists claim that immoral law can be valid if it is enforceable and accepted. See Aleksander Peczenik, "Taking Laws Seriously," *Cornell Law Review* 68 (1983): 660, and more generally on legitimacy and law obedience Robert L. Holmes, "State-Legitimacy and the Obligation to Obey the Law," *Virginia Law Review* 67 (1981): 133, and Hydén, Normvetenskap, 303 *et seq.*

103 On the lack of legitimacy, see e.g., Xin, "What Kind of Judicial Power Does China Need?" 62.

gal concepts as well as of course the present political system. The incentives for improvement are arguably stronger for the judiciary than for instance the procuratorate, given its central role. The judiciary is by now also composed of comparatively well-educated judges, which is another reason for the relatively progressive developments. The central position of the judiciary with implications on all legal matters but also with implications on political issues makes reform even more sensitive. For these reasons, the problems in law implementation that the judiciary is facing may be more particular.

It is easy to give armchair advice. Law implementation in itself is complicated with numerous factors to consider. The Chinese political and legal system is hugely complex just because of its sheer size, and the specific problems inherent in a one-party state must be added to this. The plurality of actors in a legal system centrally occupied by the Chinese courts makes coordination and cooperation in reform processes highly difficult. Moreover, the multilayered hierarchical system of courts and corresponding institutions at each level further complicates the picture, not least in reform processes with multiple conflicting agendas and loyalties.

Nevertheless, law in China is seen as the cure to much ill: by solely adopting more legislation with more details while the problem may rather lie in the field of implementation. The resulting overlaps, contradictions, ambiguities, and an often impenetrable system of various levels and sources of law do not help the implementation deficit. Rather, realization of universal shortcomings of law as well as those particular to China is needed, as is the construction of a more coherent, transparent, and credible system of law. Ensuring the existence of institutions clearly designated, well funded, and with sufficient power and mandate to ensure the implementation of law seems to be a fundamental and essential step. These coupled with a more coherent and rational system of law will make more headway than adopting more—often symbolic—pieces of legal and political instruments without clout. A system failing to consider this risks not only falling short of its aims, but, even more importantly, risks undermining the very credibility of the whole legal system.

Yet, the cautious emperor does not provide a clear mandate, or sufficient incentives, until the outcome is beyond doubt. Judicial independence is a central part of the Chinese reform agenda. Many efforts are made to ensure increased judicial independence, and by and large the courts are acting independently. In extreme cases—where the "stability," the status quo of the present state of affairs, is challenged or perceived as such—the state and the party retain the ultimate control over the judiciary.[104] The independence is then reduced to a mere slogan; reform is stalled; and the credibility of the legal system, and with it the success of law implementation, is radically reduced.

Bibliography

Aubert, Vilhelm. *In Search of Law: Sociological Approaches to Law*. Totowa: Barnes & Noble Books, 1983.

Balme, Stéphanie. "The Judicialisation of Politics and the Politicisation of the Judiciary in China (1978–2005)," *Global Jurist Frontiers* 5, issue 1 (2005).

Bardach, Eugene. "Implementation: Political." In *International Encyclopedia of the Social & Behavioral Science*, edited by Neil J. Smelser and Paul B. Baltes. Amsterdam: Elsevier, 2001.

Bardach, Eugene. *The Implementation Game: What Happens after a Bill Becomes a Law*. Cambridge, MA: The MIT Press, 1977.

Brinkerhoff, Derick W. "Coordination Issues in Policy Implementation Networks: An Illustration from Madagascar's Environmental Action Plan," *World Development* 24, issue 9 (1996): 1497–1510.

Brown, Ronald C. *Understanding Chinese Courts and Legal Process: Law with Chinese Characteristics*. The Hague: Kluwer Law International, 1997.

Cabestan, Jean-Pierre, "The Political and Practical Obstacles to the Reform of the Judiciary and the Establishment of a Rule of Law in China," *Journal of Chinese Political Science* 10, no. 1 (2005): 43–64.

---

104 See e.g., Liebman, "China's Courts," 626, 630.

Chen, Jianfu et al., eds. *Implementation of Law in the People's Republic of China*. The Hague: Kluwer Law International, 2002.

Clarke, Donald C. "Puzzling Observations in Chinese Law: When Is a Riddle Just a Mistake?" In *Understanding China's Legal System*, edited by C. Stephen Hsu. New York: New York University Press, 2003.

Cohn, Margit. "Fuzzy Legality in Regulation: The Legislative Mandate Revisited," *Law & Policy* 23, issue 4 (2001): 469–487.

Finder, Susan. "Court System," in *Doing Business in China*, edited by Bruckhaus Deringer Freshfields, New York: Juris Publishing, 2002.

Finder, Susan. "The Supreme People's Court of the People's Republic of China," *Journal of Chinese Law* 7, issue 2 (1993): 145–224.

Fu, Hualing, "Procuracy." In *Doing Business in China*, vol. 1, edited by Freshfields et al. Huntington: Juris Publishing, 2003.

Fu, Hualing. "Putting China's Judiciary into Perspective: Is It Independent, Competent, and Fair?" In *Beyond Common Knowledge: Empirical Approaches to the Rule of Law*, edited by Erik G. Jensen and Thomas C. Heller. Stanford: Stanford University Press, 2003.

Grimheden, Jonas. "The Reform Path of the Chinese Judiciary: Progress or Stand-Still?" *Fordham International Law Journal* 30, no. 4 (2007): 1000–1013.

Guo, Chunming and Zhigang Liu. "Sifa gongzheng: sifa zhidu gaige de mubiao." *Zhongguo faxue* 4 (2000).

Holmes, Robert L. "State-Legitimacy and the Obligation to Obey the Law," *Virginia Law Review* 67, no. 1 (1981): 133–141.

Hydén, Håkan. *Normvetenskap*. Lund: Studentlitteratur, 2003.

Jacob, Herbert. "Courts as Organizations." In *Empirical Theories About Courts*, edited by Keith O. Boyum and Lynn Mathers. New York: Longman, 1983.

Jacob, Herbert et al., *Courts, Law, and Politics in Comparative Perspective*. New Haven: Yale University Press, 1996.

Kahan, Dan M. "The Logic of Reciprocity: Trust, Collective Action, and Law," *Michigan Law Review* 102 (2003).

Lefevre, Silvere. "Interpretative Communications and the Implementation of Community Law at National Level," *European Law Review* 29, issue 6 (2004).

Li, Yuwen. "Court Reform in China: Problems, Progress and Prospects." In *Implementation of Law in the People's Republic of China*, edited by Jianfu Chen et al. The Hague: Kluwer Law International, 2002.

Liebman, Benjamin. "China's Courts: Restricted Reform," *The China Quarterly* 191 (2007): 620–638.
Liebman, Benjamin. and Tim Wu. "China's Network Justice," *Chicago Journal of International Law* 8 (2007): 7–143.
Liu, Sida. "Beyond Global Convergence: Conflicts of Legitimacy in a Chinese Lower Court," *Law & Social Inquiry* 31, issue 1 (2006): 75–106.
Lubman, Stanley and Leïla Choukroune. "L'incomplète réforme par le loi," *Esprit* (February 2004).
Matland, Richard E. "Synthesizing the Implementation Literature: The Ambiguity-Conflict Model of Policy Implementation," *Journal of Public Administration Research & Theory* 5, no. 2 (April 1995): 145–174.
May, Peter J. "Policy Design and Implementation," In *Handbook of Public Administration*, edited by B. Guy Peters and Jon Pierre. London: Sage Publications, 2003.
Papadakis, Vassils M. "The Role of Broader Context and the Communication Program in Merger and Acquisition Implementation Success," *Management Decision* 43, issue 2 (2005): 236–255.
Peczenik, Aleksander. "Taking Laws Seriously," *Cornell Law Review* 68 (1983): 660–684.
Peerenboom, Randall. "Judicial Independence and Judicial Accountability: An Empirical Study of Individual Case Supervision," *The China Journal* 55 (January 2006): 67–92.
Peerenboom, Randall. "Judicial Independence in China: Common Myths and Unfounded Assumptions," *La Trobe Law School Legal Studies Research Paper No. 2008/11*.
Peerenboom, Randall. "The X-Files: Past and Present Portrayals of China's Alien 'Legal System,'" *Washington University Global Studies Law Review* 2 (2003).
Prosterman, Roy et al. "Implementation of 30-Year Land Use Rights for Farmers Under China's 1998 Land Management Law: An Analysis and Recommendations Based on a 17 Province Survey," *Pacific Rim Law & Policy Journal* 9 (2000).
van Rooij, Benjamin. *Law as Event: Lessons about Lawmaking, Compliance and Enforcement, Drawn from the Regulation of Land and Pollution in South-West China*. Leiden: Leiden University Press, 2006.
Rosenberg, Gerald N. "The Implementation of Constitutional Rights: Insights from Law and Economics," *University of Chicago Law Review* 64, no. 2 (1997): 1215–1224.

Sapio, Flora. "Implementing Anticorruption in the PRC: Patterns of Selectivity," *Working Papers in Contemporary Asian Studies* 10 (2005), available at http://www.ace.lu.se.

Summers, Robert S. *Form and Function in a Legal System: A General Study.* Cambridge: Cambridge University Press, 2006.

Summers, Robert S. "How Law Is Formal and Why It Matters," *Cornell Law Review* 82 (1997): 1165–1229.

Tan, Shigui. *Zhongguo sifa gaige yanjiu.* Beijing: Falü chubanshe, 2000.

Trevaskes, Sue. *Courts and Criminal Justice in Contemporary China.* Lanham: Lexington Press, 2007.

Trevaskes, Sue. "Courts on the Campaign Path: Criminal Court Work in China's 'Yanda 2001' Anti-Crime Campaign," *Asian Survey* 42, issue 5 (2002): 673–693.

Tyler, Tom. *Why People Obey the Law.* New Haven: Yale University Press, 1990.

Winter, Søren C. "Implementation—Introduction," In *Handbook of Public Administration*, edited by B. Guy Peters and Jon Pierre. London: Sage Publications, 2003.

Woo, Margaret Y. K. and Yaxin Wang. "Civil Justice in China: An Empirical Study of Courts in Three Provinces," *American Journal of Comparative Law* 53 (2005).

Xiao, Yang. "Fayuan, faguan yu sifa gaige." *Faxuejia*, 1 (2003).

Xin, Chunying. *Chinese Courts: History and Transition.* Beijing: Konrad-Adenauer-Stiftung, 2005.

Xin, Chunying. "What Kind of Judicial Power Does China Need?" *International Journal of Constitutional Law Online* 1, no. 1 (2003): 58-78.

Xin, He. "Ideology or Reality? Limited Judicial Independence in Contemporary Rural China," *The Australian Journal of Asian Law* 6, no. 3 (2005): 213–230.

Xu, Anbiao. "A Supervisory Law Intended to Guarantee Exercise of Supervisory Power by Standing Committees of People's Congresses," *China Law* (October 2006).

Zou, Keyuan, "Judicial Reform in China: Recent Developments and Future Prospects," *International Lawyer* 36 (2002): 1039–1062.

5

People's Congresses Involvement in Law Implementation

The Case of Environmental Protection Laws

OSCAR ALMÉN

Introduction

In January 2000, a group of twenty-five legislators from the city of Foshan submitted an interpellation at the Guangdong provincial People's Congress (PC) of the provincial Environmental Protection Bureau (EPB). The people's deputies demanded an explanation as to why an electroplating plant that was polluting the nearby river could continue operation although no Environmental Impact Assessment (EIA) had been made. The EPB leaders could not give a satisfactory answer and were harshly criticized in a televised meeting. In the aftermath several polluting companies had to stop production.

In 2003, a chemical factory in Shanghai refused to pay the fine of CNY 100,000 that the municipal EPB had fined the company for polluting the water. Instead the factory sued the EPB in court but lost the case. The Shanghai PC had been active in the case as many residents in the area had petitioned it to pressure the EPB to do something about the pollution.

This chapter studies in what way China's legislatures can influence the implementation of laws.[1] Special focus will be on the implementation of environmental protection laws. Environmental

---

[1] People's Congresses (PC) are established at all state structure levels from national to township level. In this study, PC refers to all levels.

protection is an issue where PCs can be active in supervision without posing a threat to the party-state because the target is more often an enterprise rather than the government. The main focus in this chapter is on the PCs as institutions rather than on the environmental protection laws. Studies on the environmental protection laws in China are plentiful.[2] However, none of them place the PCs as important actors. As a consequence little has been written about the role of PCs in this.[3] The present chapter will add to the body of research on law implementation and environmental protection in China by including the PCs in the analysis.

---

2 Some examples include Barbara J. Sinkule and Leonard Ortolano, *Implementing Environmental Policy in China* (Westport: Praeger Publishers, 1995); Hon. S. Chan, Koon-kwai Wong, K. C. Cheung, and Jack Man-keung Lo, "The Implementation Gap in Environmental Management in China: The Case of Guangzhou, Zhengzhou and Nanjing," *Public Administration Review* 55, no. 4 (July/August 1995): 333–340; Shui-Yan Tang et al. (eds.), "Institutional Constraints on Environmental Management in Urban China: Environmental Impact Assessment in Guangzhou and Shanghai," *The China Quarterly*, no. 152, (December 1997): 863–874; Abigail R. Jahiel, "The Contradictory Impact of Environmental Protection in China," *The China Quarterly*, no. 149 (March 1997): 81–103; Abigail R. Jahiel, "The Organization of Environmental Protection in China," *The China Quarterly*, no. 156 (December 1998): 757–787; Lester Ross, "China Environmental Protection, Domestic Policy Trends, Pattern of Participation in Regimes and Compliance with International Norms," *The China Quarterly*, no. 156 (December 1998): 809–835; Michael Palmer, "Environmental Regulation in the People's Republic of China," *The China Quarterly*, no. 156, (December 1998): 788–808; William P. Alford and Benjamin L. Liebman, "Clean Air, Clear Processes? The Struggle over Air Pollution Law in the People's Republic of China," *Hastings Law Journal* 52 (2000–2001): 703–748; Benjamin Schwarz, "Environmental NGOs in China: Their Roles and Limits," *Pacific Affairs* 77, no. 1 (Spring 2004); Benjamin van Rooij, *Regulating Land and Pollution in China, Lawmaking, Compliance and Enforcement; Theory and Cases* (Leiden: Leiden University Press, 2006).

3 Cai Dingjian, "Functions of the People's Congresses in the Process of Implementation of Law," in *Implementation of Law in the People's Republic of China*, eds. Jianfu Chen et al. (Kluwer Law International, 2002), 35–53, is an exception to this, but he writes mainly on the National People's Congress (NPC) and less on subnational people's congresses.

Legislatures and Law Implementation

As a result of the increasing complexity of politics in modern societies, during the twentieth century many legislatures delegated more and more of their policymaking powers to the executive branch. The decisions to be made became too numerous and detailed and required more expert knowledge than legislators possessed. The legislatures had to concentrate on the general policy directions. In addition, the often-quoted principle "modern politics is party politics" meant that most policy-related decisions were made in the party organizations and not in the legislatures. These trends made it seem that legislatures were turning into nothing more than formal bodies without any real political power. However, legislatures all over the world have to a varying degree retained some of their political powers.

First, current research on legislatures often claims that the most important role of legislatures is not their lawmaking function but their power to supervise the executive. While it is commonly acknowledged that legislatures' power over policymaking has waned, they have instead stepped up their influence in other aspects of politics. It is particularly in the area of oversight and as "forums of scrutiny of the executive" that legislatures are today growing in importance.[4] Thus, although legislatures are not implementing organs, much of their focus has moved from the lawmaking stage to the law-implementation stage.

Second, political parties are not unitary actors but consist of individuals and groupings.[5] Depending on the degree of party disci-

---
[4] Nicholas D. J. Baldwin, "Concluding Observations: Legislative Weakness, Scrutinising Strength?" *The Journal of Legislative Studies* 10, nos. 2/3 (Summer/Autumn 2004): 302. See also Marcus E. Ethridge, *Legislative Participation in Implementation: Policy Through Politics* (New York: Preager Publishers, 1985 and Jessica Korn, "The Legislative Veto and the Limits of Public Choice Analysis," *Political Science Quarterly* 109, no. 5 (Winter 1994–1995): 873–894.

[5] Michael Laver, "Divided Parties, Divided Government," *Legislative Studies Quarterly* 24 (February 1999): 5–29.

pline, the legislature can become an important political player in the intraparty political game. The general rule is that a high degree of party discipline, commonly associated with Western European systems, gives less maneuvering space for the legislature to influence politics than in systems with less party discipline such as in the U.S. Congress. One could expect the Chinese Communist Party to be even more disciplined than Western European parties. However, PCs consist of a body of unorganized prominent members of society of which usually around 70 percent are Communist Party members. The large number of party members does not guarantee complete loyalty to the local party committee, however. Party membership in China is in many cases just a confirmation of an individual's importance in society. Successful entrepreneurs and local celebrities are often co-opted to join the party as a way of maintaining the elite in society within the party.[6] Although this might be a good way to increase party control over society's elite, it makes the party more pluralistic and less ideological and disciplined. Hence, PCs sometimes rebel against the party committee. Lack of party discipline is a source of power for legislatures. This is true in China as elsewhere.

Third, many legislatures have responded to increasing executive dominance by establishing specialized committees and subcommittees that have increased the expertise and institutional powers of the legislature.[7] This has been noted also in semiauthoritarian systems.[8] One important and indeed decisive character of Chinese PCs, as was the case for most East European communist systems, is their division between the plenary session and the standing committee (SC). Plenary sessions are only held once a year for a few

---

6 Bruce Dickson, *Red Capitalists in China, The Party, Private Entrepreneurs, and Prospects for Political Change* (New York: Cambridge University Press, 2003).

7 Kenneth Shepsle, "Representation and Governance: The Great Legislative Trade-off," *Political Science Quarterly* 103, no. 3 (1988): 461–484.

8 David M. Olson and William E. Crowther, *Committees in Post-Communist Democratic Parliaments* (Columbus: Ohio State University Press, 2002).

days. The work of the PC, including most supervision and lawmaking, is instead handled by the SC and its working committees. In fact, as its wording indicates, the People's Congress Standing Committee (PCSC) Supervision Law, only applies to the PCSC and not the plenary session.[9] This is a major difference compared to liberal democratic legislatures, where the decisions are always formally made by the whole legislature. The SC members are formally elected by the plenary session but are in practice mainly appointed by the local party committee, and hence owe their position to the party. The members can be described as semiofficials. The SC reports to the party committee. Moreover, at the local level, the chair of the SC is often also the local party secretary. Hence, SCs are more controlled by the party committee than is the plenary session.

Lawmaking

The content of law is important for its implementation. The more detailed a law, the less discretion local bureaucrats have in implementing it.[10] It therefore makes sense to also look into lawmaking when studying influence over law implementation. While many legislatures have seen their lawmaking powers diminish, the Chinese legislatures have on the contrary become increasingly influential in the legislative process.[11] This is perhaps not strange consider-

---

9 The law was passed on August 27, 2006, by the NPCSC and went into effect on January 1, 2007.
10 Korn, "The Legislative Veto."
11 Murray S. Tanner, *The Politics of Lawmaking in China; Institutions, Processes, and Democratic Prospects* (Oxford: Clarendon Press, 1999); Ming Xia, *The Dual Developmental State; Development Strategy and Institutional Arrangements for China's Transition* (Aldershot: Ashgate, 2000); Young Nam Cho, "The Politics of Law-making in Chinese Local People's Congresses," *The China Quarterly*, no. 187 (September 2006): 592–609; Young Nam Cho, *Local People's Congresses in China; Development and Transition* (New York: Cambridge University Press, 2009), Chap. 2.

ing the rubber stamp role the PCs had previously. It is in particular the working committees of Chinese legislatures that have become important. For example, in the case of environmental laws, the National People's Congress (NPC) Environment and Natural Resources Protection Committee (ENRPC) and the NPC Law Committee are usually mentioned as the most important institutional actors in the lawmaking process.[12] Overly general laws are often considered a major impediment for successful implementation of law in China. However, as noticed by van Rooij, the 2000 amendment of the Air Pollution Prevention Control Law was stricter and much more detailed than previous ones. The stricter law did not lead to more compliance, as the lawmakers had intended, but often resulted in local resistance, as it was not flexible enough. It is shown by van Rooij that too strict and detailed laws can become a problem for environmental law implementation.[13]

Law Implementation Supervision from Above

The PCSC works closely with and continuously reports to the party committee. Therefore, most supervision of the PC is done with party support and serves the purpose of improving the party's ruling. This is what I will refer to as law implementation supervision from above.

Since the 1990s PCSCs at all levels have steadily increased their capacity to supervise the government and judiciary. Whereas previously people's congresses had to make do with the odd inspection or review of the yearly reports, during the 1990s other more specific and effective methods of supervision were developed. Like so many

---

12 See Palmer, "Environmental Regulation," 793; Alford and Liebman, "Clean Air, Clear Processes?" 713; Schwarz, "Environmental NGOs." It seems, however, that PCSC working committees responsible for environmental issues at the local level have yet to reach a similar power over local legislation.

13 Van Rooij, *Regulating Land*, 87–88.

other reforms in China, these changes started out as local experiments and, as they turned out to be functional, spread to other parts of the country. The People's Congress Standing Committee Supervision Law includes a standardized practice for law implementation examination (*zhifa jiancha*). Other methods such as work appraisal (*gongzuo pingyi*) are specified in provincial people's congresses implementation rules.[14] Most supervisory methods are organized by the SC although ordinary people's deputies frequently get invited to participate in the activities. Only the SC has the resources, knowledge, and organizational capability to conduct this kind of supervision.

Law implementation examination (zhifa jiancha). The examination focuses on specific laws and, in a more systematic way than inspection (*shicha*), investigates their implementation situation. Every year, the PCSC leadership at all levels in consultation with the party committee selects a certain number of laws to be examined. Sub-provincial level people's congresses usually examine the same laws as the ones selected by the provincial level, and often the examinations involve people's deputies at different levels.[15] The process is intended to involve the detailed study of the laws and inspections at the local level at for example enterprises or government agencies. The examination ends in a report presented to the government. The report points out the problems of implementing the particular law and suggests improvements. The government is required

---

14 For more on PC supervision, see for example An Chen, *Restructuring Political Power in China* (Boulder: Lynne Rienner Publishers, 1999); Young Nam Cho, "From 'Rubber Stamps' to 'Iron Stamps': The Emergence of Chinese Local People's Congresses as Supervisory Powerhouses," *The China Quarterly*, no. 171 (September 2002): 724–740; Oscar Almén, *Authoritarianism Constrained: The Role of Local People's Congresses in China*, (Ph.D. dissertation, Gothenburg University, 2005); Xia, Ming *The People's Congresses and Governance in China: Toward a network mode of governance*, (Routledge: 2008)

15 Interview with county PCSC chairman, November 2001. Also see Cho, "From 'Rubber Stamps' to 'Iron Stamps,'" 735.

to, within a certain period of time, respond with a report containing a description of how the problems will be handled.[16]

Cai has noted that the examination of the NPCSC and its working committees has been particularly successful when it comes to environmental protection laws. In 1995–1996, examinations were carried out in three selected provinces and in Beijing, Tianjian, and Shanghai. Cai claims among other things that these examinations became an important basis for the revisions of laws by the NPCSC, including the law on prevention and control of water pollution in 1996.[17]

The role of media has become important in making the inspections effective. Media can either participate directly in the inspection or it can be used to publicize the results of the inspections. Once reported to the public, pressure will increase on the government agency to handle the law implementation problems. In order to increase the effects of the inspections, they sometimes are combined with appraisals (described below) making the implementation of law an important criterion of work achievement of the cadre.[18] The effectiveness of the inspection is clearly related to whether or not it has been previously announced, giving the target of inspection time to prepare and handle problems in advance. In this respect, ordinary spontaneous inspections can be more effective than the law implementation examinations.[19]

The limitations of the examination can be found mainly in the weak legal environment and the political structure in China. The group conducting the inspections includes members of the government branches, and this makes the legislators even more apprehen-

---

16 Xu Shiqun et al. (eds.), *Difang renda jiandu gongzuo yanjiu* [Research on Local People's Congress Supervision Work] (Beijing: Zhongguo minzhu fazhi chubanshe, 2005), 221.

17 Cai, "Functions of People's Congresses," 45–48.

18 Cho, "From 'Rubber Stamps' to 'Iron Stamps,'" 736.

19 Interview with NPCSC staff and Shanghai PCSC staff, December 2005.

sive in giving criticism.[20] Many local governments have failed to implement the changes and improvements required in the inspection report, and the local PCs often do not have the political strength to force them to do this.[21] Despite the many shortcomings of the law implementation examination, it can point out problems and put extra pressure on the government to implement the laws.

Appraisals (pingyi). The appraisal method involves a thorough evaluation of all government departments' performance. Before the supervisory law was passed in 2006, one form of appraisal called work report appraisal (*shuzhi pingyi*) was particularly powerful as it was directed toward individual government cadres. The process often involved grading the cadres by use of secret ballot voting. Cadres that received the mark not competent or basically competent risked being demoted.[22]

The supervisory law did not explicitly forbid the use of work report appraisals. However, as the method was not mentioned in the law it was clear that the NPC did not support its use. Moreover, following the passing of the law, in the yearly PC training meetings, national and provincial PC staff advised lower-level PCs on the correct use of appraisal and explained the meaning of the supervision law.[23] The main problem was a conflict between the PCSC grading of the cadre's performance and the party's authority to administer the cadres (*dang guan ganbu*). Ultimately, the party committee's control over the individual cadre's career could not be challenged. As one commentator argues, if the result of the PCSC appraisal were

---

20 Cai, "Functions of People's Congresses," 48; Lin Baihai, *Renmin daibiao dahui jiandu zhidu de fenxi yu goujian* [An analysis and setup of the People's Congress supervisory system] (Beijing: Zhongguo shehui kexue chubanshe, 2004), 108.

21 Cho, "From 'Rubber Stamps' to 'Iron Stamps,'" 735.

22 Interview with county people's congress vice chair, Zhejiang, March 2001. By 2005 all but three provinces had specified rules for voting in the appraisal. See Bi Renfa, "Piaojue: pingyi zhi zhongchui" [Voting: Appraisal's heavy stick], *Zhejiang renda*, no. 9 (2005).

23 Interview with county people's congress vice chair, Zhejiang, June 2009.

not implemented it would negatively affect the authority of the PC.[24] Today most places, for example Zhejiang province, no longer use work report appraisal but the more general appraisal method called work appraisal (*gongzuo pingyi*).[25]

Another consequence of the supervision law was to limit the power of PCs to supervise the courts. Previously, a method called individual case supervision (*ge an jiandu*), although controversial and criticized, was nevertheless widely used by many local PCs in China. It empowered the PC to intervene in individual cases and demand that the court retry cases. This form of supervision was seen as political involvement and a threat to judicial independence. Sometimes PCs even went as far as directly deciding the verdict.[26] The passing of the supervision law made clear that this practice would no longer continue.[27]

In addition to these institutionalized supervisory methods, the PCSC is also equipped with more ad hoc methods of supervision that can be applied depending on the situation. One example of this in relation to environmental protection issues was the Tuojiang River pollution disaster in Sichuan. In 2004 two serious toxic spills in the Tuojiang River occurred within a period of a few months. The seriousness of the pollution and the fact that a second spill happened just a few months after the first one made this a case of national concern. After the first spill, the Sichuan government reported to the provincial PCSC. Some members of the PCSC thought there were some problems in the government's handling of the case.

---

24 Xie Puding, "Difang renda fazhi jianshe he zhidu chuanxin" [Rule of law development and system innovation of the local people's congress], in Yang Xuedong et al. (eds.), *Difang de fuxing, defang zhili gaige 30 nian* [Bring the local back in: Reform and changes of China local governance since 1978] (Beijing: Social Science Academy Press, 2009).

25 Interview with staff at Zhejiang PCSC April 2009.

26 Young Nam Cho, "Symbiotic Neighbour or Extra-Court Judge? The Supervision over Courts by Chinese Local People's Congresses," *The China Quarterly*, no. 176 (December 2003): 1068–1083.

27 Interview with Zhejiang provincial people's congress staff, April 2009.

Responsibility for the accidents was not clearly specified. In an unusual act of confrontation, the PCSC demanded the government rewrite its report and present it at the next PCSC meeting in June when the PCSC would make a joint review (*lianzu shenyi*) of the report. The second report was later passed by the PCSC.[28]

Law Implementation Supervision from Below

Sometimes the PC initiative to supervise the government and the judiciary comes from sources other than the SC, what I have termed supervision from below. I identify two forms of PC supervision from below. First, citizens could contact the PC by way of the letters-and-visits system (*xinfang zhidu*) or they could contact their local people's deputy directly. Second, people's deputies could initiate supervision themselves. In contrast to much of the SC supervision, which is largely routine overview, supervision from below is usually a reaction to existing problems.

First, we shall consider the use of the letters-and-visits system as a form for contacting the PC. Although the system is commonly described as uniquely Chinese, similar systems exist in democratic countries. In the United States, "casework" is considered an important part of constituency work for legislators.[29] In the casework system, citizens' contact with legislators provides information based upon which the legislators can sometimes supervise the executive organs, quite similar to the letters and visits system. Instead, what makes the letters-and-visits system in China special is that it exists in an authoritarian system. In a society where the authorities always

---

28 This case was widely reported in the media. Information on the PCSC involvement can be found at Sichuan People's Congress magazine *Minzhu yu fazhi jianshe* [Building democracy and a legal system], http://www.mzfzjs.net/disppage.php3?time=1170330546&id=1352 (accessed July 2, 2007).

29 John R. Johannes, "Casework as a Technique of U.S. Congressional Oversight of the Executive," *Legislative Studies Quarterly*, IV (1979): 347.

have put a lid on public criticism, this system has provided one of the few means of redress for people. At the same time, the letters-and-visits system provides a source of information on law implementation problems for the PC, as well as for other state organs.

Since the introduction of market reforms, and in particular during the last decade, the number of complaints has increased manyfold. In 2005 the government petition office received more than ten million petitions, but only a fraction were resolved.[30] The increase in petitions shows that the present political and judicial system is unable to handle and solve the new problems that appeared as a result of the reform policy.[31] Unfortunately, the letters-and-visits system is a poor substitute for a functioning legal system. Many complaints are ignored or get passed on in the system until the petitioner gives up. The system is not unified, but most important state bodies, including courts, public security bureaus, people's congresses, and party organizations, have their own letters-and-visits office at all levels. Many petitioners either find it hard to differentiate between these organs or find it best to use all available channels and therefore they send their letters to all organs.[32] It has become obvious that the present form of the letters-and-visits system cannot handle the increasing number of complaints.

After an intense debate on the need to reform the system, in January 2005 the State Council issued a revised version of the letters-and-visits regulation. The party has since stated that it in-

---

30 Ting Shi, "Petition system reform due after Party Plenum," *South China Morning Post*, October 6, 2006.

31 Kevin J. O'Brien and Li Lianjiang, "The Politics of Lodging Complaints in Rural China," *The China Quarterly*, no. 143 (September 1995): 756–783; Isabelle Thireau and Hua Linshan, "One Law, Two Interpretations: Mobilizing the Labor Law in Arbitration Committees and in Letters and Visits Offices," in *Engaging the Law in China: State Society and Possibilities for Justice*, eds. Neil Diamant, Stanley B. Lubman, and Kevin O'Brien (Stanford: Stanford University Press, 2005), 84–107.

32 Interview with former staff at district level judicial legal department and with Shanghai PCSC official, December 2005.

tends to further reform the system.³³ One suggestion for reform was to, in the long run, abolish all letters-and-visits offices and incorporate them into the PCs. This would increase the legal status and legal protection of the petitioners. People's congresses would use their legal authority to supervise the government and judiciary, and people's deputies would collect petitions in their district and turn them into formal motions or suggestions.³⁴ To some extent this is already practiced. In Shanghai, the letters-and-visits staff can and sometimes do write legislative suggestions based on citizen complaints.³⁵ One problem with this approach is that PCs do not have the political strength or institutional capability to handle all complaints. The PCs would have to be empowered first, but this would mean a restructuring of the political power relations of the whole political system.

The second form of law implementation supervision from below is when the initiative comes from the people's deputies themselves. People's deputies are legally equipped with many supervisory tools. They have the authority to, for example, make unannounced inspections at enterprises, a method commonly used to investigate pollution.³⁶ People's deputies also have the authority to submit motions or suggestions that are forwarded to the relevant government departments for implementation. The real political powers of the people's deputies are exercised during the annual plenary session when they elect government leaders and vote on bills and government reports. It is also during the plenary session that the people's deputies have the chance to organize in groups and use the more

---

33 Ting Shi, "Petition system reform due after Party Plenum."
34 Yu Jianrong, "Zhongguo xinfang zhidu pipan" [Critique of China's letters and visits system], *Zhongguo gaige*, no. 2 (2005), based on a speech at Beijing University in 2004; Yu Jianrong, "Dui xinfang zhidu gaige zhenglun de fansi" [Reflections on the debate on the letters and visits system reform], *Zhongguo dangzheng ganbu lunyun*, no. 5 (2005); Yu Jianrong, "Ba xinfang jigou jizhong dao ge ji renda" [Concentrate the letters and visit body to people's congresses at all levels], *Nanfang zhoumo*, May 21, 2009, p. 31.
35 Interview with Shanghai PCSC letters and visits official, December 2005.
36 Ibid.

powerful supervisory functions such as interpellations. During the year, people's deputies can also be invited to participate in the supervisory activities organized by the SC such as appraisals or law implementation examination.

Citizen-Initiated Supervision from Below: Shanghai Residents Complain to the People's Congress about Water Pollution

In 2003, residents in the district of Qingpu, Shanghai complained to the local authorities about a foul smell, a strange color, and dead fish in a nearby river. When district authorities did not react to the complaints, the residents turned to higher levels. Using the letters-and-visits system, they complained to the Shanghai EPB and to the Shanghai PC, claiming that chemical factories were the source of the pollution. The Shanghai EPB sent inspectors to Qingpu and found that three companies were responsible for the cause of the polluted water.[37]

Two of the companies were found guilty of intentional excessive pollution and were ordered by the Shanghai EPB, to pay a fine of CNY 100,000, the maximum fine that the EPB was authorized to access. The companies were also to ensure that the pollution ceased. One of the companies, Gaowei chemical plant, did not obey the administrative decision of the Shanghai EPB. Gaowei sued Shanghai EPB according to the Administrative Litigation Law, demanding the fine be revoked. This was the first time the Shanghai EPB faced administrative litigation, and the case was referred to in the media as "the first environmental protection administrative litigation lawsuit in Shanghai."[38]

---

[37] Shanghai Environmental Hotline, October 17, 2003, http://www.envir.gov.cn/info/2003/10/1017977.htm (accessed June 28, 2007).

[38] "60 wan fuchu huanlai 10 wan fajin, hu shou lie huanbao guangsi shenli

Gaowei claimed that the pipe, which was the source of the polluted water, did not belong to them. The drain that had been examined was from a public rainwater pipe. In 2001, when the property of the plant was extended, the pipe came within the walls of the factory. Since then, this pipe had not been maintained.[39] The case was first tried in the district court of Zhangning, which in April 2004 ruled in favor of the government. Gaowei then appealed to the first intermediate court of Shanghai, but the court confirmed the previous verdict.

Most media accounts of the case confirm the official picture presented by Shanghai EPB and the local courts. The company is described as the guilty party, and the main problem has been that the expenses for the EPB, which spent more than CNY 500,000 in investigating the pollution, turned out to be far higher than the CNY 100,000 the company was fined. Interviews with people with insights in the case also confirm this picture. According to some, the head of the Qingpu EPB had failed to act on the pollution problem, and this was described as local protectionism, with the company being protected by the EPB. The Qingpu EPB director was removed from office as a consequence of the case.[40] According to a local judge, the case was crystal clear. The company was the source of the pollution. The factory manager might have had some good points

---

zhongjie" [600,000 paid for a 100,000 fine, Shanghai's first environmental protection administrative litigation lawsuit has come to an end], *Jiefang ribao*, April 7, 2004, http://news.xinhuanet.com/newscenter2004-04/07/content_1405802htm (accessed July 3, 2007).

39 Yang Jun, "Shanghai huanbao di yi an beihou gongping de yinyou" [Some afterthought worries regarding the fairness of the first environmental protection case in Shanghai], *Nanfang zhoumo*, January 27, 2005, http://www.nanfangdaily.com.cn/southnews/zmzg/200501271035.asp.

40 *Shi Huangbaoju lingdao xinxiang qingkuang fankui* [Feedback on the situation of the Environmental Protection Bureau leader mailbox], internal report, 2006, on file with author; interview with Shanghai PCSC staff, December 2005; interview with environmental expert, Shanghai, December 2005.

in his reasoning, but nothing that changes the basic fact that the company was responsible.[41]

However, one report stands out in stark contrast to the rest. The outspoken *Nanfang zhoumo* in early 2005 instead took the side of the company owner, arguing that he was correct in his claim and that the local authorities, the district government, and its environmental protection bureau in particular wanted to get rid of the company. In the article, the company owner is portrayed as the victim of a local government plot. The district authorities branded the company a losing company and instructed banks and energy companies to restrict their services to the company. Before the inspection of the chemical factories Qingpu had already launched its policy "Green Qingpu," with which apparently many of the chemical plants in the district were not in line. From this perspective, the district government more or less chased the company out of Shanghai. The report also pointed out the stark contrast with how the enterprise was treated when it was invited to invest in Qingpu fifteen years earlier.[42] In fact, Qingpu has a history of lax environmental enforcement. In the 1990s, twelve projects in Qingpu were constructed without the required environmental impact assessment, even though they discharged pollutants directly into the Huangpu River.[43]

The relocation of Gaowei company seemed to be a matter of fact by 2005. The article in *Nanfang zhoumo* reported that the company was forced to relocate and was currently planning to do so. Also, staff at the Shanghai PCSC said that the company planned to relocate to Subei in order to escape Shanghai's tough environmental law enforcement.[44] However, when I visited the factory in late 2006 it

---

41 Interview with judge at Shanghai High People's Court, December 2005.

42 Yang Jun, "Some afterthought worries."

43 Shui-Yan Tang et al., "Institutional Constraints on Environmental Management in Urban China: Environmental Impact Assessment in Guangzhou and Shanghai," *The China Quarterly*, no. 152 (December 1997): 871.

44 Interview with Shanghai PCSC staff, December 2005.

was still running, and company representatives confirmed this by saying that the company was not relocating but staying in Qingpu.

In 2008 this case took a new turn that finally sealed the fate for Gaowei's future business in Shanghai. In June 2008 Qingpu EPB again fined Gaowei CNY 100,000 for excessive air pollution. However, in August residents in the area complained about a foul smell. This time the area affected included international schools and many foreign residents. Four expatriates were sent to a hospital suffering from nausea. The case was first reported in *Dongfang zaobao* and then again in the English language *Shanghai Daily*.[45] This time citizens actively used the Internet to spread information and organize. A "clean air campaign" was started in order to safeguard the air quality of the district. The campaign was directed against Gaowei chemical plant.[46] On October 24 a group of around forty residents even tried to deliver a letter directly to Shanghai Party Secretary Yu Zhengsheng. The letter had almost two thousand signatures from twenty-eight different nationalities. The group failed to deliver the letter and was told by police to go through the proper channels. In late November, the group's website published a response letter from the Shanghai EPB to some of the complaining residents. The letter stated that Shanghai EPB, Qingpu government, and SEPA had conducted investigations at Gaowei plant. The inspections found that after Gaowei had returned to normal production in October, the emissions again clearly exceeded the legal limits. The Qingpu government with the assistance of Shanghai EPB had therefore decided

---

45 Li Wei, "Echou huanrao si ming jumin yishi qiti zhong du" http://www.news365.com.cn/wxpd/sh/qp/200810/t20081023_2068370_1.htm; Chen Xingjie and Cai Wenjun, "Four neighbours complain as chemical factory pumps out foul odors" http://www.shanghaidaily.com/article/shdaily_sing.asp?id=377994&type=Metro&page=0

46 See campaign website: http://hi.baidu.com/cleanair2008/blog/index/1 The details of the case has been confirmed in interviews with residents engaged in the campaign.

to initiate legal procedures to shut down Gaowei.[47] In August 2009 the factory was finally shut down.[48]

The exact relationship between the company and the district authorities remains unclear. If the district authorities were not trying to get rid of the company, why was the district EPB head fired because he failed to act against the company? Most accounts claim that the district authorities acted only after they received pressure from the municipal-level EPB. Also, the fact that Gaowei was still operating in 2008 indicates that the local authorities were interested in keeping the company in operation. The company chairman complained that over 730 environmental checks from different authorities were conducted between 2003 and 2008. Despite this, the company still managed to avoid being shut down until 2009.[49]

Although this case is mainly a conflict between Gaowei company, the local residents, and the EPB, the Shanghai PC was quite active as well. The role of the PC was to try to be a channel for residents' complaints. In their first complaintß, some residents went to the Shanghai PC in hope that they could pressure the local government to act. One informant in the Shanghai PC letters-and-visits office personally went to the residents and investigated the case.[50] The residents had selected one representative to be in contact with the authorities. This person was a previous government employee and had both the knowledge and verbal capacity to represent the residents. However, according to him he did not find the PC very helpful so he focused the petition on the EPB.[51] According to figures from the Shanghai EPB letters-and-visits office, in 2004 Shanghai PC transferred sixty-two letters-and-visits cases to Shanghai EPB,

---

47 An English version of the letter can be found at: http://hi.baidu.com/cleanair2008/blog/item/dc24490858cb16c83ac7637d.html

48 Interview with residents engaged in the protest, June 2009; http://hi.baidu.com/cleanair2008

49 Chen Xingjie and Cai Wenjun "Neighbours complain."

50 Interview with staff at Shanghai PCSC, December 2005 and November 2006.

51 Interview with petitioner, June 2009.

of which seventeen were about Gaowei not obeying the administrative ruling of the Shanghai EPB.[52] When cases are transferred from the PC rather than directly to the government department, the case will have the backing of PC supervision. The EPB is requested to report back to the PC how the case has been handled. The fact that so many cases came from the PC increased chances that the PC would follow the case closely and make sure the EPB took the case seriously.

Interestingly, the group of protesters in 2008 did not go through the people's congress or the letters-and-visit system. They had tried to contact their local people's deputy but were unsuccessful so they called the EPB directly and made use of the Internet to organize a protest campaign. The main reason this group of protesters used less traditional ways of complaining was that this time the most active residents held foreign passports. This meant that they were less vulnerable to pressure from the authorities and also that they were less familiar with the Chinese political system.[53]

Compared to other parts of China, Shanghai is often considered better at its efforts in environmental protection. Shanghai representatives have been pushing for stricter national environmental protection legislation, and the local regulations are also stricter than national ones.[54] However, while the Shanghai PCSC is considered strong in terms of legislation, it has never stood out as particularly bold or active in supervision when compared to, for example, PCs in Guangdong.[55]

This case revealed many problems with the implementation of the environmental protection laws. The fact that the cost of investigating the case far surpassed the excessive pollution fee that the

---

52 Report from the Shanghai environmental protection bureau letters and visits office, 2004, on file with author.
53 Interview with residents engaged in the protest, June 2009.
54 Alford, "Clean Air, Clear Processes?" 715; Tang, "Institutional Constraints."
55 Cho, "The Politics of Lawmaking"; Interview with staff at Shanghai PCSC, December 2005.

company had to pay was pointed out by the local authorities as one of the main problems. The case was also referred to when Shanghai PC drafted its new water pollution law. The new law was stricter and aimed to counter local protectionism.[56]

People's Deputy–Initiated Supervision from Below: A Group of Guangdong Provincial People's Deputies Attacks the Provincial Environmental Protection Bureau

In January 2000, during the yearly Guangdong provincial PC session, a group of twenty-five people's deputies from Foshan, a district-level city, submitted an interpellation to the provincial EPB. The background for the interpellation was that the EPB had failed to act on a heavily polluting factory in Sihui, an upstream county-level city under Zhaoqing city neighboring Foshan, despite Foshan people's deputies having pointed out the problem several times. The EPB leaders were called to the PC to answer the interpellation in a televised meeting. The EPB leaders' answer did not satisfy the people's deputies who claimed that the EPB had seriously failed in its work to implement the environmental protection laws.[57] The incident caused a heated media debate in Guangdong and was reported by most major media in China. In the aftermath nine factories were temporarily shut down. Another nine factories were stopped from being built.[58]

This case became widely known in China not only because of the unusually bold act by the people's deputies but also because

---

56 Interview with Shanghai people's congress staff, November 2005.
57 *Renmin zhi sheng* [People's Voice], no. 3 (2000): 4–9.
58 Qing-Jie Wang, "Transparency in the Grey Box of China's Environmental Governance: A Case Study of Print Media Coverage of an Environmental Controversy from the Pearl River Delta Region," *Journal of Environment & Development* 14, no. 2 (June 2005): 278–312.

of the massive media reporting. However, shortly after the interpellation, the media stopped reporting about the incident, and only a few short notices have appeared since. The case is often referred to when describing the increasing assertiveness of PCs. Two articles by Wang have shed light on the political game behind the media scene. Wang's studies reveal that the actual outcome of the PC interpellation was less substantial than what had been reported in media at the time. [59]

Foshan city government had for some time tried to contend with its serious pollution problems by enforcing strict environmental regulations. This chased away some of the polluting industries who opted to move to Zhaoqing or other locations rather than invest in expensive environmental protection equipment. One such company was the Nanjiang industrial group electroplating plant (NIP), which was building eighteen electroplating factories. NIP was located in Sihui, a county-level city under Zhaoqing. Three of the factories owned by Nanjiang had been relocated from Nanhai in Fo-shan.

When the plant, which was being built close to the Beijiang River, started operations, some residents in Foshan reacted to the pollution from the factories and contacted their local people's deputy. A group of provincial-level people's deputies from Foshan, led by Han Ying, chair of the Foshan PCSC, went to the Nanjiang plant to conduct inspections in early September 1999. Han was also a member of the Guangdong PCSC. The inspections resulted in a report requesting the Guangdong EPB to stop construction of the plant as it would cause serious pollution to the Beijiang River. The report also pointed out that an environmental impact assessment, which was required by law, had not been conducted for the project before construction commenced. Nine of the factories had already begun to

---

59 Wang, "Transparency in the Grey Box"; Jing-Qie Wang and Mark Yaolin Wang, "Mission Possible? Chinese Provincial Congress Deputies' Involvement in an Environmental Dispute in Guangdong," *Asia Pacific Viewpoint* 47, no. 2 (August 2006): 195–216.

operations. The report was given support by Chen Zhiquan, director of the environmental committee of the Guangdong PCSC. The Guangdong EPB did not respond to the report and acted only after vice governor Tang Bingquan ordered them to. The EPB conducted an investigation in October and did not inform the Foshan PC until December that the factories had been ordered to stop production until an environmental assessment had been conducted. However, some of the Foshan people's deputies made a new inspection and collected evidence showing that the factories had continued operations and were discharging pollutants directly into the river.

In the interpellation meeting in January 2000, the EPB vice director responsible for the case could not answer why no EIA had been made before the factories were being constructed. The Foshan deputies were unsatisfied with this and harshly criticized the EPB leaders. In a vote on the answer of the interpellation, twenty-eight people's deputies participated, twenty-three voted "not satisfied," and only five voted "satisfied." According to the rules, the EPB was now required both to submit a written answer as well as meet with the deputy group the following day. The key problem according to the people's deputies was that the EPB had already seriously failed in its work to implement the law. The construction project had been approved by the EPB without prior assessment. The question now was whether the EPB should be held legally responsible. Despite new efforts from the EPB to appease the people's deputies, they submitted a suggestion to the people's congress presidium to remove the vice director from his job on the ground that he was lacking in legal, environmental, and PR knowledge.[60]

A heated debate started in the Guangdong media. Opponents to the Foshan deputies included officials and people's deputies from Zhaoqing and the owners of the factories, mainly Hong Kong businessmen. The Sihui officials claimed that factories in Foshan were even worse polluters and that the Foshan deputies were simply jealous. The Hong Kong businessmen threatened to sue the gov-

---

60 *Renmin zhi sheng* [People's Voice], no. 3 (2000): 4–9.

ernment if the plant did not start production again. During these turbulent days, the nine factories were ordered to stop production. It was further claimed that the vice head of the EPB was fired and the EPB head replaced.[61] However, as it turned out, none of them were actually fired.[62] Guangdong media mainly sided with the people's deputies, and this put extra pressure on the authorities to act according to their requests. Hence, the first impression was that the people's deputies managed to strongly influence the situation. However, in the longer perspective the actual result was less clearcut.

Wang in his analysis of media reporting of the incident noted that after the unusually open media reporting surrounding the PC interpellation in late January, media suddenly stopped reporting the case after February 2. According to Wang, the media censored itself because the Guangdong authorities had verbally instructed it to stop reporting on the case. In the following months, the case was handled internally in the government. The nine companies stopped production for some months. On June 28 a decision was made to allow production to resume at the nine factories but that they were required to follow EIA stipulations. An additional nine factories were not permitted to be built. Apparently, the Guangdong government, including the EPB, was concerned about the unemployment and loss of economic growth as a result of shutting down the factories.[63] The Zhaoqing leadership was quite successful in influencing the final decision by the provincial leadership.[64] The NIP factories that were allowed to continue operation were to be supervised in future years. The Foshan people's deputies continuously inspected the development of the remaining electroplate factories and submitted motions requesting a solution to the environmental prob-

---

61 Jennifer Ehrlich, "Soiled Side of Environmental Protection on the Mainland," *South China Morning Post*, March 10, 2000.
62 Wang and Wang, "Mission Possible?"
63 Wang, "Transparency in the Grey Box."
64 Wang and Wang, "Mission Possible?" 210.

lem.⁶⁵ Wang concludes that most of the Foshan people's deputies were dissatisfied with the final result of the interpellation.⁶⁶ However, apparently the case lived on even after Wang's study. Amid more reports on the worsening of the water quality of the Beijiang River, it was decided by the provincial EPB and the provincial procuratorate in early 2006 that the nine factories were to be relocated to a location that did not affect the Beijiang River.⁶⁷ The relocation was reportedly under way in late 2006.⁶⁸

In the case of the Foshan people's deputy group's interpellation it was not, as often is the case, only the PCSC that used its powers to supervise the government. It was a group of people's deputies who used their legal status as people's deputies to handle a problem in their locality. To be sure, the political status and contacts of the Foshan PC chair Han Ying were also important. It appears that the PCSC was divided over the handling of the case. In January 10, just two weeks before the congress, a group led by Chen Zhiquan, the director of the Guangdong PCSC environmental committee, investigated the NIP and wrote a report that supported the Sihui industries. This was surprising since the same group had in September required these plants to stop production.⁶⁹ Hence, the Foshan people's deputy acted contrary to the will of the PCSC leader responsible for environmental issues. Officially the PCSC leadership showed

---

65 Foshan PC webpage, http://www.fsonline.com.cn/misszj/07lh/htzj/200701080030.htm (accessed 2007).

66 Wang and Wang, "Mission Possible?" 212.

67 Liu Xitong, "Sheng Huanbaoju jianchating lianhe zhifa gongpo wuran 'laodanan,,'" [Provincial EPB and procuratorate together break through in enforcing an old pollution problem], *Nanfang ribao*, January 18, 2006, http://gd.sohu.com/20060118/n241493028.shtml (accessed July 3, 2007).

68 Xie Pingsheng, "Beijiang bian 9 ke 'wuran zhadan' chunjie qian chaichu" [Nine pollution bombs at the Bei river to be removed before spring festival], *Guangzhou ribao*, December 12, 2006, http://gzdaily.dayoo.com/html/2006-12/12/content_19394324.htm (accessed July 3, 2007).

69 Wang, "Transparency in the Grey Box," 284; Wang and Wang, "Mission Possible?" 202.

support for the interpellation. On February 24 the chairman of the Guangdong PCSC, Zhu Senlin, held a speech at a seminar. In his speech he clearly stated his support for the Foshan deputy group's interpellation and criticized the environmental protection cadres for not being willingly supervised.[70] At this stage, however, the provincial leadership had taken over the case, and the PC had little chance of exerting influence over its handling.

To a large extent the case is a conflict between two competing localities. Pollution problems are often transboundary, and the factory causing the pollution sometimes does not affect the area in which it is situated and under whose jurisdiction it falls but instead affects a neighboring area that has no authority over the factory. According to Lieberthal, "after China imposed water discharge fees for adding pollutants above the permissible levels to rivers and streams, there was noticeable movement of offending enterprises to the downstream boundaries in various townships and counties."[71] The people's congress became a political institutional weapon used by one of the localities against the other. Such cleavages weaken the authority of the PC in relation to the executive. The pollution in Sihui seriously affected the water in neighboring Foshan. Foshan has no authority over Sihui as it falls under Zhaoqing, but the provincial level has authority over Zhaoqing. By using the PC, the Foshan people's deputies could forward local interests to a higher level. They could have pursued the issue by, for example, contacting the provincial EPB informally, but the PC gave the claims legal and moral legitimacy. In addition, the media played an important role in the process. By presenting the interpellation in the presence of media, the issue became public, which made it much more difficult for the local leadership to handle the problem in the traditional informal way. However, once the media was silenced, the provincial party leadership could reassert control over the decision-making

---

70 *Renmin zhi sheng* [People's voice], no. 4 (2000): 4.

71 Kenneth Lieberthal, "China's Governing System and Its Impact on Environmental Policy Implementation," *China Environmental Series* (1997): 6.

process. It appears that the Zhaoqing leaders were more successful than the Foshan side in influencing the final decision on the matter.[72]

Although the Foshan people's deputies failed to achieve their stated purpose, their action was not a complete failure. Attention was given to the pollution problem, and the status and legitimacy of the PC was strengthened by the media attention. In this case the PC impact on the implementation of the environmental protection laws was more obvious than in the Shanghai case. The Foshan people's deputy group became a main actor in pressuring the Guangdong government to close the polluting factories and ensuring that the regulations were followed.

All over the province of Guangdong PCs have been known to flex their political muscles to a much greater extent than in other parts of China, frequently in relation to environmental problems. This is often referred to as the "Guangdong phenomenon," a concept used to describe the politically more open and confrontational atmosphere in Guangdong.[73] In Guangdong, in particular Guangzhou and Shenzhen, PCs have been in the forefront of reforming the PC system.[74] Also, environmental protection issues have been

---

72 Wang and Wang, "Mission Possible?" 210.

73 People's congress staff in other parts of China have pointed this out in several interviews. Some of them have visited Guangdong and noticed the difference in openness and assertiveness of people's congresses. The Guangdong phenomenon is also often mentioned in Chinese media and research articles on people's congresses. See for example Wang's comparison of the Beijing Haidian district PC phenomenon and the Guangdong PC phenomenon: Wang Weiguo, "'Guangdong renda xianxiang' yu 'haidian renda xianxiang' bijiao" [Comparing the "Guangdong Phenomenon" and the "Haidian Phenomenon"], *Renda yanjiu*, no. 5 (2006).

74 Xia uses Shenzhen as a special experimental case in his study of provincial PCs, "The Dual Developmental State." Shenzhen was the first city to use an online PC in 2000 in which local citizens could follow the meeting over the Internet and send e-mail suggestions directly, *Renmin zhi sheng*, no. 9 (2000): 32. This method has since spread to other local people's congresses in China. In April 2000 Guangzhou was first to use a public hearing (*xunwen hui*) in which the media participated when legislators asked questions of the government in a reportedly con-

increasingly on the agenda for the Guangdong provincial PC. In the 2006 provincial PC the environmental protection related motions increased by 40 percent to 78 out of a total of 1,006 motions.[75]

Implementing Environmental Protection Law: Actors and Interactions

As PCs are not implementing organs, their involvement in the law implementation process is indirect: by influencing the implementers. Except for the most obvious actors involved in the implementation, such as the Environmental Protection Agency (EPA), the PCs also have to relate to other actors that are directly or indirectly involved in the implementation game. These actors include other government departments and agencies, polluting companies, residents affected by the pollution, the media, and the courts. Many of these actors are engaged at different levels in the administrative hierarchy.

First of all we must remember that PCs are not single units but consist of several institutions. This fact complicates the whole discussion on the relationship between PC and other actors as this relationship differs a lot between the plenary session and its SC. Many factors affect the possibilities of the PCSCs to actually conduct meaningful supervision over the government. One aspect concerns the PCSC internal structure. Dealings between the PCSC and the government on environmental protection issues are mostly handled by the PCSC working committee responsible for environmental issues and the EPA. The organization and establishment of the working committees is, with the exception of some obligatory committees, up to the provincial PC to decide. As a consequence, this differs

---

frontational style, *Renmin zhi sheng*, no. 6 (2000): 8; *Nanfang zhoumo* (April 21, 2000): 2.

75 *Zhongguo huanjingbao*, March 16, 2006, http://www.gdepb.gov.cn/ztzl/lh2006/xgbd/t20060316_36322.html.

quite a lot between provinces. In the case of environmental protection, many provinces have established single working committees responsible for the protection of environment and natural resources.[76] However, another common solution is to combine the environmental protection affairs with city construction. In Shanghai the working committee responsible for environmental protection is called the Environmental and City Construction Working Committee.[77] According to staff at the Shanghai PCSC, city construction and environmental protection often have contradictory goals. As a result, a conflict between environmental protection and city construction becomes an internal conflict within the PCSC working committee rather than a conflict between two separate PCSC working committees or between the PCSC and a government department. This weakens the capacity of the PCSC to handle environmental issues.[78] Interestingly, as a comparison, the Guangdong PC has changed from the model practiced in Shanghai to a single working committee responsible for environmental protection.

While the internal work structure of the PCSC can be reorganized, the special relationship between the SC and the government and the party is more complicated. The SC members are picked by the local party committee, and the party committee is constantly present in the form of a party group within the SC.[79] Many SC mem-

---

76 This is the case, for example, in Guizhou, Ningxia, Jiangxi, Guangdong, Hainan, Shaanxi, Hubei, Fujian, and Hunan. In Zhejiang the committee also handles agricultural affairs.

77 This model is used not only in provincial-level municipalities like Shanghai, Beijing, Tianjin, and Chongqing, but also in provinces like Jiangsu, Anhui, Sichuan, and Shandong, where it is called Urban and Rural Construction and Environmental Protection Committee.

78 Interview with Shanghai PCSC staff, November 2006.

79 The party maintains political control over state institutions by controlling the political careers of the leaders. According to the nomenclature system, directors, vice directors, and the general secretary of the PCSC are nominated by the party committee one notch above. Ordinary SC members are nominated by the party committee at the same level. In addition local party committees establish party groups in most state institutions consisting of the top leaders in the institution that are also

bers have previously worked in the government structure. In addition, the working committees within the SC have developed working relations with the government departments in their respective field. The SC is thus to some extent embedded in both government and party structures.[80] The closeness of the relationship makes formal SC supervision of the government a delicate and complicated matter. Instead of using the formal channels of supervision, many SC members prefer to present their views to the government informally through personal communication. This way the government can listen to the views of the SC and make necessary adjustments in their practices without publicly appearing to have differences. It should be noted that such informal problem-solving is of course not unique for the Chinese political system. Compromises and informal deals are necessary parts of politics in most countries. However, the entwinement of the SC with the government and party structures and the lack of transparency in the Chinese political system make such behavior more common in China than in most countries. This is an important aspect of how the PC can influence the implementing organs. It could also be argued that individual deputies exert influence in this way. It has, for example, been noted that SCs can use the discontent of ordinary people's deputies as a form of pressure on the executive or the party.[81] Because of their relative independence vis-à-vis the party and government compared to the SC members, many of the individual people's deputies

---

party members. Party groups mainly deal with personnel issues and are responsible for communication between the local party committee and the particular state institution.

80 Kevin O'Brien, "Chinese People's Congresses and Legislative Embeddedness: Understanding Early Organizational Development," *Comparative Political Studies* 27, issue 1 (1994): 80–107, made this observation early. Cho, also writes about the "cosy" relationship between special committees and executive agencies, in the "The Politics of Lawmaking," 604.

81 Ming Xia, "Political Contestation and the Emergence of Provincial People's Congresses as Power Players in Chinese Politics: A Network Explanation," *Journal of Contemporary China* 9, issue 24 (2000): 185–215.

are less constrained in criticizing and supervising the government. But it is the SC that has the political tools to perform effective supervision.

This discussion is important in light of the two cases described above. They constitute examples of how PCs use the formal legal channels of influence. Because they are unusual and conflict laden, they have also attracted media attention. In both cases, the local environmental bureau was punished for failing to implement the law. In Shanghai, the district environmental protection office head was fired as a result of pressure from the municipal EPB, and indirectly from the municipal PC. In Guangdong, it was the provincial EPB that had failed and received criticism from the people's congress. Those cases where PCs work together with the EPB and successfully ensure that the law is implemented and polluting companies change their behavior have no news value and will not be reported in the media in the same way.[82] Neither will those cases where the PCs exert influence informally because this information is simply not available. In this analysis, the informal influence of the SC is treated as an integral part of the SC supervision from above.

The EPA is the main body responsible for environmental law implementation at respective administrative levels The EPAs do not have an easy job enforcing the law. Despite the recent strengthening of the environmental protection bureaucracy, the EPAs are still comparatively weak at the local level where most enforcement takes place. The reason for this is the decentralized nature of Chinese environmental protection enforcement. Local EPAs are politically subordinate to and financially dependent on the local government. Local governments often have economic development as their top priority, and environmental protection is often perceived as an obstacle to this. In the eyes of many local government leaders, environmental protection laws restrain production and force companies to invest in expensive environmental protection equipment. Eco-

---

82 For a discussion on this see Randall Peerenboom, Chapter 2 in this volume.

nomic development is an incentive for locally led development, both in terms of personal enrichment and as a basis for political promotion. Now environmental protection has been included as one of the performance criteria upon which cadre promotion is calculated, but it still weighs lighter than economic and social development.[83]

Environmental protection law implementation often affects government departments other than the EPA, which can result in a conflict of interest. The typical case is a conflict between environmental and commercial interests when the EPA wants to fine a local enterprise but the industry and planning bureau or other powerful government departments protect the enterprise. In such a case, the EPA might find the PC a useful ally in the struggle, particularly since the PCSC sometimes can muster party committee support. Often in environmental law implementation problems the PC and government are on the same side against the violators, usually a company. Fighting on the same side obviously makes implementation of the law easier, as in the Shanghai case. Sometimes, however, the government and the company are allied, and the government protects the company. In these cases the PC has the difficult task of fighting both government and enterprise. Although this makes PC supervision harder, it is not entirely impossible, as was shown in the Guangdong case.

In recent years, the State Environmental Protection Administration (SEPA) has strengthened its position within the Chinese bureaucracy. In what has been termed the "environmental storm", SEPA has started to publicly reveal violations of the environmental protection laws, in particular violations of the environmental im-

---

83 Interview with staff at environmental institute under Shanghai EPB, December 2005. See also Schwarz, "Environmental NGOs in China," 33. Following the Tuojiang River pollution in Sichuan 2004, the local government claimed that government cadres that have had major pollution mishaps in their jurisdiction will be considered unqualified for promotion. See http://www.china.org.cn/english/2004/Jun/97245.htm.

pact assessment law, in projects where other government departments are directly responsible. Such conflicts have traditionally been handled within the bureaucracy without the public's knowledge. Government departments' use of the law against other departments is a new way to gain political power and legitimacy in Chinese politics.[84]

Conflicts between different government departments do not (yet) involve mediation by courts but are ultimately solved within the administration. Courts are, however, increasingly being used by private actors as a way to handle perceived injustices. In the Shanghai case, the company owner claimed to have been treated unjustly by the local government and took the case to court in what was termed the first environmental protection administrative litigation in Shanghai. In the Guangdong case, Hong Kong-based investors also threatened to sue the local government, but in the end never followed through with their threat. Courts in China suffer from lack of independence from the political structure. The corruption problem that prevails in many courts is an obstacle for judicial independence. Judicial corruption has been the main argument for many local PCs to engage in very strong supervision over local courts.[85]

Violations of environmental protection laws are often revealed as a result of reactions by local residents who are affected by the pollution. As discussed above, the complaint system is a source of information for the authorities regarding environmental problems. However, as argued by Dasgupta and Wheeler, the system also has many flaws. The complaint system cannot be used as a reliable source of information on where the environmental problems are the worst. Those who scream the highest and are the most articulate are not necessarily those who have the greatest problems.[86] Simi-

---

84 Cai Dingjian, "The Development of Constitutionalism in China," *Columbia Journal of Asian Law* (Spring/Fall 2005): 24.

85 For more on the role of courts, see Randall Peerenboom's and Jonas Grimheden's chapters 2, 4, respectively, in this volume.

86 Susmita Dasgupta and David Wheeler, "Citizen Complaints as Environ-

larly, a survey in 1999 by researchers at Beijing University found that almost 4 percent of the respondents had taken part in lawsuits or petitions in relation to environmental problems.[87] The same survey also found that environmental awareness and knowledge were significantly higher in urban areas than in rural areas and also in relation to level of education.[88] Hence, the extent to which citizens can influence their situation when a violation of the environmental protection laws occurs differs greatly between regions. Citizens in developed and urban areas complain about pollution problems to a much higher degree than in less developed rural areas, although pollution is often greater in poorer areas.[89] This fact is amply illustrated by the Shanghai case where the protestors were high-income residents and in some cases held foreign passports. In poorer areas the problem sometimes goes on until it develops into a major conflict involving mass protests and violent clashes between citizens and local authorities. The lack of political participation in environmental protection policy in China has been mentioned by many observers.[90] More recent studies have noted that society has become a more important actor in environmental protection. Domestic as well as international environmental nongovernmental organizations are becoming more important.[91] People's deputies could have an important role to play in representing the interests of residents affected by environmental pollution. From the perspective of the authorities this could help in averting serious clashes between citizens and the local government. More and more local people's deputies play an increasingly active role in representing their constituency, and some

---

mental Indicators, Evidence from China," *World Bank Policy Research Working Papers* 1704 (1997).

87 Yang Ming, ed., *Huannjing wenti yu huanjing yishi* [Environmental awareness and perceptions] (Beijing: Huaxia chubanshe, 2002), 96.

88 Yang, Environmental Awareness and Perceptions, 76–88.

89 Van Rooij, Regulating Land, 284, 285.

90 Sinikule and Ortolano, *Implementing Environmental Policy*, 202; Tang, "Institutional Constraints."

91 Schwarz, "Environmental NGOs in China."

PCs have developed reforms to improve and facilitate contacts between citizens and people's deputies.[92]

The media's increasing importance in China is particularly apparent in cases of environmental law violations. This fact is also exploited by other actors. In the Guangdong case, the people's deputies used the presence of the media in the questioning of the EPB. Once the accusations of the people's deputies had been made public, the Guangdong government found it politically costly to ignore the people's deputies' action. This would have been true even if the media had not been involved, but the presence of the media added the power of public opinion on the side of the people's deputies. Once the media was ordered to stop reporting, the people's deputies' chances of influencing the outcome decreased. Often PCSCs have the media participate in law implementation inspections. Of course the media is still often used as a classical propaganda weapon to produce an image of a strong PC also in those cases where the supervision has no practical function but is merely a show for the public. Increased media freedom in reporting on environmental issues has made the media an important actor in its own right. National media constantly reports on violations of the environmental protection laws by local governments. Here, the importance of vertical relationships in the social and administrative structure becomes apparent. While local media, which is typically the mouthpiece of the local party committee, is inhibited from reporting on local problems unless it is first cleared by the local party committee, national media have to worry less about this. National media or-

---

92 For examples of reforms in relations between people's deputies and citizens, see for example, Li Fan, *Zhongguo xuanju zhidu gaige* [Reform of the electoral system in China] (Shanghai: Shanghai jiaotong daxue chubanshe, 2005); Zou Pingxue, *Zhongguo daibiao zhidu gaige de shizheng yanjiu* [Research evidence of China's representative system reform] (Chongqing: Chongqing chubanshe, 2005); He Junzhi, *Zhidu dengdai liyi: zhongguo xianji renda zhidu moshi yanjiu* [Institutions in search of roles: The growth of China's County People's Congresses] (Chongqing: Chongqing chubanshe, 2005).

gans will find it much more difficult to critically report on issues regarding the national leadership.

The interaction between different administrative levels creates a dynamic to the law implementation situation. One actor can act at several levels simultaneously, while others are restricted to one level. Actors also move both vertically and horizontally in the socio-political system; PCs can use this vertical structure to their advantage since they frequently coordinate actions, such as law implementation inspections, between different levels. Also some people's deputies are representatives at several levels at the same time. The Guangdong people's deputies are a case in point. Despite relocating, the company could not escape the Foshan government as the people's deputies used their position as provincial people's deputies to influence provincial authorities to control the company. In a similar way, the Shanghai municipal EPB and the Shanghai municipal PC acted when the Qingpu district EPB failed to handle the environmental pollution problem. Also in this case the company was considering relocation to an area with less strict law enforcement.

The problem of companies escaping environmental protection enforcement by relocating shows how implementation of laws differs in different localities in China, and sometimes even within provinces. It is thus usually not the law that differs but to what extent the law is implemented by the local bureaucracy.[93] The regional difference with regard to the environmental protection situa-tion roughly follows the pattern of economic development. In regions where economic development has already reached a relatively high level, people are getting more interested in environmental protection, and the environmental protection authorities have more resources and power. The behavior of enterprises fol-

---

93 There are also differences in laws between regions. In addition, at the national level, leaders of poorer regions have opposed strict environmental protection legislation, while leaders in richer regions have pushed for stricter legislation. See Alford and Liebman, "Clean Air, Clear Processes?" 715.

lows the same logic that drives multinational corporations to move from (often economically developed) countries with strict environmental regulations to countries (often economically weak) with less stringent regulation, or less active implementation of existing regulations.

Concluding Discussion

I have argued that PC influence over the implementation of laws can be channeled in mainly three different forms based on the source of the initiative: SC-initiated supervision from above, citizen-initiated supervision from below, and the people's deputy-initiated supervision from below.

Comparatively speaking, the supervision from above is a form of institutionalized supervision. The SC can mobilize some resources and have a close and continuous contact with the executive organs. In this way this form of supervision can influence the law implementation situation continuously in several stages of the implementation process. However, the embeddedness of the PCSC with the party and government organs also makes this form of supervision weak when there is a real conflict situation. In contrast, law implementation supervision from below lacks the capacity and the institutionalization of supervision from above. But this form of supervision is not to the same extent restricted by its embeddedness with the party and government structure. Hence, for example, law implementation examination is more thorough and involves more people than ordinary inspections, but the effect of this advantage is diluted by its formalization. A spontaneous individual people's deputy inspection can therefore be more effective. Ordinary people's deputies can, when they manage to mobilize their organizational capability, to a greater extent confront the government. The effects of such a confrontation are more dramatic than the institutionalized supervision from above, but it is far rarer. In most PCs such confrontations never occur. Nevertheless, the mere potential of such a conflict will work as a constraint on the government not to violate or ignore the law and the PC.

Returning to the cases described above, how can we understand them in terms of successful and unsuccessful law implementation? First, the cases are hardly representative of PC work in general. They have been given attention because they are unusual and show PCs that actively engage in influencing the law implementation situation. In addition, the success of the PCs studied in influencing the law implementation situation turned out to be somewhat limited, at least if we measure this in terms of how the violators were handled. Although the direct action of the PCs resulted in strict measures being taken against the law violators, in the longer perspective the effects were less obvious. The Shanghai chemical factory could continue operating for many years before being shut down in 2009, and in Guangdong most companies were only temporarily shut down. Also if we measure success based on the exercise of power by the PCs over the executive, the result is ambiguous. Although the PC actively used its authority, it is difficult to know whether its engagement had any practical consequence over government actions.

Finally, we shall consider PC involvement in the implementation of law in relation to Hydén's analytical framework of legal norms presented in this volume. According to Hydén, the successful implementation of a certain law requires a correspondence with existing norms in society. Norms consist of three dimensions: will, knowledge, and possibilities. The successful influence of PCs in the implementation of laws requires a will driving the PC to act, knowledge enabling the PC to act, and systemic conditions that make this action possible. In order to understand the involvement of PCs in the implementation of, for example, environmental protection laws, we must consider the laws that regulate the actions of PCs. The constitution and the laws regulating the activities of PCs equip the people's deputies with many legal responsibilities and possibilities to uphold and ensure the implementation of laws. However, in this case there is an evident gap between the law and the norms of the people's deputies.

People's deputies will to actively ensure the implementation of the law is in general limited. Being a people's deputy is still for many an honor, and their role is to support the party and the executive, not to question and confront them. The incentive structure to actively influence the implementation of law is weak. However, as the organization of people's deputies is based on regional division, deputies from a geographic area often have shared interest. People's deputies can engage in an environmental protection issue because they genuinely worry about the environmental damages caused to their locality. But they can also use environmental protection arguments as a weapon in the regional competition with other localities. Both motives, local concerns and inter regional competition, work as favorable incentives to implement the environmental protection laws.

In terms of knowledge, the SC members are equipped with resources, knowledge, time, leadership, and organizational capability that far surpass what ordinary people's deputies can muster. Yet the PCSC still finds itself struggling with a knowledge gap in relation to the executive branch. Leadership is an important factor as this differs a lot between PCs. A PCSC led by a strong and resourceful chairman can be very assertive in influencing the law implementation situation.

According to Hydén, the systemic conditions that decide the possibilities for action are the most important factor. This is also where the greatest obstacles for law implementation can be found. The party's position as the ultimate arbiter in all political matters significantly constrains the possibilities of PCs to actively get involved in the implementation of law. PCs have to handle relationships with the party and executive carefully. Legislators that skillfully handle different leaders and groupings within the party committee can exert influence over the implementation of laws. Other systemic factors include the attitude of the party committee leadership toward environmental issues as well as towards the role of the PC, the political climate in China in general during the particular time period, and the local political culture. The boldness of

PCs in Guangdong is related to the more open political climate in the province compared to other parts of China.

The norms that support the active engagement in the implementation of law for the PCs are weak. However, in all three dimensions there is a change toward a strengthening of these norms. More people's deputies are made up of entrepreneurs and intellectuals that actively use their position as people's deputy to influence society.[94] Knowledge of the law increases both among individual people's deputies and the PCSC, which can use this knowledge to assist individual people's deputies. Change is also taking place in the crucial systemic conditions. The general status of the PC and of the law has increased in China. PCs are officially encouraged to be active, and some reforms have been made in order to facilitate more active and engaged legislatures in China. Though the gap between the law and the norms of the PC is still wide, it is slowly getting smaller.

Bibliography

Alford, William P., and Benjamin L. Liebman. "Clean Air, Clear Processes? The Struggle over Air Pollution Law in the People's Republic of China," *Hastings Law Journal* 52 (2000-2001): 703-748.

Almén, Oscar. *Authoritarianism Constrained: The Role of Local People's Congresses in China*, Ph.D. dissertation, Gotherburg University, 2005.

Baldwin, Nicholas D. J. "Concluding Observations: Legislative Weakness, Scrutinising Strength?" *The Journal of Legislative Studies* 10, no. 2/3, (Summer/Autumn 2004): 295-302.

Bi, Renfa. "Piaojue: pingyi zhi zhongchui" [Voting: Appraisal's heavy stick], *Zhejiang renda*, no. 9, (2005).

Cai, Dingjian. "Functions of the People's Congresses in the Process of Implementation of Law." In Jianfu Chen et al. (eds.), *Implementation of Law in*

---

94 He, Institutions in Search of Roles, 137, 138, has showed that there is a great discrepancy between the official occupational categorization of PC deputies and their real occupation. For example, the category of workers usually consists of a great majority of entrepreneurs.

the People's Republic of China, 35–53. The Hague: Kluwer Law International, 2002.

Cai, Dingjian. "The Development of Constitutionalism in China," *Columbia Journal of Asian Law* (Spring/Fall 2005).

Chan, Hon S., Koon-kwai Wong, K. C. Cheung, and Jack Man-keung Lo. "The Implementation Gap in Environmental Management in China: The Case of Guangzhou, Zhengzhou and Nanjing," *Public Administration Review* 55, no. 4 (July/August 1995): 333–340.

Chen, An. *Restructuring Political Power in China*. Boulder: Lynne Rienner Publishers, 1999.

Cho, Young Nam. "From 'Rubber Stamps' to 'Iron Stamps': The Emergence of Chinese Local People's Congresses as Supervisory Powerhouses," *The China Quarterly*, no. 171 (September 2002): 724–740.

Cho, Young Nam. "Symbiotic Neighbour or Extra-Court Judge? The Supervision over Courts by Chinese Local People's Congresses," *The China Quarterly*, no. 176 (December 2003): 1068-1083.

Cho, Young Nam. "The Politics of Law-Making in Chinese Local People's Congresses," *The China Quarterly*, no. 187 (September 2006): 592–609.

Cho, Young Nam. *Local People's Congresses in China, Development and Transition*. New York: Cambridge University Press, 2009.

Dasgupta, Susmita, and David Wheeler. "Citizen Complaints as Environmental Indicators, Evidence From China," *World Bank Policy Research Working Papers* 1704 (1997).

Dickson, Bruce. *Red Capitalists in China, the Party, Private Entrepreneurs, and Prospects for Political Change*. New York: Cambridge University Press, 2003.

Ethridge, Marcus E. *Legislative Participation in Implementation: Policy through politics*. New York: Praeger Publishers, 1985.

He, Junzhi. *Zhidu dengdai liyi: zhongguo xianji renda zhidu moshi yanjiu* [Institutions in search of roles: The growth of China's county people's congresses]. Chongqing: Chongqing chubanshe, 2005.

Jahiel, Abigail, R. "The Contradictory Impact of Environmental Protection in China," *The China Quarterly*, no. 149 (March 1997): 81–103.

Jahiel, Abigail R. "The Organization of Environmental Protection in China," *The China Quarterly*, no. 156 (December 1998): 757–787.

Johannes, John R. "Casework as a Technique of U.S. Congressional Oversight of the Executive," *Legislative Studies Quarterly* IV (1979): 325–351.

Korn, Jessica. "The Legislative Veto and the Limits of Public Choice Analysis," *Political Science Quarterly* 109, no. 5 (Winter 1994–1995): 873–894.
Laver, Michael. "Divided Parties, Divided Government," *Legislative Studies Quarterly* XXIV (February 1999): 5–29.
Li, Fan. *Zhongguo xuanju zhidu gaige* [Reform of the electoral system in China], Shanghai: Shanghai jiaotong daxue chubanshe, 2005.
Lin, Baihai. *Renmin daibiao dahui jiandu zhidu de fenxi yu goujian* [An analysis and setup of the people's congress supervisory system]. Beijing: Zhongguo shehui kexue chubanshe, 2004.
Lieberthal, Kenneth. "China's Governing System and Its Impact on Environmental Policy Implementation," *China Environmental Series* (1997): 3–8.
O'Brien, Kevin J. "Chinese People's Congresses and Legislative Embeddedness: Understanding Early Organizational Development," *Comparative Political Studies* 27, issue 1 (1994): 80–107.
O'Brien, Kevin J., and Lianjiang Li. "The Politics of Lodging Complaints in Rural China," *The China Quarterly*, no. 143, (September 1995): 756–783.
Olson, David M., and William E. Crowther. *Committees in Post-Communist Democratic Parliaments*. Columbus: Ohio State University Press, 2002.
Palmer, Michael. "Environmental Regulation in the People's Republic of China," *The China Quarterly*, no 156 (December 1998): 788–808.
Ross, Lester. "China Environmental Protection, Domestic Policy Trends, Pattern of Participation in Regimes and Compliance with International Norms," *The China Quarterly*, no. 156 (December 1998): 809–835.
Schwarz, Benjamin. "Environmental NGOs in China: Their Roles and Limits," *Pacific Affairs*, vol. 77, no. 1, (Spring 2004).
Shepsle, Kenneth. " Representation and Governance: The Great Legislative Trade-off," *Political Science Quarterly* 103, no. 3 (1988): 461–484.
Sinkule, Barbara J., and Leonard Ortolano. *Implementing Environmental Policy in China*. Westport: Praeger Publishers, 1995.
Tang, Shui-Yan, et al. "Institutional Constraints on Environmental Management in Urban China: Environmental Impact Assessment in Guangzhou and Shanghai," *The China Quarterly*, no. 152 (September 1997): 863–874.
Tanner, Murray S. *The Politics of Lawmaking in China; Institutions, Processes, and Democratic Prospects*. Oxford: Clarendon Press, 1999.
Thireau, Isabelle, and Hua Linshan. "One Law, Two Interpretations: Mobilizing the Labor Law in Arbitration Committees and in Letters and Visits

Offices." In *Engaging the Law in China: State Society and Possibilities for Justice*, edited by Neil Diamant, Stanley B. Lubman and Kevin O'Brien, 84–107. Stanford: Stanford University Press, 2005.

van Rooij, Benjamin. *Regulating Land and Pollution in China, Lawmaking, Compliance and Enforcement; Theory and Cases*. Leiden: Leiden University Press, 2006.

Wang, Qing-Jie. "Transparency in the Grey Box of China's Environmental Governance: A Case Study of Print Media Coverage of an Environmental Controversy from the Pearl River Delta Region," *Journal of Environment & Development* 14, no. 2 (June 2005): 278–312.

Wang, Qing-Jie, and Mark Yaolin Wang. "Mission Possible? Chinese Provincial Congress Deputies' Involvement in an Environmental Dispute in Guangdong," *Asia Pacific Viewpoint* 47, no. 2 (August 2006): 195–216.

Wang, Weiguo. " 'Guangdong renda xianxiang' yu 'haidian renda xianxiang' bijiao" [Comparing the "Guangdong peonomenon" and the "Haidian phenomenon"], *Renda yanjiu*, no. 5 (2006).

Xia, Ming. *The Dual Developmental State: Development Strategy and Institutional Arrangements for China's Transition*. Ashgate: Aldershot, 2000.

Xia, Ming. "Political Contestation and the Emergence of Provincial people's Congresses as Power Players in Chinese Politics: A Network Explanation," *Journal of Contemporary China* 9, issue 24 (2000): 185–215.

Xia, Ming. *The People's Congresses and Governance in China: Toward a Network Mode of Governance*. New York: Routledge, 2008.

Xie, Puding. "Difang renda fazhi jianshe he zhidu chuanxin" [Rule of law development and system innovation of the local people's congress]. In *Difang de fuxing, difang zhili gaige 30 nian* [Bring the local back in: Reform and changes of China local governance since 1978], edited by Yang Xuedong et al. Beijing: Social Science Academy Press, 2009.

Xu, Shiqun, et al., eds. *Difang renda jiandu gongzuo yanjiu* [Research on local people's congress supervision work]. Beijing: Zhongguo minzhu fazhi chubanshe, 2005.

Yang, Ming, ed. *Huannjing wenti yu huanjing yishi* [Environmental awareness and perceptions]. Beijing: Huaxia chubanshe, 2002.

Yu, Jianrong. "Zhongguo xinfang zhidu pipan" [Critique of China's letters and visits system] (based on a speech at Beijing University 2004). *Zhongguo gaige*, issue 2 (2005).

Yu, Jianrong. "Dui xinfang zhidu gaige zhenglun de fansi" [Reflections on the debate on the letters and visit system reform], *Zhongguo dangzheng ganbu lunyun*, no. 5 (2005).

Yu, Jianrong. "Ba xinfang jigou jizhong dao ge ji renda" [Concentrate the letters and visit body to people's congresses at all levels], *Nanfang zhoumo* (May 21, 2009): 31.

Zou, Pingxue. *Zhongguo daibiao zhidu gaige de shizheng yanjiu* [Research evidence of China's representative system reform]. Chongqing: Chongqing chubanshe, 2005.

6

From Nothing to Something

Development of a Legal Aid System in China

HATLA THELLE

Law is made to serve a society that is formed of government, community, and individuals. In this way, ordinary citizens themselves become active players in efforts to make law effective, both as users and as enforcers. To make law work is a complicated process that involves making, enforcing, and using law in a dynamic interaction in which the makers are also the enforcers and users. In this interaction enforcers influence makers, and users force makers and enforcers to adapt legislation or change their practices. These interacting movements result in implementation, which can be more or less successful, that is, more or less effective in achieving the goal of a certain law or regulation, which in turn is shaped by problems in society. Other chapters in this book describe the role of different actors such as legislative bodies, the courts, the Communist Party, and the media in relation to implementation; this chapter discusses legislation made to secure citizens' access to the legal system in order to solve their problems or to defend themselves against violations perpetrated by state organs or other citizens. The topic here is implementation of a law that is made to guarantee implementation of other laws. This chapter first describes the situation in terms of legislation and practice, then the statistics and possibilities of measuring outcome will be discussed, followed by an analysis of the problems of implementation in this case.

In 2003 an administrative regulation was adopted, stipulating that a system of legal aid institutions be set up in all localities to provide poor people with the "necessary" legal services to protect their rights. This has been done in a great majority of counties so the stipulation has been complied with, in a formal sense. However, relatively few people have access to legal aid and few funds have been allocated to provide this service when compared to the area's estimated needs and those of international standards. While the immediate consequence of the regulation is that institutions are gradually being set up across the country and local regulations put in place, the wider outcome is that many poor people still have to rely on their own resources to defend their rights and interests. The reasons for the still weak protection mainly lie in the lack of allocated funding, the design of the regulation, as well as in the attitude of the most important group of professionals, i.e., the lawyers.[1]

A New Policy

The goal of establishing a system to help poor people gain access to justice in China was formulated in official circles in 1994 and found its current form in the Legal Aid Regulation (LAR) in 2003, which is the core document in this study. According to Article 1 of the LAR: "This regulation is formulated in order to ensure that citizens with financial difficulties obtain the necessary legal services and to promote and standardize legal aid work." The system to reach this goal has evolved gradually during the last decade; the vision behind the policy as it is expressed in official rhetoric is linked to legal, social, and economic concerns. The system developed from scratch, which is stressed as important by policymakers.[2] It is said to be an objective necessity in the development of China's socialist market economy and establishment of the rule of law; a further im-

---

[1] See Håkan Hydén's discussion of will, knowledge, and capacity, Chapter 3 in this volume.

[2] An often used phrase is "from nothing to something," or "from small to big."

petus is that many advanced countries in the world have such a system in place.[3] The arguments for the policy are formulated as follows: (1) the regulation serves to realize the constitutional principle of equality before the law; (2) it guarantees social justice and helps to complete the social security system; and (3) it promotes progress in social civilization.[4] In other words the emphasis on legal aid during this period is caused by the policy of realizing rule of law, of establishing a comprehensive system of social security, and of securing social order. These three aims are of course connected. The growing social inequality caused by the economic reforms leads to frustration and social unrest, which in turn can be eased by an effective system for access to justice organs. In the end the stability of the regime is at stake, and the regime has to do something to lead frustrations and discontent into formal channels.

New Regulations

The Chinese authorities announced the intention to draft a national legal aid policy for poor people in 1994,[5] as mentioned above, preceded by unofficial steps from the early 1990s when law faculties at universities began to establish legal aid centers, beginning in Wuhan in 1992.[6] The legalization process followed the well-known path

---

3 Gong Xiaobing, *Zhongguo falü yuanzhu zhidu. peixun jiaocheng* [The legal aid system in China. Training lectures] (Beijing: Zhongguo jiancha chubanshe, 2002), 26.

4 *Zhongguo falü nianjian 2004* [Law Yearbook of China 2004] (Beijing: Zhongguo falü nianjian she), 541.

5 Then minister of justice Xiao Yang officially proposed the establishment of a legal aid system on March 1, 1994. See "Legal Aid Chronicle of Events," *Renmin Ribao*, September 8, 2004. For development of the legal profession and legal services for the poor before the mid-1990s, see Benjamin L. Liebman, "Legal Aid and Public Interest Law in China," *Texas International Law Journal* 34, no. 2 (1999): 215–219.

6 Francis Regan, "Legal Aid in China: An Analysis of the Development of

of experimenting, studying and summing up experiences, convening national forums, drafting local regulations, setting up new institutions, publishing national circulars and decisions. During the first two years, different models with different distribution between public and private responsibility were experimented in Guangzhou, Beijing, Shanghai, Zhengzhou, Wuhan, and other big cities. At the same time notably mass organizations such as the Women's Federation and some universities outside the fields of responsibility of the Ministry of Justice system began offering legal aid services.

National Level Regulations

After evaluating results of the experiments, the basic principles surrounding the institutional setup were put in place in early 1997. The National Legal Aid Center (NLAC) was established within the Ministry of Justice, and the Legal Aid Foundation (LAF) was set up in May.[7] The following years saw the establishment of many local legal aid centers. Other legal developments at the time underpinned the building up of legal aid mechanisms, notably the promulgation of a revised Criminal Procedure Law (CPL) and a Lawyers Law (LL), both went into effect on January 1, 1997. Article 34 of the revised CPL stipulated that if the defendant is a minor, deaf, blind, mute, or facing a possible death sentence, the court has to provide defense counsel if the defendant has not hired a lawyer. In other cases the court may appoint a lawyer if the judge finds it appropriate. According to Article 42 of the LL, lawyers are obliged to provide legal aid for free upon request from the local bar association or legal aid center. The CPL and the LL are normally quoted as the basic sources of the administrative regulations governing the legal aid system, and

---

Policy," *Civil Justice Quarterly* 24, no. 3 (July 2004): 175. The first center in Wuhan was called Wuhan University Center for Protection of the Rights of Disadvantaged Citizens, and the Ford Foundation funded it.

    7 The aim of the Legal Aid Foundation was to raise funds for legal aid from various social forces and propagate its cause.

the local regulations refer explicitly to them. Regulations for special groups were also set up during this period, for example, the Law on Protection of Interests of Senior Citizens, in effect since October 1, 1996, stipulated that the elderly who could not defend their interests because of economic difficulties could get legal aid. Legal aid in labor cases was addressed later in the Circular of November 6, 2004, titled, "Solving Problems of Delaying Payment of Construction Fees and Workers Salaries in the Construction Area." This circular, promulgated jointly by the Ministry of Justice and Ministry of Construction, urges lawyers to represent migrant workers in collecting back salary. In 2005 a similar provision was included in the revised Law on Protection of Rights and Interests of Women.

With the basic design in place, local governments began to adopt legal aid regulations first from Guangdong Province in August 1999, followed by those in other provinces. At least half of the provinces had adopted local regulations before the national regulations were adopted by the State Council with effect from September 1, 2003. At that point the relevant organs such as the justice bureaus and local procuratorates began immediately to promulgate the legal aid regulations through conferences, media coverage, and training classes. They stipulated that local justice bureaus establish legal aid institutions from county level and above, and that these institutions would be responsible for supervising and managing all legal aid activities within their area. The bureaus shall receive and examine applications from citizens and provide defendants with defense counsel upon request by the courts. Local lawyers associations shall assist with legal aid work, and the state encourages social organizations and institutions to participate.

Important in all systems of legal aid across the globe are the questions of *who* could apply, and in *what* situations one would be eligible for free legal services. In the Chinese LAR in principle anyone can apply for legal aid, provided they are poor and their rights or interests have been violated. These two facts have to be backed by documentation, and the identity of the applicant verified by valid identification. It is the prerogative of the local authorities to define the level of being "poor"; a level that is not lower than the minimum living standard (MLS) for the region.[8] Regarding the scope of coverage, the LAR lists six kinds of civil cases in which legal aid can be applied for by citizens. These include

1. claims for state compensation in accordance with the law;
2. claims for social security payments or minimum living guarantee payments;
3. claims for pensions for the disabled or bereaved or welfare payments;
4. claims for payments for the support of parents, child support, or alimony;
5. claims for labor remuneration; or
6. matters in which they are advocating civil rights and interests that arise as a result of actions taken in the interest of justice.

The local authorities are allowed to broaden the scope but they may not narrow it further. In criminal cases the legal aid centers shall provide legal aid when the court appoints defense counsel for a defendant, which it is obliged to do—as mentioned above—in cases where the defendant is minor, blind, deaf, mute, or facing a death penalty charge, and which it can do in other cases where the defendant does not retain a lawyer for economic reasons.

Local Level Regulations

The local regulations adopted both before and after the summer of 2003 are almost identical to the national regulation. Fifteen provincial regulations have been studied for this chapter, those of Guang-

---

[8] The MLS is a social security measure. The local government sets a standard, normally CNY 200–300 a month. See the Ministry of Civil Affairs website http://www.mca.gov.cn for precise figures. If the average income of persons in a household is below the standard, the family will receive a subsidy from the state.

dong (1999), Guangxi (2004), Henan (2002), Hubei (May 2003), Hunan (2002), Jiangsu (2005), Liaoning (2004), Ningxia (2006), Shandong (2001), Shanxi (November 2003), Shaanxi (2001), Sichuan (2001), Xinjiang (2004), Yunnan (2001), and Zhejiang (2005). The years in parentheses indicate the versions read during the study. Many places adopted legal aid regulations prior to July 2003 and then amended or reissued them after the adoption of the national regulation by the State Council in that month.

The margins for local discretion are not wide, or at least they are not widely used. The basic concepts of local regulations are defined in almost the same. One example is the Xinjiang regulations that were adopted as late as April 2006. According to these regulations legal aid is defined as the process by which a legal aid entity organizes, guides, and coordinates legal aid personnel (lawyers, notaries, and legal workers) to secure the reduction or exemption of fees for legal services for the poor or people in special circumstances. Legal aid organizations according to the Xinjiang regulations are law firms, notaries, and county legal service offices. A legal aid center (LAC) is established and entrusted with the following tasks: to draw up plans for providing legal aid; to organize and supervise all legal aid work in the region; to educate legal aid personnel; to designate personnel at the request of the court; to collect and administer legal aid funds; and to disseminate knowledge about the legal aid system to the public. The LAC has a supervisory function in relation to the law firms and basic-level legal services offices, in which these two offices are obliged to provide service to the centers. It is not mandatory to set up a center according to the LAR but most provinces seem to have done so. If no center is set up, the above-mentioned tasks rest with the justice bureau. Legal aid regulations encourage social groups, including organizations such as the Women's Federation and the Youth League, to participate in the provision of services and be rewarded for their contributions. There are no strict demands on what qualifications are required for people to serve as advisors. For example, regulations in Ningxia stipulate that people "with legal knowledge" could participate as advisors but they would have to register as volunteers with the local legal aid centers. Legal aid services provided by social groups and volunteers are supervised, guided, and coordinated by the local legal aid centers.

Although it is mandatory for the LAC to designate a lawyer when the court asks for one, request for a lawyer is made directly by the applicant. As mentioned above, the localities not only could broaden the scope of situations in which people can apply for legal aid, they also set the standard for financial affordability. Most localities allow a few more situations in the scope for acceptance than does the national regulation; most mention occupational injury, traffic accidents, and health disputes, and some include incidents of domestic violence. Liaoning Province has a provision related to pollution and public health and safety, while the Ningxia regulations provides for cases relating to accidents that involve farm tools and pesticides. The City of Jiayuguan in Gansu Province includes a point on issues linked to personal property.

Most localities set the standard for financial difficulty at the level of the local minimum standard of living, which means that few people could apply for legal aid. Some localities choose a slightly higher standard, and some submit to individual means testing so a fixed ceiling will not always be applied. It is also quite common to name certain groups as "natural" beneficiaries of legal aid services, this applies mostly to the disabled or the elderly. For example, the Jiangsu regulations name specific vulnerable groups who automatically are entitled to legal aid. These include disabled persons or persons without close relatives to support them. The Beijing Municipality in 2008 adopted a new regulation incorporating migrant workers as one such group, which means the migrant workers do not need to document economic hardship in order to be eligible for legal aid.

All in all there are no significant variations among the localities or when local regulations differ from the national rule. Some localities are more lenient than others on admission but not enough to really solve emerging problems with the entire establishment of legal aid centers.

The system described above portrays an interesting characteristic on legislation and law implementation in China. Experiments were conducted; institutions were established; and local regulations were adopted before the national regulations were promulgated. Several legal documents—from ministerial decrees to State Council regulations—built upon each other and gradually developed the principles that were then confirmed in a document with national application, probably to form the basis of a law in due time.

Legal Aid in Practice

Even though the LACs run by the Ministry of Justice are not predominant in terms of funding and human resources, the system is supposed to have an important function as coordinator and supervisor of legal aid activities in general. It is through the LACs that the state lives up to its obligation as expressed in Article 3 of the LAR, "Legal aid is the responsibility of the government." The state-run centers function both as direct organizers of legal aid activities and to guarantee that other centers provide free legal services and provide them in the right way. Many local regulations include an article on ethics and correct behavior, such as lawyers must abide by codes of conduct of the profession, or confidentiality rules shall be observed. Interviews conducted with legal aid center personnel did not yield the practical definition of the terms, "coordinate," "guide," "organize," or "supervise." Most staff members would focus on the word "guide" and stress that it is not a hierarchical relationship but an exchange between equal partners for mutual benefit. To illustrate how the relationship between the LACs and other entities providing legal aid manifests itself in practice, different institutions and settings visited during the spring and summer of 2006 will be described.

The following examples from a rural county and one city district are based on interviews and visits conducted in 2006 in the Beijing municipality and in Shaanxi Province. The institutions visited were selected to include local legal aid centers, social organizations, and university clinics based in both urban and rural areas. The situation concerning legal aid in the big coastal cities is interesting because their organization points in the direction of what the policy can be expected to develop into in the future, but it is also necessary to visit the economically backward areas to get a sense of the gaps between rich and poor areas. Institutions in the big urban centers were much more accessible but it was difficult to gain access to rural areas. The choice of examining Beijing and Shaanxi was based on a desire to compare an economically developed region such as the political center of China with a backward rural area, while relying on previously established contact persons since personal choice and access to field sites may be difficult without such contacts.[9] Apart from questions about number, procedures, etc., the study focused on how the different organizations cooperate at the local level and how the ministerial system plays its role.

Rural County

In Hua County, a farming area of Shaanxi Province,[10] the different organs available to provide legal aid counseling were small in size and close in proximity, providing a miniature picture of the system as such. The county had a population of 360,000, and its government was placed in the center of the county town along a muddy road. The offices that were allowed to provide legal aid services consist of one letters and visits office, one legal center, two law firms, and two basic-level legal service offices. Just outside the gate of the

---

9   As is well known to social scientists doing fieldwork in China the researcher is not free to choose just any site. Within the criteria of finding a poor area I had to choose among places which I could gain access to through existing contacts and this explains why Shaanxi and not another poor place was selected.

10   Hua County is not a leading example or well known among researchers. The choice of this county came through the personal connections of my collaborator. The information noted here was obtained during a visit to the county on March 20–21, 2006.

government compound and to the left, the county letters and visits office[11] was housed in a small building with two or three rooms that were furnished to receive visitors. On the opposite side of the street was the legal aid center, with a room to receive visitors. The two law firms were located within a three-minute walk down the street, one on each side of the street. The two basic-level legal service offices and the headquarters of the county party committee were in a large three-story building. This building also housed the local branches of the Women's Federation, the Youth League, and the Trade Union, where people could come to their offices at designated hours and receive counseling. On the first floor by the entrance was the letter and visits office of the local party committee, where staff members would receive visitors every Monday morning.

The letters and visits office in front of the compound is run by the government and had been there since the 1950s. The petitioning system of letters and visits is practiced nationwide but it is not an effective practice and the services it provides do not fall under the category of legal aid. It is mentioned here as it provides another channel through which poor people could claim their rights and because the close proximity of the two offices (county and local) meant that the staff from either office referred clients to each other. The letters and visits office would receive complaints from individuals or groups of people and transfer the complaints to the relevant authorities. Its staff comprised administrative personnel with no special training. It usually did not follow through the cases it received and its actions have no legal implications.[12]

The LAC facing the government compound was set up in September 2005 under the aegis of the county justice bureau, and it had four full-time staff members. These were not law graduates but had been given a license to work as legal workers through a special training for justice bureau personnel in the local government. Thus

---

11 Part of the petitioning system mentioned below.
12 For discussion of the system as such see Minzer (2006) and Yu Jianrong (2005).

they belonged to the category of legal service personnel and basic-level legal workers mentioned earlier. The establishment of the LAC was based on the State Council LAR in 2003. From 2003 to 2005 a legal aid office in the justice bureau had three people who received cases and transferred them to law firms in the town if the applicants could prove that they were unable to pay for a lawyer themselves. The current LAC does the same kind of work, but the legal workers could also solve cases if they are not complicated. This LAC had formally accepted fourteen cases in the six-month period since its establishment in September 2005 until March 2006, when the director of the LAC was interviewed; nine of these cases were civil cases, five were criminal cases.

The two law firms down the street worked mostly on commercial terms, and they employed eight lawyers total, five in one and three in another. These eight were the only lawyers in the county so in addition to their normal activities they had to take in legal aid criminal cases assigned by the court since the basic service office did not accept criminal cases. This was possible as there were only about six criminal cases each year where the defendant was eligible for legal aid. The county court dealt with six hundred to seven hundred cases each year and only 1 percent of these were legal aid cases. The two basic-level legal service offices also employed a total of eight people who were licensed legal workers, like the ones in the LAC. The basic service offices are the lowest organs in the judicial pyramid. Legal aid workers there provide cheap services in civil cases; the workers could also receive cases from the LAC in the same manner as does the law firms.

All these units were connected in different ways, and more or less formally. The LAC had a leading role over the basic service offices and could demand that they take in cases. The LAC staff also had the cooperation of the letter and visits offices, the Women's Federation, or the Association for Disabled People and for Senior Citizens. In the offices of the LAC was a center for women and children, run jointly by the Women's Federation and the LAC. The LAC benefits from the Women's Federation being present in all villages when they wished to address cases such as domestic violence, and the Center staff could benefit from the Women's Federation's position in the party committee building in relation to access to contacts and dissemination of information. Reciprocally, legal aid workers trained women cadres in legal issues. These cadres would then send cases to the LAC if women who were eligible for legal aid contacted them. Even though the LAC here is new and small it is part of a larger network of mechanisms and institutions that are close to each other both geographically and socially. In judging the effectiveness of the LAC one has to include the other organs and their procedures, which together create a kind of safety net for poor people in trouble. The coverage though is still deemed to fall short of the demand, as will be discussed later.

City District

A city district is administratively on the same level as a county, which represents the next lowest level in the state apparatus. The Haidian district LAC in Beijing is the subject of discussion here.[13] There are 2.4 million people living in the district, and the local LAC has a staff of ten. At the time of research there were 177 law firms in the district. The LAC occupied the same building as the district prosecution services and its staff patronized the same cafeteria as the prosecutors. In spite of an agreement on mutual cooperation, there seemed to be no close links or collaboration between the two organs other than their sharing of a target group. The LAC ran a hotline and a website through which people could contact them directly to receive preliminary advice. In 2005 the center accepted 743 cases, of which 370 were criminal, 372 civil, and 1 was administrative. The scope of cases had been broadened by the Beijing Munici-

---

13 Note that this district, as the university area of the capital, is one of the most advanced in the country. The district LAC handled the most cases in the city in 2004 (*Haidian Bao*, August 10, 2005, 1). The information given here comes from an interview on March 29, 2006.

pal LAC, which in February 2005 issued a notice that three kinds of cases should be added to the six mentioned in the national regulation as stated above (see list on page 192). It is possible now for people to apply for legal aid in cases related to work injury, traffic accidents, and domestic violence because reports from the district centers in Beijing Municipality identified these kinds of problems as serious for poor citizens. In addition, migrant workers also became eligible for legal aid without means testing. There seems to be a national consensus to include these categories and groups of clients as these categories appear in other areas where the local government has chosen to broaden the scope.

Under the district level are the street-level offices and community-level offices. Twenty-nine working stations responsible for legal aid at the street office level. Most of these are housed in one of the street offices, but some are attached to mass organizations such as the Women's Federation and the Association for Disabled People. Each station has at least three staff members. They receive legal aid applications to pass along to the district level offices for approval and they offer legal counseling and representation in court in civil cases. They are economically independent, and their fees are relatively low, except when they are assigned legal aid cases from the district and will have to work for free. At the community level below the street offices the LAC appoints a contact person who often will be the head of the mediation committee. This person will transfer cases upward in the system if mediation fails and the client qualifies for legal aid. In theory people can approach a low-level office at the community or street level and gradually be directed to the right place. However, only the district LAC can approve applications for legal aid so if people apply through a lower organ for such aid, this organ will have to get permission from the district level. There is a small fee paid to the law firm for legal aid cases; in Beijing this fee is set at CNY 800 for civil cases and CNY 500 for criminal cases. The district legal aid center pays the fee to the law firm, but since it is not enough to cover the actual expenses associated with handling a case, the lawyers work the remainder of the case for free.

Apart from cooperation with the offices at the lower levels, the district LAC also cooperates laterally with the offices of the prosecutor, the police, the government, universities, and law firms. In May 2004 agreements were signed between the district justice bureau (which supervises the LAC) and the district prosecution services, police, and court, respectively, spelling out procedures for the interaction between these organs and the LAC. In these agreements it is stipulated that meetings between the organs shall be held twice a year. All parties commit themselves to conduct investigations, analyze typical cases, and exchange experiences. Furthermore the LAC has agreements with 54 of the 177 law firms in the district that are willing to handle cases accepted for legal aid. Similar agreements are signed with selected universities. The LAC transfers special cases not eligible for legal aid to the legal aid units at participating universities, in turn the university units will send the LAC cases they deem to qualify for legal aid. The district LAC signs agreements on different matters with different universities: with Peking University Law School they have established a so-called Legal Aid Research Center to better combine theory and practice. The university center researches representative cases and provides the LAC with suggestions and advice. The LAC also works with the Women's Federation, the Trade Union, the Association for Disabled People, which all at the street, community and district levels appoint a liaison officer responsible for legal aid work.

It appears from interviews with staff of legal aid centers that the cooperation with police and prosecutors is not as close or productive as cooperation with universities and mass organizations. However, these formal agreements demonstrate recognition on the part of state authorities that individual rights and interests need a voice and a channel into the legal system. Not surprisingly, the coverage in the city district is much wider than in the poor county. There are more lawyers in relation to the population as well as more support of volunteers in university settings and civil society organizations.

Nonstate Level

According to Articles 7 to 9 of the Legal Aid Regulations social forces are encouraged and supported in taking part in legal aid work through measures adopted by the justice bureaus.[14] The two organizations outside the government sector discussed here represent two different kinds of institutions that provide legal aid or similar services to vulnerable groups of the society.[15] One is a university-based organization advocating women's rights and the other is a small independent group working to protect the rights of migrant workers.

In Xi'an, Shaanxi Province, the Center for Women's Development and Rights of Northwestern Polytechnical University was established in 2000, and its work was to research the rights of female workers.[16] The goal was to promote gender equality through networking, research, and combining research and practical work, including handling individual or collective cases for free. Since the center aspired to influence legislation and administrative practice, they only took cases they thought could have a broader impact in society, and in these cases they would do everything for free. Analysis of the cases helped to handle future ones and was used as mate-

---

14 In a Chinese context "social forces" refer to groups, individuals, or businesses that are not part of the state apparatus. The term carries an air of charity or voluntary donation, but the activities can be quite orchestrated by for instance local government organs.

15 Several organizations of this kind are discussed elsewhere: see Liebman, "Legal Aid and Public Interest Law in China," 248–250; Peter Ho, "Greening Without Conflict? Environmentalism, NGOs and Civil Society in China," *Development and Change* 32 (2001): 908; Mary Hennock, "Legal Aid for China's Workers," *BBC News Online*, October 15, 2003; *China Development Brief*, November 14, 2004.

16 The staff of the center was interviewed on March 22, 2006.

rial in training legal aid workers and volunteers. There were about twenty scholars, lawyers, and activists affiliated with the center, and they worked closely with the Women's Federation, in particular, and the All-China Federation of Trade Unions. The volunteer lawyers conducted training for young people and laid-off women on employment rights and helped them to cooperate with other organizations. The Center was funded by the Ford Foundation[17] and Oxfam, Hong Kong. It rented office space on university grounds but receive no support from the university except for the protection implicit in being housed by the university. The municipal and district legal aid centers allocated cases to the center. In such instances the center received CNY 300 per case, which is the rate set by the Xi'an justice bureau. Apart from this payment there were no special links between the LAC and the work done by the university center for protection of women's rights.

In a Beijing village a small group of young migrant workers has set up an office to help and support migrant workers in the area.[18] The group is also partly funded by international donors. It uses music and street theater as tools for raising awareness and also offers legal counseling for migrant workers who have conflicts with their employers. Three full-time staff members organize courses for volunteers in ways of helping construction workers and maids from outside Beijing to know and claim their rights. The philosophy of this group is to educate people in order to help themselves so the courses offer some legal knowledge, some discussion techniques, some psychology, and more practical skills such as how to use the

---

17 The Ford Foundation has since 2002 been very active in funding legal aid institutions at Chinese universities. The centers combine legal counsel with an educational purpose in so-called legal clinics. Students perform counseling supervised by teachers. In 2006 there were more than thirty-six of these kinds of institutions gathered in a network also supported by the foundation. The Xi'an center described above is a bit special in that it does not use legal aid activities in an educational context.

18 The group has been visited several times in the period 2004–2006, and talks have been conducted with staff and volunteers.

Internet. The volunteers are partly young students from institutions of higher learning in Beijing and partly migrant workers themselves. They are recruited through word of mouth and through the media as the activities of the group are publicized in newspapers and TV programs. The group cooperates with and gets help from a number of legal scholars and established intellectuals in Beijing. Communications with the LAC of Chaoyang District (where the village is situated), however, is scarce or almost nonexistent, though the group members sometimes use the name "legal aid center" when defending an employee and approaching his/her employer.

The group is active in reaching out to the community in which it lives. It rents former factory buildings in a village where two-thirds of the inhabitants are migrants and it runs a primary school for migrant children in the village. In addition it has facilities for housing a few migrant workers who have become homeless as a result of conflicts with their employers. Being homeless puts the worker in an extremely vulnerable situation, and many workers are hesitant to confront their bosses because they live in quarters provided by the companies they work for. Hence, the group maintains an insightful view of the situations employees might face and looks at every aspect when trying to help its "clients."

The work of the social groups described above is a necessary supplement to the formal legal aid institutions, which cannot answer to the need for advice and support in the face of social or legal problems. However, the contribution is problematic in the way that the individual is not guaranteed full enjoyment of the rights he or she holds. Given the limited resources and leverage the social groups only represent a stopgap measure, better than nothing under the present circumstances. However, according to an understanding shared by members of the groups, a dynamic and vibrant social movement can to a high degree raise issues and put problems on the agenda, which in the long run will benefit the establishment of a more effective system for rights protection.

Development of a Legal Aid System

Two Cases of Legal Aid

The two cases described here show the manner in which different actors are able to facilitate legal assistance, depending on their place in the official hierarchy, their mandate, and their personal capabilities. The different kinds of outcomes and their implications are also discussed.

The first is a LAC case from Shanghai. A Shanghai taxi driver named Wu had terminated his contract with the taxi company and subsequently discovered that it had not contributed as much to the social security fund as he thought it should have. It appeared that there was a discrepancy between the demanded social security contribution stipulated in relevant labor regulations and the minimum contribution noted in the contract he had signed. The driver had no fixed salary as he received compensation only after having paid his contracted sum to the company; thus, it was difficult to document his exact salary. Wu contacted the district LAC to apply for legal aid. His case was accepted. The staff helped him collect and forward relevant documents to the labor arbitration committee of Shanghai. However, the case was lost since the committee believed the company was right and the client was wrong in the interpretation of the relevant legislation. Wu accepted the decision and on top of this had to pay his part of the fee to the arbitration committee.[19]

The second case is from the migrant group in Beijing, a nonstate organization. A twenty-one-year-old girl from Gansu named Fang had been employed for four years at an elevator company. Her family wanted her to return home to get married. When she told the company she wanted to leave, her remaining salary, after deductions, left her with CNY 50! An average salary at that time might have been around CNY 500 a month, therefore CNY 6,000 a year for four years amounted to CNY 24,000. The company had deducted fees for several different things. Fang protested to the district

---

19 Interview Shanghai LAC, April 2005

labor bureau, where she was confronted with a host of questions she could not answer: where the company was registered, who was legally responsible for the company, what was stated in her contract, which telephone number could be used for reaching her boss, etc. At the labor bureau and by accident Fang met a person from the migrant group named Wen who was helping another migrant worker. After hearing her story Wen decided to help her. He phoned the company and pretended to be from a legal aid center. The company accountant first denied having cut the salary, but after persuasion and threats the company agreed to pay Fang an additional CNY 300 so she would have enough money to buy a train ticket home. Fang was in a hurry to return home and was willing to compromise as long as she had enough money for a ticket. Wen had threatened the company with a lawsuit and a big fine if they did not negotiate a solution immediately. There was no doubt that the company had broken the Labor Law, but there was more doubt whether in reality Wen would have succeeded in bringing the company to court, bearing in mind that Fang did not even have a valid contract. In the end the client received enough compensation from the company to save her from her immediate predicament, but she did not get the salary she should have received according to the Labor Law and related regulations.[20]

These two—quite typical—cases show that sometimes "more" can be achieved through nonformal channels than through the established complaint procedures. More money was gained in the Beijing case than in the Shanghai one, and the young girl in Beijing was more content with the "informal" solution to her troubles than the taxi driver in Shanghai was happy with the "formal" solution to his problem. The different outcomes reflect the differing objectives of the two systems. Most cases handled by the nonstate groups are "pragmatic" in the sense that they use different kinds of tactics to solve an immediate problem, but their main concern is to strength-

---

20 Interview with anonymous migrant workers group, Beijing October 2005,

en people's will and self-confidence in the process. Whether justice is done to the letter does not count as much as enabling people to act and fight for their rights.[21] On the other hand the LACs' main objective is to find and try out the formally "correct" avenues, and they care less about whether the client learns anything. If the correct avenues fail, the result will be a disappointed citizen who has lost a bit of faith in the legal system. Both approaches are necessary and beneficial in their own right that they can both exist and survive is a sign of the diversity of Chinese society as it has developed during the last decades.

Statistics

A few words on figures will be necessary to place the legal aid system in its context and illustrate the problem of how to judge whether the demand for legal aid is satisfied.[22] On the one hand there are several important problems in making such a judgment, tempting one not to do it at all; on the other hand one cannot neglect the issue of how many people get what kind of help through the system. How many is already difficult to answer precisely, but even worse is the question of whether the help is sufficient and how to define "the system."[23]

The centers under the Ministry of Justice constitute one part of a wider picture where people who feel wronged can use different

---

21 Mary Gallagher's interesting study from a legal aid center in Shanghai shows how contact with the legal system strengthens people's inclination to interact with it in spite of negative feelings about the efficacy of the implementation of law (Mary Gallagher, "Mobilizing the Law in China: 'Informed Disenchantment' and the Development of Legal Consciousness" *Law & Society* Review, Vol. 40, no. 4, 2006).

22 See also Randall Peerenboom's discussion on official statistics and government information in Chapter 2 of this volume.

23 Again Gallagher, "Mobilizing the Law in China" is relevant here. On defining the system one can take only the narrow focus of the Ministry of Justice legal aid centers or one can take a broader view including all the mechanisms people can turn to when they need to solve a conflict.

channels to obtain compensation or redress, as could be seen in the cases described above. A large group of institutions and units in China today receive complaints and provide legal advice and defense for people who have experienced violations of their rights in different ways or face criminal charges. Some of these channels can be used for free or are very low-cost; hence, they are available to the groups targeted by the legal aid system. Like in any other society in the world most problems and grievances are not solved in the courtroom or even in a consultation setting but are negotiated or mediated between the involved parties, sometimes with the help of a third party, be it a legal professional, a social group, or an administrative unit. People will try different avenues at the same time and use formal as well as informal agents to claim their rights or help their relatives or friends. Some of the means for dispute resolution or problem-solving in China are traditional and even stem from imperial times while others have been newly created and based on modern legal thinking, like the legal aid system.

According to official statistics the development of the ministerial legal aid system has been dramatic, from 133 legal aid centers in 1999 to 3,000 in 2004, and the expenses have followed the development with a rise from CNY 28 million allocated in 1999 to CNY 246 million in 2004.[24] In 2004 legal aid was given in a little more than 190,000 cases (108,000 civil, 79,000 criminal, and a few administrative and notary cases) involving close to 300,000 people, and almost 2 million people received legal advice in the same year. To get advice one need not conform to the poverty standards; in principle anyone could walk into a legal aid center and obtain advice without going through the formalized procedures so the 190,000 cases are those that were accepted through the procedures described in the various regulations. This figure should be considered in relation to

---

24 *Zhongguo nianjian 2005* [Law yearbook of China 2005] (Beijing: Zhongguo *falü* nianjan she), 1079; *Legal Aid and Law Reform in Transitional Societies* (Beijing: Law Institute, Chinese Academy of Social Sciences, 2004), 18 (papers presented at the Second Dongfang Form on Public Interest Litigation).

a number of other figures, and a few examples will be discussed here. In addition to the 190,000 cases accepted by the LACs, more than 100,000 legal aid cases were solved in the offices of the All-China Federation of Trade Unions, All-China Women's Federation, the Youth League, the Association for Disabled People, and the Association for Elderly People.[25] The work of these mass organizations is contained in the annual report of the NLAC, and as such they must be counted as part of the ministerial legal aid system. Other channels for dispute resolution are mediation committees, which solved 4.4 million civil conflicts in 2004, and the petitioning system, which is judged to receive more than 11 million complaints each year.[26] Both these systems offer services for free and are thus potential avenues for people who feel their rights have been violated. There are no formal connections between the LACs and mediation committees or petition offices, but the latter two contribute toward solving problems for people even though their decisions are not legally binding. The different organs could also make use of each other's resources, for example, when the Haidian district LAC reported that liaison officers are appointed at the community level, these officers could also act as heads of the mediation committee.

Local variations are great as they always are in China. A few figures from the cases discussed above illustrate the differences. The Haidian city district in Beijing accepts one *legal aid case* per 3,200 inhabitants, while the rural county of Huaxian takes a case for every 12,800 inhabitants; Haidian district has one *law firm* for every 13,500 persons, while Huaxian has one *lawyer* for every 45,000. But there is more to this comparison. Other channels can be open in the rural areas that are not available in an urban district,[27] and again the han-

---

25 *Legal Aid and Law Reform in Transitional Societies*, 28–29.

26 *Zhongguo falü nianjian 2004*, 1078; Carl Minzer "Xinfang: An Alternative to Formal Chinese Legal Institutions," *Stanford Journal of International Law* 42, no. 103 (2006): 2.

27 See for example Zhu Suli's analysis of how basic-level judges can serve as arbitrators of disputes in the countryside in *Sending Law to the Countryside* (Beijing: University of Politics and Law Publishing House), 176–196.

dling of cases tells us very little about the outcome: was justice achieved in each single case? The measurement of outcome, understood as efficient protection, still has a long way to go.

The number of Ministry of Justice legal aid cases can also be compared in relation to all court cases. In 2004 more than 5 million cases of first instance went through the Chinese courts, of which 4.3 million were civil cases and 647,000 were criminal cases.[28] With regards to *civil* cases the actual need for legal aid is difficult to gauge, but the 108,000 civil cases involving legal aid only made up 2.5 percent of the 4.3 million civil cases that went through the Chinese courts in 2004. As not all civil cases accepted for legal aid go through the courts—they could also go to arbitration or before a mediation committee—the proportion of legal aid cases to civil court cases is actually lower. People engaged in a civil lawsuit might tend to be among the more resourceful numbers of the population, for example, compared to defendants in criminal cases, but the number of inquiries directed at other complaint mechanisms indicates a greater need. The proportion between civil cases in court and conflicts presented in other forums might reflect the fact that most disputes are not solved in the courtroom; so in answering the question of whether there is an unfulfilled need for legal aid in civil cases requires more documentation and comparative research. The daily reports of social problems, however, leave little doubt that people need more help than they can get.

More precise evaluations can be made regarding *criminal* cases. According to the CPL *all* underaged defendants and *all* persons charged with a death penalty crime shall have a lawyer appointed by the court if they do not appoint one themselves. Calculations by the NLAC show that the 39,000 cases appointed by the court in 2004 concerned minors and 25,000 cases were death penalty cases.[29] At the same time we know that 70,000 minors were charged with a crime in the same year and 146,000 received a sentence of five years

---

28 *Zhongguo falü nianjian 2005*, 1064.
29 *Legal Aid and Law Reform in Transitional Societies*, 22.

of imprisonment or more, including the death penalty.³⁰ So 45 percent of the minors and 11 percent of those charged with a serious crime received the help of a lawyer through the legal aid system. For the death penalty category it is hard to gauge need as we do not know how many of the 158,562 serious cases involved the death penalty, but concerning the minors it seems strange that only half of them got a lawyer through the legal aid system. They could have appointed and paid for defense counsel by themselves or through their guardians, but it seems unlikely that only half of them would be able to do so.

Another method of evaluation was suggested by Ben Liebman in 1999. With 85 million people in China living under the low-income line the 300,000 people who got legal aid in 2004 constitute only 3.5 percent of all poor people.³¹ It is difficult to imagine that such a small proportion of poor people were in need of legal aid in a country where income inequality is high and rising, the economic and political structure is under drastic transition, and a serious problem of corruption exists.

Problems in Law Implementation

A range of different problems in reaching the goal of ensuring "necessary legal services" to citizens with financial difficulties through implementation of the LAR is discussed in the Chinese and Western literature and appears from the interviews and case material.

---

30 *Zhongguo falü nianjian 2005*, 1064–1065.
31 The National Bureau of Statistics in 2004 reported that twenty-nine million live under the poverty line of CNY 637 per month, while fifty-six million live between the poverty line and the low-income line of CNY 882 per month. The low-income line roughly corresponds to the "one U.S. dollar a day concept" usually used to define absolute poverty. See *Poverty Statistics in China* (Rural Survey Organization of National Bureau of Statistics, 2004), 3, 7. Liebman also mentions eighty-five million poor people in China, quoting a 1997 source in Liebman, "Legal Aid and Public Interest Law in China," 241.

Some of these concern weaknesses in the legislation, i.e., in the content of the regulations; others relate to implementation of the existing regulations. These two aspects are interrelated in the way that some implementation problems are not directly caused by the wording of the legislation but point back to weaknesses in the basic thinking or "ideology" behind the legislation.

The first problem is with funding. While the regulations demand that local authorities earmark funds for legal aid activities, they do not set a lower limit for the amount of money set aside, neither in absolute nor in relative terms. There are no direct sanctions imposed on local governments who do not set funds aside. The decentralization of funding obligations to lower levels is a general practice of post-reform social policies—of which legal aid officially is a part, as mentioned above—and the distorting consequences of such an approach is also a general phenomenon in China today.[32] The distortion lies in regional differences. A vicious circle is set in motion where governments in poor areas with the biggest need tend to provide poor services to local residents because the government is poor in resources. Governments in poor areas will to a higher degree prioritize expenses that lead to economic development, such as efforts to attract investment, and will naturally have fewer surpluses available to nonproductive activities such as legal aid. On these grounds the central government has in recent years established a redistribution mechanism for legal aid by earmarking a sum of money to be distributed to backward areas. In 2005, CNY 50 million was distributed by the NLAC to subsidize local areas. The NLAC took into account the caseload and the gap between resources and expenditures in each place, and on that basis distributed the extra funds.[33] The National Legal Aid Foundation sup-

---

32 Note for example the disastrous consequences in the educational sector, where even primary schooling becomes an economic problem for poor families. See Hatla Thelle, *Better to Rely on Ourselves* (Copenhagen: NIAS Press, 2004), ch. 7.

33 Interview with National LAC, September 5, 2006.

ports poor areas in various ways, such as arranging for law students from Beijing to serve as interns in remote places. Some local governments also reallocate funds toward legal aid. For example, in Guangdong in 2005, eighty of the poorer counties received CNY 10 million from the provincial government.[34] Total expenditures nationwide in 2006 were CNY 370 million for legal aid,[35] of which 90 percent came from the government.[36] In 2003 it was reported that nongovernmental donations were primarily collected in the rich eastern part of China, and one-third of the provinces did not collect any donations at all.[37] It is not easy to collect donations for this purpose and not likely that it will be much easier in the years to come. State funding has to cover the greater parts of the expenditures.

The second problem is that legal aid centers are set up and funded by the local governments. The staff and the funds of a district or county LAC are controlled by the local people's congress. The local authorities set the price for one legal aid case and pay the LAC the fee that is meant to cover expenses related to the cases. There is usually one fee for criminal cases and one (higher) fee for civil cases, ranging from approximately CNY 300 to 800. Centers are judged on the basis of how many cases they take in and they receive a fee for each prosecuted case. Therefore LACs tend to take in mostly easy cases and cases in which they do not risk coming into conflict with powerful local interests. One LAC also mentioned the conflict

---

34 Interview with Guangzhou LAC, March 8, 2006.

35 Including criminal and civil cases the figure amounts to CNY 0.3 per person in China. The corresponding figure for selected Western countries was between 2.25 dollars in the United States and 26 dollars in the United Kingdom by the mid-1990s. See Edwin Rekosh "Access to Justice: Legal Aid for the Underrepresented," in *Legal Aid and Law Reform in Transitional Societies*, 243. These last figures, however, only cover legal aid in civil cases.

36 *China Daily*, February 6, 2007. The funding has increased more than nineteen times from CNY 19 million in 2000. See *Legal Aid and Law Reform in Transitional Societies*, 18.

37 "Statistical Analysis to the Legal Aid Nationwide in 2003," *Zhongguo Sifa* [Justice of China]: 79–80.

between the desire to avoid litigation on the one hand and the fact that only prosecuted cases will earn them a fee. The government does not subsidize mediated cases.[38]

A third problem is that the conditions for getting legal aid are very strict. The regulations stipulate that economic hardship is defined by the provincial authorities. The normal practice, spelled out in a ministerial circular in December 2003 and repeated in the local regulations, is to set the standard equal to the minimum living standard (MLS) valid in the community, as mentioned above. This standard is low. People with higher income than the MLS can easily have problems hiring a lawyer at their own expense, but they will thus not be able to get free legal services. The grounds for applying for legal aid are also narrow, confined to the kinds of cases mentioned earlier, such as seeking state compensation or claiming missing pensions. Some local LACs have expanded the list a bit, but still there are strict limitations as illustrated below. It is also a significant problem that those who apply for legal aid would have to show valid identity papers. This means that migrant workers who did not receive a temporary permit to stay in the city cannot apply. Unfortunately, migrant workers constitute one of the most vulnerable groups in Chinese society, and many of them could use legal assistance. In criminal cases only a small group of persons is guaranteed defense counsel, such as minors and people facing death penalty. For the rest a proper defense by a competent lawyer does not become a right but only a possibility for those who can pay for it. Further, the mandatory defense counsel is only introduced ten days before the trial, according to Article 151 of the Criminal Procedure Law, leaving an appointed lawyer very little time to prepare an effective defense.

As a fourth point, the whole system rests on the basis of the willingness and capacity of one professional group—the lawyers—to work for free. To force such an obligation on the lawyers does not

---

38 Interview with Chaoyang LAC, March 30, 2006.

ensure commitment and work of good quality.[39] Only lawyers are obliged by law to provide legal aid for free, while other groups such as the social organizations, are only encouraged to contribute to the legal aid cause by way of a moral obligation. As a result the quality of legal aid lawyers tends to be low. Further, they are supervised by a bureaucratic system, not a professional one. Debates on the legal aid system are often focused on the morale of lawyers being low,[40] and ethical codes of lawyers have been adopted by the bar associations, including making demands on lawyers to sacrifice their time. The LAC personnel are mostly bureaucrats so they are not able to supervise the quality of the lawyers' work but confine themselves to exercising quantitative control by insisting that each lawyer takes at least one or two cases a year. Many lawyers are unwilling to take *pro bono* cases and prefer the better income and less trouble of handling commercial cases,[41] and they could even sometimes pay off their obligation to provide legal aid for free. It is also a problem that the fee for a case is the same no matter how much time the lawyers spend on it—again the system works with a disincentive for lawyers to engage seriously in legal aid cases.

Last, many sources complain of the lack of a truly legal basis. The Legal Aid Regulations are only administrative rules and lack the weight of a law passed by the National People's Congress. Most importantly a law would involve obligations of other professional

---

39 The attitude of lawyers toward *pro bono* work is discussed in Ethan Michelson, "The Practice of Law as an Obstacle to Justice: Chinese Lawyers at Work," *Law & Society Review*, 40, no. 1 (2006). Michelson rather categorically characterizes lawyers as "an obstacle to justice." I would not go that far, but most lawyers certainly are not willing to work for free. See also Cai Yongshun and Yang Songcai, "State Power and Unbalanced Legal Development in China," *Journal of Contemporary China* 14, no. 42 (February 2005).

40 Interview at National LAC, September, 2006.

41 Cai Yongshun and Yang Songcai, "State Power and Unbalanced Legal Development in China," *Journal of Contemporary China* 14, no. 42 (February, 2005): 117–134.

groups, like prosecutors and judges, and could involve sanctions for violators, the LARs only cover a limited field of actors and actions.

The Influence of Motives

The motivation behind adopting certain legislations may also complicate their enforcement. The impetus for initiating the new policy of building a system for legal aid came from above, as we have seen, but there is no doubt that the rising tide of social unrest from below created a need among the leadership to find ways to deal with people dissatisfied with the changes in their daily lives and uncomfortable with the corrupt and politically influenced legal system. The occurrence of more and more demonstrations and events during the reform years is well documented, as is the growing awareness of individual rights and legal justice among the population.[42] External actors such as the institutes of higher learning and engaged individuals reacted to the challenges of popular protests by providing channels for complaints and by providing basic legal services, often inspired by foreign experiences.[43] To quote Francis Regan: "China's legal aid reflects the quite common pattern of a combination of bottom-up and top-down initiatives."[44] At the outset was a social problem or many social problems, and government policies were designed to channel these problems into solutions that could be ac-

---

42 *Engaging the Law in China*, eds. Neil Diamant, Stanley Lubman, and Kevin J. O'Brien (Stanford: Stanford University Press, 2005); *Rightful Resistance in Rural China*, eds. Kevin O'Brien and Linjiang Li (Cambridge: Cambridge University Press, 2005); Ethan Michelson, "The Practice of Law as an Obstacle to Justice: Chinese Lawyers at Work," *Law & Society Review* 40, no. 1.

43 Notice the important role played by the American Ford Foundation mentioned earlier. The Asia Foundation and Canadian International Development Agency (CIDA) have also been very active in supporting the ministerial system.

44 Regan, "Legal Aid in China," 174.

cepted by the people, thereby promoting social stability and support of the existing regime. The connection between legal aid and social stability is mentioned in too many official writings to deny that establishing law and order was an important motive for the legislators.[45] In fact there are signs that the political will to help poor people access the justice sector is not very strong or at least decision-makers are ambivalent toward the endeavor. The international media has cited numerous cases of harassment of lawyers who try to help poor villagers from being relocated or protesting against illegal appropriation of collective property. In many cases protecting local authorities prevails over seeking justice for ordinary people, especially those living in the countryside.[46] This leads one to assume that the leadership is wary of allowing too much latitude in individuals' claiming of rights and that such ambivalence may be the result of meager funds allocated toward providing legal aid at the local level. Funding for legal aid measures has to compete with funding for a host of other social services and all of them in fact seem to receive too little. New norms among the people have forced the authorities to act, and they looked to the world around them to find solutions. The legal aid system in making is influenced by similar systems around the globe; there is basically just one special Chinese characteristic, that is, that the obligation to do *pro bono* work is a legal obligation contained in the Lawyer's Law, a requirement not found in many other places.

---

45 One example among many is Jiang Jianfeng, "Legal Aid's Functions in Maintaining Social Stability and Its Realization," *Zhongguo Sifa* [Justice of China], no. 4 (2005).

46 See for example *Xinhua*, January 30, 2007, where government officials are urged to treat farmers' petitions concerning land confiscations with respect. *China Daily*, January 30, 2007, reported that workers' claims for delay in wage payments and other problems are drawn out when "rich people delay the proceedings." I read the official demand to treat farmers with respect and complaints about wage delays as proof that this is really a serious problem.

Law Implementation as Attainment of Goals

In judging whether law works in our discussion, it is necessary to differentiate between problems with the law itself and problems with implementation of the law, understood here as the realization of various articles in the Legal Aid Regulations. It has been shown above that there are many problems with the regulations. To focus on whether these regulations are correctly implemented is not sufficient to judge whether the goal of the law is met. Regulatory law is probably an exception in being highly instrumental in forcing people or institutions to do things they would normally not do, instead of preventing them from doing things.[47] Different obstacles to an *effective* implementation are interconnected, for example, in that text of the law presupposes the cooperation of key actors such as lawyers without providing them with sufficient incentives to comply with these orders. When they do not comply it constitutes both a problem of the text and of the implementation. The text itself taken at face value might seem to enable a policy that would lead to the goal, but reality shows something different, and one has to return to the text or the commands and change these.

The LAR mandates an administrative organ to "guide" and "coordinate" legal aid work, but the exact content for guiding and coordinating seems unclear, as is the mandate of the LACs in relation to other actors providing legal aid. The local LACs do not seem to be keen in monitoring or controlling legal aid activities; on the other hand they do not seem to be able to mobilize substantive resources from outside their own system as charity funds are hard to come by. The relation with the semigovernmental legal aid conducted by the mass organizations seems to be close and based on equality and mutual benefit. The truly nongovernmental legal aid providers like the group of migrants do not see the LAC as an important player in their work. They do not receive support from the LAC in funding or in encouragement. In fact they do not have much

---

47 See Håkan Hydén, Chapter 3 in this volume.

contact except in special cases coming from the relatively rich Beijing district of Haidian. If the intent is for the local government to help expand the scope of services, the system fails because of lack of incentives in mobilizing civil society. The LACs have no resources to encourage alternative players and do not possess the means to impose sanctions if the quality of the work provided by lawyers is not up to standard. The general impression is that the legal aid system is not a politically strong actor; the small scope of situations where legal aid can be provided, scarce financial resources, and lack of effective sanctions all point to a weak organ, reflecting the traditionally low esteem of lawyers in Chinese society. The disrespect for lawyers is most clearly seen in the field of handling criminal cases. It is common knowledge that the "equality of arms" between the defense and the prosecution during the investigation and trial process is unbalanced in favor of the prosecution. Lawyers are most often unable to meet clients in private; they could only access materials the prosecutors allowed them; and numerous other kinds of obstructions stand in the way of an effective defense counsel. Coupled with the inherited socialist principle that state interests reign supreme over individual interests these factors together all paint the picture of strong norms against helping poor people claim their rights. A change is underway, but the boat has barely left the harbor.

The law is quite clear on where the burden will finally land. It basically protects the interests of a group of vulnerable people by forcing another group, the lawyers, to work for free; in other words it creates a legal obligation based on a moral idea of charity and mutual help. This moral obligation in legal disguise could maybe serve as a "clear and consistent rule" but its legitimacy is weak. As a consequence the help given becomes insufficient in quantity and quality because many (and probably the more qualified) of the lawyers do not accept this moral obligation. The trends in development of the law profession in China point in different directions. On the one hand lawyers are forced to fight for survival in private business; there are few financial rewards in handling impact litigation; it can be risky to defend poor people, especially in labor disputes;[48] and lawyers are generally unwilling to represent defendants in criminal cases.[49] On the other hand a whole new vocabulary and attitude is being born, signaling new ways of thinking and acting. The phrase "to protect lawful rights and interests" is widely used in all official and popular writings. Sociologists propose "sending" law down to the basic level;[50] the concept of barefoot lawyers is well known, and reports of brave lawyers risking life and health to protect citizen's social, civil, or political rights are published by international human rights organizations. External actors such as university students, women activists, or environmental groups are willing to engage in legal aid work. Their actions can in the long run be helpful in supporting the development of a healthy civil society and create new norms of "strategic" or "alternative" lawyering.[51]

Conclusion

The above scenarios present a system where formal and nonformal channels interact closely and public and private actors supplement each other, though in different ways in different localities.

---

48 Michelson, "The Practice of Law as an Obstacle to Justice," 19.

49 Cai and Yong, "State Power and Unbalanced Legal Development in China," 134.

50 Under slogans such as "to send law to the countryside" or "law entering the community." See *Zhongguo falü nianjian 2005*, 783. See also Albert H. Y. Chen, "Socio-legal Thought and Legal Modernization in Contemporary China: A Case Study of the Jurisprudence of Zhu Suli," *Law, Legal Culture and Politics in the Twenty First Century*, eds. Guenther Doeker-Mach and Klaus A. Ziegert (Stuttgart: Franz Steiner Verlag, 2004), 227–249.

51 Expressions from a report of a 1999 legal aid practitioners' forum in Bangkok, *Rule of Law, Human Rights and Legal Aid in Southeast Asia and China* (International Human Rights Law Group and Asian Human Rights Commission, 1999). Strategic lawyering points to the idea of law being an instrument of social change while the meaning of alternative lawyering is the empowerment of the recipients of legal aid.

This interaction is important for securing access to justice for the poor that is backed by the law, albeit in somewhat vague terms. With regards to poor people "obtaining the necessary legal services," the services in the cities seem at first glance to be more varied as there are volunteers and educational institutions and social groups at play, while in the countryside the formal system lack the support of social forces. On closer inspection, rural areas are found to have other, traditional measures for resolving disputes, which are not within the scope of this study so it is not possible to conclude from the data presented here whether poor people in the countryside in reality are less protected than city people.

In implementing a new legal aid policy some of the problems with the law have themselves become problems in implementation, as the practical application of the law clarifies and reflects a weakness in legislation. The failure of local government to set aside *sufficient* funding is actually a problem in implementation, pointing back to the failure in the law to specify exact demands on the local people's congresses when setting budgets. However, if local governments lived up to the "spirit" of the regulation, they would have to set more funds aside. The local people's congresses do set aside funds, but not enough. Similarly, the low quality of the work done by lawyers points back to the fact that they have to work for free, which is written in the regulations. The lawyers, too, do not comply with the "spirit" of the law as they do not put enough effort into the mandatory defense cases. They take the case, as they are obliged to do, but they do not put sufficient energy into the work.

With respect to institution building, it is fair to say that the regulations are implemented or are in the process of being implemented. The number of LACs and people benefiting from legal aid has risen dramatically, as has the amount of funding allocated for the purpose nationwide, especially since the adoption of the LAR in mid-2003. The NLAC has also begun to allocate additional funding for needy areas, introducing or strengthening a redistributive element. Most localities now have local regulations and more are coming. There is a steady increase in people volunteering to provide legal services, and the idea of legal aid for poor people is gaining ground in the public debate, contributing to the transition toward a system based on rule of law.

In sum, the law is ambiguous in certain respects. It involves a plurality of actors, but the relation between them is not clear. The law is clear in other areas, which should be an achievement and meet the criteria of legal certainty, but in these areas it affects the commitment of the key actors in a negative manner. The law stipulates that the expenses related to compliance are put on the shoulders of the local government, while no economic obligation is formally borne by the central government. Article 3 of the LAR admits that legal aid is the responsibility of the government, but in the next sentence delegates the responsibility down to "People's governments at the county level and above," implying that the central level is not economically responsible for implementation but only for regulation. The document thus constitutes an act of decentralization, which is in conformity with government policies in other areas of social security, and which carries the risk of unequal protection of access to justice across the country. Furthermore, decentralization policies allow more room for local protectionism.

The discussion above implies that at stake here are a liberal ideology of charity and not of rights, of a moral obligation instead of an economic incentive, as well as independence from the courts and the demands of market economy. The charity discourse is implicit in the design of the institutional structure and the official explanations of it; so it basically must be viewed as a policymaker top-down discourse, while a rights discourse is emerging from the bottom, as discussed above. The problems of implementation reveal lack of commitment on the part of key actors and lack of sanctions as important elements complicating the process of realizing the goal expressed in Article 1 of the LAR of ensuring poor citizens the necessary legal services. The lack of commitment is mainly caused by lack of incentives; so a focal point for reform of the existing system could be to create more incentives for lawyers and legal workers to live up to the obligation that is put on them.

Bibliography

Cai, Yongshun, and Yang Songcai. "State Power and Unbalanced Legal Development in China," *Journal of Contemporary China* 14, no. 42 (2005): 117–134.

Chen, Albert H. Y. "Socio-legal Thought and Legal Modernization in Contemporary China: A Case Study of the Jurisprudence of Zhu Suli." In *Law, Legal Culture and Politics in the Twenty First Century*, edited by Guenther Doeker-Mach and Klaus A. Ziegert, 227–249. Stuttgart: Franz Steiner Verlag, 2004.

Diamant, Neil, Stanley Lubman, and Kevin J. O'Brien, eds. *Engaging the Law in China*. Stanford: Stanford University Press, 2005.

Gallagher, Mary. "Mobilizing the Law in China: 'Informed Disenchantment' and the Development of Legal Consciousness," *Law & Society* Review 40, no. 4 (2006): 783–816.

Gong, Xiaobing. *Zhongguo falü yuanzhu zhidu. Peixun jiaocheng* [The legal aid system in China. Training lectures]. Beijing: Zhongguo jiancha chubanshe, 2002.

Hennock, Mary. "Legal Aid for China's Workers," *BBC News Online*, October 15, 2003.

Ho, Peter. "Greening Without Conflict? Environmentalism, NGOs and Civil Society in China," *Development and Change* 32 (2001): 893–921.

Jiang, Jianfeng. "Legal Aid's Functions in Maintaining Social Stability and Its Realization," *Justice of China*, no. 4, 2005.

Legal Aid and Law Reform in Transitional Societies (papers presented at the Second Dongfang Forum on Public Interest Litigation, Beijing, December 2004). Beijing: Law Institute, Chinese Academy of Social Sciences, 2004.

Liebman, Benjamin L. "Legal Aid and Public Interest Law in China," *Texas International Law Journal* 34, no. 2 (1999): 211–286.

Michelson, Ethan. "The Practice of Law as an Obstacle to Justice: Chinese Lawyers at Work," *Law & Society Review* 40, no. 1 (2006): 1–38.

Minzer, Carl. "Xinfang: An Alternative to Formal Chinese Legal Institutions.," *Stanford Journal of International Law* 42, no. 103 (2006): 1–69.

O'Brien, Kevin, and Linjiang Li, eds. *Rightful Resistance in Rural China*. Cambridge: Cambridge University Press, 2005.

Regan, Francis. "Legal Aid in China: An Analysis of the Development of Policy," *Civil Justice Quarterly* 24, no. 3 (2004): 169–186.

Rekosh, Edwin. "Access to Justice: Legal Aid for the Underrepresented," *Legal Aid and Law Reform in Transitional Societies* (2004): 53–96.

Rong, Yujian. "Xinfang zhidu diaocha ji gaige silu [Current system of letters and complaints and its reform]." In *Analysis and Forecast on China's Social Development (2005)*, edited by Ru Xin, 212–219. Beijing: Shehui kexue wenxian chubanshe, 2004.

Thelle, Hatla. *Better to Rely on Ourselves*. Copenhagen: NIAS Press, 2004.

Zhongguo falü nianjian 2004 [Law yearbook of China 2004]. Beijing: Zhongguo falü nianjian she, 2005.

Zhongguo falü nianjian 2005 [Law yearbook of China 2005]. Beijing: Zhongguo falü nianjian she, 2006.

Zhu, Suli. *Fa song xiaxiang* [Sending law to the countryside]. Beijing: Zhongguo zhengfa daxue chubanshe, 2006.

Norms, Politics, and the Law

7

Cultural Heritage Protection in the People's Republic of China

Preservation Policies, Institutions, Laws, and Enforcement in Zhejiang

MARINA SVENSSON

Cultural Heritage Issues in China: A Growing Public Debate

Cultural heritage issues have become a hot topic in China in recent years. Many factors explain this development, including increasing state and nonstate activities in the cultural heritage field, a growing interest in Chinese traditions and local history among Chinese citizens, growth in domestic tourism, as well as rapid changes of the Chinese cityscape and rural landscape. Although one needs to acknowledge the Chinese state's increased spending on cultural heritage sites, nobody can be immune to the destruction of the built heritage in many Chinese cities and villages. There is an obvious gap and contradiction between, on the one hand, the official celebration and commercialization of the Chinese heritage, which among other things has led to the building of mock historic structures and, on the other hand, the neglect and outright destruction of authentic historic environments.[1]

---

[1] On Beijing, see e.g., Aurore Merle and Peng Youju, "Peking Between Modernisation and Preservation," *China Perspectives*, no. 45 (January–February 2003): 37–41; and Michael Meyer, *The Last Days of Old Beijing: Life in the Vanishing Backstreet of a City Transformed* (New York: Walker & Company 2008).

The challenges and threats to the built heritage in China are many and varied. They range from poverty, to economic growth, to commercialization and tourism, and to rapid urbanization. The cultural heritage is also threatened by misguided preservation efforts. Some of the problems are institutional in character and related to weak institutions and poor knowledge and understanding among those responsible for cultural heritage protection. The threat to the cultural heritage is also a result of weak laws and poor enforcement. Many Chinese citizens, cultural heritage officials, and legal experts have expressed a strong concern about the weak legal protection and destruction of valuable heritage sites. These issues have been hotly debated in the media and other forums, such as people's congresses and people's political consultative conferences at different levels, leading to increased activity in the legal field. There have been both revisions and amendments of old laws and adoptions of new laws and regulations, as well as efforts by concerned departments and people's congresses to improve supervision and enforcement of existing laws and regulations. The Cultural Heritage Law (CHL) from 1982, the main law in the field, was amended in 2002 in order to adapt it to the current situation and improve protection.[2] In reality, however, legal protection remains quite weak. Many problems continue to persist and new problems have emerged as a result of conflicts between the amended law and other laws and recent policies.

This chapter studies the policies and laws that govern cultural heritage protection, the institutional setup of cultural heritage management, and some of the current problems with implementing laws and regulations.[3] The focus is on both national and local laws, poli-

---

2 A minor revision of the CHL took place in December 2007, see Cultural Heritage Net at http://www.ccrnews.com.cn/100004/100005/15599.html, accessed on February 27, 2008.

3 The sources used for this study include media reports, policy documents, regulations and laws, internal working publications by the State Administration of Cultural Heritage (SACH) and the Zhejiang provincial cultural heritage bureau, as well as academic works. I have also interviewed scholars, officials in the

cies, and institutions, and the interaction between them, using Zhejiang province as a case study.[4] The study surveys relevant laws and institutions with the aim to try to identify and explain both problems and the measures undertaken to address them. It also attempts to identify and highlight factors that explain differences and trends in preservation work, including the role of the political leadership, the role and strength of different institutions, levels of economic development, reforms that have strengthened the administrative and legal power of heritage management institutions, citizen activism, legal awareness, change in norms, and media exposure. It is interesting to study implementation of the CHL because it was amended as recently as 2002, and partly as a response to earlier problems of enforcement. As a result of the amendments, the State Administration on Cultural Heritage (SACH) has worked to strengthen the legal competence and enforcement mechanisms of the cultural heritage bureaus (CHB), resulting in new in-house legal bodies and more legal training of cadres and officials.

Underlying these developments is the emergence of new norms and values in society related to what should be preserved, how, and by whom. The dramatic socioeconomic and ideological changes in Chinese society have led to the construction of new individual and group identities, historical narratives, and memory-making that challenge the earlier revolutionary-nationalistic master narrative. Cultural heritage issues today engage a much more diverse group of people and institutions than in the past, which reflects the growing pluralism in Chinese society. These new groups include ordinary

---

cultural heritage bureaus at different levels, and ordinary citizens, as well as made site visits and attended several conferences in China.

4 My first visit to Zhejiang took place in 1988, and since 2000 I have visited the province on an annual basis. I have conducted interviews with cultural heritage officials at the provincial and local level, local political leaders in some villages and townships, as well as ordinary citizens and scholars. I am very grateful for the help and patience people have shown me throughout the years. Needless to say, I am responsible for any errors, as well as for the interpretation and analysis of the information obtained during my visits.

citizens, professionals in CHBs, city planners, real estate companies, tourism bureaus, and political leaders. Since they have very different views and conflicting interests, problems and conflicts often arise in both the policy- and lawmaking phase and when these policies and laws are to be implemented. The impact of civil society and media is quite striking and distinguishes the cultural heritage field from some of the other cases discussed in this book.[5]

The focus in this study is on the protection of historic buildings and monuments in villages and cities. The reason for limiting the study to the built heritage is because this is a particularly debated and pressing topic in view of China's rapid economic development and urbanization. It also clearly brings out the complex relationship and conflicts that exist between different laws, institutions, and economic and other interests, as well as reveals that cultural heritage protection is related to many other pressing issues in China today, including property rights and land use rights.

Cultural Heritage Management in China:
Institutions, Laws, and Forms of Protection

It is not always easy to understand or grasp the institutional and legal framework for cultural heritage management in China, especially since it is in a state of flux.[6] Cultural heritage work in China is handled by different bodies and at different levels of the state administration. The most important bodies in the cultural heritage field are SACH and the Ministry of Construction, and their equivalents at the provincial, municipal, district, and county levels. Cultural heritage work also involves other departments, such as those

---

5 Civil society and media, however, also play a quite important role in the environmental field, see Almén and van Rooij in this volume.

6 This complaint is also made in *Cultural Heritage Management in China: Preserving the Cities of the Pearl River Delta*, eds. Hilary du Cros and Yok-Shiu F. Lee (London: Routledge, 2007).

responsible for culture, tourism, and religious affairs, as well as those dealing with financial and land issues. The players in cultural heritage work have different administrative status, and they are under both vertical and horizontal jurisdiction. Like other administrative bodies, the CHBs are thus responsible to and dependent on funding from the local government and supervised by people's congresses at the same level.

Cultural heritage law encompasses several different areas, including protection of archaeological sites, preservation of historic structures and the built environment, preservation of the intangible cultural heritage (including folk customs, music, and traditional handicraft), regulations of the arts and antiquities market, regulations of museum work, and the recovery of stolen or illegally obtained antiquities.[7] In many countries one major law covers most of these areas, but cultural heritage protection is also regulated and affected by other laws and regulations, such as laws and regulations concerning land use, city planning, and environmental protection.

The major law related to cultural heritage and preservation work in China is the CHL adopted in 1982 and revised in October 2002. The National People's Congress (NPC) Standing Committee adopted the revised law after four rounds of deliberations. The number of articles increased from thirty-three to eighty, and the new law is not only more detailed but also has a partly new content. In July 2003 the State Council adopted the implementing regulations (*shishi tiaoli*). Discussions on legal weaknesses and problems with enforcement, as well as recent findings from NPC investigation missions and media reports, had fed into the debate and work to revise the

---

7 The field of cultural heritage law is understudied and often ignored by legal scholars. For recent Western works in the field, see Robert Pickard (ed.), *Policy and Law in Heritage Conservation* (London: Spoon Press, 2000); Barbara T. Hoffman, *Art and Cultural Heritage: Law, Policy, and Practice* (Cambridge: Cambridge University Press, 2006); and Patty Gerstenblith, *Art, Cultural Heritage and the Law: Cases and Materials* (Durham: Carolina Academic Press, 2004).

law. Other laws that entail provisions regarding preservation of old buildings and historic sites are the City Planning Law and the Construction Law, as well as regulations regarding demolitions and compensations. For all of these laws and regulations there also exist provincial and local provisions and regulations. Since the new law was adopted most provinces have revised their provincial and local regulations to comply with the new law. Zhejiang adopted its new provincial regulations in 2005.[8] A new trend both nationally and locally is to adopt regulations for individual sites of special significance, such as World Heritage Sites and the Great Wall. It can be debated whether this is necessary or whether the CHL and local regulations would not offer enough protection. There also seems to be a tendency to clamor for a new law whenever new problem areas have been identified. Amid concerns that new rural policies would threaten the vernacular heritage on the countryside, some scholars and officials have thus advocated a special regulation or law in this field.[9]

The forms of protection and management of the built heritage vary depending on type of site and level of administration. The State Council is responsible for promulgating protected sites (*wenwu baohu danwei*) on the national level, while lower-level governments announce provincial and local-level heritage sites. The sites are protected in accordance with stipulations in the CHL, and overseen by SACH and CHBs at the provincial, municipal, and county levels. There are currently 2,351 national level protected sites, some 9,300 provincial-level sites, and around 60,000 lower level sites (i.e., at

---

[8] Some provinces moved quicker than others and had already by 2004 adopted new regulations (examples include Jiangsu and Guangxi), whereas others (including Shaanxi, Inner Mongolia, Hubei) did not adopt new regulations until 2006. The differences would primarily be due to the legislative workload of local people's congresses.

[9] Such views were for example expressed at the conference on the protection of the vernacular heritage of the countryside arranged by the Zhejiang Cultural Heritage Bureau and Construction Bureau, Hangzhou, June 2007. Personal observations.

the municipal, district, and county levels).[10] This is a relatively small number for a country of China's size and long and rich history. It can be compared with Sweden, where some 450,000 graves and ruins, 2,260 historic buildings, and 3,000 churches enjoy state protection.

The CHL also includes stipulations regarding protection of so-called historic areas. A much looser protection befalls what are called historic cities, townships, and villages. The State Council announced the first group of twenty-four national-level historic cities (*lishi wenhua mingcheng*) in 1982; today there are 107 historic cities nationwide. In 2003, China began to select so-called historic townships and villages; currently there are forty-four townships and thirty-six villages. Since the late 1990s, there have been calls for the adoption of a national law for the protection of historic cities and townships, but for various reasons this work has been difficult and delayed. The Ministry of Construction finally circulated a draft in 2007, and in April 2008 the State Council adopted the "Regulation on the Protection of Historical Cities, Townships and Villages."[11] Many provinces like Zhejiang had early on adopted local regulations and also selected provincial historic cities, townships, and villages.[12]

---

10 The first round of 180 national level sites was announced in 1962. Since then new rounds have followed on irregular intervals (1982, 1988, 1996, 2001, and 2006). Compared with a mere 750 protected sites in 1996, the total number of national sites grew to 2,352 in 2006. For complete lists of protected sites in China, see China Cultural Relics Daily (eds.), *Zhongguo wenhua yichan baohu chengjiu tonglan* [A layout of the results in protecting the Chinese cultural heritage] (Beijing: Wenwu chuban she, 2007).

11 The general public was invited to send in suggestions, see http://www.cin.gov.cn/zcfg/gwwj/200707/t20070727_117914.htm. For the adopted regulation, see http://www.gov.cn/zwgk/2008-04/29/content_957280.htm It should be noted that since it is not a law but a regulation it has less status.

12 For information about preservation of historic cities more generally, see Ruan Yisan, Wang Jinghui, and Wang Lin, *Lishi wenhua mingcheng baohu lilun yu guihua* [The theory and planning of protection of historic and cultural cities] (Shanghai: Tongji daxue chubanshe, 1999). For a compilation of local regulations

The problems and contested issues in heritage management and enforcement differ between countries and over time.[13] Liu Mingwei, head of the law enforcement department at SACH, has argued that violations of CHL can be divided into three categories.[14] Destruction and removals during city re-development is the largest category, followed by tourism-induced destruction and illegal excavations and thefts. Although statistics are incomplete, available information suggests that the majority of violations prosecuted are illegal excavations of tombs, thefts of cultural relics, and trafficking of antiquities.[15] This being said, there are many problems in this field too, such

---

in the field, see Zhang Song, *Chengshi wenhua yichan baohu guoji xianzhang yu guonei fagui xuanbian* [A collection of international charters and domestic laws and regulations on protection of the urban cultural heritage] (Shanghai: Tongji daxue chubanshe, 2007).

13 The majority of crimes in Sweden for example consist of thefts of relics in churches and illegal excavations. See recent reports by the Swedish National Council for Crime Prevention, available at http://www.bra.se/extra/pod/?action =pod_show&id=10&module_instance=18.

14 Quoted in Liu Jing, "Wenwu zhifa jiujing nan zai nar?" [What are the problems with implementing the Cultural Heritage Law?], *Renmin ribao*, June 23, 2005.

15 It is difficult to get complete and reliable figures, see Li Xiaodong (ed.), *Wenwu baohu danwei fangfan tixi yanjiu* [A study on the system of safeguarding protected sites] (Beijing: Xueyan chuban she, 2007). A SACH survey of eleven provinces found that there had been illegal excavations of some 40,000 graves during the period 1988–1990. As a consequence harsher punishments and new regulations were adopted in the early 1990s, eventually being incorporated in the revised Criminal Law of 1997. The number of reported and prosecuted cases of illegal excavations and thefts in the late 20th and early 21st centuries are very few, around 30–40 annually according to Li (in *A study on the system of safeguarding protected sites*). However, other sources indicate higher figures. In the province of Shanxi alone, 219 cases were reported during a five-year period (2001–2005), whereas 10 cases were reported in the province of Liaoning in 2002 (see China Cultural Relics Daily, eds., *A Layout of the Results in Protecting the Chinese Cultural Heritage*, 68, 81). SACH in 2004 reported 36 cases of thefts from museums and temples in the whole country, only 7 cases of which were solved. In Zhejiang some 40 cases of thefts and illegal excavations were dealt with by the police in

as a low rate of discovery, poor knowledge of the law among both officials and ordinary citizens, and weak enforcement. But the Chinese state takes strong measures against thefts of cultural relics and illegal excavations, which are crimes that in serious circumstances may even carry the death penalty. Since the culprits in these cases are individuals, including poor peasants, criminal prosecution is relatively easy as it does not threaten or challenge the state's power or legitimacy. For nationalistic and ideological reasons the Chinese government also seems to pay more attention to the repatriation of looted cultural relics than to the destruction of the built heritage within China's borders.[16] The culprits in cases of demolitions and destruction of historic buildings and environments are furthermore usually officials or local government and departments, which makes criminal prosecution much more difficult and quite rare.[17]

The Impact of International Work on Cultural Heritage Protection

Although the legal and institutional setups vary between different countries, international cooperation and exchange have led to the adoption of international conventions and charters and some uni-

---

2007, compared with 32 the previous year. See the Zhejiang CHB 2007 report, accessed at http://www.zjww.gov.cn/affiche/2008-02-20/1964802.shtml.

16 For a discussion on repatriation, see Richard Kraus, "When Legitimacy Resides in Beautiful Objects: Repatriating Beijing's Looted Zodiac Animal Heads," in *State and Society in 21st-century China: Crisis, Contention, and Legitimation*, eds. Peter Hays Gries and Stanley Rosen (New York: Curzon, 2004), 195–215.

17 For similar arguments, see Cai Dingjian, "Dao mu zhe zhong xing, dian cheng he zui?" [Those who illegally excavate tombs are severely punished, but what crime are those who destroy cities charged with?], originally published in *Zhongguo qingnian bao*, August 21, 2000, reprinted in Cai Dingjian, *Heibai yuanfang: Fazhi, minzhu, quanli, zhengji lunji* [A collection of articles on rule of law, democracy, rights, and justice] (Beijing: Falü chubanshe, 2003), 210–211. See also Liu, "What are the problems."

formity as to best practices in cultural heritage protection. International exchanges and projects have also influenced the preservation debate in China and strengthened awareness among both authorities and the general public. China has to date signed four international conventions, including the United Nations Education, Scientific, and Cultural Organization (UNESCO) *Convention Concerning the Protection of the World Cultural and Natural Heritage*, in the field of cultural heritage.[18] It is an active member in international organizations such as UNESCO and the International Council of Monuments and Sites (ICOMOS). It is obvious that SACH is making good use of international activities and charters to publicize and promote cultural heritage work at home. China currently has thirty-one World Heritage Sites (cultural and mixed cultural and natural).[19] The status and cultural capital associated with these sites are much coveted by central and local authorities that compete for nominations. Since World Heritage Sites are under the scrutiny of UNESCO and the international community, China is expected to fulfill certain criteria when it comes to the protection and management of these sites. International organizations, supported by Chinese experts and journalists, have on occasion raised concerns about the management of some sites.[20] Partly as a result of this critique,

---

18 On these conventions and other international agreements, see Stefan Gruber, "Protecting China's Cultural Heritage Sites in Times of Rapid Change: Current Developments, Practice and Law," Sydney Law School, Legal Studies Research Paper, No. 8/93, August 2008, accessed at http://ssrn.com/abstract=1236382

19 For the current list, see http://whc.unesco.org/en/statesparties/cn

20 When China was awarded a new World Heritage Site in June 2007, the Chinese media hinted at poor protection, an allegation that was promptly refuted by SACH. See Wang Shanshan, "Heritage sites 'not in danger,'" *China Daily*, June 29, 2007, and Sun Po, "*Zhongguo mei you shijie wenhua yichan lieru 'she wei minglü'*" [China doesn't have a world heritage site on the endangered sites' list], *Zhongguo wenwu bao*, July 6, 2007. In the past, UNESCO criticized developments in, for example, Chengde; see Peter Wonacott, "Development of China's scenic spots

SACH has tried to improve management and adopted special regulations for the protection of these sites. In November 2006, the Ministry of Culture, for example, adopted the Administrative Measures for the Protection of World Heritage Sites. China is also engaged in bilateral and multilateral cooperation programs on specific sites, and in the development of new conservation and heritage management practices.[21] A few World Bank projects have also addressed cultural heritage protection.[22] These projects and the work to develop and implement best heritage practices are both constrained by and have had an impact on the development of domestic laws and regulations.

International work and cooperation no doubt influence the discourse on cultural heritage in China. While in the past revolutionary sites and grand and imperial sites were privileged, today new types of heritage sites, such as vernacular heritage buildings and modern industrial sites, are also appreciated and protected. International cooperation has furthermore helped foster professional-

---

sparks debate over privatization," *Wall Street Journal*, May 22, 2001. Other international organizations have also raised concern about the protection of Chinese heritage sites. In 2000, ICOMOS, for example, voiced concerns about developments in Lijiang (see http://www.international.icomos.org/risk/china_2000.htm). The World Monument Foundation (WMF) has also on several occasions listed Chinese sites among the world's one hundred most endangered sites (see http://www.wmf.org). In 2005, as a result of WMF's listing, journalists from *Xin Jingbao* made a special investigative trip to one of these sites, the border town Huailai, see news report on June 24 and 26, 2005.

21 The China Principles was developed in cooperation between SACH, the Getty Institute, and the Australian Heritage Board, see http://www.getty.edu/conservation/field_projects/china/

22 Two World Bank projects in particular have focused on heritage protection, one in Lijiang, a World Heritage Site in Yunnan, and one in Ningbo, Zhejiang. In the Ningbo case, the World Bank seems to have had a beneficial impact on preservation work in the city. See Katrinka Ebbe and Donald Hankey, *Case Study: Ningbo China. Cultural Heritage Conservation in Urban Upgrading* (World Bank, 1999).

ism and created a domestic heritage community consisting of experts and scholars who play an active and vocal role.[23] One could describe this growing community as an "interpretive community" that is active in shaping and framing cultural heritage policy by analyzing problems and pushing for legal reform.[24]

Zhejiang: A Prosperous Province with a Rich Cultural Heritage

Zhejiang is one of China's most prosperous provinces with a per capita income of CNY 42,214 in 2008, to be compared with the national average of 22,697. But there are great differences within the province and between cities and the countryside. Zhejiang has a quite developed industrial economy although development is rather uneven. Pockets of poor areas continue to exist in the mountainous areas in the central and southern parts of the province. Farmland is getting increasingly scarce, especially at the outskirts of bigger cities where new residential areas and industrial development zones are being built. In many places in Zhejiang, land confiscations have resulted in resentment and protests. It is expected that the countryside will see even more rapid changes in the coming years as a result of the adoption of a new rural policy in late 2005. The pace of urbanization has been dramatic in cities such as Hangzhou, Ningbo, and Wenzhou, where radical transformations of the cityscape have destroyed much of the traditional housing stock.

Zhejiang has a rich built heritage in the form of temples, historic monuments, and vernacular houses in different architectural

---

23 On the growing professionalism, see also du Cros and Lee, *Cultural Heritage Management in China*.

24 On the concept of interpretive community and the selective adaptation of international law more generally, see Pitman B. Potter, "Legal Reform in China: Institutions, Culture, and Selective Adaptation," *Law & Social Inquiry* (2004): 465–495.

styles. With the growth in tourism, the built heritage has become a valuable economic asset for many cities and villages. Hangzhou and Shaoxing have spent large sums of money to develop and renovate certain sites while destroying vernacular buildings not regarded of equal importance and value.[25] Both cities have recently adopted conservation plans and regulations, and there is today a higher awareness and commitment to heritage protection than in the booming years of the 1990s.[26] This new concern and consensus was preceded by rather heated debates and struggles during the years of rapid inner-city redevelopment and demolitions. Had it not been for protests from local residents and a vocal media in Hangzhou, Hefang Street and an old house on Hai'er Lane, discussed below, for example, would have been demolished. Today Hangzhou authorities are more open and have on several occasions solicited views from the public regarding preservation plans and city planning more generally.[27]

As of 2007 there were 132 national-level protected heritage sites in Zhejiang, 387 provincial-level protected sites, and around 3,000 municipal- and county-level sites.[28] There were 6 national-level historic cities and 14 national-level historic townships and villages. Zhejiang has itself listed 11 provincial-level historic cities and 78 provincial level protected historic districts and villages. With 132

---

25 In Hangzhou critique has been voiced regarding the renovation and upgrading of Hefang Street, Lei Feng Pagoda, and the West Lake, whereas in Shaoxing critique has focused on the upgrading of the area surrounding the author Lu Xun's old home.

26 For Hangzhou, see Song, *A Collection of International Charters and Domestic Laws and Regulations*, 245–252 and 289–294.

27 Personal observations at the city planning office's exhibition of the preservation plan, readings of media reports, and interview with city planner in 2004. Whether ordinary citizens' views have any effect is another question.

28 For an overview of protected sites in Zhejiang, see Zhejiang Cultural Heritage Bureau (ed.) *Zhejiang lishi yichan wenhua pin du* [The splendor of artistic conception by savoring the cultural heritage in Zhejiang province] (Hangzhou: Zhejiang renmin meishu chubanshe, 2004), and the Zhejiang CHB web site at http://www.zjww.gov.cn/index.jsp

national-level protected sites out of the total 2,352, Zhejiang province ranks number five in the country.

Zhejiang has in many ways been in the forefront of cultural heritage work. This is evident with respect to the number of protected sites, cultural heritage management, financial support, and legislative work. There, however, exist many problems in the province, many of which are similar to those found elsewhere in the country. The correlation between economic development, administrative setup, and enforcement is not straightforward as political will and public pressure plays an important role.

The Institutional Setup: Weak Cultural Heritage Bureaus and Fragmentation of Authority

The administrative status of individual departments and the complex institutional relationship have an impact on cultural heritage work. SACH has a so-called vice ministerial–level status (*fubu ji*) under the Ministry of Culture.[29] This means that some important documents and policies are issued by the ministry or in cooperation with the ministry rather than by SACH itself. Not all provinces have independent CHBs, and in many provinces they instead sort under the provincial cultural department (*wenhua ting*). In 2004, only four out of thirty-one provinces and autonomous regions and cities had a separate CHB, a so-called real department (*zhengting ji*), eleven had the status of vice-departmental level (*futing ji*), whereas the rest were so-called placard cultural relics bureau (*guapai wenwuju*), meaning that they were a bureau to the outside but, administratively speaking, a lower-level branch (*chu*).[30] Many ex-

---

29 For a discussion on the administrative status of different CHBs, see Sun Jiahua, head of the Jiangxi CHB, "Wenwu gongzuo zhong xuyao jiejue de san da wenti" [The three big issues that needs to be solved in cultural relics work], *Wenwu gongzuo*, no. 7 (2004): 23–26.

30 See Sun, "The three big issues." Information also comes from interview

perts argue that the latter type should be abolished in order to strengthen the CHBs and the status of cultural heritage work.[31] The administrative status is important in relation to other departments and local governments. It is also decisive for the bureau's ability to issue administrative measures and secure financial and personnel resources. The administrative setup is decided by each province and depends on financial resources and support from the local leadership and people's congresses. It is therefore a result of a complex bargaining process undertaken in competition with other departments.

In 2000, as a result of the administrative streamlining under Zhu Rongji's premiership, the Zhejiang provincial cultural heritage bureau saw its status falling from a *futing ji* level bureau to a *guapai wenwuju*.[32] In 2004 its position was, however, restored as a result of new policy priorities in the province that resulted in the financial and personnel support needed to upgrade the bureau. At the municipal and lower levels there exist a whole range of models and combinations that reflect different priorities. Most municipalities do not have independent CHBs, and they are then instead incorporated in bureaus that include departments working on culture, media, education, tourism, and sport. In Zhejiang there exist some ten to fifteen different institutional setups.[33]

There is a general consensus that the current institutional setup is not beneficial. Cultural Heritage Bureaus are often understaffed and financially strapped, and differ in size. The Zhejiang CHB is

---

with Li Xiaodong in November 2005. Beijing, Shanghai, Shaanxi, and Shanxi, for example, all have independent cultural heritage bureaus, whereas vice-departments are found in Hebei, Henan, Hubei, Hunan, Yunnan, Gansu, Xinjiang, and Zhejiang.

31 See Sun, "The three big issues."

32 Interview with former head of the bureau, October 2005. The Zhejiang cultural heritage bureau had actually been a *zhengting ji* bureau from its setup in the 1950s and into the 1980s.

33 Interviews with local cultural relics officials in Zhejiang. The situation is similar in other provinces. In Shanxi there are twenty-two different institutional setups, see *Shanxi fazhi ribao*, June 27, 2005.

rather small with a staff of only twenty-five people, a number that has not increased in many years, although the number of protected sites, and thus the workload, has increased considerably.[34] The Jiangxi provincial cultural heritage bureau, albeit being a so-called *guapai wenwu ju*, has a similar setup to that of Zhejiang but with fewer staff, only nine people as of 2005.[35] The size of an average county-level bureau seems to be around ten people in Zhejiang. In 2007, the Wuyi county bureau thus had a staff of eight people but only two of them had a specialization in cultural heritage affairs. Few among the staff have a background in law. Only one staff member at the Zhejiang CHB has a law degree, which creates problems when trying to inform about and implement relevant laws. The institutional, financial, and personnel problems are exacerbated at the lower levels of the administration, especially at the county level.[36] The problems become even more acute as the majority of all listed and nonlisted historic structures are found at the county level.

Many CHBs suffer from limited economic resources. At the national level, there has, however, been a quite dramatic rise in the SACH's budget. During the tenth Five Year Plan (2000–2005) total investment in protection reached CNY 7.889 billion.[37] The financial situation varies in the country but also within individual provinces

---

34 Concern voiced in interview with official, July 2007.

35 Interview with Jiangxi cultural heritage official, October 2005.

36 This issue is frequently addressed in SACH's publications, see various issues of *Wenwu gongzuo*. Sometimes lower-level bureaus have to accept transfers from other departments that are motivated by political and personal connections rather than qualifications. In one county in Zhejiang the head of the cultural heritage bureau thus came from the military, whereas in another county the head came from the business sector; neither of them had any education or previous experience in the cultural heritage field. Interviews with local officials in the two counties, July 2007.

37 "China's cultural heritage protection progressive, yet not optimistic," *People's Daily*, May 25, 2006, http://english.peopledaily.com.cn/200605/25/eng2006 0525_268598.html, accessed on February 29, 2008.

due to level of economic development and priority put on cultural heritage work. Zhejiang province has increased its spending on protection of heritage sites from CNY 3 million in 2000 to CNY 6 million in 2007. In the 2007 budget, a further CNY 8 million was set aside for large archaeological sites and another CNY 6 million earmarked for the protection of covered bridges (*langqiao*) in the central and southern parts of the province.[38] National-level sites can get funding from SACH and provincial-level sites from the province, although competition is fierce. But many county-level CHBs have no money for protection work, and the joke has it that their staff are "beggars who eat out of golden bowls." However, one cannot draw the conclusion that a higher budget necessary implies better protection or law implementation since shortage of money is but one reason for poor protection.

The State Administration for Cultural Heritage and the different provincial and lower level CHBs have somewhat different internal institutional setups. A separate legal department is a rather recent phenomenon. In the 1990s, SACH had a political and legal affairs office (*bangongshi*) that later was elevated to the status of branch (*chu*), and in 2005 to a department (*si*) level. When the State Council decided on its elevated status, the department also got approval to increase its staff to ten people.[39] The Zhejiang CHB is divided into three departments, a general department (*zonghe chu*), which apart from general issues also is in charge of legal work, a department working on cultural relics and archaeology (*wenwu kaogu chu*), and a department for museum work (*bowuguan chu*). In 2005 a special unit for law enforcement was set up. This new body also incorporates staff from an organization that earlier was responsible for regulations of the culture and antiquities market. The Zhejiang CHB is a mid-

---

38 Information provided by Bao Xianlun, the head of the Zhejiang Provincial Cultural Heritage Bureau, in a presentation delivered on June 21, 2007, Hangzhou. See also *Zhejiang wenwu*, no. 1 (2007).

39 Interview with former head of legal affairs bureau, November 2005. Interview with current head of the laws and regulations section, October 2005.

sized bureau when it comes to staff and institutional setup, although it has a comparatively rather large budget for protection work.[40] The institutional setup at the municipal and county level also varies. Most CHBs are divided into a department working on museum affairs and one on cultural heritage protection and archaeology. Of the ninety-four CHBs in Zhejiang province, some 60 percent had by 2007 set up special law enforcement bodies.[41]

There is a division of responsibility between CHBs and construction bureaus when it comes to management of different types of sites. One of the tasks of SACH and its local bureaus is to oversee the administration and protection of protected heritage sites, whereas the Ministry of Construction oversees the administration of so-called historic cities and villages. But there is much overlap. The construction bureaus are responsible for overall construction and planning work, and this of course also has an impact on individual sites. Since cultural heritage protection is vested with different departments, and is somewhat overlapping in character, or, differently put, touches upon and conflicts with other interests (economic development, land use, ownership issues, etc.), coordination and cooperation between different departments are very important. In order to improve coordination work, many provinces and cities have set up special committees for the protection of the cultural heritage (*wenwu baohu guanli weiyuan hui*) and/or committees for the protection of historic cities (*lishi wenhua mingcheng baohu weiyuan hui*), or similar such bodies, with staff from concerned departments, including the police, and often headed by political leaders such as mayors or provincial governors. In many cases the CHB is the weakest part in these organizations.[42] Many of these

---

40 As a sign of its improved status in 2007 the bureau moved from its cramped offices to a new building of its own close to the West Lake. It also has a new and very informative website. See http://www.zjww.gov.cn/index.jsp

41 Interview with the head of the Zhejiang CHB law enforcement body, June 2007. See also *Zhejiang wenwu*, no. 1 (2007).

42 The CHBs are often overrun by the more powerful construction bureaus,

committees had already been set up in the 1980s. In most places they only seem to meet a couple of times per year, when new policies and laws are adopted, or if problems have been reported.[43] In 2003, the Zhejiang provincial government established the Zhejiang Historic and Cultural Heritage Protection Committee (*Zhejiang lishi wenhua yichan baohu guanli weiyuan hui*). Zhejiang also has a special committee for the protection of historic cities as well as an advisory board of experts. The latter is mostly made up of retired officials from concerned departments. One-third of all cities/counties in Zhejiang have a committee for the protection of the cultural heritage, but their impact is rather limited.[44] The need for institutions or mechanisms to improve coordination is still very pressing in many places.[45]

At the national level an interesting and potentially important development has been the establishment in 2006 of a national leading group on cultural heritage protection (*Guojia wenhua yichan baohu lingdao xiaozu*).[46] The establishment of the leading group was approved by the State Council and should thus be seen as an acknowledgment of the importance of cultural heritage issues. The group has been assigned with the work to coordinate and supervise cultural heritage work in the country. Local governments have also been called upon to set up similar bodies.

---

but the situation has improved somewhat in later years as the political interest in preservation work has become stronger. Interview with county official, July 2007.

43 Interview with the Jiangxi cultural heritage official in October 2005, and with Zhejiang cultural heritage officials in October 2004 and June 2007.

44 Interviews with county official, July 2007, and provincial official, July 2007.

45 On a recent visit I made to Yongjia county, Wenzhou, local government officials called for the establishment of such a body in the county. The visit in June 2007 was part of a tour arranged by the Zhejiang construction bureau and the Zhejiang cultural heritage bureau.

46 See speech by State Council member Chen Zhili on the first meeting of the leading group, May 8, 2006, reprinted in *Wenwu gongzuo*, no. 5 (2006): 1–4. The leading group is one of only thirteen such leading small groups in China, which seems to indicate a rather strong commitment. There are no further details of the work of the group.

Administration According to Law: Developing and Strengthening Cultural Heritage Work

The development of special in-house law enforcement bodies is a recent development that is due to the fact that the amended CHL gives CHBs more administrative power to enforce the law. This development is part of a general trend to reform and strengthen the administrative law regime (*yifa xingzheng*).[47] A number of laws and regulations have been adopted in this field, including the Administrative Compulsory Enforcement Law adopted in 2005. Several provinces, including Zhejiang, have adopted local administrative enforcement regulations in the field of cultural heritage protection.[48] Another aspect of the efforts to strengthen the administrative powers of the CHBs is the adoption of regulations concerning the responsibility and performance system for cultural heritage officials. The revised CHL and new administrative regulations have given CHBs clearer guidelines and firmer enforcement jurisdictions. Since 2003, SACH and provincial-level CHBs have adopted several policy documents and regulations that establish administrative enforcement mechanisms. SACH has also called upon CHBs at various levels to set up special law enforcement bodies.

Although some cities and provinces already had such law enforcement bodies, the development has taken off since 2003. In 2005 it was reported that one-third of all CHBs in the country, 807 of 3,882, had set up special bodies concerned with law enforcement. Some provinces moved more quickly than others for a variety of administrative, financial, and political reasons, as the setting up of a new body requires approval from the personnel depart-

---

47 On administrative law reform in general, see for example Randall Peerenboom, "A Government of Laws: Democracy, Rule of Law, and Administrative Law Reform in China," in *Debating Political Reform in China: Rule of Law vs. Democratization*, ed. Suisheng Zhao (Armonk: M.E. Sharpe, 2006): 58–78.

48 The Zhejiang regulation "Zhejiang sheng wenwu xingzheng zhifa xuncha banfa" was adopted in 2007.

ment.⁴⁹ In 2005, as already mentioned, the Zhejiang provincial government had approved the setting up of a special provincial level law implementation task force and has since then also pushed for similar organizations at the municipal and county level. In 2005, SACH carried out the first inspections of law enforcement work in several provinces. In 2006, the focus was on activities that destroyed heritage sites, especially activities that implied dereliction of duty and led to the commercialization of sites. SACH also investigated the new enforcement bodies, including their training activities. All provinces were furthermore requested to compile and submit information about at least five cases that they had handled during the past year.⁵⁰

A problem for many of the new bodies has been the poor legal knowledge of the staff. One priority for the Zhejiang enforcement body has therefore been to undertake legal training of its staff, other officials in the CHBs at various levels, and political leaders.⁵¹ The body has distributed compilations of laws and regulations to officials and cadres and it also tries to reach out to the general public with information about laws and regulations. Another aspect of the work is inspection tours to different sites and museums. These inspections take place on a regular basis but also on a more ad hoc basis when problems have been reported.⁵² In 2006, the Zhejiang law body received a prize from SACH for its work.

If problems and violations occur, the law enforcement body uses its administrative power to issue orders to stop these illegal activities, and in case of serious criminal activities notifies the police so that they can initiate criminal prosecution. But the CHBs seem to

---

49 See Li Sigui, "Xingzheng zhi fa: Wenwu baohu de fazhi baozhang" [Administration according to law: The legal protection of cultural relics protection], *Wenwu gongzuo*, no. 9 (2006): 25–27.

50 See *Wenwu gongzuo*, no. 4 (2006).

51 Interview with head of the provincial law enforcement body in October 2005 and June 2007. See also *Zhejiang wenwu*, no. 4 (2006): 6, and no. 1 (2007).

52 Provincial and local officials would join forces to make an investigation after violations have been reported. Interview with county officials, July 2007.

rely more on the use administrative measures according to which they can discipline and fine violators.[53] In 2007, the Zhejiang CHBs, for example, handled one hundred different cases, of which thirty-five were given administrative punishments and fines, whereas forty cases of thefts and illegal excavations were handed over for prosecution to the police, and the customs offices handled sixteen cases of illegal exports of cultural relics.[54]

It is not easy for CHBs to enforce the administrative measures. In June 2005, Chinese media reported that a pharmaceutical company had destroyed parts of the city wall in Linfen, Shanxi, when building a dormitory for its staff.[55] The city wall had become a municipal-level protected site as late as 2004, and the construction work violated the protection plan. When local residents notified the local CHB of the destruction, the bureau issued a notice demanding that construction work be stopped immediately. Despite this notice the illegal construction work continued for more than a month. Officials in the CHB and local residents then had to resort to blocking trucks from delivering goods to the construction site. It was not until the *People's Daily* broke the news on June 21 that the Shanxi government and the provincial CHB reacted and were able to stop the construction work. On July 12, 2005, SACH ordered the company to pay a fine of CNY 900,000 for repair of the wall and to demolish the illegally constructed building. The Linfen case was later

---

53 Interview with head of the Zhejiang law enforcement body, June 2007, and county officials in three different counties, July 2007.

54 Figures provided in the Zhejiang CHB 2007 report. There was no mention of which punishments were meted out in the criminal prosecutions. See http://www.zjww.gov.cn/affiche/2008-02-20/1964802.shtml

55 The news was first reported in *Renmin ribao*, June 21, 2005, with a follow-up report the following day. Showing the high importance put on cultural heritage protection and acknowledging current problems, the newspaper later published a lengthy, more general article on June 23, see Liu, "What are the problems with implementing the Cultural Heritage Law?" On June 25, *Zhongguo gaige bao* also carried an article on the topic. Among the local newspapers, *Shanxi fazhi ribao* published an article on the news on June 27.

cited by SACH as one of the four major cases of illegal constructions in 2005. The other cases had also been dealt with by SACH through administrative measures and the culprits ordered to demolish the illegal constructions and pay fines.[56]

Laws and Regulations: Vague Laws, Imperfect Laws, Loopholes in the Laws, and Clashes Between Laws

In general what we observe with the CHL are the same problems as with many other laws, i.e., inherent vagueness, lack of clear definitions, and vague and unenforceable regulations. Although the revised CHL in many ways is a significant improvement, it still offers rather weak protection. The law stipulates the protection of "important historic sites ... and typical buildings of modern and contemporary times related to major historic events, revolutionary movements, or famous people that are highly memorable or are of great significance for education and for the preservation of historic data." It further states that buildings of significant historic, artistic, or scientific value shall be designated as protected sites (*wenwu baohu danwei*) at different levels of the state administration. One problem is how and by whom sites are selected and designated, and which buildings and sites are deemed worthy of preservation. Individual citizens and owners of old houses cannot themselves suggest or nominate a building as a protected site. There have been several cases where owners and experts have argued that an old house slated for demolition was of significant value but been overruled by experts appointed or controlled by local governments.

One case that received much publicity in both the Chinese and the foreign media was that of Zhao Jingxin's old courtyard house in

---

56 See http://www.sach.gov.cn The total number of illegal constructions, or other instances of destruction of preserved sites and buildings, was not mentioned.

Beijing.⁵⁷ Zhao lived in a 350-year-old courtyard house that his father had bought in 1950. In 1998, Zhao received notice that his house was to be demolished due to redevelopment. But instead of accepting the decision, Zhao decided to file a lawsuit against the district CHB. Zhao received support from several famous experts who argued that the house was indeed of historic significance and worth preserving. But the court dismissed this testimony and followed the opinion of the CHB, and the house was demolished. This case illustrates the difficulties for ordinary citizens to win a lawsuit against the government when economic interests or political prestige are at stake. The government and the CHB furthermore also have the prerogative to decide what constitutes a historically valuable building, and the government may sometimes pressure the CHB to side with it on this point.

A case with a happier outcome is that of Hai'er Lane No. 98 in Hangzhou.⁵⁸ In 1998, the house was slated for demolition at the request of a nearby school that needed the land to expand. The other residents soon moved, but the son of the original owner and his family refused to move.⁵⁹ The man demanded that the house be preserved because of its historic value. Despite massive media attention and a lot of support from experts and ordinary citizens, the school won the first instance court case, and the man was ordered by the court to move. The man, however, appealed the verdict. At

---

57 On this case, see Mark O'Neill, "Deng's scholarly neighbor ousted from historic home," *South China Morning Post*, October 28, 2000; Ian Johnson, *Wild Grass: Three Stories of Change in Modern China* (New York: Pantheon Books, 2004); and Peter Hessler, *Oracle Bones: A Journey Between China and the West* (London: John Murray, 2006), 174–187.

58 Information on this case comes from several visits to the house and interviews with the old man, his lawyer, the delegate to the local people's congress, cultural heritage experts at both the municipal and provincial level, and local journalists, as well as a reading of media reports, court documents, and other documents on the case.

59 Parts of the house had been confiscated by the state in the 1950s and allocated to other families.

the same time a member of the municipal people's congress standing committee also called for a reversal of the demolition order. Somewhat surprisingly the second instance court later overturned the first instance verdict, and the house was saved from demolition. This was most probably not a purely legal victory but a result of the political intervention of the municipal party secretary who spoke out in support of protecting the house. The house was later listed as a protected site and turned into a memorial hall, and the old man moved to a new apartment. This case does not illustrate successful law implementation per se as the house was not a protected building to start with. But the old man's struggle to preserve the house shows both that norms of what is worth preserving are changing and that ordinary people take part in this debate and have started to challenge the official preservation policy. The old man's efforts and the general public debate no doubt also helped strengthen preservation work in the city.

Even though a building has been designated a protected site, such a decision is not always respected and can be overturned by the local government. In the CHL the removal or demolition of a protected building is allowed under special circumstances, such as the public interest, but the decision has to be approved by the next higher level. The public interest is sometimes very arbitrarily defined.[60] Old houses that have not been declared a protected site can be dismantled and moved to another site at will. Rich businessmen and tourism companies are now also buying up old houses around the country. Recent cases from Zhejiang include an ancestral hall

---

60 One example is the demolition of a house in Shanghai owned by relatives to world-renowned architect I. M. Pei. The house had been designated a protected building by the Shanghai municipal government as late as March 1999. But when it stood in the way of a new city park, the house was demolished in 2001. See Craig S. Smith, "Politics dictate the fate of Shanghai building," *New York Times*, June 24, 2001, at http://query.nytimes.com/gst/fullpage.html?sec=travel&res=9E00E3DD1031F937A15755C0A9679C8B63, and Hannah Beech, "Appetite for destruction," *Time Asia*, March 5, 2001, vol. 157, no. 9, at http://www.time.com/time/asia/news/magazine/0,9754,100588,00.html

sold to a tourism company in neighboring Anhui, and several houses from Anhui that were sold and moved to the West Lake in Hangzhou. There is also a booming market in wood carvings and other ornaments, which are used as decorations in fashionable city restaurants. While some are taken from dismantled houses, there are also many cases of thefts from ancestral halls and other buildings that are virtually unprotected.[61]

When a certain building has been designated a protected site, the law stipulates that the owner or user has the responsibility to protect the building. He or she cannot make any changes without the approval of the relevant CHB and must also shoulder the financial burden of the upkeep of the building. While the majority of protected sites at the national or provincial level are owned by the state, most vernacular buildings, especially in the countryside, are in private hands. This creates difficulties when the owner or the CHB lacks the economic means for renovation or restoration. In 2001, Zhang'gu ying village in Hunan was designated a national-level protected site. A peasant who lacked funding to repair a crumbling wall was turned down when he asked the CHB for financial support. The man did not see any other option but to tear down the wall but was then charged with violating the CHL.[62] Poor villages that suddenly are nominated as either protected sites or historic villages face the problem of how they would be able to shoulder this new responsibility and financial burden. The problem becomes more complex when the protected unit is a whole village rather than an individual building. Villagers are often resentful over restrictions

---

61 In several villages I have visited in Zhejiang, wood carvings have been stolen. In 2006 a case involving several people was uncovered in Jiangshan, see *Zhejiang wenwu*, no. 2 (2007).

62 This case was reported in the media and taken up by several programs on TV. See *Oriental Horizon (Dongfang shikong)*, October 18, 2003, accessed at http://www.cctv.com/oriental/sklx/jmnr/20021018/19.html , and *Law Today (Jinri shuofa)*, April 23, 2003, http://www.cctv.com/program/lawtoday/20030432/100760.shtml See also report on http://www.eeast-law.com of July 16, 2003.

on the use of their property, or demands to demolish new houses because they are suddenly illegal and violate the protection plan.[63]

The issue of construction and preservation work in the countryside is complicated by the fact that the Land Regulation Law is quite restrictive. Since land is scarce in the villages themselves, and land outside of the village often is classified as prime agricultural land, new buildings can often only be constructed on the site of an old building in the village center. Thus the reason why villagers demolish old houses is to be able to build new, modern ones. In other words, there exists a clash between the Land Regulation Law and the CHL.

Since the desire to build new houses is very strong and permission to build new houses difficult to get, villagers often build new houses without permission. The local governments can find themselves in a difficult position and in many cases choose to turn a blind eye. But sometimes they are pressured by higher authorities to enforce the law and demolish illegal constructions.[64] In Guodong village, a national-level historic village in Zhejiang, illegal constructions had over the years destroyed the historic ambience and led to much criticism. As a result of this criticism and a visit by a famous national expert in spring 2007, the local authorities decided to demolish all the illegal buildings, at great financial loss for the villagers.[65] These harsh and campaign-like actions certainly do not improve the CHB's and local government's relationship with the villagers, or make villagers more supportive of preservation. In order to improve the situation and make law implementation easier, authorities would have to involve the local community in both decision-making and preservation work.

---

63 Discussions and observations in several villages in Zhejiang.

64 Observation from field visits to villages in Jiangsu, August 2005, Zhejiang, July 2007, and Jiangxi, October 2005.

65 See Lou Qingxi "*Zhongguo gu cunluo: Kunjing yu shengji—Xiangtu jianzhu de jiazhi ji qi baohu*" [China's old villages: Problems and victories. The value and protection of vernacular architecture], *Zhongguo wenhua yichan*, no. 2 (2007). Personal observations in the village during visits made in 2004 and 2007.

Clashes of Power and Interests: Horizontal and Vertical Clashes

In cultural heritage work we see both horizontal and vertical clashes that reflect the complex Chinese institutional and administrative structure and the crisscrossing of levels of jurisdiction and authority. The horizontal power structure leads to clashes between CHB, on the one hand, and local governments, construction bureaus, real estate companies, and tourism companies, on the other hand. Local governments and individual political leaders are more concerned about promoting the local economy and thus willing to let protection take a backseat, or even go so far as to violate the CHL. Chinese cities have in the past ten years seen many conflicts as a result of city redevelopment schemes that have led to relocations of residents and to the destruction of historic environments. The vertical clashes and conflicts occur between national bodies and local bodies, and between national bodies and local governments. Horizontal and vertical conflicts often intersect and reinforce each other, which makes policy and law implementation even more difficult.

Cultural Heritage Bureaus depend upon local governments for financial and other support and therefore come under a lot of pressure. The problem of local protectionism can be illustrated with the Dinghai case. Dinghai (or Zhoushan) was assigned status as a provincial-level historic city in 1991.[66] In 1997 the local government nonetheless embarked on an ambitious city redevelopment scheme that threatened many of the city's old buildings. Several of the families whose houses were to be demolished protested this in letters and petitions to the local government. They were also supported by local cultural heritage officials as well as by some delegates to the local people's congress who wrote motions asking for the houses to

---

66 Information on this case comes from interviews conducted with people involved in the lawsuit and scholars and journalists familiar with the case, as well as from a reading of letters and petitions, court verdicts, government documents, and articles in the Chinese media, and watching relevant television programs.

be saved. When the protests fell on deaf ears, a group of eleven families decided to take their case to court. The media picked up this story, and the demolitions and lawsuit were a hot topic in the Chinese media between 1998 and 2000. Many famous cultural heritage experts and legal scholars voiced strong criticism of the Dinghai authorities. National and provincial authorities joined this criticism, and experts from the Ministry of Construction and the Zhejiang People's Congress visited the city and criticized the ongoing destruction. Despite this strong criticism from national and provincial authorities, experts, and the media alike, the local authorities turned a deaf ear and did not put a halt to the destruction. The court of first instance, which was pressured by the local government, ruled in favor of the local authorities. In the end a compromise of sorts came about. The house within the protection plan that nonetheless at first had been slated for demolition were saved before the trial of second instance took place. The four other families, whose house was outside of the protection plan, however, lost the second instance trial, and the house was quickly demolished. The Dinghai case illustrates the difficulties of preserving old houses in the face of economic interests, the strength of local authorities to withstand criticism from national and provincial authorities, and the existence of local protectionism. This is a clear case where vertical and horizontal power structures, coupled with vested economic interests, interact and create problems for law and policy implementation at the local level.

At the village level we also find clashes between CHBs, on the one hand, and local governments, village committees, and tourism companies, on the other hand. In many villages there is a tension and struggle between protection and economic development that affects both individuals and collectives. With the growth of tourism, several CHBs have been tempted to relinquish management of protected sites to tourism companies, or have themselves set up such enterprises. But in some cases the village leadership and the CHB have instead joined forces and tried to fight off township governments and tourism companies that try to promote tourism and reap benefits without consideration of either protection or the interests of the local community. Like in many other villages, it was villagers in Zhuge village, Zhejiang, who first got together and collected money toward restoring the village's ancestral halls.[67] It was not until the village was listed as a national-level protected site in 1996 that the local and provincial-level CHBs became engaged in preservation work in the village. In the early 1990s, the villagers began a modest tourism enterprise. But when tourism took off, the Lanxi Municipality decided that tourism should be managed by the township and not by the villagers themselves. The villagers were unhappy with this decision and were not very cooperative, with the result that one year later the tourism company was returned to the villagers with the village party secretary as director. The tourism company/village committee is able to offer some help toward renovation and has set aside land outside the old village center for families who prefer to move to a modern house.

One important reason why Zhuge village has been able both to benefit from tourism and to protect its cultural heritage is the good management and farsightedness of the current party secretary, who came to power in 1997. The party secretary has been very receptive and has built up a network consisting of nationally known experts and officials in the SACH and the provincial bureau.[68] This support has enabled the village to withstand pressure from township and municipal authorities to develop tourism without consideration of preservation. Due to fairly good economic development, the party

---

67 Information on developments in Zhuge village comes from extensive fieldwork in the village since 2003, interviews with local officials, cultural heritage experts, and residents, as well as from a reading of both unpublished and published materials on the village.

68 The village has recently been launched as something of a model village for its ability to secure local ownership, protect the heritage, and promote the economy. The party secretary has been invited to several conferences on preservation issues and has also published articles on the topic. See for example *Zhejiang wenwu*, no. 1 (2007). An interview with the party secretary was also published in *Nanfang zhoumo* on December 7, 2006.

secretary has also been able to convince his fellow villagers to continue to invest in preservation work and has managed to strike a good balance between protection and villagers' demands for economic development. The village committee has also worked to raise awareness of cultural heritage protection in the village through various educational activities.

There is at present a strong concern among cultural heritage officials that the launching of the New Socialist Countryside (*xin nongcun jianshe*) policy initiated in late 2005 would be the signal for a massive destruction of the remaining cultural heritage in the countryside.[69] They fear that the new slogan will prove as harmful as the slogan "old city redevelopment (*jiucheng gaizao*)" was for the cities.[70] Official policy documents and statements from national political leaders, however, stress that the new policy should not be interpreted as a go-ahead for massive destruction/construction. There are also many statements to the effect that the policy should be implemented with sensitivity and respect for the villagers' property rights, etc. But it is too early to say whether this awareness also will be reflected in the actual implementation phase. There have already been some reports of large illegal constructions in violation of both the spirit and the letter of the new policy. The adoption of new policies, however well intended, can have unforeseen consequences or conflict with other policies and laws.

The Role of the Political Leadership

It is often on the direct order of or intervention from political leaders that the cultural heritage is either saved or demolished. In

---

69 Interviews and observations during a conference on protection and *xin nongcun jianshe* in Hangzhou, June 20–21, 2007.

70 Many articles have been published in *Wenwu bao* and *Wenwu gongzuo*. For a selection of articles on the topic by Zhejiang CHB officials, see *Zhejiang wenwu*, no. 1 (2007).

other words, cultural heritage protection does not rely on laws alone but needs to be backed up with political will and a strong leadership. Furthermore, as the Linfen case shows, good will at the local level is often not enough, as local officials and leaders also need to have backing from higher levels. On the other hand, as the Dinghai case shows, political will among higher authorities does not guarantee protection if local officials can circumvent national policies or orders, and when they do not feel that they have a stake in protection. In Zhuge village the party secretary has been instrumental for the protection of the village but at times has met strong resistance from township and municipal authorities. It should be noted that local officials and village cadres do not benefit from taking preservation seriously as they are only evaluated on the basis of the economic development and social stability of their locality. Although political leaders are not, strictly speaking, accountable to their constituency, public opinion and the media may nonetheless sway political leaders as the Hangzhou case also shows.

In-House and External Supervision of Cultural Heritage Protection

SACH and local bureaus undertake inspection tours on both a regular and an ad hoc basis when problems have been reported. They acknowledge, however, that outside supervision from more powerful agencies such as people's congresses is very crucial. Much of the supervisory work is quite reactive in character and often takes place after an incident or violation has taken place, or else is more pro forma and part of a ritualized and politicized routine. Delegates to the NPC have on several occasions raised concern about the widespread destruction of the cultural heritage. In 1999, for example, more than ten standing committee members wrote a letter appealing for an investigation into violations of the CHL. During the 2000 annual session of the NPC, six motions concerning protection of historic sites were made. The NPC also sends delegations to investigate the situation of cultural heritage protection. In 2000 such delegations visited Henan, Shanxi, and Fujian, and in 2001 they visited Guangdong. Local people's congresses are also active and make investigative studies or propose motions on heritage issues as the cases from Dinghai and Hangzhou show.

In 2004, several provincial people's congresses (including to my knowledge those of Zhejiang, Jiangxi, Henan, Shanxi, and Shaanxi) carried out the first supervision of the CHL since it was amended in 2002. According to media reports, the findings revealed many of the same problems, including conflicts between construction and protection, lack of funding, especially at lower-level bureaus, institutional problems, for example, with respect to CHB vis-à-vis other departments and local governments, and poor management of heritage sites.[71] In March and April 2004, the Zhejiang provincial congress committee for educational, scientific, cultural, and health affairs carried out its own investigation.[72] The committee listened to reports from the provincial construction bureau and CHBs and also visited selected cities and counties in the province, including Ningbo, Shaoxing, Jinhua, Taizhou, and Lishui. In their report they listed some recent examples of destruction of historic buildings and insensitive and illegal constructions close to heritage sites. The report stressed the need to popularize and spread information about the CHL among both officials and the general public. The report also advocated the setting up of a special law enforcement body at the provincial level as well as in cities and counties with a rich heritage. In 2007, the NPC decided to undertake a nationwide investigation of the implementation of the CHL.[73] Four provinces, Hainan, Gan-

---

71 There were some media reports in *Zhongguo wenwu bao* during 2004, but unfortunately it has been impossible to get the full internal reports from these investigations.

72 For a summary report see *Zhejiang wenwu nianjian* (2004): 363–367.

73 Interview with NPC official, July 2007. No full reports are available, only brief notices in the media.

su, Shanxi, and Xinjiang, were selected, and inspection tours undertaken.

The People's Political Consultative Conference (PPCC) and its local organizations are also quite active on cultural heritage issues as many cultural heritage officials and experts are members of these bodies. The PPCC offers suggestions, writes reports, and also undertakes its own investigations.[74] Although the body does not have the same clout or power as the people's congresses, it does have some impact on public opinion and the general debate. The PPCC also arranges conferences and interacts with scholars on cultural heritage issues.[75]

The Role of Civil Society and Local Communities in Preservation and Supervision Work

Although the party and state organs continue to dominate cultural heritage policy in China, the reform period has seen the emergence of new players and voices in the cultural heritage field. In many villages in Zhejiang it was on the initiative of local residents that ancestral halls were recovered from other uses and restored to their former glory.[76] In recent years there has also been a growing interest in preserving the cultural heritage among experts, journalists, and ordinary citizens, who increasingly have begun to join forces in calling upon the government to protect threatened houses and his-

---

74 In 2006, the Communist Party of China Central Committee thus made an investigative trip to Zhejiang. See *Zhejiang wenwu*, no. 5 (2006) 4, 7.

75 In August 2005, I participated in a conference on preservation of the rural heritage coorganized by the Suzhou PPCC.

76 On people's commitment to restoring temples and ancestral halls, see Marina Svensson, "In the Ancestors' Shadow: Cultural Heritage Contestations on the Chinese Countryside," (Working Paper 17, Lund University, Centre for East and South-East Asian Studies, 2006), accessed at http://www.ace.lu.se/o.o.i.s/6793

toric environments.⁷⁷ This reflects both an old idealistic commitment dating back to Liang Zicheng's fight in the 1950s to save Beijing's city wall and a growing sense of professionalism. Experts and scholars also often use their seniority and position in political bodies such as the NPC and PPCC to promote their views and influence legislative and political work. There have also been some attempts to establish independent organizations to protect the cultural heritage, publish more popular magazines in the field, and set up both private and semiofficial websites.⁷⁸ An early example of an independent organization is the Beijing Cultural Heritage Protection Center. The organization tries to raise awareness and create debate on cultural heritage issues.⁷⁹ The interest in cultural heritage issues is also reflected in the increasing number of both academic and more popular books on traditional architecture, as well as in the growth of heritage tourism. Local CHBs have also come to acknowledge the importance of local community participation. Several cities in Zhejiang, for example, have appointed volunteers to visit and keep an eye on heritage sites and report any problems to the authorities.⁸⁰ They also acknowledge these local efforts, for example, by giving awards and selecting model villages.

---

77 Retired officials from museums and cultural relics bureaus are very vocal as are other intellectuals and scholars such as the author Feng Jicai. For an example of Feng's work, see Feng Jicai, *Qiangjiu lao jie* [Rushing to Save the Old Street] (Beijing: Xifan chubanshe, 2000).

78 The growing general interest has led to the establishment of popular magazines devoted to cultural heritage issues such as *Zhongguo wenhua yichan*, established in 2004, and *Zhonghua yichan*, established in 2006; both are sponsored by and associated with SACH. Web sites include, http://www.oldbeijing.org and http://www.wenbao.net

79 The organization was established in 1998 and was funded by a younger official working in SACH. Since 2003, the organization has been registered as a nonprofit enterprise. Interviews conducted with members in 2003, 2005, and 2007. See http://www.bjchp.org.

80 Interview with provincial official in 2005 and 2007. Interview with county official, July 2007.

The Role of the Media: Investigative Journalists, Media-Savvy Citizens, and Publicity-Hungry Cultural Heritage Bureaus

The growing public debate on cultural heritage issues is partly a result of the development of a more critical and market-savvy media. Journalists play an important role in highlighting cultural heritage contestations through their investigative reporting and sometimes also take on the role of activists.[81] Liu Xudun, a former journalist at the *China Science and Technology Daily*, became deeply involved in publicizing the demolition in Dinghai as it involved his own family home. He published many articles on the topic in different newspapers and magazines and was instrumental in encouraging other journalists and scholars to write about the case.

There are several instances where media attention and a strong public opinion have swayed the local governments to save old houses and areas.[82] In 1999, the Hangzhou Municipality put forward a suggestion to broaden a traditional street in central Hangzhou, *Hefang jie*, and rebuild the houses on the north side of the road. When news about this plan became known, citizens and the media strongly protested. When the local CHB was unable to stop the plan, Luo Zhewen and Zheng Xiaoxie, experts in the National Historic Cities Protection Committee, called upon the new mayor of Hangzhou to protect the street and the city's historic center. Mao Zhaoxi, the former head of the provincial CHB and at the time a member of the standing committee of the NPC, also voiced his concern. Newspapers and magazines, such as the local *Qianjiang wanbao*, set up special columns to discuss the protection of *Hefang jie*. Although

---

81 One example is Wang Jun, a journalist with the Xinhua News Agency who has published many articles on the topic, and has also written a very successful book, *Cheng ji* [Memories of the city] (Beijing: Shenghuo, dushu, xinzhi, sanlian shudian, 2003).

82 See Marina Svensson, "A Tale of Three Cities: Cultural Heritage Preservation in Zhejiang" (unpublished paper, on file with author).

cultural experts today have some reservations regarding the actual execution of the renovations, the street is now a bustling and popular commercial tourist attraction. Another case where public opinion and the media played a crucial role was the preservation of the house on Hai'er Lane, discussed above. The old man consciously courted the media and was aware of the usefulness of publicity. He pasted a whole wall in his house with press clippings from national and local newspapers and received journalists and ordinary citizens who had read about the case in the media and now sought his advice regarding their own houses.[83]

Local CHBs increasingly acknowledge the usefulness of the media and actively use it when exposing problems and trying to raise awareness on cultural heritage issues. For example, they sponsor or initiate shows on TV, reports in newspapers, and develop special web pages that can be used to inform citizens as well as gather information about violations.[84] This development not only reflects the growing power of the media but on a more negative note also reflects the continuing weakness of the CHBs and the legal system more generally.

Legal Education and Publicity Campaigns

The State Administration of Cultural Heritage and local CHBs put a lot of effort into legal awareness campaigns and educational work. They use a range of old and new methods similar to what other departments and the Ministry of Justice use during so-called dissemination of legal knowledge campaigns (*pufa yundong*). This includes

---

83 On my latest visit to the house in July 2007, after the renovations, I was met by journalists from local newspapers and TV stations, whom the old man without my knowledge had notified about my visit, which tells us something about his flair for publicity. For a report on my visit published in the local paper *Qianjiang wanbao*, see http://www.zjww.gov.cn/news/2007-07-12/86174046.shtml

84 On the Zhejiang CHB's new web site citizens can submit information about violations as well as contact the head of the bureau personally.

old-fashioned campaign-style activities, such as meetings, putting up banderols and posters on the streets and in the neighborhood, information and distribution of relevant laws and regulations in the street, exhibitions, selection of model citizens and villages, and public sentencing rallies. The authorities also use special days such as the International Museum Day on May 18, and Chinese Cultural Heritage Day, which since 2006 has been celebrated on the second Saturday in June, to spread information on cultural heritage protection through exhibitions, talks, articles in the media, and TV shows.

Provinces and cities also arrange special educational schemes targeting different groups and areas. In several villages in Zhejiang, CHBs and village committees have distributed the CHL to citizens or pasted posters with legal regulations on the village board or elsewhere in the village. In Zhuge village they have produced a calendar with a different article from the CHL for each month. It is questionable how effective these old-style campaign and educational methods really are. In many places, the posters are faded and unreadable after having been exposed to rain and wind. It is not always easy to reach people. In one village the officials had to resort to the measure of offering individuals CNY 5 to guarantee that they attended a meeting on preservation issues. In another village the authorities put on an opera and used that opportunity to spread information. It is also quite common that a village that has protected buildings or itself is a protected village incorporates regulations on protection in the so-called village contracts (*cunmin yue*) that otherwise usually have stipulations about health issues and family planning, etc. Villagers who live in protected villages also often have to sign so-called responsibility agreements (*zeren shu*) with the local CHB regarding their obligations to protect the old house and the cultural heritage more generally.

Chinese law is still very politicized, and the dichotomy between policy and law is not always very clear. Campaign-style efforts are thus still used to encourage new institutional and professional norms and reward good citizens and officials (compare van Rooij in this volume). In order to encourage and reward good officials, SACH and the Ministry of Construction, for example, each year select role models and good workplaces. In 2005, officials at the Linfen CHB, for example, got a special prize for their efforts to protect the city wall. In 2006, the Lishui CHB in Zhejiang awarded a village committee in the municipality CNY 5,000 for notifying the bureau about the discovery of a grave and promptly stopping construction work.[85] In 2006, Shaoxing was selected a nationally outstanding cultural heritage county for its protection work. In order to create law-abiding citizens, CHBs and the police often use the carrot and stick policy. In March 2006, the court in Longquan, Zhejiang, thus held a public sentencing rally in a middle school where it handed down sentences of between six and seven years to four local men for illegally having excavated the site of an old kiln.[86] At the rally several officials from the CHB also took part and informed the public about cultural heritage crimes.

Conclusion: Toward More Rule and Law-Based Cultural Heritage Work

The cultural heritage field has seen some quite remarkable and promising developments in recent years. There is a growing debate and concern among both the political leadership and the general public about cultural heritage protection as manifested in revisions of old laws and the adoption of new laws and administrative regulations that on paper at least have strengthened legal protection. These legal changes have paved the way for institutional changes, including the establishment of in-house bodies responsible for law enforcement and stricter supervision mechanisms. Although local

---

85   The case was reported in *Zhejiang wenwu*, no. 1 (2007): 48.

86   Information about the case and the rally in *Zhejiang wenwu*, no. 2 (2006): 34. The case was also discussed in an interview with a responsible official at the Lishui CHB in July 2007.

CHBs today receive more recognition and more resources, they are still quite weak in comparison to other authorities, and therefore continue to face big problems when trying to enforce laws and regulations. The administrative notifications often go unheeded, and it is difficult for the CHBs to get the necessary support and backing from local governments and other relevant departments when facing strong economic interests. However, the CHBs have found a new ally in the increasingly assertive media, which through its critical reports creates debate and puts pressure on higher officials and political leaders. The emergence of new interest groups and activists explains changing norms and views on what should be preserved that influence both preservation practices and the drafting of laws. The cultural heritage field is becoming an increasingly contested arena where ideological and economic interests challenge traditional practices and institutions. The fact that China is undergoing such rapid and dramatic social and economic changes will continue to make law implementation a difficult and challenging task for the foreseeable future.

Bibliography

Beech, Hannah. "Appetite for destruction," *Time Asia* 157, no. 9 (March 5, 2001).

Cai, Dingjian. "Dao mu zhe zhong xing, dian cheng he zui?" [Those who illegally excavate tombs are severely punished, but what crime are those who destroy cities charged with?], originally published in *Zhongguo qingnian bao*, August 21, 2000, reprinted in Cai Dingjian, *Heibai yuanfang: Fazhi, minzhu, quanli, zhengji lunji* [A collection of articles on rule of law, democracy, rights, and justice], 210–211. Beijing: Falü chubanshe, 2003.

China Cultural Relics Daily, eds. *Zhongguo wenhua yichan baohu chengjiu tonglan* [A layout of the results in protecting the Chinese cultural heritage], Beijing: Wenwu chuban she, 2007.

du Cros, Hilary, and Yok-Shiu F. Lee. *Cultural Heritage Management in China: Preserving the Cities of the Pearl River Delta*. London: Routledge, 2007.

Ebbe, Katrinka, and Donald Hankey. *Case Study: Ningbo China. Cultural*

Heritage Conservation in Urban Upgrading. Washington, DC: The World Bank, 1999.

Feng, Jicai. *Qiangjiu lao jie* [Rushing to save the old street]. Beijing: Xifan chubanshe, 2000.

Gerstenblith, Patty. *Art, Cultural Heritage and the Law: Cases and Materials.* Durham: Carolina Academic Press, 2004.

Gruber, Stefan. "Protecting China's Cultural Heritage Sites in Times of Rapid Change: Current Developments, Practice and Law," Sydney Law School, Legal Studies Research Paper, no. 8/93, August 2008, http://ssrn.com/abstract=1236382

Hessler, Peter. *Oracle Bones: A Journey Between China and the West.* London: John Murray, 2006.

Hoffman, Barbara T. *Art and Cultural Heritage: Law, Policy, and Practice.* Cambridge: Cambridge University Press, 2006.

Johnson, Ian. *Wild Grass: Three Stories of Change in Modern China.* New York: Pantheon Books, 2004.

Kraus, Richard. "When Legitimacy Resides in Beautiful Objects: Repatriating Beijing's Looted Zodiac Animal Heads." In *State and Society in 21st-century China: Crisis, Contention, and Legitimation,* edited by Peter Hays Gries and Stanley Rosen, 195–215. New York: Curzon, 2004.

Merle, Aurore, and Peng Youju. "Peking Between Modernisation and Preservation," *China Perspectives,* no. 45 (January–February 2003): 37–41.

Meyer, Michael. *The Last Days of Old Beijing: Life in the Vanishing Backstreet of a City Transformed.* New York: Walker & Company, 2008.

Li, Sigui. "Xingzheng zhi fa: Wenwu baohu de fazhi baozhang" [Administration according to law: The legal protection of cultural relics protection], *Wenwu gongzuo,* no. 9 (2006): 25–27.

Li, Xiaodong, ed. *Wenwu baohu danwei fangfan tixi yanjiu* [A study on the system of safeguarding protected sites]. Beijing: Xueyan chuban she, 2007.

Liu, Jing. "Wenwu zhifa jiujing nan zai nar?" [What are the problems with implementing the Cultural Heritage Law?], *Renmin ribao,* June 23, 2005.

Lou, Qingxi. *"Zhongguo gu cunluo: Kunjing yu shengji—Xiangtu jianzhu de jiazhi ji qi baohu"* [China's old villages: Problems and victories. The value and protection of vernacular architecture], *Zhongguo wenhua yichan,* no. 2 (2007).

O'Neill, Mark. "Deng's scholarly neighbor ousted from historic home," *South China Morning Post,* October 28, 2000.

Peerenboom, Randall. "A Government of Laws: Democracy, Rule of Law, and

Administrative Law Reform in China." In *Debating Political Reform in China: Rule of Law vs. Democratization*, edited by Suisheng Zhao, 58–78. Armonk: M.E. Sharpe, 2006.

Pickard, Robert, ed. *Policy and Law in Heritage Conservation*. London: Spoon Press, 2000.

Potter, Pitman B. "Legal Reform in China: Institutions, Culture, and Selective Adaptation," *Law & Social Inquiry* (2004): 465–495.

Ruan, Yisan, Wang Jinghui, and Wang Lin. *Lishi wenhua mingcheng baohu lilun yu guihua* [The theory and planning of protection of historic and cultural cities], Shanghai: Tongji daxue chubanshe, 1999.

Smith, Craig S. "Politics dictate the fate of Shanghai building," *New York Times*, June 24, 2001.

Sun, Jiahua. "Wenwu gongzuo zhong xuyao jiejue de san da wenti" [The three big issues that needs to be solved in cultural relics work], *Wenwu gongzuo*, no. 7 (2004): 23–26.

Sun, Po. "*Zhongguo mei you shijie wenhua yichan lieru 'she wei minglü'*" [China doesn't have a world heritage site on the endangered sites' list], *Zhongguo wenwu bao*, July 6, 2007.

Svensson, Marina. "In the Ancestors' Shadow: Cultural Heritage Contestations on the Chinese Countryside." Working Paper 17, Lund University, Centre for East and South-East Asian Studies, 2006, http://www.ace.lu.se/o.o.i.s/6793

Svensson, Marina. "A Tale of Three Cities: Cultural Heritage Preservation in Zhejiang." Unpublished paper on file with author.

Wang, Jun. *Cheng ji* [Memories of the city], Beijing: Shenghuo, dushu, xinzhi, sanlian shudian, 2003.

Wang, Shanshan. "Heritage Sites 'Not in Danger,'" *China Daily*, June 29, 2007.

Wonacott, Peter. "Development of China's Scenic Spots Sparks Debate over Privatization," *Wall Street Journal*, May 22, 2001.

Zhang, Song. *Chengshi wenhua yichan baohu guoji xianzhang yu guonei fagui xuanbian* [A collection of international charters and domestic laws and regulations on protection of the urban cultural heritage], Shanghai: Tongji daxue chubanshe, 2007.

Zhejiang Cultural Heritage Bureau, ed. *Zhejiang lishi yichan wenhua pin du* [The splendor of artistic conception by savoring the cultural heritage in Zhejiang province], Hangzhou: Zhejiang renmin meishu chubanshe, 2004.

8

The Legitimacy of Law in China
The Case of "Black Internet Cafés"

JOHAN LAGERKVIST

Introduction

An Internet café called Lanjisu was burned to the ground in Beijing's Haidian District on June 16, 2002. Twenty-four young people died in a building in which the emergency exits had been blocked from the outside. When it became known that two teenagers had set fire to the café to protest not being admitted to the premises, it triggered an intricate interplay between lawmakers, bureaucratic entities, parents, and the mass media. What was to unfold was clearly a case of event lawmaking,[1] or rather law as event, which is something that often takes place in connection with accidents in profitable and, for various reasons, hard-to-control industry sectors. From this followed a new, tougher set of regulations that specifically targeted the Internet café industry.[2] This set of regulations, Regulations on the Administration of Internet Access Service Business Establishments, followed three previous national-level measures concerning Internet cafés that had been issued by various

---

1 Benjamin van Rooij, *Law as Event: Lessons about Lawmaking, Compliance and Enforcement, Drawn from the Regulation of Land and Pollution in South-West China* (2006), 383, 408.
2 The mining industry in China is another case in point. Local mining companies' disregard of national regulations on safety measures for miners has also given rise to *ad hoc* regulations.

government agencies since 1998. These national-level measures are sometimes enforced in conjunction with various local government rules directed toward Internet cafés.

This chapter sets out to analyze the social and normative context in which the legal measures, issued by the central government, regulate and control the Internet café industry. A particular focus is on the set of regulations that followed the Lanjisu fire in 2002, since it illustrates a case of successful law implementation in China, and the factors that are conducive to such an end result. Successful, in the eyes of authorities, was the effort to wipe out unregistered and illegal Internet cafés during an intensive phase of the legal campaign. Therefore, I specifically analyze the overlapping sphere where agencies of the state, citizens, party intellectuals,[3] and big business on the normative level shaped public opinion *vis-à-vis* rules and regulations targeting the growth of an Internet industry producing content deemed "unhealthy" by the authorities, although a particular focus is devoted to illegal *hei wangba*, or so called black Internet cafés.

The regulation of different parts of Chinese cyberspace today, like online news sites, bulletin board systems (BBS), and blogs, has a forerunner in the regulation of the physical meeting places called Internet cafés, or *wangba* in Chinese. These Internet access points became very popular in the late 1990s. While demand for them was huge, the authorities were slow in issuing business licenses to would-be operators. As a result, many illegal Internet cafés mushroomed. When asked why the authorities keep statistics on the development of karaoke halls but not Internet cafés, the chief statistician of Shanghai's statistical yearbook said it was impossible to keep track

---

[3] Most of the intellectuals debating the Internet cafés and the Internet demonstrate a negative attitude toward the Internet as they in its development see dangers for Chinese youth and threats to the ruling ideology of the regime and Communist Party. Because they want the Communist Party to increase its legitimacy among the populace, something more independently minded intellectuals might be ambivalent about, they are in this chapter called "party intellectuals."

of them since there were so many, not least all the unregistered, illegal ones.[4] The mushrooming of the Internet café industry worried different government ministries and the Chinese Communist Party but it also gave rise to anxiety among parts of civil society. The formation of norms is shaped differently in democracies and authoritarian-run states, where the existing popular norms are sometimes more easily engineered. But as this chapter shows, without a spark of underlying support, compliance and implementation of rules may become seriously hampered—also in an authoritarian context. First and foremost, the official discourse was of a moral kind, and arguments that Internet bars should be shut down because they contributed to offline and online crime, illicit political activity, and youth vice were given plenty of space in mass media, academic writings, and policy documents.

The double strategy of promoting and containing Internet usage in mainland China is well-known. The state actively encourages businesses, schools, and private individuals to go online. In this respect it has been very successful. In July 2009, according to China Internet Network Information Center (CNNIC), the country's online population reached 338 million, surpassing the United States.[5] At the same time, the state enforces rules that limit free speech in all electronic meeting places with a heavy hand. International media frequently reports how China's police crackdown on the Internet and furiously battle for control of the Chinese consciousness in the digital territory. This realm is walled in by "the great firewall of China."[6] For many Chinese the Internet cafés are, or in the bigger cities were, the first place where they encountered cyberspace.

The history of Internet regulation in China is about lawmaking

---

4 Interview by the author in Shanghai in June 2001.
5 China Internet Network Information Center, www.cnnic.com.cn
6 Ronald J. Deibert, "Dark Guests and Great Firewalls: The Internet and Chinese Security Policy," *Journal of Social Issues* 58, no. 1 (2002): 143–159. See also "The Great Firewall: China Faces the Internet," http://www.cpj.org/Briefings/2001/China_jan01/China_jan01.html (accessed February 20, 2007).

bent on catching up with the quick development of modern communications technology, and how it enables horizontal sharing of information between citizens. In accordance with the needs of an authoritarian party-state, the bureaucracy and the police around the country hunt down any information or content creators who seek to delegitimize the Communist Party's hold on power. The great firewall of China, just like the physical Great Wall of China, actually consists of several independently built and operated virtual firewalls operating on different levels and provinces around China. Together they form a larger structure, not intact without loopholes as experienced users can circumvent the blocks and filters by using proxy servers or advanced software. But, according to recent reports and analysis, it is now the most sophisticated Internet-filtering project in the world.[7] Together with government propaganda, self-censorship among businesses and individual users, and cooperation between industry leaders and the bureaucracy, these firewalls work in tandem.

The enforcement of Internet café laws is one of several means to contain the Internet in the virtual and physical landscape of China. They all serve the strategy to blocking out or filtering news and information from the outside world that in itself or if acted upon by organized interests such as labor rights activists and religious groupings like Falun Gong would constitute a threat to social stability or the power of the current regime. In recent years the phenomenal growth of the Internet in China means that more than 180 million netizens regularly go online for news stories, for email, or just to find entertainment. National Chinese and foreign information technology (IT) companies alike have to bow to the demands of the authorities, which aim at resisting the influx of Western ideas and cultural influences on the Chinese Internet. Human rights groups have accused Cisco Systems of selling the sophisticated equipment that is needed by China's security organs to effectively build its cen-

---

7 OpenNet initiative, *Internet Filtering in China in 2004-2005: A Country Study*.

sorship infrastructure. And Microsoft, Yahoo, and Google are regularly pointed out as acquiescing so much to government pressure that they are censoring content produced by their users. In June 2005, it became known that Microsoft censors Spaces, its blog-hosting service, from words deemed inappropriate by the Chinese authorities.[8] Thus, these Western firms have assisted the authorities in effectively limiting freedom of expression and Internet searches, but even more alarmingly they have possibly contributed to the arrests of journalists and dissenters in Chinese cyberspace.[9]

Internet Café Regulations in China

In December 1998 the first directive explicitly targeting the Internet industry was the Notice of the Ministry of Public Security, the Ministry of Information Industry, the Ministry of Culture, and the State Administration for Industry and Commerce on Regulating the Operation of, and Strengthening the Administration of, Security in Connection with Internet Cafés.[10] This first directive consisted only of six articles. Its main feature was the demand that Internet cafés had to register with the local branch of the public security bureau. The second, more expanded, and important directive to focus on the Internet cafés promulgated in April 2001 was the Measure for the Administration of Internet Access Centers.[11] It consisted of

---

8 "Microsoft censors its blog tool," http://www.rsf.org/article.php3?id_article =14069.

9 See "Google omits controversial news stories in China," NewScientist.com news service, September 4, 2004, http://www.newscientist.com/article.ns?id= dn6426; "Google-Yahoo market battle threatens freedom of expression, reporters without borders calls on U.S. officials to impose code of conduct on Internet firms," July 26, 2004, http://www.rsf.org.

10 For Document Gong Tongzhi <1998>, effective from December 25, 1998, no. 90, see *China and the Internet: Essential Legislation* (Baker & McKenzie, 2001), 133–135.

11 This regulation was issued by the Ministry of Information Industry, the

twenty-five articles and highlighted the need for both physical safety and "healthy and civilized online activities" in Internet cafés. The third directive, Regulations on the Administration of Internet Access Service Business Establishments, following the tragic Lanjisu fire, was absolutely crucial for the transformation of the whole Internet café industry in China.[12] With the Ministry of Culture superseding the Ministry of Information Industry as the number one regulatory agency in this particular area, the regulations focused even more than before on ideological aspects, such as "building a socialist spiritual civilization." Before the implementation of the new regulation, approximately 220,000 Internet cafés existed in China. After the crackdown this number was halved.[13]

Article 23 of the 2002 regulations clearly explains how the government expects the owners of Internet cafés to monitor and keep detailed books on their customers' surfing habits. It demands that Internet cafés "shall examine, register, and keep a record of the identification card or other effective document of those customers who go online. The contents of the registration and records shall be maintained for at least 60 days, and shall be provided to the cultural and public security agencies for examination in accordance with the law. Registration contents and records shall not be altered or destroyed during this period." The fourth directive targeting the industry was the Ministry of Culture's proposal for a national chain-store model, which can be viewed as the final phase of the overall crackdown on illegal black Internet cafés. The vision in the text clearly envisaged the remaining Internet cafés to be firmly checked, and to operate "in chains." Xinhua News Agency reported that the

---

Ministry of Public Security, the Ministry of Culture and the State Administration for Industry and Commerce on and effective from April 3, 2001. See China and the Internet: Essential Legislation, 370–382.

12 This regulation was jointly promulgated on September 29, 2002 by the Ministry of Culture, the Ministry of Public Security, the State Administration for Industry and Commerce, and the Ministry of Information Industry.

13 Quoted by Cnet, http://news.com.com/2100-1028_3-5097379.html (accessed February 20, 2007).

remaining 110,000 Internet cafés that existed after the huge crackdown on illegal *wangba* after the Lanjisu fire would be brought under the management of large state-owned companies.

This is important as it promotes one mode of operation of Internet cafés as superior. As Qiu and Zhou argue, with the incremental buildup over time, each new measure has become more detailed and formal, which indicates increased control, especially the 2003 announcement (in this chapter referred to as the fourth directive) marks a new course combining "strict control" and "positive guidance."[14] Hereafter, the four above-mentioned national level directives will be referred to as "the net café regulations."

It is difficult to estimate to what extent the detailed Article 23 of the 2002 regulations has been successfully implemented across regions, provinces, and within cities of China. Given the well-known difficulty of implementing law in China, one would surmise that like many other laws under implementation in the People's Republic laws targeting Internet cafés would also face serious administrative "lag" when encountering the concrete realities of administrative fragmentation and competition between various agencies. In China, law implementation suffers from many problems. The persistent dilemma of locally implementing centrally made laws is widely recognized and rooted in a long history of precedents.[15] Another obvious problem is the public's lack of trust in the judicial system.[16] The judiciary is seen as corrupt, inadequate to handle issues of justice for ordinary people, since the court system is subject to potentially very heavy influence from the Communist Party. Since the founding of the PRC,

---

14 Jack Linchuan Qiu and Liuning Zhou, "Through the Prism of the Internet Cafe: Managing Access in an Ecology of Games," *China Information* 19, no. 2 (July 2005): 281.

15 Thomas Metzger, *The Western Concept of the Civil Society in the Context of Chinese History* (Stanford: Hoover Essays, 1998), 17.

16 Jonas Grimheden, "Themis v. Xiezhi: Assessing Judicial Independence in the People's Republic of China Under International Human Rights Law" (Lund: Ph.D. Dissertation, Lund University, 2004), 229.

citizens have continued to approach bureaucrats through the formal bureaucratic system of *xinfang*, letters-and-visits system, to plead their causes. The popularity of this procedure, often involving complaints about the courts, has continued to increase in recent years despite the government's emphasis on strengthening the rule of law in China.[17] The use of lawyers for civil lawsuits is increasing but is generally not seen as the most useful way to correct grievances. Thus, although the agencies of the central government are quite abstract, people still put their trust in central agencies of the party-state, taking their problems to the central letters-and-visits office in Beijing, thus deferring more legitimacy on it than on the court system. However, in the overall context of problems of implementing laws, especially on the regional and local levels, what is interesting with the Internet café regulations is that there seems to be an efficient implementation of these particular laws. In the following sections of this chapter, I will explain why, at least in the bigger cities, the laws targeting Internet cafés are exceptions to conventional wisdom about problems of law implementation in China.

Legal Ideals and Normative Realities

For an understanding of how Chinese society, its citizens, mass media outlets, and companies have reacted toward recent Internet regulations involving both enterprises and individuals, the ideas put forward by law scholar Håkan Hydén may be taken as a point of departure. According to him, legal regulations are never issued in a social vacuum. He argues that there are always existing norms operating in society with which the legal norms will compete or that they will complement in one way or another, and that a law cannot

---

17 Sara Davis, "China's Angry Petitioners," *Asian Wall Street Journal*, August 25, 2005, A7.

be expected to have any sustainable effect if it does not correspond to these norms.[18] This norm model has three dimensions. The first dimension of a norm is that it is an expression of a person's will. The second dimension is knowledge and cognition, the prerequisites needed to carry out one's will. The third dimension is related to the systemic conditions characterizing the situation or the society in which the action occurs and consequently where the norm is perpetuated. It is not enough that someone wants to do something and that the person has cognitively adequate knowledge on how to go about it. One also has to have factual possibilities to do what one wants and can in order for a norm to be cultivated. While the first two dimensions are related to subjective factors among actors, this third factor is related to objective factors, i.e., factors not at the actors' disposal.

Hydén argues that for normative changes to be realized, the systemic conditions of the third dimension are the most important. And he takes the final battle in the implementation process to be when the legal ideals of the law meet the normative realities of society. It is when the normative content from above meets the undercurrent of existing norms in society that tensions are at their highest in the implementation process. In the Chinese context, although the personal freedom to cultivate one's own opinion and norms has increased in the post-Mao era, the systemic condition characterizing China today is that the party-state, given its control of the news media, still manages a hegemonic discourse over social and political change. Among other factors, the fluctuations in this discourse are what contribute to normative change or status quo thinking on a particular social issue.

---

18 Håkan Hydén, "Implementation of International Conventions as a Socio-Legal Enterprise: Examples from the Convention on the Rights of the Child," in *Human Rights Law: From Dissemination to Application*, eds. Jonas Grimheden and Rolf Ring (Martinus Nijhoff Publishers, 2006).

A Party-State Intent on Molding Citizen Norms

Stephen Cherry has argued that the question of how long China's censorship of and harsh policies toward the Internet will continue is no longer a question of technology. With increasingly sophisticated Internet technologies, the issue is now more about politics than technology.[19] If government policy is more decisive than technological features, then some sort of popular legitimacy is necessary. Even in a repressive authoritarian state, the laws are more easily implemented and enforced if they are legitimate in the eyes of the population.

Given the difficulty of successful law implementation in China, it is intuitive to believe that the regulations targeting Internet cafés also met problems when they were to be implemented in the concrete reality of Chinese daily life. Legal legitimacy is always dependent on the mainstream norm tacitly or actively supporting a law. Thus, one must ask if there were any visible tensions when the normative content in the Internet café regulations formulated from above met the undercurrent of existing norms in Chinese society. In order to successfully win the public's trust, it was necessary for the authorities to draft the four Internet café regulations in such a way that they reasonably corresponded to norms held in Chinese society. Needless to say, the state-controlled media also attempts, often successfully, to bend and engineer public opinion in support of government policies.[20] In the case of the implemtation of the third law, following the Lanjisu fire, implementation proved to be fairly easy since one strong driving force for harsher regulation

---

19 Steven Cherry, "The Net Effect: As China's internet gets a much-needed makeover, will the new network promote freedom or curtail it?" http://www.spectrum.ieee.org/jun05/1219 (accessed June 27, 2007).

20 Johan Lagerkvist, "In the Crossfire of Demands: Chinese News Portals Between Propaganda and the Public," in *Chinese Cyberspaces: Technological Changes and Political Effects*, eds. Jens Damm and Simona Thomas (London: RoutledgeCurzon, 2006); Johan Lagerkvist, *China and the Internet: Unlocking and Containing the Public Sphere* (Lund: Lund University Press, 2006).

came from the parents of children spending considerable time in the Internet cafés. Thus the Internet café regulations, particularly the third one, corresponded well with mainstream and majority views on the matter. Few protests from either owners of Internet cafés or Chinese youth followed the implementation. Thus, in line with Hydén's ideas, it is reasonable to argue that the normative ideals (i.e., party-state norms) in the legal text complemented one of the most important and powerful norms in society in this particular case, what I would call the "parental norm." Interestingly, this also shows that a bottom-up normative change from society's grass roots was transferred via the mass media having an impact on decision-makers. This can mean either that the systemic relations between rulers and citizens in China are changing because listening to public opinion is becoming important for regime legitimacy, or that bureaucratic agencies found public opinion useful in this case for achieving other objectives. Or both of these processes perhaps occurred simultaneously, where different forces all got something from the final outcome.

In order to grasp the normative changes concerning the Internet café regulations, we need to survey the different opinions that existed in society and the context that contributed to the growth of a norm consensus. Although there exists no single seminal document that specifies an official ideology on what constitutes the negative effects of the Internet, many academic texts and policy documents argue that Western values must be resisted in the ongoing war against this risky cultural dissemination on the Internet. The usual culprits associated with these values are pornography, online gaming, religious superstition, the slandering of China, defaming the Communist Party and its highest leaders, or encouraging secession from the Chinese state. For many years the Internet cafés have been viewed or depicted as being the host of all these vices tempting the nation's youth.[21] A paragraph from the booklet "Some views of the Central Committee of the Communist Party and the State Council

---

21 Duncan Hewitt, "China acts on net 'addicts,' Chinese police want to moni-

regarding the further strengthening of young people's moral thinking" illustrates well the position of the party vis-à-vis Internet cafés. This position is "the party-state norm," which in many ways goes hand in hand with the parental norm in this particular case. The document emphasizes the importance of strictly enforcing the regulation that does not allow youngsters below the age of eighteen into Internet bars, and of enforcing the installation of filtering software blocking pornographic and other unhealthy content in the equipment of Internet bars. Moreover, it is argued that

> [p]opularizing green Internet software is an effective means for parents to supervise children's online behavior also at home. In earnest, carry out "the Regulations on the Administration of Internet Access Service Business Establishments" and the State Council's regulations, transmitted through the Ministry of Culture and other ministries: "Notice on views regarding the specific order of business establishments initiating electronic gaming" and "Notice on views regarding the punishing of net bars and other Internet access service business establishments", and further optimizing the environment surrounding school yards. There cannot exist any net bars or business establishments with electronic gaming within 200 meters of primary and secondary schools.[22]

This paragraph reveals that government agencies have the possibility to make money as a by-product when ensuring social stability. This is especially true if censorship strategies are framed in such a way as presenting opportunities for parents to improve on their children's schoolwork by buying filtering software from the authorities—

---

tor Internet activity," BBC News Online, http://news.bbc.co.uk/1/low/world/asia-pacific/1448423.stm (accessed July 20, 2001).

22 *Some Views of the Central Committee of the Communist Party and the State Council Regarding the Further Strengthening of Young People's Moral Thinking* (Beijing: China Legal Publishing House, 2004), 17.

software that is sponsored, developed, and sold by state-owned companies often run directly under the Public Security Department.[23] An enormous amount of money is involved in the surveillance and control of Internet cafés. It was estimated that the advanced surveillance system to be installed in about one-thousand Internet cafés in the southern city of Shenzhen would produce more than three million dollars in revenue during its first year of operation.[24]

As law scholars He Bing and Zhao Peng have shown, considerable economic interests were behind the fourth national-level net regulations, which forced individual operators out of business while new licenses have been exclusively granted to chain operators subordinate to the Ministry of Culture.[25]

Interestingly, financial concerns are apparent also in some local resistance against the Internet café regulations. Although most bureaucrats and lawmakers have adopted the official party line on what constitute the hazards of Internet development, there have been differing voices among Chinese provincial legislators regarding the regulation of Internet bars. Members of the standing committee of Guangzhou's people's congress, for example, expressed fear that excessively harsh registration would limit the development of the Internet cafés in Guangzhou to the detriment of both the public and these businesses. In fact they argued that "these administrative measures embody an obvious interference with business.

---

23 The central government reported in 2004 that it would reduce the requirements for market access to information security products. Obviously the business must grow to keep censorship budgets within limits. See "Information security system to be built," www.chinaview.cn, April 6, 2004.

24 PR Newswire, "China Security and Surveillance Technology Inc. signs contract as exclusive surveillance system provider for Shenzhen city Internet cafes," http://www.prnewswire.com/cgibin/stories.pl?ACCT=104&STORY=/www/story/03-21-2006/0004324623&EDATE= (accessed February 20, 2007).

25 He Bing and Zhao Peng, "Quanli ruhe shenru shichang? Cong wangba guanzhi, xi wo guo xingzheng lifa de wenti" [How is power seeping into the market? Analyzing china's lawmaking problems from the administrative legislation regarding internet bars], unpublished paper, 2003, on file with the author.

The city of Guangzhou should free the development of Internet cafés."[26] Apparently, in late 2006 there were growing indications that Guangzhou would end the two-year moratorium, started in March 2004, on licensing new Internet cafés. The shift in policy was expected to double the number of legal Internet cafés during 2007.[27] The Guangzhou people's congress exemplifies local politicians and bureaucrats who have adopted a more liberal approach toward Internet cafés. Also, as Oscar Almén's chapter in this volume shows, in issues pertaining to environmental law, the rather "liberal" Guangzhou people's congress has advocated on the part of citizens' rights to both livelihood and their economic interests. If this liberal minority across the country had not voiced its concern, all privately owned net cafés in China could have been out of business today. These voices represented less strong norms in society that argued on behalf of less powerful interests like small-scale operators, low-income groups unable to access the Internet from their homes, or Chinese youths in general. This weaker norm could be termed "the youth and subaltern norm," to be contrasted with the "parental norm" and the "party-state norm." According to one manager of an Internet café chain in Nanjing, some hardliners did advocate a very tough stance toward the Internet café businesses during 2002. This informant was convinced it was arguments about economic growth that softened the final wording of the 2002 regulation. This is a plausible statement. Even though the net cafés may be at the low end of the information industry's value chain, they were an important source of income since there were approximately two thousand of them and therefore they contributed in no small part to the revenues of telecom companies, manufacturers of computer hardware, and suppliers of electricity.[28]

---

26 "Should Guangzhou Internet cafés be allowed more freedom?" News item, online opinion poll, and discussion at http://www.sina.com (accessed September 23, 2003).

27 Kevin Huang, "Freeze on Internet cafes to end, number of legal cyber bars in Guangzhou expected to double," *South China Morning Post*, August 18, 2006.

28 Interview in Nanjing, March 5, 2005

With economic globalization impacting strongly on China, one wonders if the policies of cultural protection and containment of domestic media industries are simply a futile war of resistance. Nevertheless, there are powerful cultural policy models like Singapore's to emulate that fit well with the Chinese government's wish to boost the economy while blocking a pluralistic discourse on politics in the digital media landscape. Singapore's cultural policies are meant to propel the growth of a new creative economy, which is premised on the innovative energies that can come out of each creative Singaporean. One may, of course, doubt whether this small Southeast Asian city-state can act as a working model for the world's most populous nation, but one cannot help notice some striking similarities. In Singapore, the economic potential of culture is appreciated while strict boundaries of political and social exchange are still enforced.[29]

This endeavor is not easy. Speaking of censorship policies and cultural protection becoming impediments for creativity in China, Michael Keane has argued that "concerns about cultural identity and regulatory regimes must be handled carefully, or at least skillfully moderated."[30] The reason for this is, of course, that if the heavy hand of the state stifles creative industries, audiences, markets, and investors will gradually lose interest. Therefore, in the interest of continued economic growth, there may be a "best before date" on the cultural models of both Singapore and China.

Citizen Norms and Internet Cafés

What role have ordinary Chinese citizens played in the process of implementing the Internet café regulations? Ordinary citizens and larger businesses in the Internet industry have not been passive by-

---

[29] Terence Lee, "Creative Shifts and Directions: Cultural Policy in Singapore," *International Journal of Cultural Policy* 10, no. 3 (2004): 295.

[30] Michael Keane, "Brave New World: Understanding China's Creative Vision," *International Journal of Cultural Policy* 10, no. 3 (2004): 267

standers to the process of unregistered Internet cafés targeted by law and cracked down upon by local police forces. An often quoted motivating force behind these closures and justification of the state's actions is said to be parents of young children. As Chinese media has frequently reported on violence occurring inside or in the vicinity of Internet cafés and the dysfunctional effects of hours of playing games online, parents have feared their children becoming addicted to online computer games and teaming up with juvenile delinquents at these public places.[31] In Nanjing, one father of an "Internet worm" was quite happy with the enforcement of tougher regulations against Internet cafés in his native city. Moreover, he was convinced all parents were of the same opinion, especially after the unfolding of the story about the arson at the Lanjisu Internet café in Beijing.[32]

Some researchers have argued that rather than being an excuse for cracking down on freedom of expression, the Internet café closures had more to do with pressures on government to act strongly to the complaints of parents, schoolteachers, or reports in the media. Others, like Chinese law scholars He and Zhao, have argued to the contrary that the Internet café businesses were already too heavily regulated already *before* the Lanjisu fire. Therefore people eager to start a business due to rising demand for these business establishments saw no option other than setting up unregistered Internet cafés.[33] One can interpret He and Zhao's argument that before the Lanjisu arson the already strong 1998 regulations were not legitimate in the eyes of the public, and that tension regarding implementation of Internet café regulations was prevalent in society as citizens demanded more outlets, and businesses were unsatisfied with too much red tape to register with the authorities. It was only after the media coverage of the arson and the subsequent me-

---

31 See chinaview.cn, "Power cuts to kick kids off the net", September 26, 2004, http:/www.chinaview.cn.

32 Interview in Nanjing, February 2002.

33 He and Zhao, "How Is Power Seeping into the Market?"

dia storm that even harsher measures were met with outright applause from Chinese civil society. Lanjisu proved to be a turning point that defused tensions regarding the previous Internet café regulations. Nonetheless, I would also argue that using moral arguments in this case created an opportunity for bureaucratic agencies to regulate a hitherto neglected trade in line with their own economic interests. This does not mean that the Chinese government and Communist Party do not try to advance political interests by using moral arguments to win over public opinion on issues dealing with social stability.[34] They do. But in the case of the Internet café regulations, political interests played second fiddle.

Intellectuals' Writings on the Internet Peril: Threatening Culture and Youth

One wonders how the turning point in normative change had such an immediate transformative effect. Plenty of arguments utilizing parental and party-state norms were raised well before the 2002 Lanjisu fire. These norms became embedded in the discourse of society, although without having any sudden effect on public opinion or policy. I believe the reason to be that the tragic Lanjisu arson served as a catalyst for ideas and opinions already embedded in society but whose latent force had not yet been fully uncovered. Party intellectuals and many academics have for a long time debated the negative impact of Internet cafés. In writing news stories, academic articles, or ideological texts, they have worked hard for these ideas to become urgent issues to act upon. Therefore, an understanding of how mainstream norms in Chinese society interplay with the intellectual rationale behind the policies of protecting Chinese iden-

---

[34] Since then the government has continued to see the usefulness of engaging the public for endorsing new Internet laws. In October 2004 there was also an effort to engage "the masses" to report any unhealthy tendencies on Chinese websites.

tity in the age of globalization also yield significant insights about the legitimacy of laws directed at the Internet industry in general.[35]

The Chinese government has recently halted further liberalization of Sino-foreign joint ventures in cultural industries, such as television and the Internet, which are content-sensitive businesses. There is good reason to believe that recent policy changes reflect that the rationale of the party intellectuals influence the policymakers who decide the extent and levels of cultural regulation. Few Chinese intellectuals who have devoted themselves to analysis of the influence of the Internet on society have hopes of an intercultural paradise in the future. According to most writers who stay close to the party line, the interconnected global village is nothing but an arena for "the electronic clash of the civilizations" and foreign "cultural invasions." There is, however, no question of technophobia. The most optimistic commentators point out the incredible opportunities for communicating Chinese culture in the other direction.

Not all intellectuals debating cultural regulation of the Internet industry are conservative party intellectuals. Positive visions are sketched out: the Chinese language will be strengthened, bonds between Chinese people worldwide will be tightened, and a Chinese view of world events will finally reach out to a Western-manipulated world opinion. There have been scholars arguing for a less conservative approach. Zhang Wei, for example, has argued that "although Internet cafes indeed have some negative effects, they should not be banned." According to Zhang, they should only be "cleaned up."[36] But later events have shown that defense of the Internet cafés and the social benefits delivered by providing cheap access to information for the poor was not strong enough. In general the negative

---

35 After the fire in the Lanjisu Internet café, the interplay between parents, mass media, and lawmakers resulted in new regulations on the Internet café industry.

36 BBC, "China Internet cafe debate hots up," http://news.bbc.co.uk/1/hi/world/monitoring/media_reports/1302309.stm (accessed April 29, 2001).

voices dominate, i.e., those who think that Chineseness is being watered down in a cultural soup of globalization and Americanization. Utter moral panic appears, as in all human affairs, when the welfare of youth is being discussed. The young are generally considered to be a particularly vulnerable group of users as they so easily lose their moral compass, a view public opinion also seems to support. A strong paternalistic attitude recurs on the part of the writers. Their simplified equation involves defenseless young people being attacked in a one-dimensional manner by an immoral Western culture. Some of them follow the party line very closely, despite the fact that they are published in academic journals or popular magazines. One illustrative example is Xiao Lingnuo's analysis:

> The Internet has added fuel to the fire recently, with material appearing on the Web as each Western festival—Christmas, Valentine's Day, and so forth—rolls around, as though it must be celebrated all over the world. Guided by advertisements in the media, Chinese people who have always considered their national dishes very nutritious have begun to develop a taste for foreign food. This is especially so for the generation of youth growing up now. [. . .] These things clarify one issue: In this information age, everyday aspects of our national culture have already come under attack from Western culture.[37]

In her opinion, easily led and defenseless young Internet users are "devoured" by Western cultural products. The deplorable end-result of this process is a general public suffering from an inability to be able to identify which culture they really belong to. It pains her to see how people "can no longer find their way home" and have "difficulties in distinguishing between good and evil and between true and false." Part of this picture is also how Western nations are exploiting a China in the midst of rapid development and therefore

---

37 Xiao Lingnuo, "Informatization and the National Culture," *Contemporary Chinese Thought* 35, no. 2 (Winter 2003–2004): 74.

unable to defend itself against the expansion of unsound values.[38] Among the worst of these are individualism, egoism, money worship, sexual promiscuity, and hedonism. And all of these are said to lead to the corruption of China's youth. Even if nowadays few intellectuals fear China's imminent ruin, many are still drawing from the same dystopian well when they look at the world.[39] Despite the opportunities of the market for alternative intellectual careers, *youhuan yishi*, or the "worrying mentality," which is the moral task of intellectuals, continues to form a strongly educative undercurrent within many different discourses and in widely differing sectors of society.

Proposals for necessary countermeasures to protect the party's legitimacy, Chinese youth, and the Chinese nation from so-called unhealthy phenomena transmitted through new information and communications technology show how the buildup of norms regarding Internet cafés has been incremental and has become embedded in social discourse over a long time. Moreover, the party-intellectuals' texts are also a clear expression of the strategic thinking that goes on within the party-state propaganda apparatus. It is time to realize, these intellectuals say, that creative change must be carried out in the traditional work of propaganda. The overarching aim is to have young people follow and accept the party's plan for

---

38 See Hui Shuguang and Huang Tianhan, "Hulianwang dui sixiang zhengzhi jiaoyu de xiaoji yingxiang ji duice yanjiu" [Research on the negative impact of the Internet on ideological education and countermeasures to it], *Beijing youdian daxue xuebao* [Journal of Beijing Post and Telecommunications University], no. 2 (2002): 48–53; Li Zhuoying and Wang Jian, "Hulianwang dui sixiang zhengzhi gongzuo de yingxiang ji duice" [The Internet's impact on ideological and political thought: Work and ways of addressing it], *Xin changzheng* [The New Long March], no. 3 (2001): 31–33.

39 Fu Xiaoping and Zhang Lei, "Hulianwang dui daxuesheng xinli, xingwei de fumian yingxiang ji duice tanjiu" [The negative effect of the Internet on the behavior and psychology of tertiary students and a thorough look at ways of dealing with it], *Sichuan shifan xueyuan bao* [Journal of Sichuan Teachers College Philosophy and Social Sciences], no.1 (January 2002): 88–92.

the development of Chinese society. Cultural globalization via the Internet therefore constitutes a tangible threat to the rich and refined, but all too vulnerable, Chinese culture.[40]

Mutual Understanding Between Big Business and the Government

Big international Internet companies such as Google, Yahoo, and Microsoft play another important role in creating a normative understanding in society and legal legitimacy for the net café regulations and other Internet laws in China. By not standing up for principles not to censor their customers, web logs, websites, or chat room postings, they make it easier for the government to mold public opinion on the information industry to their liking. From being very slow in the beginning, Chinese legislators and the judiciary have become increasingly apt at accommodating every advent of a new web application that carries the potential of fomenting public opinion on the net. Keeping track of new web applications is important as they form alternative spaces for expression of dissent and criticism of current policies. As for the large Nasdaq-listed Chinese web portals like Sina, Sohu, and Netease, they have no choice but to acquiesce to the ever-changing maze of old and new laws, notices, and regulations from various government bodies.[41] There is really no alternative course for them to take either, for in order to operate an Internet business in China they need to obey the law. They must also follow the instructions from government censorship bodies

---

40 Chris Buckley, "China Issues New Restrictions Aimed at Protecting Its Culture," *New York Times*, August 4, 2005.

41 The most recent regulation that web portals and other companies carrying online news must follow is Rules on the Administration of Internet News Information Services, promulgated by the State Council Information Office and the Ministry of Information Industry. See http://www.cecc.gov/pages/virtualAcad/index.phpd?showsingle=24396 (accessed October 1, 2005).

closely, as the managing director of web portal Sina's Shanghai branch clearly elaborated in an interview:

> Actually, we work very, very close with the government, the propaganda department, or the Ministry of Information Industry. We follow the guidelines and have to be working partners with the government. It is not a choice to work with them, but on the other hand it is a choice ... We are not allowed to have our own correspondents; we are dependent on the government for news. It is a good way; saves cost also.[42]

From the above paragraph it may seem like the managers of web portals are not necessarily unhappy about the current situation. They make good money and stay in business as long as they do nothing to affront the government or the Communist Party. But big web portals and Internet start-up companies are under pressure from their own shareholders to break new market ground. Therefore, they have to tread a delicate path between pleasing the government and serving the rather unfaithful hordes of Internet surfers who easily shift to other web pages if the atmosphere in one web portal gets stuffier or less cutting edge in providing the latest information.[43] When supervision of Internet law today to a large extent is delegated to Internet content providers themselves, this means companies must invest resources in eavesdropping on the public that is using their web portal services, chat rooms, BBS, and instant messaging systems. On the surface, and in official statements, the delegation of Internet law enforcement is loosely sketched out in the joint statements between the industry and the government to promote "a healthy Internet." The Sina manager also wanted to emphasize the casual and nonconflictual nature in the relationship between his company and the publicity department (formerly the propaganda department), and his view on the joint statements on a

---

42 Interview in Shanghai, April 2003.
43 For more on this dilemma, see Lagerkvist, "In the Crossfire of Demands."

healthy Internet issued by the government and the industry are also revealing:

> We are good friends with the propaganda department—casual. You have to treat people as partners... The joint statements are good: copyright issues and "the three represents."[44] I think it is correct. Basically it's a good thing. Well, the government has their views on reform. Still in China, this is our own situation. Democracy does not come overnight. It would not be good for the Chinese government or the people, not good either way, like in Russia. A statement like this is voluntary because I think not every Internet company is part of it. Many government departments want us to join this or that; that is (actually) up to us.[45]

The views of this informant are very straightforward and telling of the general situation for Internet technology businesses in China. Big Internet companies like the web portal Sina have to work in close cooperation with the government in order not to upset the latter, or risk discriminatory sanctions that would put them out of business. But more interesting is that these often highly educated young men, often with degrees from Western universities, who work in the information sector do not lament the current antifree speech policies of the Chinese government. More often than not, they seem convinced that freedom of speech is not necessarily something that benefits society at large. In this they share the view of the government—unhealthy information or web content undermines social and political stability, and in the end business profits.

---

44 Former president Jiang Zemin's contribution to the Chinese Communist Party's theoretical canon is called *san ge daibiao*, or "the three represents," by which is meant that the party shall represent "the advanced forces of production," "advanced culture," and "the interests of the majority." Basically it means that the party nowadays also recognizes the value of entrepreneurs for China's future welfare.

45 Interview in Shanghai, April 2003.

At least they would have us believe that changes should be brought about in agreement and in a cooperative manner with the government.[46] Thus, there is no solidarity on the part of the big Internet technology entrepreneurs toward their smaller brethren on the Internet café level. This is indicative of how skillful the Chinese party-state has been in controlling and coopting different parts of Chinese society in accordance with their interests to contain a very dynamic phenomenon—the Internet café venue.

Concluding Remarks

In this chapter I show why implementation of measures targeting Internet cafés in China has been successful. The reason is that the measures directed against illegal "black Internet cafés" and Internet cultural regulation reflect sentiments not just in the Chinese Communist Party but also more generally among Chinese parents, party intellectuals, and big private Internet technology firms. National-level laws and regulations all face problems of implementation when they encounter the concrete realities of administrative fragmentation and corruption in China's provinces and cities. How did implementation amount to a success? With regard to physical space, i.e., the Internet café premises, civil servants of the state continued to use old-time measures of control and law enforcement to check on the ground if rules were followed. If they were not, owners were fined or, worse, had to close down. As to virtual space, supervision of correct and lawful behavior has to a large extent become delegated and outsourced to Internet content providers and web portals, public or semiprivate.

What is interesting with the four national-level Internet café regulations, however, is that from the initial difficulties when the first measure was announced in 1998, it has since become an easier

---

46 David Sheff, *China Dawn: The Story of a Technology and Business Revolution* (New York: Harper Business, 2002), 254.

task to supervise them and contain their development. I argue that the main reason is that the legal norms of the party-state, in this chapter called the party-state norm, increasingly resonated well with some of the existing norms in society (establishment intellectuals and parents) in this case. Implementation proved to be fairly easy since one strong driving force for harsher regulation came from the parents of children spending considerable time in the net cafés. In this chapter I have called this norm the parental norm. Thus, the government won the public's trust (or at least the stronger elements and norms of the public) for harsher regulation of the trade. But this was the result of a normative change that seemingly was dependent on a random incident in society, namely, the tragic arson at Beijing's Lanjisu Internet café in 2002. I believe, however, that society and the public was already prepared to change its opinion on the Internet café business scene because the normative change was already embedded in public discourse. It merely took a tragic catalyst like Lanjisu to gain enough momentum and unfold.

What looks like a bottom-up normative change from society's grass roots, transferred via the mass media to a government perhaps becoming more attentive toward public opinion, could actually be something completely different. Another interpretation is that the Lanjisu fire served as a window of opportunity for the bureaucracy to act swiftly out of economic interest in regulating a lucrative segment of the Internet technology market. And many party intellectuals prepared the ground by launching discursive arguments in journals and the mass media against foreign-produced cultural pollution contaminating China's young sitting in front of unregulated screens. Naturally, parents afraid of their game-playing children getting low grades in a very competitive society were attentive to these kinds of arguments. And out of fears of bureaucratic penalties, big Internet technology businesses agreed with the general calls from the government to clean up China's Internet world, resulting in a "green and healthy Internet."

Against the stronger norms of the party-state and Chinese parents were voices among a minority of liberal academics and lawmakers who represented what I call the youth and subaltern norm. Out of different concerns, all the above actors have played important parts in the norm- building processes that have made law implementation vis-à-vis the Internet cafés an increasingly easy affair. It is important to acknowledge that not all of the norm holders in society support the authorities' position regarding the Internet café industry. Although society is split on this issue, it is not split in half. In fact, there is no way to know for sure; perhaps there was a majority of café owners and a variety of customers out there were unable or too fatalist to raise their voices? Nonetheless, the sheer force of the more powerful norms marginalized these weaker norms. I would argue that using moral arguments of cultural regulation in this case created an opportunity for bureaucratic agencies to regulate a hitherto neglected trade in line with their own economic interests. In other words, the political and moral concerns, effectively advanced by Chinese intellectuals and the mass media, served as an effective disguise for economic interests. This does not mean that the Chinese government and Communist Party do not try to advance political interests by using moral arguments to win over public opinion on other issues dealing with social stability.[47] They do. But in the case of the Internet café regulations political interests certainly played the second fiddle.

The legitimacy of the four national-level regulations that started the crackdown on the Internet cafés continues to be strong. Arguably, with the forces of economic globalization today impacting heavily on China, increased travel, a youth often educated abroad, and foreign-produced TV programs, to name just a few, the war against the myriad of interconnecting cultural influences to be found in China's online networks will be increasingly difficult to wage over time. Thus, one wonders if the party-state's policies of cultural pro-

---

47 Since then the government has continued to see the usefulness of engaging the public for endorsing new Internet laws. In October 2004 a strong effort was made to engage "the masses" to report any unhealthy tendencies on Chinese websites.

tection and containment of pollution of the cultural environment will not erode due to further normative changes in society as a result of this development. Nonetheless, at least for the time being, it seems like the strongest determining factors for molding norms and legal legitimacy about Internet developments in general and Internet cafés in particular in China are domestic ones.

Bibliography

BBC, "China Internet cafe debate hots up," http://news.bbc.co.uk/1/hi/world/monitoring/media_reports/1302309.stm (accessed April 29, 2001).
Buckley, Chris, "China Issues New Restrictions Aimed at Protecting Its Culture," *New York Times*, August 4, 2005.
Cherry, Steven, "The Net Effect: As China's internet gets a much-needed makeover, will the new network promote freedom or curtail it?" http://www.spectrum.ieee.org/jun05/1219.
China and the Internet: Essential Legislation. Hong Kong: Baker & McKenzie, 2001.
Davis, Sara, "China's Angry Petitioners," *Asian Wall Street Journal*, August 25, 2005, A7.
Deibert, Ronald J. "Dark Guests and Great Firewalls: The Internet and Chinese Security Policy," *Journal of Social Issues* 58, no. 1 (2002): 143–159.
Fu, Xiaoping and Zhang, Lei, "Hulianwang dui daxuesheng xinli, xingwei de fumian yingxiang ji duice tanjiu" [The negative effect of the Internet on the behavior and psychology of tertiary students and a thorough look at ways of dealing with it], *Sichuan shifan xueyuan bao* [Journal of Sichuan Teachers College Philosophy and Social Sciences], no. 1 (January 2002): 88-92.
"Google omits controversial news stories in China," NewScientist.com news service, September 4, 2004, http://www.newscientist.com/article.ns?id=dn6426;
"Google—Yahoo market battle threatens freedom of expression, reporters without borders calls on U.S. officials to impose code of conduct on Internet firms," July 26, 2004, http://www.rsf.org.
Grimheden, Jonas. "Themis v. Xiezhi: Assessing Judicial Independence in the People's Republic of China Under International Human Rights Law." Lund: Ph.D. Dissertation, Lund University, 2004.

He, Bing, and Zhao, Peng. "Quanli ruhe shenru shichang? Cong wangba guanzhi, xi wo guo xingzheng lifa de wenti" [How is power seeping into the market? Analyzing China's lawmaking problems from the administrative legislation regarding Internet bars], unpublished paper, 2003, on file with the author.

Hewitt, Duncan. "China acts on net 'addicts,' Chinese police want to monitor Internet activity," BBC News Online, http://news.bbc.co.uk/1/low/world/asia-pacific/1448423.stm

Huang, Kevin. "Freeze on Internet cafes to end, number of legal cyber bars in Guangzhou expected to double," *South China Morning Post*, August 18, 2006.

Hui, Shuguang, and Huang, Tianhan. "Hulianwang dui sixiang zhengzhi jiaoyu de xiaoji yingxiang ji duice yanjiu" [Research on the negative impact of the Internet on ideological education and countermeasures to it], *Beijing youdian daxue xuebao* [Journal of Beijing Post and Telecommunications University], no. 2 (2002): 48–53.

Hydén, Håkan. "Implementation of International Conventions as a Socio-Legal Enterprise: Examples from the Convention on the Rights of the Child." In *Human Rights Law: From Dissemination to Application*, edited by Jonas Grimheden and Rolf Ring, Leiden: Martinus Nijhoff Publishers, 2006.

Keane, Michael. "Brave New World: Understanding China's Creative Vision," *International Journal of Cultural Policy* 10, no. 3 (2004): 265–279.

Lagerkvist, Johan. "In the Crossfire of Demands: Chinese News Portals Between Propaganda and the Public." In *Chinese Cyberspaces: Technological Changes and Political Effects*, eds. Jens Damm and Simona Thomas. London: RoutledgeCurzon, 2006.

Lagerkvist, Johan. "China and the Internet: Unlocking and Containing the Public Sphere," Ph.D. Dissertation, Lund University, 2006.

Lee, Terence. "Creative Shifts and Directions: Cultural Policy in Singapore," *International Journal of Cultural Policy* 10, no. 3 (2004): 281–299.

Metzger, Thomas. *The Western Concept of the Civil Society in the Context of Chinese History* Stanford: Hoover Essays, 1998.

"Microsoft censors its blog tool," http://www.rsforg/article.php3?id_article=14069.

Li, Zhuoying and Wang, Jian, "Hulianwang dui sixiang zhengzhi gongzuo de yingxiang ji duice" [The Internet's impact on ideological and political thought work and ways of addressing it], *Xin changzheng* [The New Long March], no. 3 (2001): 31–33.

OpenNet initiative. *Internet Filtering in China in 2004–2005: A Country Study.*

Qiu, Jack Linchuan and Zhou, Liuning. "Through the Prism of the Internet Cafe: Managing Access in an Ecology of Games," *China Information* 19, no. 2 (2005): 261–297.

Sheff, David. *China Dawn: The Story of a Technology and Business Revolution*, New York: Harper Business, 2002.

China Legal Publishing House. *Some Views of the Central Committee of the Communist Party and the State Council Regarding the Further Strengthening of Young People's Moral Thinking* Beijing: China Legal Publishing House, 2004.

van Rooij, Benjamin. *Law as Event: Lessons about Lawmaking, Compliance and Enforcement, Drawn from the Regulation of Land and Pollution in South-West China*. Leiden: Leiden University Press, 2006.

Xiao, Lingnuo. "Informatization and the National Culture," *Contemporary Chinese Thought* 35, no. 2 (Winter 2003–2004): 68–78.

9

Twists and Turns

Anticorruption Law in Beijing

FLORA SAPIO

Introduction

This chapter examines how Beijing Municipality implemented anticorruption laws in the 1990s.[1] Anticorruption policy is one of the most sensitive areas of legislation where the Chinese Communist Party (CCP) is still a key actor. The party has relinquished the micromanagement of several areas of the legal system, delegating lawmaking and implementation to other actors. Anticorruption legislation, however, has remained outside this trend: the party still controls its drafting, content, and implementation.

Other chapters in this volume have pointed out how implementation failures can result from a lack of awareness of legislation, the weakness of sanctions and of implementing agencies, local protec-

---

1 Beijing was chosen as the site of this case-study because of its political and symbolic importance, and the relevance anticorruption has in city governance. Besides being China's administrative and political center, the capital is also China's showcase to the world. Any unrest or scandals taking place there would be interpreted as an omen of the CCP's collapse. Therefore, the main task of its leaders has always been keeping the capital's stability. Corruption can easily spur popular unrest. This is why anticorruption was and still is one of the topmost priorities on Beijing's political agenda.

tionism, and conflicting policy priorities too. This chapter rather problematizes the CCP involvement in law implementation. While the party may not directly interfere in the enforcement of environmental or housing legislation, it clearly plays a paramount role in the enforcement of anticorruption norms. This simple truth has been acknowledged by most scholarship on corruption.[2]

A decline in the CCP political interference, and the party's retreat from the micromanagement of society are generically regarded as beneficial to various aspects of governance. The absence of any political interference by the CCP is, on the other hand, one of the key requisites for the transition toward a form of rule of law, and the achievement of a meaningful judicial independence. From a rule-of-law perspective, there is no doubt that any involvement of the CCP in law implementation would be detrimental and go against the very principles of judicial and procuratorial independence. Yet, the rule of law and the outcome of anticorruption are distinct conceptually and empirically. Conceptually, the former pertains to the realm of legal and political philosophy, while the latter belongs to a subfield of political science. Analytically, thin or thick models of the rule of law have, as their constitutive element,[3] the requirement that "the gap between law in the books

---

2 A few of the more important studies are Andrew Wedeman, "Anticorruption Campaigns and the Intensification of Corruption in China." *Journal of Contemporary China* 14, no. 41 (2005): 93–10. Of the same author see also "The intensification of corruption in China," *The China Quarterly*, no. 180, (2004): 895–921, "Great Disorder under Heaven: The Paradox of Endemic Corruption and Rapid Growth in Contemporary China," *China Review* 4, no. 2 (2004): 1–32, and finally "China's War on Corruption: Progress or Stalemate?" *CSIS Freeman Report* (2007): 1–2 Yan Sun, *Corruption and Market in Contemporary China* (Ithaca: Cornell University Press, 2004). Shawn Shieh, "The rise of collective corruption in China: the Xiamen smuggling case," *Journal of Contemporary China*, vol. 14, no. 42, (2005): 67–91. Lü Xiaobo, *Cadres and Corruption. The Organizational Involution of the Chinese Communist Party*. Stanford: Stanford University Press (2000). Gong Ting, "Corruption and local governance: the double identity of Chinese local governments in market reform," *The Pacific Review*, vol. 19, no. 1, (2006): 85–102.

3 For a listing of the constitutive elements of either of these models see Ran-

and law in practice must be narrow."⁴ Yet states whose legal systems meet the formal standards of a neoliberal rule of law can be plagued by corruption. Taiwan and South Korea can barely reach the mid-rungs of the Corruption Perception Index (CPI). On the other hand, Hong Kong, where the CCP interference can suffocate rule of law mechanism, ranks at the twelfth least corrupt country. ⁵ The existence of a form of rule of law is often not sufficient to fulfill the requirements that laws be implemented. In theory, the strong hand of an authoritarian single-party could. Singapore, which CPI score is higher than Switzerland, provides the most apt illustration. From the narrower point of view of law implementation, the question of whether CCP involvement is beneficial or detrimental is hence no trivial question. Thus far, scholarship on corruption has just assumed that party interference makes things worse. This is tantamount to saying that if the CCP gave up its control over anticorruption law probably party cadres would refrain from engaging in graft and bribery. Yet, the democratic transition of the former Soviet Union has been plagued by high levels of corruption, and there was no Communist Party of the Soviet Union (CPSU) to control legal implementation. From a purely theoretical point of view, it is justified to ask whether *some* policies may *actually benefit* from CCP involvement for two reasons. First, some policies launched and controlled by the party have been a success. The policy of reform and opening up is perhaps the most striking example. Second, scholarship's assumptions have thus far not been tested through empirical case studies. This is what this chapter does. The novelty of this study also lies in the choice of an analytical perspective seldom used in the field of China studies: the concept of networks is applied both to law implementing agencies and to actors involved in corruption.

---

dall Peerenboom, *China's Long March Towards the Rule of Law*. (Oxford: Oxford University Press, 2002): 65 and ff.
  4 *Supra* at 65.
  5 Transparency International, *Corruption Perception Index 2008*.

To better understand the importance of political variables on law implementation, this chapter explores answers to the following questions:

- How was anticorruption law implemented in Beijing? Did the party's control over it distort the outcome of implementation?
- Could implementation be a success in spite of distortions? Or did distortions simply cause—or contribute to—implementation failures?

Implementation of anticorruption legislation was a case of mixed results. Local authorities in Beijing successfully built up a network of law implementing agencies, but something hampered its workings. A clash between the policy priorities devised by the Center[6] and those actually pursued in Beijing was at play. But the single most important factor was the political leadership's direct involvement in implementation. The leadership of Beijing was involved in a conflict of interest. Economic decentralization resulted in the local economy being directly managed by local leaders and the promotion of economic growth was one of their most important tasks. However, direct management of the economy gave them a stake in profit-making activities. Politically, the local leadership was an agent of the Center and had to implement anticorruption legislation. To this end, it enjoyed a certain autonomy in designing and implementing law. But how could anticorruption legislation be implemented by those exploiting economic growth for private interest? Under such circumstances, how could anticorruption legislation produce its intended results? How did the Beijing leadership solve this dilemma?

---

6 From here onward, "the Center" will be a shorthand for all the central-level party and state organs responsible for defining and implementing anticorruption law described below.

Wicked Problems

Until the mid-1980s, crimes of corruption were unsophisticated. They involved single individuals and took place in single institutions. Simple methods were used to exchange bribes or to steal public funds. Official speculation (*guandao*), small-scale bribery, and the theft of state resources and their use to finance private consumption were the main forms of corruption in prereform China and in the early years of the reform era. These acts seldom involved conspiracy among people belonging to different organs, or among officials and other social groups. Commissions for Discipline Inspection (*jilü jiancha weiyuanhui*, CDIs), the party's anticorruption organs, could easily investigate these crimes. CDIs are established in *each* organ of the party-state and have jurisdiction *only over crimes committed in the organ hosting them*. For instance, crimes committed in a tax office are investigated by the tax office's CDI but it cannot investigate crimes committed in other agencies. Insofar as corruption was very simple, this arrangement worked sufficiently well. In the early 1990s, decentralization of economic decision-making resulted in a "mushrooming" of decision-making organs. Allocation of economic resources such as land use rights, bank credit, and licenses and permits involved a larger number of government agencies than before. Also, decision-making processes become more articulated than in the past. Attempts to distort them required the forging of a consensus among several bribers and state officials. Figuring out who the decision-makers were, reaching out to them, and devising the right strategy to corrupt them was not easy. No single individual could perform such a task. Rather, prospective bribers would need to join the officials' social networks, and use their connections as avenues and try to deliver bribes to all the decision-makers they wanted to pay off. This gave rise to complex forms of corruption. The need to use such bribery strategies caused the emergence of flexible, far-reaching networks composed of officials and business people, and involving several state and party organs.[7] The size and reach of these networks also meant that corruption could spread at a considerably faster pace than in the past. Corruption had become a "wicked problem," which could be solved only by the concerted action of several agencies,[8] and which fell under several areas of legislation. Accordingly, the power to implement anticorruption legislation belongs to various organs. None of them alone possesses the resources or the expertise needed to investigate a case from beginning to end.[9] Investigation of any case requires the involvement of both CDI and party committees. The first stages of the investigations are normally conducted by these *party organs*. They decide whether suspects can be punished lightly with party discipline sanctions. If so, the "culprit" is most of the time warned, transferred to a different organ, or demoted.[10] The official, however, is not criminally prosecuted. If CDI and party committees believe the case warrants further investigation, then a series of nonparty organs comes into play. These are public and state security organs, audit and tax offices, bureaus of industry and commerce, and inspectorates of customs. The most complex cases are handled by ad hoc investigative groups composed of personnel from each of these organs. These groups are responsible for evidence collection and investigative procedures. After investigation, if the CDI believes that the official is guilty of a crime, the case is

---

7 Gong Ting, "Dangerous Collusion: Corruption as a Collective Venture in Contemporary China," *Communist and Post-Communist Studies*, no. 35 (2002): 85–103.

8 Horst W. J. Rittel and Melvin Webber, "Dilemmas in a General Theory of Planning," *Policy Sciences*, no. 4 (June 1973): 155–169.

9 Brinton H. Milvard and Keith G. Provan, "Governing the Hollow State," *Journal of Public Administration Research and Theory* 10, no. 2 (2000): 359–380.

10 In these cases, a change of position is involved either as a result of a direct transfer from one position to another or as a result of demotion. Given that data on party discipline sanctions broken down by year are not available publicly, figures on the turnover of officials because of party discipline sanctions are a reliable indicator of how many people committed crimes that were not punished with criminal sanctions.

filed with the judicial organs. People's procuratorates and people's courts enter during the last stages of a case, when the political fate of an official has largely been decided by a CDI.[11] Here it is possible to see a clear conflict of competence between the party and judicial organs. Overlaps in the jurisdiction of implementing agencies exist in other areas of the legal system as well,[12] signaling its complexity. In this case, the intertwining of party and judicial organs has to do with the politically sensitive nature of corruption. The dialectic between corruption and cleanliness is a core component of political legitimacy, political power, and power struggle. This dialectic is at the core of processes of political contestation absent from other legal areas.[13] The authorities controlling the content of anticorruption legislation cannot be delegitimized and the agencies controlling how anticorruption legislation is put into practice cannot be destabilized. Political control over the implementation of other types of legislation would not yield the same results.

Beside this "dual-track legal system"[14] there is "dual-track legislation" and a certain overlap between policy (*zhengce*) and law (*falü*). Party and state law are brought together more closely here than elsewhere in the legal system and the dualistic relationship existing between law and policy makes it difficult to draw a clear boundary between them.

Finally, anticorruption legislation cuts across three different areas of legislation: regulations on party discipline, administrative law, and criminal law. Regulations on party discipline are issued by

---

11 Due to the secretive nature of CDIs, the criteria used to determine the "guilt" of an official are not known to the public.

12 See the Introduction, and the chapters by Marina Svensson (Chapter 7), Mattias Burell (Chapter 10), Oscar Almén (Chapter 5), and Hatla Thelle (Chapter 6) in this volume.

13 Arnold J. Heidenheimer and Michael Johnston, *Political Corruption, Concepts and Contexts*, 3rd ed. (New Brunswick and London: Transaction Publishers, 2002).

14 Helena Kolenda, "One Party Two Systems: Corruption in the People's Republic of China," *The Journal of Asian Law* 4, no. 2 (1991): 189–232.

party organs at all levels and set forth the behavioral norms all CCP members should follow. Acts of corruption committed by state officials, most of whom are party members, are defined and punished by administrative regulations. These are enacted by the State Council and by governments at all levels. Party discipline regulations punish crimes of corruption involving less than CNY 5,000,[15] whereas crimes involving more than CNY 5,000 are punished by the Criminal Law[16] with penalties ranging from imprisonment for one year to the death penalty.[17] Party discipline regulations and administrative regulations are implemented by CDIs,[18] whereas the Criminal Law is implemented by the procuratorates and the courts. Both criminal and criminal procedure legislation are applied by procuratorates during investigations on cases of corruption and by the courts during trial. The leading role in dictating the line to follow in

---

15 Central Commission for Discipline Inspection, *Dangzheng ganbu dangnei jiandu he jilü chufen guiding* [Regulations on the supervision of party-state cadres and discipline sanctions] (Beijing: Zhongguo Fazhi Chubanshe, 2004), 222: "Guanyu dui fanyou tanwu, huilu cuowu dangji chufende shu'e jiexiang wentide qingshide dafu" [Instructive reply on monetary limits to consider in the punishment of those responsible for mistakes of graft and bribery].

16 This is clearly stated by Article 383(4) of the Criminal Law, and by a regulation issued by the Supreme People's Procuratorate: "Guanyu renmin jianchayuan zhijie shouli li'an zhencha anjian li'an biaozhunde guiding (shixing)" [Provisions on monetary limits for filing cases falling under the people's procuratorates jurisdiction]. See *Zhonghua Renmin Gongheguo Xingfa* [Criminal law of the People's Republic of China] (Beijing: Zhongguo Fazhi Chubanshe, 1998), 328; Zuigao Renmin Jianchayuan Yanjiushi (Research Office of the Supreme People's Procuratorate), *Zuixin xingshi falü yu sifa jieshi shouce* [Handbook of the newest criminal laws, regulations and judicial interpretations] (Beijing: Falü Chubanshe, 2000), 278–302.

17 This is the range of penalties for crimes of corruption. See Chapter 8 of the Criminal Law. *Zhonghua Renmin Gongheguo Xingfa* [Criminal law of the People's Republic of China] (Beijing: Zhongguo Fazhi Chubanshe), 326–340.

18 In February 1993 CDIs and organs for administrative supervision were merged, and hence the CDIs became responsible for implementation of administrative regulations as well. "Guanyu zhongyang jiwei, jiancha jiguan heshu bangong he jigou shezhi youguan wentide qingshi," *Zhongfa* [Central Document] (1993) 4 hao (no. 4)

implementing the law belongs to the party committee of the organ where any case of corruption takes place.

Policy Priorities and Policy Tools

The changing shape of corruption was what determined the policy approach followed in the 1990s. The Center was aware of the changes taking place in corruption since the Central Commission for Discipline Inspection (CCDI) carries out research on its evolving features.[19] Rather than being symbolic, the policies designed by the CCDI reflected a will to reduce the extent of corruption to "an acceptable level."[20] Anticorruption policy consists of a list of priorities and objectives common to all Chinese provinces and is spelled out annually. Priorities and objectives in the 1990s were simple: localities had to root out and punish "big and important cases" (*zhong'an, da'an*). This is a code word for corruption networks. The peculiarities of these cases are the involvement of a large number of officials and/or state organs and the exchange of large amounts of money. Other goals to be pursued were listed in order of importance: repressing minor forms of corruption—labeled "sectoral and departmental unhealthy tendencies" (*hangye he bumen bu zhengzhi feng*); adopting preventive measures; reforming implementing agencies; ensuring a steady flow of citizen reports; and furthering the training and education of cadres. The main policy objective was summarized by the slogan "resoluteness first, exercise caution second, and continuously obtain gradual results third."[21] In other words, law implementation should have focused on the most innovative and

---

19 Interview on May 6, 2007 in Beijing.

20 Andrew Wedeman, "Anticorruption Campaigns and the Intensification of Corruption in China," *Journal of Contemporary China* 14, no. 42 (2005): 94.

21 *Yi yao jianjue, er yao chijiu, san yao buduan qude jieduanxing chengxiao*. A more in-depth discussion of this principle and of its historical origins can be found in Xiao Yang, *Zhongguo xingshi zhengce he celüe wenti* [Problems in China's criminal policy and strategy] (Beijing: Falü Chubanshe, 1996), 369–380.

virulent forms of corruption due to the fast development and the existence of regulatory flaws in certain sectors of the economy.

Anticorruption agencies were originally designed to punish crimes that took place within single organs. They lacked the personnel, resources, and expertise needed to investigate what had become "a form of social interaction" itself,[22] rather than an occasional occurrence. Investigating transprovincial cases of corruption involving entrepreneurs and agencies at different hierarchical levels of the party-state had become almost impossible for these agencies.

To cope with this entirely new set of circumstances, anticorruption agencies had to find a way to conduct simultaneous investigations of all the actors involved in a corruption network. A new approach to anticorruption was found in linking together different agencies, giving birth to an implementation network. Such a network is a

> structure(s) of interdependence involving multiple organizations or parts thereof, where one unit is not merely the formal subordinate of the other in some larger hierarchical arrangement. The institutional glue congealing networked ties may include authority bonds, exchange relations, and coalitions based on common interest, all within a single multiunit structure.[23]

Even though their content was clear,[24] this set of policy priorities and the tool to implement them had to be adapted to the conditions present in Beijing. Adaptation to local conditions is not just a feature of policy; in the case of corruption it was made necessary by the "locality-specific"[25] nature of corruption. As pointed out by Yan

---

22 Gong, "Dangerous Collusion."

23 Laurence O'Toole, "Treating Networks Seriously: Practical and Research Based Agendas in Public Administration," *Public Administration Review* 57, no. 1 (January 1997): 45.

24 Cho Nam Young, "Implementation of Anticorruption Policies in Reform-Era China: The Case of the 1993–1997 'Anticorruption Struggle,'" *Issues & Studies* 37, no. 1 (2001): 49–72.

25 Yan Sun, *Corruption and Market in Contemporary China* (Ithaca: Cornell University Press, 2004), 120.

Sun, differences in the development of the market economy and in the strength of the local state shape different forms of corruption.[26] The degree to which implementation of anticorruption legislation was successful can be judged by comparing the Center's policy priorities for Beijing to the policy Beijing actually implemented, and its outcomes.

Policy Priorities and Policy Tools in Beijing

In the late 1970s,[27] the secretariat of the CCP dictated that Beijing needed to be transformed from a gloomy industrial city into a modern capital. Its economic growth had to be based on the service and the industrial sectors, the primary sectors of the city's gross domestic product. Basically, the city had to be rebuilt from scratch. These ambitious objectives could have been reached with greater ease by a long-tenured leadership. Eventually, the Center's choice fell on Chen Xitong, a conservative leader who grew up politically in Beijing, and was a Li Peng ally.[28] In the beginning Chen seemed to be

---

26 Yan, *Corruption and Market in Contemporary China*.

27 Beijingshi Renmin Zhengfu (Beijing People Government), "Beijingshi Renmin Zhengfu guanyu yinfa Chen Xitong shizhang zai shi jiujie renda sici huiyishang zuode 'guanyu Bejingshi guomin jingji he shehui fazhan shinian guihua he dibage wu nian jihua gangyaode baogao', deng wenjiande tongzhi" [Beijing People's Government Circular on Issuing Mayor Chen Xitong a report to the Ninth Plenary Session of the People's Congress entitled "Report on the ten years programme for economic and social development and the eighth five-years Plan" and other documents], *Jingzhengfa* [Beijing Government Document] (1991) 32 hao (no. 32), on file with the author; Duan Bingren, *Beijingshi gaige shinian 1979–1989* [Ten years of reform in Beijing 1979–1989] (Beijing: Beijing Chubanshe, 1989): 19, 20.

28 Chen held various leadership positions in Beijing from 1979 to 1995. He was the mayor from 1988 until his fall. Chen was induced to resign in April 1995, and was investigated in September of the same year. He was expelled from the party on August 28, 1997, formally arrested on February 27, 1998, and sentenced to sixteen years detention on July 31 of the same year. He was released on medical parole on January 22, 2004. Earlier, Peng Zhen had led the capital for seventeen

the ideal choice. Not only did he successfully repress the Tiananmen rebellion and rule the capital with an iron fist, but also in a time span of a few years, he radically altered the shape of the city. Starting from the early 1990s, the tertiary sector underwent skyrocketing development. The financial, construction, high-tech, information technology, and tourist sectors became the pride of Beijing's leadership. The downside of this spectacular development, however, was that Beijing began to show forms of corruption that could not be found either in poorer inland provinces or in more dynamic coastal areas. Official speculation, the theft of state resources, and "deviant tendencies" were replaced by more articulated forms of corruption. Corruption was now carried out by networks that comprised officials, entrepreneurs, and persons belonging to several more categories. These flexible, far-reaching networks could span different provinces and different organs of the party-state. Also, corruption was particularly rife in all sectors of the economy singled out for fast development.

To counter the spread of corruption, Beijing began building an implementation network in 1987. At that point, the municipal Higher People's Procurate was ordered to foster links with other agencies and build up a "multilevel system" (*duo cengce xitong*) to investigate and punish corruption.[29] In 1988, the implementation network was born. It involved the municipal CDI, the supervision and auditing offices, the state administration of industry and commerce, the tax office, the financial office, the office for fiscal inspection, the courts, and the customs.[30] Most of the agencies were of the same rank and boasted a

---

years, from December 1948 until the spring of 1965. "Peng Zhen tongzhi guanghui zhandoude yishen" [Comrade Peng Zhen's voice and brilliant struggle], *Renmin Ribao* [People's Daily], May 3, 1997.

29 Zhongguo Jiancha Nianjian Bianjibu (Editorial Board of the China Procuratorial Yearbook), *Zhongguo Jiancha Nianjian 1988* [China Procuratorial Yearbook 1998] (Beijing: Jiancha Nianjian Chubanshe, 1989), 970.

30 Zhongguo Jiancha Nianjian Bianjibu (Editorial Board of the China Procuratorial Yearbook), *Zhongguo Jiancha Nianjian 1989* [China Procuratorial Yearbook] (Beijing: Jiancha Nianjian Chubanshe, 1990), 18.

different degree of political power. The single most important node was, however, the CDI and the municipal party committee. They were the organs that coordinated all the agencies in the network.

Links between agencies were not only horizontal and did not just involve different clusters of the party-state. They did not consist only of a vertical subordination between organs in the same functional system (*xitong*). Neither were they a replica of dual subordination (*shuangchong lingdao*). They were something different, and far more articulated. All organs within the implementation network were linked to each other and such links did not only involve municipal level agencies. Organs at the central, municipal, and district levels were involved, thereby establishing links across different "planes of governance."[31] Any anticorruption organ had to keep ties not just to its party committee and to its next higher level organ, but had to be in touch with every other agency. Links cut across hierarchical levels and administrative divisions of Beijing. If this arrangement was peculiar, even more so was the nature of the links among organs. The actions of these agencies were governed by the CCP. However, hierarchical subordinations were only part of the picture. Informal bonds, relations of exchange, and pursuing a shared objective were also important. These informal relationships not only strengthened the bonds between agencies, but also carried a certain weight in implementation. Relationships based on a shared attribute[32] could be equally—if not more—important than administrative hierarchy. Laws, regulations and other policy documents were issued at the central and municipal levels. However, all agencies in the network were involved in their drafting.[33] Judicial documents were produced

---

31 Cho Chung-Lae et al., "Translating National Policy Objectives into Local Achievements Across Planes of Governance and Among Multiple Actors: Second-Order Devolution and Welfare Reform Implementation," *Journal of Public Administration Research and Theory* 15, no. 1 (2005): 37.

32 As having a *guanxi*, being part of the same faction, being alumni of the same college, and so on.

33 Kenneth G. Lieberthal and Michel Oksenberg, *Policy Making in China: Leaders, Structures and Processes* (Princeton: Princeton University Press, 1998).

and diffused after consultations and negotiations among the network components. Information about cases and investigations had to reach all the agencies in the network. This was the only institutional arrangement that enabled anticorruption organs to investigate cases of corruption involving several party-state agencies that often were located in different provinces.

The structure of this implementation network changed little in seventeen years.[34] Hence, Beijing law implementers were ready to investigate the newer, more complex forms of corruption.[35]

The Other Side of Beijing

Soon after its establishment, the Beijing implementation network began showing its coercive powers. Mass sentencing rallies (*qunzhong dahui*)[36] and several other propaganda activities were used. This "bright network"[37] and the laws it had to put into practice to curb corruption could easily be demonstrated. An equally impor-

---

34 Cheng Jie and Zhang Yuzhu, "Beijing: sannian jiluo 114 ming tingji tanguan" [Beijing: 114 officials at the *ting* level investigated over three years], *Jiancha Ribao* [Procuratorial Daily], http://www.jcrb.com/zyw/n365/ca297222.htm.

35 The Center posed this request—albeit in unsophisticated terms—as early as 1982: "Problems entailing a violation of penal laws must be dealt with by judicial organs according to the law. Public security organs, procuratorates, courts, and *other organs at each level* must maintain close coordination and fully carry out the important tasks (*zhuangyan zhize*) each of them is responsible for." Fantanwu yu Huilu Zhengce Fagui Quanshu Bianxiezu (Editorial Board of the Compendium of Anticorruption Policies, Laws and Regulations), *Fantanwu yu huilu zhengce fagui quanshu* [Compendium of Anticorruption Policies, Laws and Regulations] (Beijing: Zhongguo Fangzheng Chubanshe, 2004), 692–699, quote on p. 699, author's translation, emphasis added.

36 Zhongguo Jiancha Nianjian Bianjibu (Editorial Board of the China Procuratorial Yearbook), *Zhongguo Jiancha Nianjian 1991* [China Procuratorial Yearbook 1991], 26.

37 Jörg Raab and H. Brinton Milward, "Dark Networks as Problems," *Journal of Public Administration Research and Theory* 13, no. 4 (2003): 413–439.

tant part of anticorruption consisted in policy priorities. In Beijing anticorruption policy was defined by the Ten Year Program for Economic and Social Development,[38] a document drafted by the municipal government. It was elaborated upon in an eighty-page document that only devoted nine lines to anticorruption. Still, in the early 1990s, anticorruption work was the Center's top priority. What was going on in Beijing? Why did and how could one of the most closely controlled cities in China openly ignore the Center's orders? Again, the answer lies in networks.

Networks are the "fittest governance form able to deal with complex problems."[39] Implementation networks can be used in anticorruption, antiterrorism, and health care delivery. Tasks executed by implementation networks are legitimate and beneficial. They are performed openly and rest upon a solid legal foundation. There is no need for the network to act covertly. However, a network is nothing more than a form of organization. As such it can be used not only to implement the law, but it can become a means to coordinate illegal activities. Officials who intend to carry out "covert and illegal"[40] activities can also adopt this organizational form. In China, the Yuanhua smuggling case is the best example. The Yuanhua group carried out smuggling of goods worth over CNY 10 billion over a period of roughly ten years.[41] Conducting such a massive smuggling operation was largely possible because the coordination mechanism used to govern the activities of its 416 members was a network.

---

38 Beijingshi Renmin Zhengfu (Beijing People Government), Beijing People Government Circular on Issuing the Ten Years Program for Economic and Social Development.
39 Raab and Milward, "Dark Networks as Problems."
40 Ibid., 415.
41 The Yuanhua case took place in Xiamen between 1989 and 1999. Yuanhua Group Limited, a private enterprise group chaired by Lai Changxin, smuggled in raw oil, cars, and consumer goods. Shawn Shieh, "The Rise of Collective Corruption in China: The Xiamen Smuggling Case," *Journal of Contemporary China* 14, no. 42 (2005): 67–91.

One of the most virulent corruption networks to ever emerge in China was based in Beijing. Its formation began around 1985–1986,[42] and its activities continued until the mid-1990s. The ring was exposed between 1995 and 1997. Investigations revealed that it had involved not only the former Beijing mayor, Chen Xitong, and his deputy, Wang Baosen, but a host of individual officials[43] who colluded with each other and with Chen and Wang to carry out criminal activity. Their actions involved the diversion of municipal funds and investment in an illegal fundraising scheme orchestrated by the Beijing State Security Office. What made this case stand out was the level of organization displayed by the network, and the fact that it included all administrative levels of Beijing Municipality and was linked to other provinces.[44] In addition, Beijing's criminal network involved officials whose political power extended over anticorruption organs. The removal of this network took place between 1995 and 1997, which had important consequences for law implementation and was a turning point in the history of the municipality. In the period 1990–1996, implementation of anticorruption law was not set aside, but it underwent several noticeable distortions. In the period 1997–2000, such distortions have persisted, but on the whole implementation seems to have become more fair.

---

42 Xian Qi, *Zhongguo Fanfu* [Anticorruption in China] (Chengdu: Sichuan renmin chubanshe, 1998); Yan, *Corruption and Market in Contemporary China*.

43 Some of the organs involved were the following: the party committee, the municipal government general office, the people's congress, the people's political consultative conference, the financial office, the public security office, the commission for foreign trade, various municipal offices involved in the administration of heavy industry, Shougang, and companies owned by officials, their personal secretaries (*mishu*), or their children and operating in the construction and hotel industry, besides a number of private companies.

44 Bo Zhiyue, "Economic Development and Corruption: Beijing Beyond Beijing," *Journal of Contemporary China* 9, no. 25 (2000): 467–487; Qin Gang, *Wushinian lai Beijingshi fanfubai dashijian yanjiu* [Research on major events occurred during the last fifty years of anticorruption in Beijing] (Beijing: Zhongguo Fangzheng Chubanshe, 2003).

Implementing Agencies

As intriguing and as effective as they may be, networks have a weakness: they can be disarticulated. Disarticulating a criminal network is easy: its members can be arrested, the flow of communication between them can be interrupted, etc. The same logic is true for implementation networks, but with some qualifications. Agencies in an implementation network cannot be physically removed or closed down. To be disrupted an implementation network *needs to be controlled* by external actors pursuing a different agenda. This is what happened in Beijing. We have already seen how implementation networks were controlled by CDIs and party committees. Furthermore, in Beijing anticorruption organs received their orders from a corrupt leadership.

Hence, three weaknesses of the implementation network were highlighted: the definition of the network's tasks, the mandate each agency received,[45] and their dependence on the same resources.[46]

To implement law successfully, each of the agencies making up the network must clearly know what its tasks are. If policy tasks overlap or are not well defined, agencies become ineffectual. The logic applies to each agency's mandate. The jurisdiction and scope of action of each agency must be clear. Any overlaps or gray areas in jurisdiction can cause the actions of agencies to conflict. Finally, agencies must be endowed with an amount of financial resources that allows them to carry out their tasks. If these elements are not present, even the best of implementation networks becomes ineffectual.

---

45 Giandomenico Majone and Aaron Wildavsky, "Implementation as Evolution," in *Implementation*, 3rd ed., eds. Jeffrey L. Pressman and Aaron Wildavsky (Berkeley: University of California Press, 1978).

46 Derek W. Brinkerhoff, "Coordination Issues in Policy Implementation Networks: An illustration from Madagascar's Environment Action Plan," *World Development* 24, no. 9 (1996): 1497–1510.

Redefining the Agencies' Tasks

As mentioned earlier, all of the policy objectives in Beijing had been spelled out by the Ten Year Program for Economic and Social Development. The program had set the objectives of economic growth in a hair-splitting manner. When it came to anticorruption, this document blurred the objectives that had been clearly defined by hundreds of pages of central-level documents. In addition, the priority between different policy tasks had been reverted.[47] In Beijing the top priorities of anticorruption were cadre training and curbing minor forms of corruption, while punishment of more complex crimes—the Center's top priority—received meager attention in Beijing. This task was moved to the bottom of the agenda. Rather than trying to root out corruption networks, law implementers in Beijing were assigned the task of punishing individual crimes of corruption, and those which occurred in the least dynamic sectors of the economy.

The clash between central and provincial plans involved not only the content of anticorruption, but also their duration of implementation. Plans issued by the Center were flexible and adapted annually to the changing patterns of corruption. Beijing's policy program, however, covered a ten-year period, and once set its anticorruption priorities could not be easily changed in spite of changes in corruption.

Blurring the Agencies' Mandate

The definition of agencies' tasks was not the only element that affected coordination among law implementers. The other element was the nature of the law implementers' mandate.

Agencies in an implementation network do not need to enjoy the same degree of political power or have the same rank since equality is not a feature of networks. In the case of Beijing, the existence of a node—the CDI—which was politically more important than all the others blurred the mandate of the implementing agen-

---

47 Majone and Wildavsky, "Implementation as Evolution."

cies. The task of Beijing's CDI was to, in line with party discipline regulations, detect and punish acts of corruption not so serious as to fall under the scope of the Criminal Law. The limit when an act of corruption ceases to be a violation of party discipline (*weiji*) and becomes a crime (*fanzui*) is set to CNY 5,000. Acts involving less than CNY 5,000 fall under the jurisdiction of CDIs, whereas all acts involving more than CNY 5,000 pertain to the jurisdiction of procuratorates. In reality, the existence of this threshold was overlooked.

Party discipline legislation had dissected several different crimes of corruption—as graft, temporary misappropriation of public funds, active and passive bribery—into each of the forms they could take. Normally corruption involves the offer of material inducements to a government official with the expectation that he or she will violate his or her duties to the state. As long as an inducement is offered, corruption takes place *regardless of what is actually offered*. A public official can be bribed with the offer of cash or a car, a credit card, or travel abroad. A characteristic of party discipline legislation is instead that corruption is punished differently according to *the items* a party official accepts. Accepting cash is defined as a "mistake involving bribery" (*shouhui cuowu*) instead of the crime of passive bribery (*shouhuizui*). As such it can receive more lenient punishment. The same principle applies if a public official accepts the offer of credit cards, company shares, cars, houses, or sexual services.

Acts involving sums above CNY 5,000 and that should have been punished according to the Criminal Law were taken outside of this domain. A broad gray area was thus created between the Criminal Law, party discipline regulations, and administrative regulations.

Tightening the Funds Allocated to Law Implementers

All of the implementing agencies were on the municipal government's budget. Besides the structural constraints they were already experiencing, they had to cope with financial constraints. There is a consensus among China scholars that having law-implementing agencies depend on the local government's budget limits their independence. Scholars of policy implementation have, however, found that "letting individual actors operate independently, and *limiting their independence with supervision and control mechanisms, and resource interdependencies*"[48] can enhance their coordination, reduce waste, etc. Potentially, the financial autonomy of the organs could cause their de facto independence. This could translate into each organ going its own way rather than joining forces with counterparts in the implementation network.

In Beijing's case resource interdependency among law implementers showed the opposite effect. The tight funds allocated to implementing agencies put them in dire straits and limited their operations. One of the most prominent members of the Beijing corruption network was Wang Baosen, deputy mayor. Wang had been the director of the municipal planning committee and of the financial office. He enjoyed a substantial degree of autonomy in deciding the allocation of funds. Furthermore, Chen Xitong and other leaders in Beijing rose to power from the ranks of political-legal organs. They kept close informal links to organs in this system. As a result, it would have been natural if this "interest group" had received a somewhat larger allocation of funds. Instead, not only did the leadership engage in a massive diversion of public funds, but it also underfunded implementing agencies. Political-legal organs were the most important units in the implementation network, yet they received less funds than those allocated to agriculture, the sector that had to undergo the largest downsizing. In 1992 political-legal organs received a mere CNY 306,400,000, while CNY 384,700,000 was allocated to the agricultural sector.[49] This situation persisted until the first half of the 1990s. While the Beijing leadership was

---

48 Brinkerhoff, "Coordination Issues in Policy Implementation Networks." Emphasis added.

49 Beijingshi Difangzhi Bianji Weiyuanhui (Editorial Board of the Beijing Gazetteer), *Beijing Nianjian 1993* [Beijing Yearbook 1993] (Beijing: Beijing Nianjian Chubanshe, 1994), 21.

being reorganized in 1995–1996, an interesting phenomenon occurred. Funds allocated to law implementers tripled to CNY 1,090,750,000.[50] Once the investigations of Chen and his accomplices ended and several organs in Beijing saw their leaders being replaced, funds tripled again to CNY 3,359,160,000.[51]

Distortions

To understand how all of these different factors impacted on implementation, a sample of 253 individuals prosecuted from 1990 until 2000 was constructed and analyzed. [52] This sample illustrates the main trends implementing agencies followed in Beijing. The main goals of anticorruption in Beijing should have been to root out corruption networks and to prosecute crimes in the service sector. In retrospect, it is well known that these were the dominant forms of corruption in Beijing.[53] So, the Center had set its priorities correctly. However, Beijing had turned the policy priorities upside down, underfunded agencies, and blurred their mandate. As a result implementation of law was distorted. It focused on outdated forms of corruption, individual crimes, and sectors of the economy where corruption networks did not exist.[54] Distortions were more serious

---

50 Beijingshi difangzhi bianji weiyuanhui (Editorial board of the Bejing gazetteer), *Beijing nianjian 1997* [Beijing yearbook 1997] (Beijing: Beijing nianjian chubanshe, 1998), 51, same source for 1996 data. Funds tripled the first time in 1996, then in 1998, and then in 2001.

51 Beijingshi Tongjiju (Beijing office for statistics), *Beijing tongji nianjian 2001* [Beijing statistical yearbook 2001] (Beijing: Zhongguo tongji chubanshe, 2002), 62.

52 See the list of sources at the end of this chapter.

53 The crimes prosecuted after Chen's demise, were committed during the 1990s. Therefore they prove that these forms of corruption were dominant in the municipality. These crimes are described in the latest issues of the sources mentioned above.

54 This chapter does not claim that this outcome occurred only in Beijing. Apart from Yan's work, no other study reconstructing the trends of corruption

from 1990 to 1996 than from 1997 to 2000. The reorganization of Beijing's leadership, in 1995–1997, would signal a turning point in the history of the municipality. As a result of the end of their political interference, implementation from 1997 to 2000 would show a different trend as well.

Outdated Forms of Corruption

For most of the 1990s, law implementers in Beijing concentrated on investigating the following ten forms of corruption: occupying excess housing space; creating slush funds; feasting using public funds; engaging in moral decadence; buying imported cars, mobile phones, and personal computers; using public funds to pay for excursions and travels; and forcing subordinate units to subscribe to party magazines. These practices, typical of socialist corruption, were dominant before 1978, and persisted throughout the 1980s until 1992. Rather than exploiting opportunities created by the economic reforms they stemmed from a distorted perception of the limits between public and private spheres, a legacy of the work unit (*danwei*) system.[55] After 1992, these forms of corruption were replaced by more sophisticated acts. They, however, persisted in underdeveloped provinces. The only difference was a change in the *status symbols* officials tried to obtain. In the past the objects of their desire had been TV sets, refrigerators, and bicycles. Now they were luxury goods, imported cars, personal computers, and mobile phones. However, these outdated forms of corruption kept CDI busy for almost an entire decade. Of all the phenomena of collusion between state officials and civil society, only the acceptance of bribes disguised as gifts in cash, stocks, or credit cards and the separation

---

within a single province exists to date. This author is trying to fill in this gap by conducting a comparative study of district-level corruption in Zhejiang.

55 Lü Xiaobo, *Cadres and Corruption—The Organizational Involution of the Chinese Communist Party* (Stanford: Stanford University Press, 2000).

between governments and enterprises became part of the CDI's tasks. As the CDI are the only organs to transfer cases to the political-legal system, this was tantamount to having the whole network investigate marginal forms of corruption. In the meantime more complex forms of corruption could quietly spread in Beijing.

From 1990 to 1996, 176 individuals in the sample were prosecuted. Of these, 131 were guilty of outdated forms of corruption, and merely 45 engaged in the main forms of corruption in Beijing.

A closer look at some of these acts reveals that they were not representative of the crimes actually taking place in Beijing. An example is given by the case of Song Jie and Song Zhangwen. In the mid-1990s the two prison wardens had accepted bribes to let convicts free. This case was described by legal publications[56] as "typical."[57] Other cases saw teachers accepting bribes to forge exam papers, or workers of state-owned enterprises dividing up state property and obtaining less than CNY 200 each. Prisons, schools, and old state-run factories were not the places offering the most opportunities for corruption. In the mid-1990s, fixed investments in the infrastructure sector were growing at a rate averaging 22 percent. The service sector was growing at rates around 11 percent. The real estate sector, with a growth rate hovering around 70 percent a year, was literally booming.[58] Crimes in these sectors were

---

56 Zhongguo Jiancha Nianjian Bianjibu (Editorial Board of the China Procuratorial Yearbook), *Zhongguo Jiancha Nianjian 1997* [China Procuratorial Yearbook 1997], 430, 431; Zhongguo Jiancha Nianjian Bianjibu (Editorial Board of the China Procuratorial Yearbook), *Zhongguo Jiancha Nianjian 1998* [China Procuratorial Yearbook 1998], 998, 999.

57 Typical cases are purported to represent the kinds of crimes that are committed more often in a locality. In reality they fulfill various purposes. One of these is instructing law implementers on which forms of corruption should be prosecuted, and which ones should be treated more leniently instead.

58 Shoudu Shehui Jingji Fazhan Yanjiusuo, Beijingshi Juecexue Xuehui (Capital Research Office on Economic Development, Beijing Association for Decision-making), *1997 nian Beijing jingji zhanwang* [An outlook on Beijing, 1997] (Beijing: Shehui Kexue Wenxian Chubanshe, 1997), 45, 78, 202.

overlooked, at least when judging from the corruption cases available in this sample.

On the contrary, from 1997 to 2000 authorities focused on more complex forms of corruption. Between 1997 and 2000, 77 people in the sample were prosecuted. Of these, 58 were guilty of one of the dominant forms of corruption, while 19 had committed outdated crimes.[59]

Individual Crimes

The sample shows that law implementers prosecuted mostly individual crimes or crimes committed by no more than three people. Of the individuals sampled, 176 were prosecuted from 1990 to 1997. Of these 107 committed crimes individually, or with one or two accomplices. Only 69 people were part of a corruption network. Four networks were found, one of which comprised 39 construction workers who stole construction materials. Another was made up of workers in the coal industry who had engaged in speculative practices (*guandao*).[60] Things changed after the municipal leadership's reorganization. Of the individuals sampled, 77 were prosecuted from 1997 until 2000 as mentioned above. Of these 40 were part of a corruption network. In addition, seven networks were found. All of them had been active in the service sector for an average of ten years. The biggest network was the one composed of Chen, Wang, and 88 other members.[61] The network was active in

---

59 The fact that a lower number of people is included in the subsample for the period 1997–2000 is not surprising. In Beijing, a sharp drop in the number of crimes prosecuted occurred from 1997 until 2000: in 1990 authorities prosecuted 1,162 officials, and 577 and 419 people were prosecuted in 1997 and 2000, respectively. Beijingshi Difangzhi Bianji Weiyuanhui (Editorial Board of the Beijing Gazetteer), *Beijing Nianjian 1990–2001* [Beijing Yearbook 1990–2001].

60 The two remaining networks, engaged in corruption to obtain bank loans, were composed of eleven and twelve people respectively.

61 Only sixteen received criminal sanctions.

Beijing, Jiangsu, and other provinces. The other networks were active in Beijing only. The transition from simpler to more complex forms of corruption took place in the late 1980s.[62] Collective corruption had existed in Beijing throughout the 1990s, but was not investigated. The higher number of crimes prosecuted between 1997 and 2000 reflects better enforcement rather than a sudden increase in complex crimes. These crimes were not cases left over from the period when Chen was in power that were prosecuted only due to the change in leadership. Rather, they were new cases or cases that, although they had begun before 1997, *did not involve any of Chen's political clients.* Therefore, the change in anticorruption seems to have been systematic. However, flaws and distortions were still present. Many of the cases prosecuted between 1997 and 2000 had many ramifications and involved a large number of people, but implementing agencies prosecuted only the one or two most prominent members of these networks. Interference that hampered implementing agencies was reduced, but not completely eliminated.

Sectors Not Plagued by Corruption Networks

This argument is supported by observations of the sectors where investigations focused from 1990 to 1997 and from 1997 to 2000,

---

62 A car-smuggling ring involving hundreds of officials and based in Hainan was the first corruption network to be found in China. The case was discovered in 1986. The Yuanhua Group began its smuggling activities in 1989. It took more than ten years for Heilongjiang officials Tian Fengshang, Han Guizhi, and Ma De to build up a 260-person-strong corruption network. See "Han Guizhi jiang zai Beijing yizhongyuan shoushen, jiazhong shuren bei shuanggui" [Han Guizhi tried by Beijing Intermediate People's Court, her relatives and acquaintances detained under the double regulation], *Renmin Ribao* [People's Daily], March 24, 2005, http://unn.people.com.cn/GB/14748/3268066.html; "Xin Zhongguo zuida maiguan'an jin kaiting, Han Guizhi jiang zai Jing shoushen" [Trial for the biggest case of sale of public office, Han Guizhi will be tried in Beijing], *Renmin Ribao*, [People's Daily], March 22, 2005, http://unn.people.com.cn/GB/14748/3260647.html.

respectively. Given that the forms and extent of corruption are shaped by market opportunities,[63] corruption is most rife in those sectors of the economy undergoing fast development.[64] Had implementing agencies been fully effective, the distribution of cases should have reflected the gross domestic product (GDP) share of the primary, secondary, and tertiary sectors. From 1990 to 1997, the structure of the economy in Beijing showed a remarkable imbalance. The weight of the agricultural sector on the GDP was a mere 6 percent. However, the industrial sector, which should have undergone a dramatic reduction contributed 45 percent to the GDP instead. This was almost as big of a share of the GDP as that of the service sector (49 percent).[65]

The number of cases prosecuted in the agricultural sector reflected its share of the GDP. Of the individuals sampled, 3 percent had committed crimes in this primary sector. Law implementers should have focused their efforts on prosecuting crimes in the service sector, given that this was the fastest growing sector of Beijing's economy. Instead, they chose to focus on the industrial sector. Of the individuals sampled, 63 percent had committed crimes in the industrial sector, while only 34 percent of those prosecuted from 1990 to 1997 were guilty of crimes that took place in the service sector.

This gives a picture of organized corruption in Beijing: cronies of the Beijing leadership were exploiting opportunities and practicing corruption in the service sector. After the municipal government was reorganized, this scenario showed two changes.[66] Based

---

63 Yan, *Corruption and Market in Contemporary China*.

64 Heidenheimer and Johnston, *Political Corruption, Concepts and Context*.

65 Beijingshi Tongjiju (Beijing Office of Statistics), *Beijing Tongji Nianjian 1990–2001* [Beijing Statistical Yearbook 1990–2001] (Beijing: Zhongguo Tongji Chubanshe, 1991–2002).

66 The reorganization of the municipal leadership did not only involve Chen's fall from power and Wang's suicide. Rather, it consisted of the removal of all of those who took part in his crimes. For a list of all the officials involved in

on information yielded by the sample, the pattern of prosecution became consistent with the spread of corruption within different sectors of the economy. The agricultural sector made up 4 percent of the GDP, while the industrial sector eventually made up 38 percent. The biggest share of the GDP was occupied by the service sector (58 percent), an acceleration of its already rapid growth.[67] Consistently, 86 percent of the cases included in the sample and prosecuted between 1997 and 2000 took place in the service sector; 12 percent occurred in the industrial sector; and only 2 percent related to the agricultural sector. Slowly the prosecution of corruption in Beijing came to reflect the spread of crimes in different sectors of the economy.

Conclusion

This study has analyzed the effects of party interference in implementation of anticorruption policy. First, I surveyed the evolution corruption underwent in the 1990s, the nature and extent of party interference. Then I moved on to examine the policy priorities the Center set for Beijing, and how the municipality implemented the relevant guidelines. This study has demonstrated the existence of conflicting policy priorities between the Center and Beijing. While the Center had devised a development strategy coherent with Beijing's role as the capital of China, the leadership of Beijing subscribed to a different developmental policy. Eventually, a selective implementation of anticorruption law allowed the Beijing leadership to reverse policy targets, and protect those sectors of the local economy in which it had a vested interest.

---

this case and for the precise dates of their removal and arrest, see Xian, *Anticorruption in China*, chs. 1–7.

67 Beijingshi Tongjiju (Beijing Office of Statistics), *Beijing Tongji Nianjian 1990–2001* [Beijing Statistical Yearbook 1990–2001] (Beijing: Zhongguo Tongji Chubanshe, 1991–2002).

Implementing agencies were not only controlled by the local leadership. They were also co-opted by Chen Xitong and his cronies. As a result, anticorruption legislation was implemented halfheartedly. Outdated forms of corruption were investigated, while the most sophisticated ones were not. Individual corruption was punished, while collective corruption was tolerated. Only those sectors of the economy in which the leadership had no personal stake were cleaned up.

Clearly, the entire process was made easier by the fact that the municipal leadership was not subjected to effective monitoring mechanisms. While they could control local-level CDIs, procuracies and courts, individual leaders could still circumvent control by central-level anticorruption organs. They did so by fulfilling relevant targets: Beijing municipality met the requirements than a high number of cases be prosecuted, publicized a few typical cases, and launched periodical "drives." The Center's reliance on quantitative results eventually could not induce compliance by this locality. Beijing could blur the mandate of relevant agencies, manipulate resource allocation and so on.

These findings lead us to reconsider the questions asked at the beginning of this chapter. Negative results can be observed in this area of law. The local party-state successfully formed implementation networks. Thanks to them it acquired the capacity to overcome the structural constraints of anticorruption agencies and to bypass potentially corrupt local leaders. But eventually this capacity failed to translate into actual practice, and anticorruption law underwent several distortions. This outcome can be attributed to the interference of political actors on implementing agencies and the decentralization of lawmaking power. In this case, the party's control over implementation was the main source of its failures. First, the party disciplinary apparatus was clearly unsuited to controlling corruption, nor did state actors enjoy significant autonomy. Hence forming implementation networks provided a very weak remedy at best. Second, notwithstanding its power, the Center relied on outdated methods to monitor implementation. The most important means used are observing the trend in figures for prosecution and the absence of scandals. Figures for prosecution normally rise at the launch of any anticorruption campaign, and then show a marked decrease. As an indicator this is highly unreliable. Also, no corruption scandals broke out in Beijing until 1996 simply because no investigations were conducted on cases of collective corruption involving the leadership. The party has played a pivotal role in launching economic and legal reform. Broadly considered, these reforms have been successful, and have given greater legitimacy to the CCP. But the case of anticorruption is different. In this policy area, party intervention is more likely to yield implementation failures. Unless the anticorruption apparatus undergoes a drastic reform, no easy successes will be achieved in the fight against corruption.

List of Sources

Beijingshi Gaoji Renmin Fayuan (Beijing High People's Court), *Beijing fayuan ming'an panjie* [Important Judgements of Beijing People's Courts] (Beijing: Falü Chubanshe, 2001); Beijingshi Gaoji Renmin Fayuan (Beijing High People's Court), *Renmin fayuan caipan wenshuxuan. Beijing 2000 nian juan* [Selection of Judicial Documents of the People's Courts. Beijing, Year 2000 Volume] (Beijing: Falü Chubanshe, 2001); Beijingshi Gaoji Renmin Fayuan (Beijing High People's Court), *Renmin fayuan caipan wenshuxuan. Beijing 2001 nian juan* [Selection of Judicial Documents of the People's Courts. Beijing, Year 2001 Volume] (Beijing: Falü Chubanshe, 2002); Beijingshi Difangzhi Bianji Weiyuanhui (Editorial Board of the Beijing Gazetteer), *Beijing Nianjian 1990-2001* [Beijing Yearbook 1990-2001] (Beijing: Beijing Nianjian Chubanshe, 1991-2002); Guojia Faguan Xueyuan, Zhongguo Renmin Daxue Faxueyuan (Law School of the China People University), *Zhongguo Shenpan anli yaolan (1996-2001) nian xingshi shenpan anlijuan* [A Compendium of Judicial Cases (1996-2001)—Volume on Criminal Cases] (Beijing: Zhongguo Renmin Daxue Chubanshe, 1997-2002); Zhongguo Jiancha Nianjian Bianjibu (Editorial

Board of the China Procuratorial Yearbook), *Zhongguo Jiancha Nianjian 1988–1999* [China Procuratorial Yearbook 1988–1999]; Huairouxian zhi bianji weiyuanhui (Editorial Board of the Huairou District Gazetteer), *Huairouxianzhi* [Huairou District Gazetteer] (Beijing: Beijing Chubanshe, 2000); Beijingshi Xichengqu zhi bianji weiyuanhui (Editorial Board of the Beijing Xicheng District Gazetteer), *Beijingshi xichengqu zhi* [Beijing Xicheng District Gazetteer] (Beijing: Beijing Chubanshe, 1999); Beijingshi Fengtaiqu difangzhi bianji weiyuanhui (Editorial Board of the Beijing Fengtai District Gazetteer), *Beijingshi fengtaiqu zhi* [Beijing Fengtai District Gazetteer] (Beijing: Beijing Chubanshe, 2001); Beijingshi Fangshanqu zhi bianji weiyuanhui (Editorial Board of the Beijing Fangshan District Gazetteer), *Beijingshi Fangshanqu zhi* [Beijing Fangshan District Gazetteer] (Beijing: Beijing Chubanshe, 1999); Zuigao Renmin Jianchayuan Falü Zhengce Yanjiushi (Office for Research on Law and Policy of the Supreme People's Courts), *Dianxing yinan anli pingxi 1997–1999* [An Analysis of Typical and Dubious Cases 1997–1999] (Beijing: Zhongguo Jiancha Chubanshe, 1998–2000); Zhonghua Renmin Gongheguo Zuigao Renmin Fayuan (Supreme Court of the People's Republic of China), *Zhonghua Renmin Gongheguo Zuigao Renmin Fayuan Gongbao 1985–2000* [Gazette of the Supreme Court of the People's Republic of China 1985–2000] (Beijing: Zuigao Renmin Fayuan Chubanshe, 2001); Beijing Daxue Fazhi Xingxi Zhongxin, Beida Yinghua Keji You-xiang Gongsi (Legal Information Centre of Beijing University, Beijing Yinghua, Ltd.), *Zhongguo Falü Fagui Daquan 2001* [A Compendium of the Laws and Regulations of China 2001] (Beijing: Beijing Daxue Chubanshe, 2001); Sun Bosheng, *Zaishen anli pingxi* [An Analysis of Appellate Cases] (Beijing: Renmin Fayuan Chubanshe, 1999); Xinshiqi fanfubai douzheng dashiji bianxiezu (English), *Xinshiqi fanfubai douzheng dashiji* [A Chronicle of the Anticorruption Struggle in the New Era] (Beijing: Zhonggong Dangxiao Chubanshe, 2005); Zhou Qihua, *Dangdai Zhongguo tanwu huilu ming'an shilu* [A Record of Important Cases of Corruption and

Bribery in Contemporary China] (Beijing: Zhongguo Jiancha Chubanshe, 1999); Qin, Research on Fifty Years of Anticorruption in Beijing; Xu Haifeng, *Shoudu jiancha shida jingpin fantan anli* [Corruption Cases Investigated by the Capital's Procuratorate] (Beijng: Falü Chuban-she, 2004); Dangdai Zhongguode Beijing bianjibu, *Dangdai Zhongguode Beijing (1949-2003)* [Beijing in Contemporary China (1949-2003)] (Beiing: Dangdai Zhongguo Chubanshe, 2003); Zuigao Renmin Fayuan, Zhongguo Yinyong Faxue Yanjiusuo (Supreme People's Court, China Research Centre on the Application of Law), *Renmin fayuan anlixuan* [A Selection of Cases from the People's Courts] (Beijing: Renmin Fayuan Chubanshe, 1992); Zuigao Renmin Fayuan, Zhongguo Yinyong Faxue Yan-jiusuo (Supreme People's Court, China Research Centre on the Application of Law), *Renmin fayuan anlixuan—xingshijuan* [A Selection of Cases from the People's Courts—Volume on Criminal Cases] (Beijing: Renmin Fayuan Chubanshe, 1997); Zuigao Renmin Fayuan, Zhongguo Yinyong Faxue Yanjiusuo (Supreme People's Court, China Research Centre on the Application of Law), *Renmin fayuan anlixuan—xingshijuan* [A Selection of Cases from the People's Courts—Volume on Criminal Cases] (Beijing: Zhongguo Fazhi Chubanshe, 2000); Jiangguo yilai dangzheng ganbu weifa weiji da'an yao'an suyi bianxiezu (Editorial Board of the Compilation of Big and Important Cases of Violation of Law and Discipline by Party-State Cadres Occurred Since the Foundation of China), *Jiangguo yilai dangzheng ganbu weifa weiji da'an yao'an suyi* [Compilation of Big and Important Cases of Violation of Law and Discipline by Party-State Cadres Occurred Since the Foundation of China](Beijing: Falü Chubanshe, 2004); Jin He, *Beijing jingji fanzui yu duice* [Strategies against Economic Crime in Beijing] (Beijing: Beijing Yanshan Chubanshe, 1991).

Cases published therein were selected by the procuratorates in Beijing. The kinds of cases selected reflect the consensus about *what* actions are to be punished as corruption. They indicate to political-legal organs the acts on which they have to focus their efforts and tioned by these sources should be—and normally are—prosecuted, forms of corruption not listed by these sources are to be treated leniently, overlooked, etc. Given the well-known impossibility to obtain information about *all* the acts of corruption that take place in a certain geographical area over a given period of time, the sample can be said to be representative of law implementers' performance. The publications used to construct it were produced by law implementing agencies, and targeted law implementing agencies. Their purpose was to show what crimes should have been punished. All the forms of corruption not listed by these sources normally do not represent a priority of law implementers. In spite of these advantages, the sample does not allow us to know the real figures on corruption in Beijing.

Bibliography

Beijing daxue fazhi xingxi zhongxin, Beida yinghua keji youxiang gongsi (Legal Information Centre of Beijing University, Beijing Yinghua, Ltd.). *Zhongguo falü fagui daquan 2001* [A compendium of the laws and regulations of China, 2001]. Beijing: Beijing daxue chubanshe, 2001.

Beijing shi difangzhi bianji weiyuanhui (Editorial Board of the Beijing Gazetteer). *Beijing nianjian 1990–2001* [Beijing yearbook 1990–2001]. Beijing: Beijing nianjian chubanshe, 1991–2002.

Beijing shi Fangshan qu zhi bianji weiyuanhui (Editorial Board of the Beijing Fangshan District Gazetteer). *Beijing shi Fangshan qu zhi* [Beijing Fangshan District Gazetteer]. Beijing: Beijing chubanshe, 1999.

Beijing shi Fengtai qu difangzhi bianji weiyuanhui (Editorial Board of the Beijing Fengtai District Gazetteer). *Beijing shi Fengtai qu zhi* [Beijing Fengtai District Gazetteer]. Beijing: Beijing chubanshe, 2001.

Beijing shi gaoji renmin fayuan (Beijing High People's Court). *Beijing fayuan ming'an panjie* [Important judgments of Beijing People's Courts]. Beijing: Falü chubanshe, 2001.

Beijing shi gaoji renmin fayuan (Beijing High People's Court). *Renmin fayuan caipan wenshuxuan. Beijing 2000 nian juan* [Selection of Judicial Documents of the People's Courts. Beijing, Year 2000 Volume]. Beijing: Falü chubanshe, 2001.

Beijing shi gaoji renmin fayuan (Beijing High People's Court). *Renmin fayuan caipan wenshuxuan. Beijing 2001 nian juan* [Selection of Judicial Documents of the People's Courts. Beijing, Year 2001 Volume]. Beijing: Falü chubanshe, 2002.

Beijing shi tongjiju (Beijing Office of Statistics). *Beijing tongji nianjian 1990-2001* [Beijing Statistical Yearbook 1990-2001]. Beijing: Zhongguo tongji chubanshe, 1991-2002.

Beijing shi Xicheng qu zhi bianji weiyuanhui (Editorial Board of the Beijing Xicheng District Gazetteer). *Beijing shi xicheng qu zhi* [Beijing Xicheng District Gazetteer]. Beijing: Beijing chubanshe, 1999.

Bo, Zhiyue. "Economic Development and Corruption: Beijing Beyond Beijing," *Journal of Contemporary China* 9, no. 25 (2000).

Brinkerhoff, Derek W. "Coordination Issues in Policy Implementation Networks: An illustration from Madagascar's Environment Action Plan," *World Development* 24, no. 9 (1996): 1497–1510.

Central Commission for Discipline Inspection. *Dangzheng ganbu dangnei jiandu he jilü chufen guiding* [Regulations on the supervision of party-state cadres and discipline sanctions]. Beijing: Zhongguo fazhi hubanshe, 2004.

Cheng, Jie, and Zhang Yuzhu. "Beijing: sannian jiluo 114 ming tingji tanguan" [Beijing: 114 officials at the *ting* level investigated over three years], *Jiancha ribao* [Procuratorial Daily], http://www.jcrb.com/zyw/n365/ca297222.htm.

Cho, Nam Young. "Implementation of Anticorruption Policies in Reform-Era China: The Case of the 1993–1997 'Anticorruption Struggle,'" *Issues & Studies* 37, no. 1 (2001): 49–72.

Cho, Chung-Lae, Christine A. Kelleher et al. "Translating National Policy Objectives into Local Achievements Across Planes of Governance and Among Multiple Actors: Second-Order Devolution and Welfare Reform Implementation," *Journal of Public Administration Research and Theory* 15, no. 1, (2005): 31–54.

Dangdai Zhongguo de Beijing bianjibu. *Dangdai Zhongguo de Beijing (1949–2003)* [Beijing in contemporary China (1949–2003)]. Beijng: Dangdai Zhongguo chubanshe, 2003.

Duan, Bingren. *Beijing shi gaige shinian 1979–1989* [Ten years of reform in Beijing 1979–1989]. Beijing: Beijing chubanshe, 1989.

Fantanwu yu huilu zhengce fagui quanshu Bbianxiezu (Editorial Board of the

Compendium of Anticorruption Policies, Laws and Regulations). *Fantanwu yu huilu zhengce fagui quanshu* [Compendium of anticorruption policies, laws and regulations]. Beijing: Zhongguo fangzheng chubanshe, 2004.

Gong, Ting. "Dangerous Collusion: Corruption as a Collective Venture in Contemporary China," *Communist and Post-Communist Studies*, no. 35, (2002): 85–103.

———. "Corruption and local governance: the double identity of Chinese local governments in market reform," *The Pacific Review* 19, no. 1, (2006): 85–102.

Guojia faguan xueyuan and Zhongguo renmin daxue faxueyuan (Law School of the China People University). *Zhongguo shenpan anli yaolan (1996-2001) nian xingshi shenpan anlijuan* [A Compendium of judicial cases (1996-2001)—Volume on Criminal Cases]. Beijing: Zhongguo renmin daxue chubanshe, 1997–2002.

"Han Guizhi jiang zai Beijing yizhongyuan shoushen, jiazhong shuren bei shuanggui" [Han Guizhi tried by Beijing Intermediate People's Court, her relatives and acquaintances detained under the double regulation], *Renmin Ribao*, March 24, 2005, http://unn.people.com.cn/GB/14748/3268066.html.

Heidenheimer, Arnold J. and Michael Johnston. *Political Corruption, Concepts and Contexts*, 3rd ed. New Brunswick and London: Transaction Publishers, 2002.

Huairou xian zhi bianji weiyuanhui (Editorial Board of the Huairou District Gazetteer). *Huairouxianzhi* [Huairou District Gazetteer]. Beijing: Beijing chubanshe, 2000.

Jiangguo yilai dangzheng ganbu weifa weiji da'an yao'an suyi bianxiezu (Editorial Board of the Compilation of Big and Important Cases of Violation of Law and Discipline by Party-State Cadres Occurred Since the Foundation of China). *Jiangguo yilai dangzheng ganbu weifa weiji da'an yao'an suyi* [Compilation of big and important cases of violation of law and discipline by party-state cadres occurred since the foundation of China]. Beijing: Falü chubanshe, 2004.

Jin, He. *Beijing jingji fanzui yu duice* [Strategies against economic crime in Beijing]. Beijing: Beijing yanshan chubanshe, 1991.

Kolenda, Helena. "One Party Two Systems: Corruption in the People's Republic of China," *The Journal of Asian Law* 4, no. 2 (1991): 189–232.

Lieberthal, Kenneth G., and Michel Oksenberg. *Policy Making in China: Leaders, Structures and Processes.* Princeton: Princeton University Press, 1998.

Lü, Xiaobo. *Cadres and Corruption: The Organizational Involution of the Chinese Communist Party.* Stanford: Stanford University Press, 2000.

Milvard, Brinton H., and Keith G. Provan. "Governing the Hollow State," *Journal of Public Administration Research and Theory* 10, no. 2 (2000): 359-380.

O'Toole, Laurence. "Treating Networks Seriously: Practical and Research Based Agendas in Public Administration," *Public Administration Review* 57, no. 1 (January 1997): 45-52.

Peerenboom, Randall. *China's Long March Towards the Rule of Law.* Oxford: Oxford University Press, 2002.

"Peng Zhen tongzhi guanghui zhandoude yishen" [Comrade Peng Zhen's voice and brilliant struggle], *Renmin ribao* [People's Daily], May 3, 1997.

Pressman, Jeffrey L. and Aaron Wildavsky, eds. *Implementation*, 3rd ed., Berkeley: University of California Press, 1978.

Qin, Gang. *Wushinian lai Beijing shi fanfubai dashijian yanjiu* [Research on major events occurred during the last fifty years of anticorruption in Beijing]. Beijing: Zhongguo fangzheng chubanshe, 2003.

Raab, Jörg, and H. Brinton Milward. "Dark Networks as Problems," *Journal of Public Administration Research and Theory* 13, no. 4, (2003): 413-439.

Rittel, Horst W. J., and Melvin Webber. "Dilemmas in a General Theory of Planning," *Policy Sciences*, no. 4 (June 1973): 155-169.

Shieh, Shawn. "The Rise of Collective Corruption in China: The Xiamen Smuggling Case," *Journal of Contemporary China* 14, no. 42, (2005): 67-91.

Shoudu shehui jingji fazhan yanjiusuo, Beijing shi juecexue xuehui (Capital Research Office on Economic Development, Beijing Association for Decision-making). *1997 nian Beijing jingji zhanwang* [An Outlook on Beijing, 1997]. Beijing: Shehui kexue wenxian chubanshe, 1997.

Sun Bosheng. *Zaishen anli pingxi* [An analysis of appellate cases]. Beijing: Renmin fayuan chubanshe, 1999.

Wedeman, Andrew. "Anticorruption Campaigns and the Intensification of Corruption in China," *Journal of Contemporary China* 14, no. 41, (2005): 93-10.

———. "The Intensification of Corruption in China," *The China Quarterly*, no. 180 (2004): 895-921.

_____. "Great Disorder under Heaven: The Paradox of Endemic Corruption and Rapid Growth in Contemporary China," *China Review* 4, no. 2, (2004): 1–32.

_____. "China's War on Corruption: Progress or Stalemate?" *CSIS Freeman Report* (2007): 1–2.

Xian, Qi. *Zhongguo fanfu* [Anticorruption in China]. Chengdu: Sichuan renmin chubanshe, 1998.

Xiao, Yang. *Zhongguo xingshi zhengce he celüe wenti* [Problems in China's criminal policy and strategy]. Beijing: Falü chubanshe, 1996.

Xinshiqi fanfubai douzheng dashiji bianxiezu (Editorial Board of the Chronicle of the Anticorruption Struggle in the New Era). *Xinshiqi fanfubai douzheng dashiji* [A chronicle of the anticorruption struggle in the new era]. Beijing: Zhonggong dangxiao chubanshe, 2005.

"Xin Zhongguo zuida maiguan'an jin kaiting, Han Guizhi jiang zai Jing shoushen" [Trial for the biggest case of sale of public office, Han Guizhi will be tried in Beijing], *Renmin ribao*, March 22, 2005, http://unn.people.com.cn/GB/14748/3260647.html.

Xu, Haifeng. *Shoudu jiancha shida jingpin fantan anli* [Corruption cases investigated by the capital's procuratorate]. Beijng: Falü chubanshe, 2004.

Yan, Sun. *Corruption and Market in Contemporary China*. Ithaca: Cornell University Press, 2004.

Zhongguo jiancha nianjian bianjibu (Editorial Board of the China Procuratorial Yearbook). *Zhongguo jiancha nianjian 1988–1999* [China Procuratorial Yearbook 1988–1999]. Beijing: Jiancha nianjian chubanshe, 1989–2000.

Zhonghua renmin gongheguo xingfa [Criminal Law of the People's Republic of China]. Beijing: Zhongguo fazhi chubanshe, 1998.

Zhonghua renmin gongheguo zuigao renmin fayuan (Supreme Court of the People's Republic of China). *Zhonghua renmin gongheguo zuigao renmin fayuan gongbao 1985–2000* [Gazette of the supreme court of the People's Republic of China 1985–2000]. Beijing: Zuigao renmin fayuan chubanshe, 2001.

Zhou, Qihua. *Dangdai Zhongguo tanwu huilu ming'an shilu* [A record of important cases of corruption and bribery in contemporary China]. Beijing: Zhongguo jiancha chubanshe, 1999.

Zuigao renmin fayuan, Zhongguo yinyong faxue yanjiusuo (Supreme People's Court, China Research Centre on the Application of Law). *Renmin fayuan anlixuan* [A selection of cases from the people's courts]. Beijing: Renmin fayuan chubanshe, 1992.

Zuigao renmin fayuan, Zhongguo yinyong faxue yanjiusuo (Supreme People's Court, China Research Centre on the Application of Law). *Renmin fayuan anlixuan—xingshijuan* [A selection of cases from the people's courts—Volume on criminal cases]. Beijing: Renmin fayuan chubanshe, 1997.

Zuigao renmin fayuan, Zhongguo yinyong faxue yanjiusuo (Supreme People's Court, China Research Centre on the Application of Law). *Renmin fayuan anlixuan—xingshijuan* [A selection of cases from the people's courts—Volume on criminal cases]. Beijing: Zhongguo fazhi chubanshe, 2000.

Zuigao renmin jianchayuan falü zhengce yanjiushi (Office for Research on Law and Policy of the Supreme People's Courts). *Dianxing yinan anli ping-xi 1997-1999* [An analysis of typical and dubious cases 1997-1999]. Beijing: Zhongguo jiancha chubanshe, 1998-2000.

Zuigao renmin jianchayuan yanjiushi (Research Office of the Supreme People's Procuratorate). *Zuixin xingshi falü yu sifa jieshi shouce* [Handbook of the newest criminal laws, regulations and judicial interpretations]. Beijing: Falü chubanshe, 2000.

Distributive and Regulative Policies and Laws

10

Policy Dilution and Equity Problems

Implementing Housing Policy in China

MATTIAS BURELL

Introduction

In the course of economic reforms, the national leadership in Beijing and local authorities in China have issued numerous policies to navigate the transition to a market system. In that sense, law has been a tool of social and economic change.[1] The policies underpinning such reforms have been of varying legal status, ranging from State Council approvals of local reform plans to full-fledged laws drafted by ministries and expert groups until their promulgation by the National People's Congress.

Not all reforms have been consolidated by formal lawmaking, often because policy evolution was ongoing and plagued by controversy or deemed to require some flexibility both in its design and in enforcement. As noted by van Rooij,[2] in a country the size of China, with its regional variations in economic structure and pace of economic reform, it is difficult to design a national law that is clear and predictable on the one hand and feasible in all localities, on the other.

---

[1] See William M. Evan, "Law as an Instrument of Social Change," in *The Sociology of Law: A Social-Structural Perspective*, ed. Willam M. Evan (New York: Free Press, 1980).

[2] Benjamin van Rooij, "Law as Event: Lessons about Lawmaking, Compliance and Enforcement, drawn from the Regulation of Land and Pollution in South-West China" (Ph.D. diss., Leiden University, 2006).

In the case of housing policy such problems have been prominent. As stated by a senior housing reform official:

> In fact, it is not possible to draft a national plan which is fair and uniformly applicable for all regions, enterprises, and agencies. Nobody can design such a thing. I could not do it during my period of appointment, and I am sure no other expert can. Because of the legacies of central planning, all we can do is to aim for overall justice and allow some leeway for local adaptation.[3]

This dilemma explains why so many reform policies mainly have taken the form of regulations issued by the State Council or central ministries. Such policy documents usually allow for local adaptation. Hence, national policies have defined the general framework and direction of reform, but were subject to specifications, enforcement targets, and timetables set by city governments.[4] It can thus be problematic to reach a clear-cut definition of effective law enforcement. It is especially hard to evaluate implementation in the economic sphere, where policy shifts have been frequent.

When we discuss law implementation we must not forget the outcomes. In housing policy there are three salient issues that deserve mentioning. First, implementation of China's housing reform was contingent upon a change in *social norms*. People had to modify their habits of consumption and savings and reconceptualize the attractiveness of owning a house as opposed to renting it. This was a time-consuming process. To entice a shift in social norms, the state combined administrative coercion with economic incentives.

---

3 Interview with BJ 2004a, former Head of the State Council Housing Reform Office (1993–1997). The interviews for this article were conducted with state officials at the Ministry of Construction, city construction bureaus, housing reform offices and city-level Housing Provident Fund agencies. All interviewees have been kept anonymous.

4 Interview with BJ 2003, Head of the Housing and Social Security Division, Beijing Housing Reform Office, December 2003.

The aim was to "convince" households that it was in their own interest, in the long run, to purchase their apartments.

Second, in the course of implementation, a process occurs that I call *policy dilution*.[5] This is when existing regulations are either deliberately watered down by a set of amendments, allowing for leniency, or enforcement criteria are attenuated because state agencies find it too difficult or costly to pursue a full policy coverage. As we shall see, policy dilution took place when enterprises were too financially weak to pay their fees to the Housing Provident Fund (HPF) and their contribution rates were lowered. Another example is when local state authorities abandoned their aim to implement HPF policy among small private firms. Policy dilution is important because it gives rise to uneven enforcement, and the same rules do not apply to all units or regions.

Third, implementing a policy in a market context can sometimes lead to *equity problems* between social groups. The case of the HPF shows that the number of beneficiaries is rather low in comparison to contributors to the fund, and households who successfully apply for housing loans tend to be rather well-off. In that sense, the HPF scheme has mainly been beneficial for households with abundant resources at the expense of medium- and low-income households, who nevertheless are forced to make life-long contributions. This lopsided result is even more salient when we look at the lack of public awareness concerning the HPF. In a survey conducted in Wuhan in 2006, I found that very few households participated in the HPF scheme (15 percent). A large number (39 percent) did not even know of its existence. Evaluated from this perspective, we must conclude that implementation of China's housing policy was a failure or at most a moderate success.

The chapter begins with a discussion on the main features of housing policy and their impact on implementation. This is followed by an analysis of the shift in social norms that was required

---

5 For further discussion, see Mattias Burell, The Rule-governed State: China's Labor Market Policy, 1978–1998 (Ph.D. diss., Uppsala University, 2001).

for successful implementation of housing reform. The third section delineates the policy framework from 1988 to 2002, with a special focus on the HPF. The fourth and fifth sections describe how HPF policies were implemented in Tianjin and the problem of policy dilution, i.e., when legal standards are weakened on paper or in practice. This is closely related to the issue of uneven enforcement across both regions and enterprises. The sixth section points to the social equity issues that characterize the HPF policy and the lack of public awareness from which it suffers. In the final section, I review the main lessons that we can draw from this case study with regard to law enforcement.

The research presented here is based on a variety of sources. These include official and semi-official statistics, secondary sources in English and Chinese, newspaper reports, internal work reports, fieldwork interviews conducted between 2003 and 2006 in Beijing, Tianjin, Guangdong, Jiangxi, and Yunnan, and a household survey (N=1000) that I carried out in Wuhan in 2006.[6]

Key Features of Housing Policy

To some extent, all policy areas have their own special features, which shape the style of policymaking and create certain problems in legal enforcement. Chinese housing reform has evolved in the cross-currents of law and economics. While the law lays stress on

---

6 The survey (N=1000) was carried out in July–August 2006 in ten city districts of Wuhan and was assisted by about forty masters degree students from Wuhan University as interview personnel. I was responsible for executing this survey, as well as designing the questionnaire, translating, pilot testing, and revising. The survey entailed training of interview personnel, quality controls, coding, and data cleansing. It was based on a stratified probability sample and was carried out as interviews in the respondents' homes. Each interview lasted about one hour, and respondents answered questions about their household economy, living conditions, and attitudes on social issues. All work was carried out in Chinese.

procedural clarity and predictability, economic reforms are conditioned by fuzziness and uncertainty. In this situation, economic policymaking is not always endorsed by formal legal acts but consists of executive decisions, economic plans, and administrative rules. In China, policymakers preferred to retain flexibility in the face of a changing economy, and most attempts to standardize economic policies into law did not occur until the mid-1990s.[7] In spite of such fluctuating factors, some aspects of Chinese housing reform can be treated as constants.

A first feature in China's housing policy is the multilevel framework of leadership groups, specialized committees, and local agencies in charge of implementation. Leadership support in this area has been fairly strong, and the allocation of budgetary and personnel resources has usually been sufficient. While local housing officials may gripe about their limited authority and position in the bureaucratic hierarchy,[8] they do not suffer from institutional weakness. Therefore, conditions for legal enforcement are rather good. In the 1990s, housing reform leadership groups composed of representatives from key agencies such as the Bureau of Construction, Bureau of Finance, and the People's Bank of China were set up at the city level to coordinate policy. These leadership groups, chaired by deputy mayors, have sought to keep intra-bureaucratic conflicts at a minimum and facilitate implementation.[9] The enforcement of HPF policy has been guided by a three-level framework: the Housing Committee, the HPF Management Center and its local offices, and

---

7 Burell, *The Rule-governed State*, chapters 5, 11.

8 Interviews with TJ 2004b, the Director of Tianjin HPF Management Center, October 2004; NC 2004, the Director of Nanchang HPF Management Center, October 2004; GZ 2004b, an official at Zhuhai HPF Management Center, November 2004; GZ 2004c, the Director of Dongguan HPF Management Center, November 2004; YN 2005, the former Head of Yunnan HPF Management Center, August 2005.

9 Interview with TJ 2004a, Deputy Head of Tianjin Housing System Reform Office, October 2004; and interviews with BJ 2004a,and TJ 2004b.

designated banks handling HPF accounts. Policymaking, enforcement, and administration have been divided between these bodies. Supervision of financial accounts has been a joint responsibility of finance bureaus, auditing bureaus, and the trade unions. Representatives from people's congresses have also had supervisory functions by attending important Housing Committee meetings.[10] Hence, the overall institutional framework for housing policy and its enforcement has been rather clear.

A second feature of housing policy is the fact that the existing housing stock represents a massive amount of sunk costs. Millions of square meters of construction space had been put into place under the planned economy. That housing stock can be considered both as an asset, i.e., its potential market value, or seen as a financial burden when taking into account depreciation and maintenance costs. Reforming such a system requires careful thinking about financial issues, property rights, and how costs and benefits of housing reform should be shared between different stakeholders. But housing is not merely a physical asset. It is also the living space and a key component of social welfare for Chinese households. For these reasons, a gradual approach to housing policy reform was seen as the best solution.[11]

Third, housing policy is closely linked with other issues such as employment, social security, wage levels, and the economic viability of different firms and regions. It is therefore necessary to view interrelated policies as a whole and consider them as a set of multiple priorities. As stated by one housing official: "Housing reform cannot be done in an isolated way. It needs supplementary adjustments

---

10 Interview with BJ 2004c, Director of Beijing HPF Management Center, October 2004; GZ 2003, Director of Guangzhou Housing Reform Office, December 2003, GZ 2004a, Director of Guangzhou HPF Management Center, November 2004; and interviews BJ 2004a, TJ 2004b.

11 Interview with MoC 2004b, Director of the HPF Division, Ministry of Construction, 23 July 2004; and interviews with BJ 2003, BJ 2004a, and TJ 2004a.

in other policy areas. In other words, there is no such thing as a surgery of single policy redesign."[12]

Fourth, implementation of housing policy required a deep change in people's values. After thirty years of socialism, where private property had been banned and wages and rents were kept low, urban employees expected that the state would solve their housing needs. In the 1980s, few urbanites viewed housing as a commodity with any exchange value or as a form of investment. Households had little inclination to spend their savings on home ownership and were content with the status quo. Housing policy had to rely on economic incentives and the propagation of new norms.

Engineering a Shift in Social Norms

Housing reform required a normative shift at two levels: first a revision of official ideology concerning private ownership, and then a shift in public norms about individual responsibility for housing consumption. The shift in official ideology took place in the early 1990s and there were many policy debates about whether it was ideologically correct to sell out main parts of the housing stock. As pointed out by a senior housing official, certain leaders and departments argued that this would be a negation of "socialism." Others, from a technical point of view, argued that the sale of public housing would be a drain of state assets. Such controversies had an impact on the speed of implementation. Contested regulations were pushed cautiously, and local authorities would linger since they knew that policy consensus was weak at the national level.[13]

Once the regulatory framework was in place, the next step was to lure public opinion into accepting the policy change. Imple-

---

12 Interviews with BJ 2005, Head of Housing and Social Security Division, Beijing Housing Reform Office, March 2005, and with BJ 2003.
13 Interview with BJ 2004a.

mentation could not be based simply on sanctions and coercion. The aim was to make urbanites realize—or let them believe—that the new policies were in their own best interests. Specifically, the objective was to shape public opinion, through propaganda and incentives, so that people would adjust their economic behavior.[14]

The fundamental problem was that new policies aimed to make people spend more money on housing than previously. The rent increases, the sale of public housing, and developing the Housing Provident Fund all had this orientation. Forcing people to spend more money is unpopular. As stated by one housing official: "In preparing a policy we have to consider if it is seen as reasonable in public opinion."[15] Another official explained: "It is really important that policies are accepted by people. Otherwise the reforms simply cannot move forward."[16] There is a consensus that public-housing rent increases was a policy that ran into massive resistance and eventually fell short of targets. The strategy in Beijing and other cities was to aim for increases that would bring rents to about 8–10 percent of household incomes. The aim was to enforce this target in a gradual manner, raising rents by a few percent each year over an eight-year period. A strategy of tightening the targets very slowly hinges on the idea of minimizing resistance, but it did not work. Due to popular dissatisfaction, even in local people's congresses, the

---

14 Cf. Hydén's argument in this volume that compliance with law becomes operational when it appeals to people's *self-interests*. Thus, when state authorities change the economic incentives linked to compliance behavior, citizens are induced to recalculate the costs and benefits of abiding with a set of regulations or ignoring them. Chinese housing policy, however, is slightly different because it is not entirely coercive and involves an element of choice. For example, you cannot coerce tenants to buy public housing and abandon the rental situation. But it is possible to change their economic incentives for renting as opposed to buying.

15 Interview with TJ 2004a.

16 Interview with BJ 2004c, Director of Beijing HPF Management Center, October 2003.

process slowed down, and eventually rents had only been raised by 2.5 percent.[17]

The sale of public housing was another policy that required careful thinking about social norms. If renting a public apartment is so cheap, what is the motivation to buy it? The policy strategy for successful implementation was to appeal to people's long-term calculations and give preferential policies. Thus, after complex calculations of initial construction costs, housing reform authorities would set approximate sale prices and households were offered the possibility of buying. Preferential policies took the form of a series of rebates, e.g., in relation to the age of the building, reflecting depreciation costs. Buyers could get discounts according to their work seniority so that twenty years of work experience in a state enterprise was translated into a 20 percent reduction in the sale price. Married couples could pool their work seniority and significantly lower the price. Finally, if the buyers accepted to make a lump-sum payment instead of paying by installments, they were given a 20 percent discount.[18] Other strategies were used to encourage the sale of housing. This reform was first implemented in the suburbs. The proximity to rural areas—where farmers already had a sense of home-ownership—was expected to influence the thinking of urban households. Another method was for officials to "lead the way" by being the first to buy apartments and arrange media coverage of that event. Ordinary people might think that leaders had advance information about the personal benefits of this policy and then follow suit. In fact, propaganda efforts in housing reform were relentless, as clarified by a senior official:

> We had not just one or two discussions on housing reform and these things. You see, we are talking about hundreds of

---

17 Interview with MoC 2004a, Director of the Real Estate Department, Ministry of Construction, July 2004; and interviews with MoC 2004b, BJ 2003, BJ 2004c.
18 Interview with BJ 2004b, former Head of the State Council's Housing Reform Office, July 2004; and interviews with BJ 2003, TJ 2004a.

meetings and endless discussions. We arranged publicity drives for the new policies, information meetings, TV programs, telephone hotlines for questions and answers, etc. In each city we had several meetings with the party standing committee to seek their support and make implementation easier.[19]

The buildup of the HPF faced similar dilemmas in how to induce a shift in social norms. In fact, the HPF is in fact a form of forced-savings scheme imposed upon people. From their monthly wages, 5 percent is deducted, placed into a special account, and can only be withdrawn under special conditions such as house renovation or house purchase. From an implementation perspective, the advantage of the HPF scheme was that it offered people benefits in exchange for their participation. Individual contributions, set at 5–8 percent of the monthly salary were matched by another 5–8 percent of the employer's monthly wage payment, thus generating a joint saving equal to 10–16 percent of the salary. Although funds were locked in the HPF account, they were the private property of the employee and would benefit him/her. Hence, resistance to this policy was weak in the beginning and would gradually disappear. This policy had many advantages and introduced a new set of social norms among Chinese households. First, it facilitated the monetization of the housing system since it was based on financial flows rather than material allocations of apartments. Second, it allowed the state to intervene in people's thinking about the household economy. In the HPF scheme, a portion of people's salary was earmarked for housing consumption. Third, the policy created a huge fund for house construction and it could then be used as a mortgage lending scheme for homeowners. Fourth, the interest rates embodied in the HPF scheme created incentives for households to become homeowners. Simply put, the interest rates for HPF deposits and HPF loans were significantly lower than those offered by

---

19 Interview with BJ 2004a. This official chaired the State Council's Leadership Group on Housing System Reform between 1992 and 1997.

commercial banks.[20] Thus, households who decided to stay in rented apartments and let their HPF deposits remain idle would be in a disadvantaged position. By contrast, people using the HPF fund to buy an apartment would benefit. In other words, it was a policy that penalized people in rental housing and benefited households deciding to take loans to buy apartments.[21]

As seen in these examples, implementation of China's housing reforms required careful thinking about the norms of urban households and ideas on how economic incentives might entice them to use a larger portion of their savings for housing consumption. Enforcement of rent increases was a complete failure, but policies for sale of public housing and participation in HPF schemes were more successful, mainly because they were seen as bringing economic advantages. By the late 1990s, when market reforms gained momentum, households began to view housing as an attractive form of investment. Due to this normative shift, the HPF policy became easier to implement. State efforts to shape norms should not be underestimated, however. Instead of treating social norms as an obstacle, the state authorities viewed them as malleable and susceptible to change.[22]

Policy Evolution and Legal Framework

Like other aspects of Chinese economic reform, housing policy in the 1980s evolved in a process of trial and errors. A handful of cities was given approval to implement pilot experiments with rent in-

---

20 In 2004, the HPF interest rate for deposits was 1.71 percent (compared to 1.89 percent in commercial banks), and the HPF lending interest rate was 4.20 percent (compared to 5.20 percent in banks). If people placed their savings in a bank, rather than in the HPF account, they would have earned a higher interest, but the HPF policy did not allow them to make that choice. Interview with BJ 2004c.

21 Interviews with BJ 2004c, BJ 2005b.

22 Cf. Peter H. Corne, *Foreign Investment in China: The Administrative Legal System* (Hong Kong: Hong Kong University Press, 1997).

creases and sales of housing, but on a very small scale.[23] The first housing reform conference was held in 1988 and the State Council issued the *Implementation Plan for a Gradual Housing System Reform in Cities and Towns* to sum up pilot tests and set the agenda. The key message was that free public housing would be abandoned and that larger financial burdens would be placed on households, but policy guidelines were set rather loosely. Localities were allowed to choose their own policy mix and pace of implementation in light of local economic conditions. They were asked to proceed cautiously in "stages and batches" and submit their local reform plans to the State Council for approval.[24]

A shift came in 1991 when the State Council approved the Shanghai housing reform plan, followed by the second housing conference in October 1991. Shanghai was the first city to set up a Housing Provident Fund based on joint contributions from employees and their work units. In 1992, large cities such as Guangzhou, Beijing, and Tianjin also adopted the HPF scheme, soon followed by other provincial capitals, and by 1995 some 135 cities had adopted this policy. By the late 1990s, almost all prefecture-level cities had established HPF agencies.[25] The next impetus came in 1994 with The State Council's *Decision on Deepening Urban Housing Reform*. In this policy document both the sale of public housing and establishment of HPFs was strongly supported by central authorities, but a leeway

---

23 Interviews with BJ 2003 and BJ 2004a.

24 James Lee, "From Welfare Housing to Home Ownership," *Housing Studies* 15, no. 1 (2000): 61–76; Yaping Wang and Alan Murie, "Social and Spatial Implications of Housing Reform in China," *International Journal of Urban and Regional Research* 24, no. 2 (2000): 397–417. See China News Analysis, "Housing Reform, What Is New?" *China News Analysis*, no. 1432 (April 1991); Cf. Interview with BJ 2003.

25 James Lee, "From Welfare Housing to Home Ownership," *Housing Studies* 15, no. 1 (2000): 65; China News Analysis, "Housing Reform in the Cities," *China News Analysis*, no. 1570 (October 1996); Interviews with MoC 2004b, TJ 2004a, TJ 2004b, BJ 2004c, and GZ 2004a.

for local adaptation was retained.[26] As clarified by a Ministry of Construction official:

> All the central government did in 1995, under Premier Zhu Rongji, was to "ask" (*yaoqiu*) localities to set up HPFs. This expression has a weaker legal value than for instance a law or a departmental regulation. Nevertheless, it prompted most cities to follow Shanghai's example.[27]

In 1998, the State Council's *Directive on Deepening Housing Reform and Accelerating Housing Construction* put an end to allocation of public housing to urban employees.[28] This policy decision sent a clear signal to urban households that they had to rely on personal savings or HPF loans to afford housing. In the mid-1990s, policymakers felt that the HPF was in need of a more formal legal framework and that HPF practices should be standardized. Thus, a drafting process started in 1996 and in 1999 the *Housing Provident Fund Management Provisions* were issued. At this point the policy coverage was extended so that all urban work units and all employees hired on a contract for over one year would be covered by HPF policy.[29] Such an expansion of the policy scope was ambitious. It meant that all work units, disregarding size, ownership, or financial status were supposed to comply with these regulations. Previously, the policy had focused on staff in government units, public institutions, and state-owned enterprises. The 1999 provisions also stipulated that HPF loans should exclusively be used for individual

---

26 Lee, "From Welfare Housing to Home Ownership"; Wang and Alan, "Social and Spatial Implications of Housing Reform in China," 403–405; Hiroshi Sato, "Housing Inequality and Housing Poverty in Urban China in the late 1990s," *China Economic Review* 17 (2000): 40.

27 Interview with MoC 2004b.

28 "Welfare Housing Allocation Will Become History," *Beijing Review* (November 2–8, 1998): 14–16; cf. Sato, "Housing Inequality and Housing Poverty," 41.

29 *Housing Provident Fund Management Provisions*, issued by the State Council Standing Committee, March 3, 1999; Interview with MoC 2004b.

households. This was a break with the prior practice of granting HPF loans to work units for housing construction. After 1999 all real estate projects had to rely on commercial bank loans.[30] Finally, the new provisions standardized HPF contribution rates. Previously, some localities had adopted low rates, e.g., 1–2 percent of the wage sum. Now the minimum limit was set at 5 percent with a joint contribution of 10 percent between the work unit and the employee.

In 2002, the *Amended HPF Management Provisions* were issued.[31] The overall content of this document is basically the same as the 1999 provisions, but with added precision in some clauses.[32] In particular, the policy scope is extended to include all types of firms (including township enterprises) and nonenterprise units. More detail is added concerning supervision of HPF management as well as penalties for noncompliance, mismanagement of funds, or misappropriation of funds. Such revisions were probably the result of the quick expansion and financial sensitivity of HPF funds, and a series of corruption cases in this area.[33]

Legislation in Tianjin closely mirrored national policy. When the HPF system was introduced in 1992, the government issued the *Temporary Measures on Tianjin's Housing Provident Fund*. HPF policy continued and was consolidated in October 1997 when the Tianjin's People's Congress adopted the *Tianjin Housing Provident Fund*

---

30 Yaping Wang, "Urban Housing Reform and Finance in China," *Urban Affairs Review* 36, no. 5 (2001): 620–645; Xingquan Zhang, "The Restructuring of the Housing Finance System in China," *Cities* 17, no. 5 (2000): 339–348; Interviews with MoC 2004b, TJ 2004b.

31 *Amended Housing Provident Fund Management Provisions*, issued by the State Council, March 24, 2002.

32 The 2002 provisions contain forty-seven articles and seven chapters: (1) General Principles, (2) Institutions and Duties, (3) Collecting and Depositing Funds, (4) Withdrawing and Spending Funds, (5) Supervision, (6) Rules of Punishments, (7) Supplementary Regulations.

33 Interviews with MoC 2004b and GZ 2004a. See also "No Full House: Housing Provident Funds are Plagued by Non-Use and Embezzlement," *Beijing Review* (January 2006) (online version, accessed February 5, 2006).

Provisions. The following year, Tianjin People's Government issued the *Implementing Measures of the Tianjin Housing Provident Fund Provisions* as a detailed set of guidelines. These implementing measures were almost identical with national legislation.[34] After the amendments of national HPF legislation in 2001, Tianjin's People's Congress issued the *Tianjin Housing Provident Fund Management Provisions* in 2002. This set of regulations was supplemented in 2002, 2003 and 2005 with implementation measures concerning the collection, withdrawals, and lending procedures for HPF funds. As clarified by HPF officials in Tianjin, there is a clear hierarchy of legal documents from the national and municipal levels down to specific operating rules (*caozuoxing de guiding*).[35] The legal hierarchy for HPF policy was well established already in 1998–1999 and with the revised regulations issued in 2001–2002 this trend was reinforced.

Implementing HPF Policy in Tianjin

As I have argued elsewhere, when looking at law-in-action we must choose some indicators of enforcement.[36] One method is to examine the human and financial processing generated by existing policies, i.e., to what extent there are flows of actions going through relevant bureaucratic agencies. In HPF policy, the key actions concern the collection, withdrawal, and lending patterns of HPF funds.

This way of measuring enforcement seems to coincide with views adopted by HPF Management Centers when they evaluate their own work progress. The annual and accumulated collection of

---

34 Huaqi Sun (ed.), *Tenth Anniversary of Tianjin Housing System Reform* (Tianjin Housing Reform Committee, 2002), 78; Interviews with TJ 2004a and TJ 2004b.

35 Interview with TJ 2006, Official at Tianjin HPF Management Center, July 2006; and interviews with TJ 2004a and TJ 2004b.

36 Burell, "The Rule-governed State," 189–196.

Table 1. Tianjin HPF Collection and Withdrawals, 1996–2005 (billion CNY)

Year	Annual HPF collection	Accumulated collection	Annual withdrawals	Accumulated withdrawals
1996–1997	1.048	–	–	–
1997–1998	1.505	4.180	–	–
1998–1999	1.871	5.990	–	–
1999–2000	2.165	8.154	0.606	–
2000–2001	2.739	10.920	0.918	2.184
2001–2002	3.074	14.065	1.180	3.365
2002–2003	–	–	–	–
2003–2004	4.884	24.192	2.317	8.021
2004–2005	6.542	30.730	3.100	11.150

Data sources: *Tianjin City Housing Provident System Implementation Report* (*TJS*) *1996–2004*.

Note: A dash indicates no data. Author's calculations.

HPF funds is a performance measure that local officials mention in interviews and which they have to report to the Ministry of Construction. The influx of new funds is the precondition for all other HPF operations, and enterprise noncompliance in this area is considered a problem.[37] As shown in Table 1, the collection of HPF funds in Tianjin increased from one to over CNY 6 billion per year between 1996 and 2005. The accumulated total since the HPF started in 1992 was over CNY 30 billion. This result cannot simply be an outcome of rising salary levels. It must be linked with the expanding policy coverage and a rising number of firms complying with HPF regulations.

According to the *Implementing Measures of Tianjin's HPF Provisions*, issued in 1999, employees can withdraw funds from HPF accounts under specific conditions (Article 30), such as house purchase, renovation, or payment of HPF mortgage or interest, etc. Table 1 shows that financial flows took place in this area too. The

---

37 Interviews with NC 2004, TJ 2004b, GZ 2004a, and BJ 2004c.

Table 2. Tianjin HPF withdrawals by category, 1996–2005 (million CNY)

Year	Mortgage and interest	Renovation and house purchase	Pensions	Other	Number of beneficiaries [a]
1999–2000	57.4	378.6	153.6	16.4	174,642
2000–2001	273.9	332.8	234.8	76.3	251,143
2001–2002	247.9	410.9	365.5	156.6	327,101
2002–2003	—	—	—	—	—
2003–2004	924.5	697.4	479.5	215.3	514,447
2004–2005	1,620.0	637.3	601.7	271.8	804,045
%	30.4	36.8	24.4	8.4	

Data source: *TJS 1996–2004*.

Note: A dash indicates no data. (a) The number of beneficiaries indicates "person-times," not the actual number of persons. The total number of "person-time" beneficiaries, 1999–2005, was 2,071,378.

amount of HPF withdrawals increased from CNY 0.6 billion to 3 billion per year between 1999 and 2005. The accumulated total reached CNY 11 billion in 2005. This is a sign that HPF regulations in Tianjin were being enforced in the most basic sense of the word.

Table 2 shows the types of HPF withdrawals that took place between 1999 and 2005. The size of withdrawals increased in all categories over these seven years. For instance, withdrawals for mortgage and interest payments rose from CNY 57 million to CNY 1,620 million per year. Most interestingly, the number of beneficiaries of the HPF system also increased significantly. There were only 174,000 beneficiaries in 1999, but this number rose to over 800,000 people in 2005. Over the years, there were two million beneficiaries of HPF withdrawals in Tianjin. Since Tianjin's HPF system covers about two million contributing employees, this result should be seen as fairly impressive.[38]

The main purpose of the HPF is to provide housing loans to eligible households. To what extent was this aspect of HPF policy im-

---

38 Interview with TJ 2004b.

Table 3. Tianjin HPF loans and beneficiaries, 1996–2005 (billion CNY)

Year	Individual HPF loans	Accumulated individual loans	HPF loan beneficiaries	Accumulated beneficiaries
1996–1997	0.169	—	—	—
1997–1998	1.018	1.232	—	26,200
1998–1999	1.069	2.301	—	48,708
1999–2000	1.967	4.268	30,521	79,229
2000–2001	2.200	6.468	29,784	109,013
2001–2002	2.002	8.470	24,330	133,343
2002–2003	—	—	—	—
2003–2004	5.303	16.200	41,584	201,575
2004–2005	5.040	21.280	34,947	—

Data source: *TJS 1996–2004*.

Note: A dash indicates no data. The accumulated figures date back to 1992 when Tianjin's HPF was established.

plemented in Tianjin? Table 3 shows that annual HPF loans steadily increased from 169 million to over CNY 5 billion between 1996 and 2005. As a result, a total of CNY 21.28 billion in HPF loans had been dispensed to Tianjin households. It has also been estimated that one-third of all housing purchases in Tianjin had been fully or partially financed by HPF loans. Meanwhile, the number of persons benefiting from HPF loans reached an accumulated total of 201,000 persons, about 10 percent of the employees contributing to the HPF fund. Since the policy aim is to assist people in their housing purchases, this result is not impressive.

As mentioned earlier, the 1999 *HPF Management Provisions* stipulated that HPF loans should be exclusively offered to individuals, thereby putting an end to house construction loans. The enforcement of this policy change is displayed in Diagram 1, where the ratio between individual loans versus work unit loans shifted between 1999 and 2001.

These statistics seem to indicate a smooth enforcement of HPF policy in Tianjin, but they only reveal parts of the story. Local officials use various methods to evaluate work progress. For instance, they pay close attention to the "establishment rates" (*jianli lü*) of

Diagram 1. Individual and work unit HPF loans in Tianjin, 1996–2205

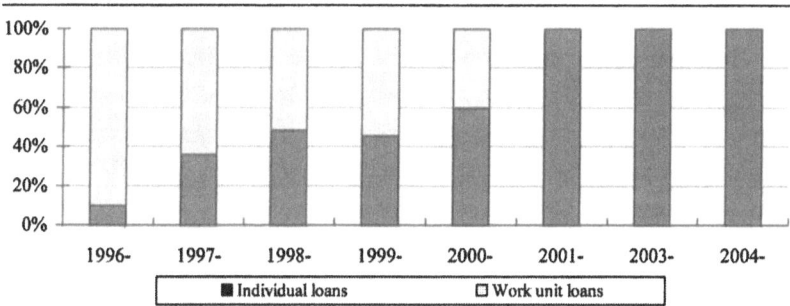

Data source: *TJS 1996–2004*.

Note: The total of HPF loans, 1992–2005, was CNY 32.35 billion, of which 65.8 percent was allocated to individuals.

HPF policy. This is the ratio between the number of employees in work units (under the scope of HPF policy), and the number of employees who have been registered into the system. If there are 2 million eligible employees in the city but only 1.9 million are registered, the establishment rate is 95 percent. Between 1996 and 2005, the HPF establishment rates have fluctuated between 89.2 and 94.2 percent in Tianjin so implementation in this area can be seen as fairly successful. The policy coverage is very low in private and foreign firms, however. Only 1,400 such enterprises had registered their staff and set up HPF accounts in Tianjin.[39]

A less frequently mentioned figure is the "payment ratio" (*jiaocun lü*). This is the share of registered staff and work units that actually make regular payments into the HPF accounts. The HPF payment ratio in 1997–1998 was 73.8 percent, which was a sign that many enterprises had difficulties making their HPF payments. Recent reports do not offer any information on payment ratios, but the problem persists as seen in official statements such as "more efforts are needed in this area."[40] From an enforcement perspective, it

---

39 *Tianjin City Housing Provident System Implementation Reports, 1996–2004* (hereafter referred to as *TJS 1996–2004*); Interview with TJ 2004b.

40 *TJS 1996–2004*. In fact, the work unit should make the joint HPF payments, i.e., its own share of 5 percent and the employees' share of 5 percent.

is problematic if only 74 percent of the contributions are paid on time, if at all.

Overdue HPF payments were a serious problem in Tianjin, although local officials are rather reluctant to admit it. In 2004 there were about twenty thousand work units in Tianjin, but over nine thousand enterprises had overdue HPF payments of CNY 1.26 billion. As a remedy, inspections were carried out and enterprises were pressured to make supplementary payments. Inspection work started in 2001 and continued in 2003 and 2005. Inspections started in 387 enterprises and then expanded to cover 5,000 work units. These inspections generated supplementary HPF payments of CNY 78 million in 2002 and CNY 320 million in 2005. Some firms were subject to administrative enforcement. A total of 127 firms were handled this way, and CNY 120 million was recovered to the HPF fund between 2001 and 2003.[41]

Many implementation problems appear to be linked with a changing economy. The reform of state-owned enterprises (SOEs) is one aspect, and the quickly growing private sector is another. It is quite difficult for HPF agencies to keep track of these changes and adjust their enforcement mechanisms. SOE reforms were particularly severe in Tianjin in the late 1990s; the consequence being that many firms became debt-ridden and had to lay off workers. For example, the textile sector downsized its workforce from 200,000 to 20,000 employees.[42] Many firms in manufacturing and service sectors face similar problems, and about 40 percent of the remaining 900,000 SOE workers in Tianjin belong to enterprises operating with deficits. It was estimated that 5,000 firms with approximately 600,000 workers were standing in debt of their HPF payments in 2004. Thus, although 2 million employees in Tianjin were registered to the HPF scheme, only 1.4 million of them belonged to units able to make regular HPF payments. Delayed payments of one to two months are common, but the longest debts can date back to ten years. Some enterprises signed up with the HPF scheme, paid the

---

41 *TJS 1996–2004*.
42 Interview with TJ 2004b.

first month and then quit.⁴³ As expressed by one senior official in Tianjin:

> Many work units just cannot pay. And if they don't make HPF contributions, although we have the right to use administrative enforcement and penalties, or turn to the court for enforcement, in fact it is really problematic. These firms don't have any money and face bankruptcy. It is quite simple: there are no assets left and no basis for implementation. What can we do?⁴⁴

The problem of financially ailing enterprises is not restricted to Tianjin. It is an obstacle for HPF implementation in many parts of China. According to national statistics, approximately eighty million urban employees were registered and covered by HPF policy in 2004 but only sixty million of them were employed in firms making regular HPF payments. The remaining twenty million employees were considered "intermittent" contributors. In fact, the official number of "on-the-post" urban employees is one hundred million; so the actual coverage of HPF policy is 60 percent. Another problem is that HPF payments compete with other insurance schemes. Most enterprises prioritize payments into pension funds and HPF contributions are given secondary importance. Hence, legal enforcement in this area is more lax.⁴⁵

Policy Dilution

As shown above, economic constraints can have a corrosive effect on the intentions of a law or policy. This is what I call *policy dilution*.⁴⁶ In a general sense, it is a deviation from the legal intent. More

---

43 Interview with TJ 2004b.
44 Interview with TJ 2004b.
45 Interview with MoC 2004b.
46 For a discussion of policy dilution in China's labor laws, see Burell, "The Rule-governed State," 204–206.

precisely, it means that originally strict standards are lowered so as to fit the underlying social reality. In other words, it is a process of adaptation that can occur in the form of legal amendments and specifications, or simply be the result of lenient practices in the course of enforcement. Policy dilution can either be seen in a favorable light or with critical eyes. On the positive side, it may be regarded as a form of pragmatism. On the negative side, it can be seen as a failure of the principle that laws should be uniformly applied and treat policy clients equally.

Policy dilution in China's housing policy has occurred in two versions. First, it is the lowering of HPF payments for firms in economic distress. This compromise already exists in legal documents but is accentuated in implementation. Since 1999, the minimum contribution rate should be 5 percent of the salary for employees, matched by 5 percent by the work unit. This standard is stated in the national 2002 *Amended HPF Management Provisions*, and in the *Implementing Measures of the Tianjin HPF Provisions* (1998). Both of these documents, however, have clauses allowing for postponed HPF payment or lowered payment rates in a situation of economic distress. Such decisions, however, must be discussed with the enterprise's trade union and approved by the Housing Committee.[47] In Tianjin, specific rules have been issued clarifying that when an enterprise has been in continuous deficit for two to three years, or if workers' salaries are set very low to cope with economic difficulties, it may apply for a lower HPF payment rate or a temporary suspension of payments. The HPF payment rate in Tianjin is actually set in a ladder-shaped pattern. Thus, it may vary between 1 and 5 percent of the enterprise's wage bill depending on its economic situation. In the words of a senior official in Tianjin: "This flexibility allows us to adjust policy so that the HPF payments are a 'reasonable burden' for each firm."[48] This position may seem fair and pragmatic, but it is still

---

47   Interview with BJ 2004c and TJ 2004b.
48   Interview with TJ 2004b.

an attenuation of the policy intentions. In that sense, it is a type of formal policy dilution.

A second form of dilution occurs in the implementation stage. Local HPF agencies may adopt a lenient attitude toward certain employing units. This approach is common vis-à-vis small private enterprises, foreign-owned firms, and work units that employ many migrant workers. Such employing units are seen as being at the margins of the policy, although HPF regulations clearly state that all urban employers must comply. For instance, in Guangdong's export zones, most enterprises do not register with the HPF scheme, although their employees represent between 50 and 70 percent of the local population, and HPF agencies are not too anxious to deal with the problem. A similar situation can be seen in inland provinces such as Jiangxi and Yunnan where it is regarded as too troublesome to enforce HPF policy among private firms, foreign enterprises, or joint-ventures.[49]

This attitude of conditional enforcement can also be found in cities like Beijing and Tianjin. Some aspects of the local economy are seen as falling outside the HPF policy coverage or being so fickle that they are difficult to monitor. Hence, originally strict standards are lowered. As expressed by a HPF official in Tianjin:

> Not all work units are included in the HPF system. They do not know about us and we don't know of their existence. New enterprises pop up all the time, and they don't register with the HPF scheme. Economic activity changes so quickly. The ideal would be to attain a 100 percent policy coverage, but it is not feasible. A coverage rate of 90 percent is already quite high and is difficult to improve. With the current rapid turnover rates of firms and workers, once we detect new forms of enterprise behavior, we are already many steps behind.[50]

---

49 Interview with GZ 2004b, GZ 2004c, NC 2004, and YN 2005.
50 Interview with TJ 2004b.

Table 4. Comparison of accumulated HPF, 1996–2005 (million CNY)

Year	Beijing	Tianjin	Nanchang	National
1996–1997	–	–		39,300
1997–1998	–	4.180		79,900
1998–1999	6,780	5.990	90	123,100
1999–2000	10,590	8.154	235	140,900
2000–2001	15,330	10.920	431	140,900
2001–2002	21,350	14.065	661	332,600
2002–2003	28,650	–	930	413,100
2003–2004	37,420	24.192	1,289	556,300
2004–2005	45,400	30.730	1,689	630,000

Data sources: *TJS 1996–2004*; *China News Analysis* 1570, October 15, 1996; *Gateway* 2006; Interviews with MoC 2004b, BJ 2004c, BJ 2005b, GZ 2004a, NC 2004, and TJ 2004. Author's calculations.

Uneven enforcement is related to policy dilution. As shown in Table 4, HPF collection rates differ between cities in China. Clearly, economic constraints have an effect on the quality of legal enforcement.[51] Uneven enforcement means that the same rules do not apply to all regions or firms. Instead, regulations are allowed to vary, de jure or de facto, in line with economic conditions. This, too, is a form of attenuation of the law. Thus, HPF collections in Nanchang rose from CNY 90 to 1,600 million between 1998 and 2005, while HPF collections in Beijing increased from CNY 6,700 to 45,400 million. The difference in population between the cities is not so great. While Nanchang has six million registered urban residents, Beijing's population is about ten million. However, the economic resources of the two cities are vastly different, and it has a significant impact on the implementation of HPF policy. According to the Ministry of Construction, HPF collections vary markedly between cities. Small cities may collect CNY 10 million to 30 million, medium-sized cities may attain one or two billion CNY, and Shanghai collects CNY 60

---

[51] For a similar argument in the sphere of judicial enforcement, se Jingwen Zhu (ed.), *Report on China Law Development: Database and Indicators*, in Chinese (Beijing: Zhongguo renmin daxue chubanshe, 2007).

billion per year.[52] This variation may either be seen as an obstacle in enforcement, as an equity problem, or both.

Equity Problems

Chinese HPF policy does not officially target any social group. The aim is simply to raise housing affordability among urban residents. However, the policy design in combination with market forces has had redistributive outcomes. As noted by some researchers,[53] HPF policy tends to benefit households with high incomes at the expense of those with medium or low incomes. Simply put, many medium-income people contribute to the HPF scheme, but their moderate salaries prevent them from fulfilling eligibility requirements for HPF housing loans. Since the HPF scheme operates with low-interest rates for both deposits and loans, low-income households suffer from a loss in interest on their deposits. By contrast, affluent households who fulfill the requirements will obtain low-interest loans and are subsidized by the scheme. In fact, the problem of low usage rates of HPF loans has been noted by Ministry of Construction officials but this problem seems difficult to solve. Local HPF agencies are unwilling to change their HPF lending procedures or adjust eligibility standards.[54]

---

52 Interview with MoC 2004b, the Director of the HPF Division, Ministry of Construction, July 2004.

53 See Lee, "From Welfare Housing to Home Ownership"; Wang, "Urban Housing Reform and Finance in China," 642; Mattias Burell, "China's Housing Provident Fund: Its Success and Limitations," *Housing Finance International* (March 2006): 46–47; Stanley Yeung and Rodney Howes, "The Role of the Housing Provident Fund in Financing Affordable Housing Development in China," *Habitat International* 30 (2006): 343–356.

54 Zhifeng Liu, "Strengthen the Management of Housing Provident Funds," speech at national housing meeting in Beijing, October 28, 2001, accessed at http://www.cin.gov.cn/meeting/01g&x/2001110602 on February 6, 2006.

Table 5. Ratio of HPF contributors and beneficiaries in Tianjin, 1998–2005

Year	Employees contributing to HPF	HPF withdrawals [a]	% of contributors	HPF loan takers	% of contributors
1998–1999	2,029,000	—	—	22,256	1.1
1999–2000	1,998,000	174,642	8.7	30,521	1.5
2000–2001	1,901,000	251,143	13.2	29,784	1.6
2001–2002	1,706,000	327,101	19.2	24,330	1.4
2002–2003	—	—	—	—	—
2003–2004	2,028,000	514,447	25.4	41,584	2.0
2004–2005	2,010,000	804,045	40.0	34,947	1.7
Average	1,945,000	414,275	21.3	30,570	1.6

Source: *TJS 1996–2004*.

Note: (a) HPF withdrawals do not refer to individual beneficiaries but "person-times" beneficiaries.

Table 5 shows that the ratio of contributors and beneficiaries in Tianjin's HPF loan activity has remained very low, fluctuating between 1.1 and 2 percent between 1998 and 2005. If we count all HPF loan takers, 183,422 persons, this equals 9.43 percent of all contributors, but this figure is still not so impressive. If only 10 percent of the HPS participants can obtain housing loans, it must be a policy failure. In addition, an inequity can be detected in the collection and dispensation of HPF funds. In the period 1998-2005, 54 percent of the funds were collected from domestic enterprises, but workers in these firms only obtained 48 percent of total HPF loans. By contrast, 35 percent of the funds were collected from government organs and public institutions, but staff in these units obtained 44 percent of total HPF loans.[55] This is due to higher salary levels in government organs compared to firms, and it signifies a redistribution from low- to high-income people.

Similar patterns can be seen in other cities (Table 6). In most places, the ratio between contributors and beneficiaries of HPF funds has ranged from 0.4 to 6 percent, and in 1998–2005 the aver-

---

55 See *TJS 1996–2004*. These figures are based on the author's calculations.

Table 6. Ratio of HPF contributors and loan beneficiaries, 1998–2005

Year	Beijing	Guangzhou	Tianjin	Nanchang	National
1998–1999	0.4	—	1.1	0.4	0.7
1999–2000	0.7	3.2	1.5	1.0	—
2000–2001	1.6	0.9	1.6	1.9	—
2001–2002	3.3	1.7	1.4	2.2	—
2002–2003	4.5	2.6	—	3.1	—
2003–2004	5.6	3.5	2.0	3.3	5.4
2004–2005	6.4	4.4	1.7	4.2	—
Average	3.2	2.7	1.6	2.3	-

Data sources: *TJS 1996-2004*; Interviews with MoC 2004b, BJ 2004c, BJ 2005b, GZ 2004a, NC 2004, and TJ 2004. Author's calculations. National percentages are based on an estimate of 60 million active HPF contributors in 2004.

age ratio was below 3 percent. A low usage rate of HPF loans seems to be a widespread phenomenon and it does not seem to vary significantly between rich and poor cities. The situation is pretty much the same in well-endowed cities like Beijing and Guangzhou and in Nanchang, which is located in the economic backwaters of China.

The limited reach of HPF policy can also be seen in the low public awareness about this scheme. Tianjin HPF agencies have recently placed more emphasis on publicity campaigns in the mass media and they have set up websites to enhance the accessibility and transparency of HPF policy.[56] Most urban employees, however, have little understanding of HPF policy. In the survey conducted in Wuhan 2006, I discovered that only 15 percent of the respondents took part in the HPF scheme and 39 percent of them did not even know it existed. Among the residents only 9.3 percent had ever applied for an HPF loan. This pattern was repeated when respondents were asked about their attitudes toward HPF policy (Table 6).

Only 24 percent of the residents agreed that the HPF scheme had improved the ability of medium-income families to afford housing. Concerning the question of whether the HPF scheme

---

56 See *TJS 1996-2004*. Interview with MoC 2004b and TJ 2004b.

Table 7. Do you think that the HPF can resolve your housing purchase?

Response	Percent
Yes, it can completely resolve	1.4
Yes, it can basically resolve	14.9
It cannot resolve. It is still quite difficult	46.5
I do not know about the HPF policy	37.2

Source: Wuhan survey conducted by the author in July 2006. N=1000

could resolve their own housing purchase, only 16.3 percent of felt that HPF loans could basically or completely solve the problem. Most importantly, almost 40 percent of the respondents had no knowledge about HPF policy.

When evaluating the effectiveness of legal enforcement we should also estimate social outcomes and public awareness. In this view, China's HPF policy clearly had a limited impact on society. The survey findings confirm the argument made by other scholars that poor and medium-income households either do not know anything about the HPF scheme or simply find it irrelevant.[57]

Conclusion

This chapter has analyzed implementation in a policy area that has neither suffered from state-society conflicts[58] nor been plagued by institutional weaknesses. Leadership support and coordination between different agencies has been rather good. On the other hand,

---

57 See Yaping Wang, *Urban Poverty, Housing and Social Change in China* (London and New York: Routledge, 2004).

58 With the notable exception, of course, of demolitions and household evictions in urban areas. These aspects of housing policy have unleashed sharp tensions between local residents, real estate companies, and local authorities in recent years.

housing reform entails a massive redistribution of resources and is therefore a sensitive policy area. This policy also required a deep shift in social norms and attitudes toward ownership, savings, and consumption. Without the propaganda efforts and a shift in economic incentives, both the privatization of public housing and the setup of Housing Provident Funds might have failed.

It has been shown that enforcement of HPF policy has a mixed record of success and failure depending on which aspect we choose to look at. The HPF collections, withdrawals, and loans have increased tremendously over the last ten years. Such transactions show that HPF policy is operational and is being enforced in a general sense. A careful look, however, reveals problems with respect to HPF collections and the allocation of HPF loans.

This case study indicates that policy dilution is a problem in Chinese law implementation. Economic realities induce a situation where original standards are lowered either through policy revisions or as de facto leniency during implementation. Some policy targets are left outside the scope of enforcement because HPF agencies find it too troublesome or costly to aim for 100 percent compliance.

Economic inequities also cast a shadow of doubt on the implementation of the HPF policy. This is the mixed result of policy design and the impact of market forces. HPF loan usage and lending patterns reveal that the benefits of this policy are mainly reaped by richer households that are, in fact, subsidized by lower-income families. This is the joint result of a forced savings scheme, HPF interest rates, the salary structure, and the eligibility criteria for HPF loans. In light of these findings, one might raise the normative question, as done by Peerenboom in this volume, whether it is really a good thing that laws are fully implemented. With respect to HPF policy, the answer to that question is uncertain. As shown in this chapter, many foreign enterprises, small firms, and ailing SOEs run the risk of falling outside the scope of enforcement. To the extent that employees in these work units only have moderate salary levels, one might speculate if they are not better off that way. In short, it is not only a question of enforcement but also the issue of fairness. Sometimes, poor law enforcement may actually contribute to less social inequality in China.

Bibliography

Beijing Review. "Welfare Housing Allocation Will Become History." November 2–8 (1998): 14–16.
Beijing Review online. "No Full House: Housing Provident Funds Are Plagued by Non-Use and Embezzlement." January (2006).
Burell, Mattias. "The Rule-governed State: China's Labor Market Policy, 1978–1998." Ph.D. dissertation, Uppsala University, 2001.
Burell, Mattias. "China's Housing Provident Fund: Its Success and Limitations," *Housing Finance International*, March (2006): 46–47.
China News Analysis. "Housing Reform, What Is New?" no. 1432, April (1991): 1–6.
China News Analysis. "Housing Reform in the Cities," no. 1570, October (1996): 1–6.
Corne, Peter H. *Foreign Investment in China: The Administrative Legal System*. Hong Kong: Hong Kong University Press, 1997.
Evan, William. "Law as an Instrument of Social Change," In *The Sociology of Law: A Social-Structural Perspective*, edited by William Evan. New York: Free Press, 1980.
Lee, James. "From Welfare Housing to Home Ownership," *Housing Studies* 15, no. 1 (2000): 61–76.
Liu, Zhifeng. "Strengthen the Management of Housing Provident Funds." Speech at the National Housing Meeting in Beijing, October 28, 2001, accessed at http://www.cin.gov.cn/meeting/o1g&x/2001110602 on February 6, 2006.
Sato, Hiroshi. "Housing Inequality and Housing Poverty in Urban China in the late 1990s," *China Economic Review* 17 (2000): 25–45.
State Council. People's Republic of China. *Housing Provident Fund Management Provisions*, issued on March 3, 1999.
State Council. People's Republic of China. RC. *Amended Housing Provident Fund Management Provisions*, issued on March 24, 2002.
Sun, Huaqi, ed. *Tenth Anniversary of Tianjin Housing System Reform*. Tianjin: Tianjin Housing Reform Committee, 2002.

Tianjin Housing Provident Fund Management Center. *Tianjin City Housing Provident System Implementation Report, 1996–2004* [in Chinese]. Unpublished internal reports on file with the author.

van Rooij, Benjamin. "Law as Event: Lessons about Lawmaking, Compliance and Enforcement, drawn from the Regulation of Land and Pollution in South-West China." Ph.D. dissertation, Leiden University, 2006.

Wang, Yaping, and Alan Murie. "Social and Spatial Implications of Housing Reform in China," *International Journal of Urban and Regional Research* 24, no. 2 (2000): 397–417.

Wang, Yaping. "Urban Housing Reform and Finance in China," *Urban Affairs Review* 36, no. 5 (2001): 620–645.

Wang, Yaping. *Urban Poverty, Housing and Social Change in China.* London and New York: Routledge, 2004.

Yeung, Stanley, and Rodney Howes. "The Role of the Housing Provident Fund in Financing Affordable Housing Development in China," *Habitat International* 30 (2006): 343–356.

Zhang, Xingquan. "The Restructuring of the Housing Finance System in China," *Cities* 17, no. 5 (2000): 339–348.

Zhu, Jingwen, ed. *Report on China Law Development: Database and Indicators* [in Chinese]. Beijing: Zhongguo renmin daxue chubanshe, 2007.

11

Regulating Land and Pollution at Lake Dianchi

Compliance and Enforcement in a Chinese and Comparative Perspective

BENJAMIN VAN ROOIJ

Introduction

Long before development opportunities arrived, Lake Dianchi, located right below Kunming city in southwest China, had been rich in natural resources. "The lake's water was pure and clean. We would swim there and even wash our clothes," explained an old woman from Jiacun[1] village, which borders the eastern side of the lake. In addition to clean water, local farmers, though not rich, used to have plenty of fertile land. However, in the last two decades, development has brought change for the better and for the worse. The inhabitants of this periurban region—like many Chinese—have been able to share in the prosperity that rapid industrialization and rural urbanization brought. Farmers switched to off-farm jobs in the new industries. On the more developed eastern side of the lake, farmers even turned to real estate development, building second houses while leasing their old ones to newly arrived migrants. In addition, villages have earned income by renting out farmland for enterprise construction. Lake Dianchi thus witnessed its inhabitants trans-

---

[1] All localities and names of persons and companies have been replaced with fictitious names whenever the identity of informants was at stake and when possible.

form from relative rural poverty to an initial stage of periurban riches.

Economic development had its price: it was disastrous for the natural resources of the lake's catchments. A combination of industrial pollution, municipal waste discharge, soil erosion, and various kinds of nonpoint pollution from chemical fertilizers, solid wastes, and pesticides used in horticulture severely atrophied the lake's water. In addition, the numerous new paper and chemical fertilizer factories polluted the rivers of the lake's catchments and the region's air. Last but not least, arable land, once an abundant resource, also suffered from development. Kunming's unstoppable expansion devoured whole villages, while in those villages left intact, the farmers' own housing craze combined with the construction of village enterprises and new highways caused the amount of arable land to decrease even further, to the extent that some villages lost most of their land.

Lake Dianchi is but one of the many localities in China where development has adversely affected natural resources. Throughout the country, economic development in combination with urbanization and industrialization has led to natural-resource degradation. Most of China's larger cities suffer from serious air quality problems. The country's major lakes and rivers have been severely polluted, and accidents involving highly toxic spills such as those at the Tuojiang River in 2004 and the Songhua River in 2005 continue to occur. A World Bank study on air pollution found in 2005 that sixteen of the world's most polluted cities were in China.[2] Furthermore, the country's arable land continues to decline, in part because of urban and rural construction, but also because of land transformation to stop further soil erosion.[3] Such erosion led to serious desertification

---

2 Jonathan Watts, "Satellite data revels Beijing as air pollution capital of world," *The Guardian*, October 31, 2005.

3 Zhimin Feng et al., "Grain-for-Green Policy and Its Impacts on Grain Supply in West China," *Land Use Policy* 22 (2005).

that in turn led to severe water shortages throughout northern China and sandstorms reaching all the way to South Korea.

China's foremost approach to stop resource loss has been the use of the legal system. Initial legislation made in the 1980s was vague and weak, and therefore unable to protect natural resources. China's legal reconstruction and the country's special circumstances were an important reason why China's original natural-resource protection laws had been vague and weak. Lacking legal experience and faced with an enormous and rapidly changing society, during the early days of reform (in the 1980s and early 1990s), Deng Xiaoping's credo *mo shitou guo he* (crossing the river by feeling the stones) had been central for China's legal development. Following a piecemeal approach, the country at first used an incremental method of lawmaking.[4] This meant that the country first established abstract general laws that could later be specified in easily changeable administrative regulations. As legislation was the result of extensive bargaining between various stakeholders, for natural-resource protection this meant watered-down legislation that sacrificed environmental for economic and social concerns.

After 1995, national leadership was convinced that by strengthening antipollution and land legislation in force, mainly enacted in the 1980s, the improved legislation could stem resource loss more effectively. This belief was based on reports by scholars and policymakers blaming the ongoing deterioration of natural resources on the existing legislation.[5] Thus, for natural-resource protection law, the piecemeal approach and the bargaining practices were partly

---

4 Jianfu Chen, *Chinese Law, Towards an Understanding of Chinese Law, Its Nature and Development* (The Hague: Kluwer Law International, 1999).

5 William P. Alford and Yuanyuan Shen, "Limits of the Law in Addressing China's Environmental Dilemma," in *Energizing China, Reconciling Environmental Protection and Economic Growth*, eds. Michael B. McElroy, Chris P. Nielsen, and Peter Lydon (Cambridge, Massachusetts: Harvard University Press, 1998), 134; Eric W. Orts, "Environmental Law with Chinese Characteristics," *William and Mary Bill of Rights Journal* 11 (2003): 561.

abandoned in the mid-1990s. In 1998, the amended Land Management Act (LMA) established a strict arable land protection system that limited the conversion of arable land into nonarable use. In a similar fashion, pollution laws were amended and new laws introduced. While the amended 1995 Air Pollution Prevention and Control Law failed to realize most of the ambitious legislative proposals of environmentalists, the amended 1996 Water Pollution Prevention and Control Law (WPPCL), the 2000 Air Pollution Prevention and Control Law (APPCL), and the 2002 Environmental Impact Assessment Law did introduce stricter and more specific norms to protect the nation from pollution.

Around the same time, apart from blaming legislation, scholars and policy-makers also attributed ongoing resource loss in places such as Lake Dianchi to weak enforcement.[6] They held that weak enforcement—whether of natural-resource protection law or any other locally unfavorable national legislation—was caused by *difang baohu zhuyi* (local protectionism). Local protectionism meant that local governments let their own local interests prevail over national concerns. Local governments were able to exercise such protectionism through their control over the budgets and personnel management of their local bureaucracies—including courts, procurates, police, and administrative departments such as land bureaus, industrial bureaus, and environmental protection bureaus (EPBs).[7]

After 1995, in order to overcome the local protectionist influence on law enforcement, China's leadership decided to strengthen central control over local inspections and sanctions for violations. Accordingly, in a seemingly Maoist fashion, China organized national political campaigns aimed to enhance the enforcement of natural-

---

[6] Due to the limitations of this paper and its focus on local data from Lake Dianchi, this large body of work cannot be fully reproduced here. Here and further in this paper such literature will be referenced indirectly by directing readers to the thesis this paper was based on where a full literature overview can be found. For an overview of this literature, see van Rooij, *Regulating Land and Pollution in China*, ch. 13.

[7] Ibid.

resource protection law. Since 1996, there have been continuous rounds of campaigns for arable land protection law enforcement and for pollution law enforcement.[8] These efforts were similar to the political-legal campaigns Beijing has organized against other illegal practices caused by weak enforcement such as drug trafficking, corruption, pirated goods, and illegal Internet cafés.[9]

Since the second half of the 1990s, China's central-level leadership has thus changed the existing legislation and organized law enforcement campaigns to control or at least slow down the ongoing deterioration of natural resources at places such as Lake Dianchi. The question is what these changes have accomplished at the local level. Can these changes prevent a future with shortages of water to drink, air to breathe, and arable land for food to eat? To what extent have stricter norms been better equipped to prevent the local conversion of arable land or control local air and water pollution? Have legal enforcement campaigns been able to overcome local protectionism and serve as a sufficient deterrent to end ongoing local violations and prevent violations from occurring in the future?

In order to answer these questions, the larger research on which this chapter is based sought to identify what influence China's post-1995 legislative changes and law enforcement campaigns have had on compliance with natural-resource protection law at Lake Dianchi. A threefold study was prepared to find the answers to these questions. First, the legislative history of the legislative changes was studied by analyzing how the process of how the laws were made affected their implementation in terms of compliance and enforcement. Second, compliance and violation behavior at Lake Dianchi was studied by analyzing what factors influenced regulated actors

---

8 Ibid., Chapter 14.
9 For an overview see Benjamin van Rooij, "China's War on Graft: Politico-Legal Campaigns Against Corruption in China and Their Similarities to the Legal Reactions to Crisis in the U.S.," *Pacific Rim Law and Policy Journal* 14, no. 2 (2005). See also van Rooij, *Regulating Land and Pollution in China*, ch.14.

to either obey or break the law. Third, enforcement work was studied by looking at why regular enforcement was problematic and what impact political campaigns had on such enforcement work. An interdisciplinary methodology was used that combined a year of local fieldwork and interviews with an extensive study of existing research concerned with Kunming city in China and other localities in other countries.

This chapter provides an overview of the findings of this research about compliance and law enforcement at Lake Dianchi. It first summarizes the study's findings about compliance with and violation of arable land protection and pollution law at Lake Dianchi, providing a typology of types of compliance and violation and analyzing why they occurred as they did. Second, it summarizes findings about why regular law enforcement was so weak and the extent to which law enforcement campaigns helped to create added compliance at Lake Dianchi. Finally, in its conclusion the chapter further analyzes what the findings about Lake Dianchi signify when compared to findings from other parts of China and when compared with existing theories and studies about regulatory law from other both Western and non-Western countries, looking at the influence of market forces and civil society on compliance and enforcement, the challenges of complexity for effective regulatory law, and the political rationality and ad hoc nature of lawmaking and enforcement. It ends with an outlook on the future that seeks to understand what hope there is for a better control of pollution and arable land loss at Lake Dianchi.

Compliance and Violation at Lake Dianchi

Around Lake Dianchi, land and pollution regulation have had both positive and negative responses. While some targeted actors abided by the newly introduced norms, others blatantly broke them, sometimes causing considerable damage to the natural environment and to those living there. Understanding the implementation of law in

China does not only require an understanding of how the state implements such law, but also involves an understanding of how those whose behaviors are targeted by the law (the regulated actors) respond to the norms.

Two observations need to be made. First, there are different types of actors involved here. For pollution regulation the main regulated actors are enterprises, of which there are many kinds: both industrial and nonindustrial, both large and small, and both rich and poor. For arable land protection regulation, regulated actors are even more varied as those who may build on such land are many. Such actors include farmers, village leadership, various governments (at township level or above), enterprises, social organizations (such as schools or temples), and land development companies. Second, there is no clear binary boundary between compliance and violation, and in many cases there are mixes of both. At Lake Dianchi there have been several types of violations of land and pollution regulation. In many of the villages surrounding the lake, enterprises have been constructed illegally on leased, collectively owned arable land without following the proper procedures that require conversion of ownership from collective to state, compensation for collective land ownership and land use rights, approval of land use conversion, and paying land use taxes to the state.[10] In Jiacun village, for example, the improved connections with Kunming city and the demand for light-industry products led to growth opportunities for enterprises. Such small, privately owned enterprises were erected on collectively-owned arable land that the village leased to the enterprises. In return, the enterprises paid an annual rent that the subvillage collectives distributed to their villagers, about CNY 2,000 per person per year. In Jiacun, most actors involved thus benefited from illegal land transactions as villagers got more money than they would have normally earned by working on their land, village leadership could develop the village, and enter-

---

10 This is in violation of Land Management Law §§ 43, 44, 45, 46, 47, 48, 49, 63.

prises could find land to start businesses without having to pay the immense lump sum payments official requisitioning, conversion, and compensation would cost them. Such illegal practices also occurred in Licun, a Hui minority village on the western side of the lake. Village leaders here forced villagers to rent their arable land to the village leadership, which in turn rented it out again to enterprises and for housing construction. The profits made here were, however, not distributed to the villagers but were withheld, probably embezzled by the village leaders. A second type of land violation mainly occurred in the richer eastern part of the lake. For example, here in Jiacun village, households illegally constructed second residential houses while renting their old houses to migrant workers.[11] Again villagers benefited as they got a better house and extra income, even much more than they would have made from their land. A third type of violation that occurred at the lake concerned the embezzlement of compensation fees to be paid to farmers losing their land use rights when the land was appropriated by the state for construction projects. In these cases the proper procedure for construction approval on collective land was followed and steps were taken to convert ownership and land use purposes and even compensation was agreed upon. However, in the end compensation was not paid in full to the farmers but embezzled by government or village leadership during the process.[12] This happened, for example, in Xiaocun, where the construction of a new road ended in riots once villagers suspected that their village leaders had taken part of the agreed compensation for land loss, while in fact it was the township leaders that took this money.

The most prevalent type of pollution violation at Lake Dianchi concerned enterprises that had the proper environmental installations but secretly switched them off during the night in order to cut costs. In Chinese this is called *toupai* (secret discharges). This happened for example in Baocun, where Huafei—a large, privately

---

[11] This is in violation of Land Management Law § 62.1.
[12] This is explicitly forbidden in LMA § 49.2.

owned chemical fertilizer plant for years known as a model clean enterprise—secretly switched off its pollution installations at night to increase its profits.[13] Huafei's discharges, which went for a long time unnoticed by local environmental authorities, had a significant impact on the local villagers whose rice was polluted and whose water buffaloes got so sick that they could no longer be used in the rice paddies. Another example of illegal secret discharges occurred when small chemical fertilizer companies producing sodium silicofluoride[14] (SSF) also failed to use their environmental installations at night as clean production was economically not feasible for these small enterprises. The effects were terrible for farmers and enterprises downstream the Tanglang River from where the polluters were located. Enterprises had to halt production as the acidic water could no longer be used, while farmers complained of ruined paddies. This case even drew nationwide media attention when a CCTV news team reported on how the pollution affected the operation of China's oldest hydroelectric power plant.[15] The second type of pollution violation concerned enterprises that did not have the proper environmental installations at all. One example is the Kunming porcelain enamel factory, which supports six hundred employees and another three thousand pensioners from its state-owned past. The factory was unable to compete with the decreasing prices of plastic products, and with declining income and continuing staff costs, it had been unable to make the necessary environmental investments. As such the factory was obsolete and should have been closed,[16] but continued to exist nonetheless. Apart from such industrial dinosaurs, such violations also occurred in small enterprises

---

13 Violating several provisions of law: WPPCL §§ 14.2, 29, 37; APPCL § 13; Dianchi Protection Regulations (DPR) § 17.1; 1996 Integrated Water Discharge Standard, GB 8978-96; and 1995 Discharge Standard of Water Pollutants for Phosphate Fertilizer Industry, GB 15580-95.

14 Na2SiF6

15 CCTV, "'Jinri Shuofa' Fushi de Beihou" ['Talking of Law Today' Corrosion's Background], http://202.108.249.200/news/society/20040317/100967.shtml.

16 APPCL § 19.

producing light industrial or food-related products.[17] One example that received attention in Kunming in 2004 was inner-city restaurants whose air, water, and noise installations did not meet the national and municipal standards. Such restaurants could often not pay for such installations largely because they were as expensive as the initial startup capital of the company.

While land and pollution regulations have been extensively violated at Lake Dianchi, there have been notable cases of compliance. Understanding these cases is important as it may hold the key to change existing violations into compliance. There have been different levels of compliance though. First of all, there have been cases where there was no opportunity to break the law, and thus compliance was not an option. An example is that the lack of demand for migrant housing in the poorer western part of the lake prevented housing violations in Baocun and Licun villages. Second, there are compliance cases where the regulated actor(s) involved could no longer break the law. In these cases compliance was also not the result of a conscious choice of the regulated actor(s), but rather the result of changes in circumstances. The clearest example of this type of compliance occurred in cases where former heavily polluting enterprises ceased operations after bankruptcy. The best example here is the Yunzhi paper company, whose pollution had for years had a disastrous impact on the Tanglang River and the many farmers and enterprises that depended on its water. For years nothing was done against this dominant local employer, until years of mismanagement following its privatization caused it to cease operation and thus its polluting activities.

In other compliance cases, violations of law ended or did not occur because of an effort made by the regulated actor(s). Such efforts occurred first of all when local communities put pressure on regulated actors to comply with the law, or even go beyond that and

---

17 Violating APPCL § 14; Kunming Restaurant Environmental Protection Rules (KMEPR) §§ 8, 11; DPR § 21.2.

exceed the minimum requirements of the law. Such pressure occurred for example when villagers protested against pollution at the Ningshi chemical fertilizer company. Villagers called the local EPB and the media every time they suspected that the factory was illegally discharging, sometimes even when they were not. In addition, these farmers cut the factory's discharge pipes and led the flow of the factory's waste water onto their land in order to increase compensation. The pressure made Ningshi invest in compliance, and unlike Huafei prevented it from carrying out secret discharges at night since such discharges would have been detected straightaway due to the watchful eyes of the local communities. Similarly, protesting farmers have in certain cases also been able to get statutory minimum (or beyond statutory minimum) compensation for loss of their arable land use rights. Good examples are the community protests in Jiacun village that erupted first when villagers feared that a Buddhist temple construction project would not compensate for all the land taken. In protest, villagers nominated a mentally disabled villager as village chief in the 2001 elections. As a result of such pressure, the temple project was forced to go well beyond the statutory minimum for compensation and even twice beyond what was common practice in the village. In 2002 this led to another round of protests when farmers found that a school construction project did not pay enough compensation since it did not pay as much as the temple construction project did. This time villagers petitioned higher-level governments, and angry protesters sabotaged the construction work by cutting down power cables and surrounding the village committee headquarters to force their demands on the village's democratically elected leaders. This led to a compromise where farmers received a little extra compensation and small plots of land for shops adjacent to the school.

In few of the cases researched compliance was the result of an effort by the regulated actor following state law enforcement action. In most compliance cases, such enforcement was absent, and compliance occurred due to other reasons outlined above. One example where enforcement did lead to compliance was when the heavily polluting paper factory in Fucun village ended its violations[18] after a campaign-time enforcement decision forced company management to move the factory out of the sensitive lakeside area to new compliant premises in the more remote Mincun village.

Understanding why compliance or violation occurred at Lake Dianchi involves understanding the specifics of each case and deriving generalities from the cases studied. Such exact analysis goes beyond the scope of this chapter, but was made in the thesis it was based on. Nonetheless, several findings from that study are relevant for this chapter. Compliance and violation can first of all be analyzed by looking at a combination of factors related to the regulated actors (internal factors) and to their context (external factors). A first internal factor important for pollution behavior is the size of the regulated actor. In the cases studied, we find that size matters, but in different manners. For instance, there were pollution violations in both small as well as large enterprises. While this is not surprising as smaller enterprises have fewer financial resources and less knowledge to comply with the law, the larger study showed that large enterprises may actually be able to break the law undetected by using their position as a dominant employer to ward off pressure from local communities and even law enforcement. A second internal factor is the manner in which regulated actors viewed costs and benefits of compliance and violation. The cases demonstrate that regulated actors stressing economic goals, having a short-term perspective, and aiming at profit maximization rather than minimizing losses were more prone to violating the law. A third internal factor is the social responsiveness of the regulated actor.[19] The larger study finds that in some cases a stronger openness of the regulated actor

---

18 WPPCL §§ 14.2, 29, 32, and 37, and the 1998 State Council Regulations on Environmental Protection Management at Construction Projects § 16.

19 Influenced by Henk G. van de Bunt, *Organisatiecriminaliteit* [Organizational Crime] (Arnhem: Gouda Quint, 1992), 19–21, and John Braithwaite, *Crime, Shame and Reintegration* (Cambridge: Cambridge University Press, 1989), 136.

toward its external context (especially its local community) and also stronger participation of such local community in the decision-making of the regulated actor led to greater compliance. However, this only happened when the interests of the law and those of the local community were aligned. If they were not and local communities actually benefited from violations of law, a regulated actor's increased awareness of community concerns or increased community participation did not lead to compliance, but could even support violation. It should be noted that the study of such internal factors is highly challenging, and more data is necessary to fully understand how the values and characteristics of the regulated actor(s) influence compliance and violation behavior.[20]

As possible drivers of change it is essential to understand how forces external to the regulated actor(s) have shaped compliance and violation behavior at Lake Dianchi. As noted above, community pressure can be a possible driver toward compliance. Examples are the cases of community protests against pollution at the Ningshi fertilizer factory and protests for a larger amount of compensation in Jiacun village. Similarly, a lack of community pressure correlated with continued violations. This occurred in Baocun village where Huafei factory could continue to pollute the local environment without any opposition. Another example is Licun village, where local leaders could make illegal profits from other people's lands unopposed. While no such study has been made concerning land violations, the findings on community pressure at Lake Dianchi are in line with research on pollution concerning other parts of China. Studies about pollution control have found that a lack of commu-

---

20 Here much can be learned from research about land conversions by Sargeson. See Sally Sargeson, "Subduing 'The Rural House-Building Craze': Attitudes Towards Housing Construction and Use Controls in Four Zhejiang Villages," *China Quarterly* 172 (December 2002), and research by Fryxell and Lo about how environmental values shape the pollution behaviors of enterprises. See Gerald E. Fryxell and Carlos W. H. Lo, "Organizational Membership and Environmental Ethics: A Comparison of Managers in State-Owned Firms, Collectives Private Firms and Joint Ventures in China," *World Development* 29, no. 11 (2001).

nity pressure correlates with continued pollution.[21] It is interesting to note that China has been witnessing increased collective action against pollution,[22] and a decrease in compensation payments for arable land loss.[23]

An analysis of the cases further demonstrates that state enforcement measures had a limited effect on compliance. At the same time, in most violation cases enforcement was weak, at least until 2004, making the costs of violation lower than the expected benefits. This teaches that while enforcement is not an important variable for explaining compliance, in the cases studied a lack of enforcement does correlate with violation behavior, and increased enforcement may have an influence toward compliance. Present studies about arable land loss and pollution in other parts of China have held similarly that these practices continued due to weak enforcement.[24] However, none of the studies consulted have looked at what the effects of enforcement on compliance are.

The political context also played a role in compliance and violation at Lake Dianchi as the political system as a whole, local political institutional changes, local leaders, and local power configurations affected regulated actors and local communities. A first finding is that local governments have played an important role in condoning violations that were an important part of the local economy. This happened in many of the land and pollution violation cases. Until late 2004, local governments, from township to provincial

---

21 For an overview of the literature, see van Rooij, *Regulating Land and Pollution in China*, ch. 6.

22 For an overview of recent pollution protests, see Andy Rothman, "Thirsty China, Its Key Resource Constraint is Water," *CLSA Asia Pacific Markets* (Summer 2006). Cf. with Jun Jing, "Environmental Protests in China," in *Chinese Society: Change, Conflict and Resistance*, eds. Elizabeth Perry and Mark Selden (London: Routledge Curzon, 2004), 143–161.

23 For an overview see Benjamin van Rooij, "The Return of the Landlord, Chinese Land Acquisition Conflicts and Tenure Security illustrated by Peri-Urban Kunming," *Journal of Legal Pluralism* (forthcoming in 2007).

24 See van Rooij, *Regulating Land and Pollution in China*, ch. 6.

level, never urged their land bureaus to act against violations of the LMA, e.g., Jiacun. Local governments also condoned severe violations at Yunzhi paper and the SSF companies even after receiving complaints. A second finding is that the local power configuration prevented local villagers from protesting when violations damaged their interests in some of the cases studied. Such local power configurations were to a large extent related to China's political system, under which local governments have a considerable amount of autonomy from superior authorities and also lack democratic participation and control by local citizens. Local power configurations were also related to local family and connections (*guanxi*) networks. An example is Licun, where the local configurations of power that connected leaders in the village with leaders at the township and district level made protest even through elections difficult. Another example is Baocun, where Huafei and the other local enterprises had close relationships with village and township leaders who successfully prevented protests. Village democratization had in some cases a positive effect on compliance, while in others it had no effect. In the land cases in Jiacun, villagers actively used the increased room for participation rural democratization had given them, while in Licun such democratic powers were not used even though formally available. The reason for the difference is most likely the dependence of Licun farmers on their leaders and the strong relationship between their leader's networks and higher-level authorities. China's national political system has also been influential. Nonlocal nongovernment organizations did not play a role at Lake Dianchi, and protests against violations only occurred on a local basis. A likely reason for this is that the state provides strict limitations on the organization of nonstate interests groups, and as a result nonstate groups working on sensitive issues have had trouble organizing in a manner that would indicate that they had reach throughout the country. National political support to act against violations can potentially help enhance compliance. Shifts in national policy led to enforcement campaigns, which, as we saw, influenced compliance in one pollution case. Studies on pollution and arable land from other parts of China have found some similar findings, most notably the impact of decentralized political structures on violations of law and local governments condoning violations.[25] However, in the current literature little attention has been paid to the effects of democratization, local power structures, political campaigns, and political limitations to organized protest on compliance and violation or even on the continuation of pollution and arable land loss.

The economic context, which consists of market forces, such as the markets for labor, land, housing, and industrial and agricultural products, was a major influence on compliance and violation behavior, both affecting it directly and indirectly through influencing other internal and external factors. Market forces played a role in Licun and Baocun villages, where there were no illegal housing construction as there was no demand for such houses. Another example of pollution compliance due to market forces occurred in connection with the Yunzhi paper factory, a case where the factory's bankruptcy, following years of mismanagement after privatization, halted its polluting activities. Economic forces also made violations lucrative when there was a demand for illegal products. One example is the demand for illegal land conversion for enterprises and extra houses in Jiacun. Another example is the small SSF enterprises and the restaurants in Kunming whose products, which could largely be made only in violation of pollution regulations, was in high demand. The economic context also had an indirect effect on compliance behavior as it shaped the possibilities and willingness of local communities and local authorities to address such violations. When there was a homogeneous local economy with dominant employers or sources of income, local communities and local authorities became more dependent on such employers or sources of income. A good example is the difference between the independent and actively protesting farmers in Ningshi, which had a heterogeneous urbanized economy, and Baocun village's dependent

---

25 See van Rooij, *Regulating Land and Pollution in China*, ch. 6.

and meek local population, who have all depended on income from the polluting industrial giant in their village due to a lack of other sources of income. Such dependence also existed in villages where most farmers had local jobs and were dependent on the village committee (VC) leadership and where such VC leadership was well connected in the village as well as with higher-level governments. A good example of this is Licun, where local villagers did not protest against illegal land practices of their own VC. Dependence on violation-related income also led to less community pressure. For example, the lack of protests or political pressure on violations of housing and enterprise construction regulation in Jiacun village existed because income from these violating activities benefited most local villagers and governments, and land conversions had become an important local source of income. Finally, the economic context sometimes affects factors related to the regulated actor itself, and especially how costs and benefits were weighed and the moral attitudes related to such weighing. Here the clearest example is the difference in how farmers deciding on building extra housing thought about protecting arable land in urbanizing Jiacun, with a high demand for construction land and where arable land was not perceived to be important, and the remote and rural Baocun, where land was still seen as sacred and not built on for second houses since there was little demand for the latter. The findings here resonate with existing studies about arable land loss in other parts of China that argue that land loss and pollution continue due to economic growth, urbanization, and industrialization.[26] However, studies about pollution in China have paid little attention to how the economic context is related to pollution. In addition, the fact that violating activities can be dominant local sources of income, which are more difficult to regulate, has not been recognized in the literature assessed here.[27]

---

26 Cf. with van Rooij, *Regulating Land and Pollution in China*, ch. 6.
27 Ibid.

Law Enforcement: Regular and Campaigns

Regular enforcement against pollution and land violations—carried out by the three main bureaus in charge, i.e., the Environmental Protection Bureau (EPB), the State Land Management Bureau (SLB), and the Dianchi Management Bureau (DMB)—was difficult at Lake Dianchi. In none of the cases of compliance studied has regular enforcement been an important factor influencing the regulated actor to comply with the law. In most of the cases of violation studied, regular enforcement was weak. Regular inspections had trouble detecting violations that had been ongoing and of long duration. With regard to detected violations, in none of the cases studied were sanctions issued during regular enforcement.

Two sets of variables can help to explain why regular enforcement was so problematic at Lake Dianchi. First, there are variables related to the enforcement agency itself. The bureaus studied lack financial resources. As a result, bureaus lack enforcement staff and equipment needed to carry out inspections. The origin of the bureaus' financial resources has also negatively affected their enforcement work. EPB officials have told me confidentially that the fact that their EPB receives all of its funding from the local government has enabled this government to exercise considerable influence on their bureau. Officials at the land bureaus have told me a similar story. Township land offices, for example, used to be managed and funded directly by the township government. Under this structure, the land offices failed to play a proactive role as agencies detecting and reporting illegal land practices. The township land office followed its township government closely, and made land management subordinate to local economic development and social stability. As one SLB agent said: "The land office would be crazy to bite the hand that feeds it." A second reason why the origin of bureau resources may lead to goal displacement is that part of the bureau's resources is derived from continued violations of law. This problem is most apparent for EPBs. The Kunming EPB, for example, depends for 30 percent of its resources on pollution discharge fees. The bureau collects such fees as part of its work to implement national law. Fees are paid based on how much pollution enterprises discharge. EPBs are thus dependent on continued pollution, without which they are no longer able to pay for 30 percent of their staff.[28] The Kunming SLB shows similar problems. Its enforcement department has a staff of twenty-two, of which only sixteen are paid for through regular funds.

Wide de facto discretion has further hampered effective law enforcement at all three bureaus. This is first of all related to the fact that internal bureau personnel procedures offer weak incentives and controls for job conformity. Stimulating and controlling agents has thus been difficult, especially since bureau management cannot verify what happens during inspections and the fact that the outcome of enforcement work is difficult to measure. Meanwhile, enforcement procedures in practice offer agents and bureau leaders considerable freedom when deciding on sanctions. As a result of the weak personnel procedures and the enforcement procedures, those deciding on sanctions have a large amount of discretion. When using this discretion, agents seem to be risk averse, trying to do their work in such a manner that it will not upset any of the relationships with management, the regulated actors, local politicians, and higher-level agencies.

A second set of variables hampering regular enforcement work is those related to the external context of the enforcement agency. The agency first of all is influenced by the regulated actor, who in several cases directly obstructed enforcement work. One example is that, especially at larger construction sites, inspection agents are

---

28 For good examples from other regions in the 1990s and how this problem affected enforcement there, see Xiaoying Ma and Leonard Ortolano, *Environmental Regulation in China* (Lanham: Rowman & Littlefield Publishing Group, 2000), 123–126. Cf. with Homer Sun, "Controlling the Environmental Consequences of Power Development in the PRC," *Michigan Journal of International Law* 17, no. 4 (1996): 1028, who argues that not just fees but also regular enforcement fines that form part of the normal bureau budget cause enforcement agents to favor violations over compliance.

sometimes not let onto the premises and have to force their way in by getting police support. Resistance against enforcement agents is particularly cumbersome for pollution inspections. A good example is the Huafei factory. The factory was until late 2004 listed as being in compliance, although most local villagers knew that the factory was secretly discharging at night. Huafei did so to evade daytime inspections as it knew well that nightly inspections were practically not feasible. The relevant EPBs are all located in Kunming city. All roads from Kunming to Baocun village, where Huafei is located, are not easy to travel and are very dangerous at night. Nightly discharges were therefore never detected during regular inspections. Furthermore, EPBs carry out few nightly inspections because personnel costs are higher and there is a significant chance that factory management is not present to let agents into the factory. Some miles further down the Tanglang River, the SSF companies have taken resistance a step further into what could be termed as blatant obstruction. "Those enterprises engage in *guerilla warfare* with us," a frustrated EPB inspection agent remarked. If before the media coverage enforcement action never stopped the ongoing violations because of local protectionism, after the coverage the Kunming EPB made a real effort to detect the violations. They have even installed around-the-clock discharge-monitoring equipment at one of the smaller enterprises to prevent the possibility of secret discharges at night. Agents found out later, however, that this particular factory was bold enough to build an extra illegal discharge pipe that circumvented the EPB's detection equipment. Thus, it took months before the EPB was able to gather proof of violations. Apart from the difficulty of detecting violations at uncooperative or fully obstructive enterprises, regular enforcement has also been difficult because of a lack of support from local communities. In many of the cases where regular enforcement was difficult, local communities depended largely on the violating activities as major sources of income, or on some of the violators who had considerable power. For land, local communities supported and even engaged in violations, while for pollution some localities still failed to report pollution even though they suffered from it. The fact that local communities depended on violating activities had several consequences. First, there were fewer complaints about violations, making detection more difficult. Second, violation of law formed a source of local income, making it more difficult to deal with such violations stringently. Finally, local governments made regular law enforcement difficult as they failed to support more stringent action and sometimes obstructed the use of strong measures against violations. Local governments control natural-resource law enforcement through their influence on agency budgets and the appointment of bureau leadership. It is thus no surprise that interviewed enforcement agents state that they pay attention to local government concerns on economic growth and social stability in their regular sanction decisions.

As a result of these variables, law enforcement agents have difficulty detecting violations, and once violations are discovered, they issue nonstringent sanctions, paying special attention to the social and economic consequences of such sanctions. The result of this is that some violations could go on for years. Examples are the pollution violations at Huafei, Yunzhi, Kunming porcelain enamel factory, and the SSF companies, and the land violations in Jiacun, Baocun and Licun villages.

The study's findings are in many aspects similar to existing research on other parts of China.[29] Such studies have especially blamed "local protectionism," i.e., local governments protecting their own interests instead of enforcing national legislation. This study also found that local protectionism influenced regular law enforcement. Instead of just seeing this as an abject and corrupt phenomenon, the study sought to understand the causes of this practice. First, it finds that local protectionism was more widespread than existing studies led to believe. It concerned more than just corrupt, self-interested local politicians. In some of the cases studied, strict law enforcement was supported by a wide range of local actors, includ-

---

29 For an overview of these sources van Rooij, *Regulating Land and Pollution in China*, ch. 13.

ing local citizens, whose livelihoods depended directly or indirectly on ongoing violations. Second, it thus finds that local protectionism may have legitimate causes. Such protectionism has in some of the cases studied maintained local livelihoods and necessary local products, which if the law had been fully enforced would have come under pressure. The best examples are the violations of the LMA's prohibitions on housing and enterprise construction on collective arable land. Other examples are the protection of Kunming porcelain enamel factory, the SSF companies, and local restaurants. Third, this study finds that local protectionism was at times a coping mechanism for risk averse law enforcement officials when lacking resources, having to enforce legislation with a wide scope of application that was widely violated, facing powerful regulated actors opposed to the law, and receiving limited support from local communities and local governments. As current scholarship holds, local protectionism is first caused by the high level of autonomy of local governments and their enforcement agents. This study, however, further finds that another important cause for local protectionism is the law's lack of local feasibility, for regulated actors, local communities, local governments, and enforcement officials. In the existing studies on other parts of China, few scholars have addressed this cause or recognized the possible legitimacy of local protectionism. Meanwhile, regular enforcement has been weak, and the law's equally legitimate goals of protecting arable land and preventing and controlling pollution proved difficult to achieve. Thus, while local protectionism may at times be an understandable phenomenon helping to adapt the law to local circumstances, it has also undermined the law and obstructed natural-resource protection.

Since 1996 Chinese leadership has recognized the danger of weak natural-resource protection law enforcement. To deal with the existing weak enforcement, campaigns were organized. The campaigns were organized through political pressure from the center, using cadre evaluation systems to overcome local protectionism, making campaign targets into priority policy on the basis of which local leaders were to be evaluated. The original campaigns had started at a time when there was a sense of urgency about natural-resource losses due to alarming reports about China's rapidly declining arable land quantity[30] and a series of pollution incidents attracting widespread media coverage that led to the adoption of strong measures against pollution in the ninth five-year plan and in new legislation.[31] The campaigns made enforcement measurable, setting formalistic targets of numbers of inspections, strict sanctions, and model cases. During the campaigns, local actors were thus less allowed and less able to take local concerns into account.

Until 2004, the campaigns had little effect on ongoing violations studied at Lake Dianchi. Only in the case of the Fucun paper factory did a campaign directly end violations. Even though in 2004 land and pollution campaigns seemed to initiate a change in land violation cases in Jiacun, Licun, and Baocun villages, and pollution violations at Huafei and the SSF companies, the findings seem to indicate that these changes were to be short-lived.

The land campaigns aimed to force a legalization of existing illegal leases of collectively owned land to enterprises, by getting the enterprises and the village authorities involved to implement the proper procedures involving transfer of ownership from collective to state, approval of land use change from agriculture to construction, compensation for land rights losses, and payment of land use fees to the state. Plans were made to implement these changes, first by detailing the amount of illegal land use in the villages, and second by setting deadlines for the completion of the procedures. For several months no progress was made, as the fees that had to be paid for the procedures had not yet been determined. When in No-

---

30 Lester R. Brown, "Who Will Feed China?" *World Watch* (September/October 1994).

31 State Council, *Guowuyuan guanyu Huanjing Baohu ruogan Wenti de Jueding* [State Council decision on several problems concerning environmental protection], *Environmental Work News Report*, no. 8, 1996, 10; Zhongda Qin, *Guanyu Zhonghua Renmin Gongheguop Shui Wuran Fangzhi Fa Xiuzheng An (Caoan) de Shuo Ming* [Explanation on the PRC Proposed (Draft) Amendment to the Water Pollution Prevention and Control Law], *NPC SC Gazette* 1996, 356.

vember 2004 these fees were finally set, the worst rumors were confirmed as the fees and land rents were high. First enterprises would have to pay a land conversion procedure fee (*banzhengfei*) of CNY 80,000 per mu (667 square meters), to be paid to the land bureau. Second, enterprises had to pay a lump sum for renting the land use right from the subvillage, which was set at CNY 200,000 for a fifty-year period. In Jiacun village, which is in many aspects the richest of the three villages studied, more than two-thirds of the enterprises were reported not to be able to pay these new fees and rents. By the end of this research in December 2004, it seemed unlikely therefore that the campaign would actually be implemented according to plan. As one of the village leaders told me two months earlier: "If we want to maintain our current level of development and continue to develop in the future, we must and will find a way around the campaign."[32]

While in some of the cases studied, such as Kunming porcelain enamel factory and air pollution violations by restaurants, the 2004 pollution campaign brought no apparent change, it did seem for a while that it would have an effect on violations at Huafei and the SSF companies, both located on the Tanglang River. Extra nightly inspections carried out during the campaigns were finally able to detect the violations at these enterprises that had for a long time gone unpunished. As a result, the EPB fined the SSF factories and ordered them to halt production, and issued a CNY 50,000 fine against Huafei and told the company that it would publicize the violation and the sanction. Huafei management was upset as it feared losing its good name and perhaps even investments from its American partners once word of their violations got out. The EPB used the factory's anxiety to strike a deal. The EPB would not publicize the violation and sanction, in return for which the enterprise would set up its own SSF production and quit supporting the highly pol-

---

[32] Due to time limitations the present research does not cover the period after November 23, 2004, in Jiacun. Therefore we do not know what has happened after this date.

luting, cheap, small-scale production. However, it seems that even in these two cases the campaign effects could not be sustained. First of all, nearly two months later, weeks after the campaign had ended, the SSF factories resumed production, even in broad daylight. This is a clear indication not only that the SSF companies could continue business as usual once the campaign had ended, but also that Huafei's promise to start its own SSF production had not affected these companies. A second indication of the campaign's failure to maintain success was that Huafei did not seem to live up to its promise of cleaning up its production process. Quite the contrary, the company initiated an expansion of its phosphor ammonium installations, enlarging production by 1.2 million tons a year. A State Environmental Protection Agency (SEPA) investigation of projects with a possible effect on the environment ranked Huafei's expansion as one of China's twenty worst new environmental hazards, stating that the company contained "hidden problems."

The reason why campaigns had difficulty causing sustainable compliance at Lake Dianchi was that they were not able to provide a structural solution to the obstacles of regular law enforcement. Once a campaign ended, many problems remained as the bureaus lacked resources or support, local communities still depended on violating sources of income, violators were still powerful as dominant employers, and local governments still cared about maintaining economic growth and social stability, which some of the law's norms if fully enforced or complied with would endanger.

There are different ways to evaluate these campaigns. From a direct compliance perspective, as adopted mostly in this book, the campaigns were largely unsuccessful. While the campaigns mark a tougher stance on natural-resource violations, the temporary toughness does not overcome structural problems, as we saw, and is unable to create compliance. From a pragmatic perspective, the campaigns are the only way to deal with the existing violations, given China's present central-local relationships and the structural conflict of interests between short-term local livelihoods and long-term natural-resource protection. Using campaigns offers an incremental tool to address the worst violations that the regular enforcement system fails to address. From a symbolic perspective, the campaigns may be more successful than they seem at first glance. The campaigns may actually be a symbol of change, demonstrating that what was condoned for years must end. The symbolic function of campaigns may be enhanced because of their increasing use of public participation mechanisms creating awareness for law enforcement and natural-resource protection. From a rule-of-law perspective,[33] one could argue that the campaigns are dangerous as they may set a bad example instead of a positive one. The constant conjuncture of weak enforcement followed by strong campaign enforcement makes the legal system as a whole less consistent. During campaigns, campaign objectives are more important than legal procedure. In addition, the campaigns are law based on politics, instead of China's recent adoption of *Yifa Zhiguo* (governance based on law). Using campaigns to enforce normally nonenforced law may endanger the legal system as a whole and the beginning stages of a rule of law doctrine in China.[34] A final perspective on the use of campaigns is a political perspective. One can wonder why, although China is losing land and pollution is damaging many interests, these problems have only recently received so much attention. Perhaps the answer

---

33 With rule of law we here mean both in general the law's meaningful restraints on government action, as well as the thin formal rational rule of law conceptions that require that the law should provide clear unambiguous procedures that should be applied in a consistent manner. Cf. with Brian Z. Tamanaha, *On the Rule of Law History, Politics, Theory* (Cambridge: Cambridge University Press, 2004); Randall Peerenboom, *China's Long March Toward the Rule of Law* (Cambridge: Cambridge University Press, 2002); Rachel Kleinfeld, "Competing Definitions of the Rule of Law," in *Promoting the Rule of Law Abroad, In Search of Knowledge*, ed. Thomas Carothers (Washington, DC: Carnegie Endowment for International Peace, 2006).

34 For debates on the development of rule of law in China, see Ronald C. Keith, *China's Struggle for the Rule of Law* (Basingstoke, Hamshire: Macmillan Press LTD, 1994); Ronald C. Keith and Zhiqiu Lin, *Law and Justice in China's New Marketplace* (New York: Palgrave, 2001); Peerenboom, *China's Long March Toward the Rule of Law*.

is that politicians truly wished to solve these problems and used the incidents to trigger changes not possible before. Moreover, more cynically and following Edelman,[35] stakeholders may have used the growing urgency about pollution and arable land loss to attain goals not directly related to them. For the cases described here and for all of China's political-legal campaigns, this line of argumentation holds attraction as most campaigns have been about enhancing the state's vertical reach into the local bureaucracy. Boosting the legal system through campaigns serves this purpose, and social problems such as pollution, food security, corruption, crime, religious practices, copyright piracy, and disabuse of village power may all serve as fora for enhancing the center's vertical reach.

Conclusion: A Broader Look at Compliance and Enforcement

Land and pollution regulation at Lake Dianchi has been a challenge. Given the incentives to break the law with the need for land, jobs, and products produced by polluting enterprises and the weak checks and balances either from law enforcement or from society, violations continue. At Lake Dianchi problems are intertwined as weak community pressure and weak enforcement are closely related to the direct and indirect dependency of local state and society actors on the violators as sources of income. To a certain extent this has meant that the goals of the law in protecting natural resources stand opposed to dominant local interests. Centrally organized law enforcement campaigns have tried to enhance state enforcement and thus break current local opposition to successful implementation. However, their efforts have proved to have limited effects or have had effects that could not be sustained. This was largely so

---

35 Murray Edelman, "The Construction and Uses of Social Problems," *University of Miami Law Review* 42 (September 1987) and *Constructing the Political Spectacle* (Chicago: University of Chicago Press, 1988).

because the basic problem that the incentives for violation continued to dominate state and society actors could not be solved.

In order to deepen the understanding of these local findings and to analyze their contribution to existing knowledge, it is important to place them in a larger comparative context. First of all we need to know how these findings here compare with other studies on different areas of China. Second, the findings presented here as well as those in other studies about China need to be compared with existing theories about compliance and enforcement from other countries. Doing so helps deepen the understanding of findings analyzed here and adds data to such existing theories. Finally, a broader perspective of the future of natural-resource law compliance and enforcement at Lake Dianchi is warranted, analyzing to what extent there is hope for amelioration in the future.

The findings about why compliance and violation occurred at Lake Dianchi are largely similar to earlier studies about arable land loss and pollution in other parts of China.[36] There are some noteworthy differences and new insights, however. First is the fact that existing studies about pollution violations have not looked at how important sources of local income have received less external pressure to comply with the law. They have not looked at the position of dominant employers, regulated actors who directly and indirectly provide a significant amount of income for people in a given locality. Second, existing studies have generally not looked at how local power configurations affect compliance and violation of law. Neither has there been attention to how village democratization has influenced arable land and pollution cases. Third, while this study, similar to other studies, found that small regulated actors were more likely to violate pollution law, such studies did not address how large enterprises have been able to use their economic power to violate the law with little risk.

For the enforcement of natural-resource protection law, the

---

36 For an overview of such studies, see van Rooij, Regulating Land and Pollution in China, ch. 6.

present study confirms many findings from existing studies concerning other parts of China emphasizing that weak enforcement arises out of local protectionism, a lack of resources, and close relationships between the enforcement agents and the regulated actors.[37] There are two main differences, however, between existing studies and the present findings. First, this study has sought to understand why local protectionism exists, finding that it occurs because local governments, enforcement agents, and local communities have condoned the violation of norms that if complied with could affect dominant sources of local income. Second, this study has looked at the effect of political campaigns, a phenomenon not yet studied for natural-resource protection law enforcement. Campaigns studied here are examples of Chinese political-legal campaigns. These campaigns have been used to enhance the implementation of law in China.[38] Given the weak regular enforcement that exists in certain areas of law, such campaigns may be necessary to overcome local resistance. However, their effect may be limited as long as structural problems and power relations are not addressed. In addition, their political and ad hoc character stands opposed to a long-term process of rule-of-law formation.

The findings here can also be compared with studies about regulatory compliance and enforcement from other both Western and non-Western countries. A first central conclusion such comparison brings forward is that compliance, the main objective of regulation, results from a convergence of variables related to the regulated actor itself, law enforcement, social pressures, and stimuli from the market. While existing research from Gunningham et al. and the World Bank is optimistic that such convergence can be attained,[39]

---

37 Ibid., ch. 12.

38 For a more detailed discussion of this phenomenon, see van Rooij, "China's War on Graft."

39 Neil Gunningham, Robert A. Kagan, and Dorothy Thornton, *Shades of Green, Business Regulation and Environment* (Stanford: Stanford University Press, 2003); World Bank, *Greening Industry, New Roles for Communities, Markets and Governments* (Oxford: Oxford University Press, 2000).

the case of Lake Dianchi shows that when regulation opposes vested local economic interests and powerful stakeholders, an opposed convergence to violation may develop that is difficult to address through stricter laws and stricter enforcement. At Lake Dianchi the economic context affected enforcement agents, local communities, local governments, and regulated actors in such a way that violation rather than compliance resulted. This happened despite efforts to strengthen legislation and law enforcement.

Lessons from other countries teach that unless there are social pressures and economic incentives for alternative behavior, compliance will be difficult to attain.[40] We do not believe, however, that compliance can be attained without a basic level of state law enforcement. Enforcement inspections, when successfully carried out, produce the basic information necessary for alternative regulatory approaches, whether they include public disclosure, fees, or tradable rights. In addition, only state enforcement can successfully pressure truly bad apples, i.e., socially unresponsive firms,[41] over which social and market pressures have little influence. Comparative research teaches that within the convergence of community pressure, market incentives, and state enforcement, especially community pressure can be an important driver toward compliance, more stringent legislation, and enforcement.[42] However, in contexts such as that of Lake Dianchi, this will only happen if there is either a local community independent of the violating activity that

---

40 Gunningham, Kagan, and Thornton, *Shades of Green, Business Regulation and Environment*; World Bank, *Greening Industry: New Roles for Communities, Markets and Governments*.

41 van de Bunt, *Organizational Crime*; Braithwaite, *Crime, Shame and Reintegration*, 136.

42 Hemamala Hettige et al., "Determinants of Pollution Abatement in Developing Countries: Evidence from South and Southeast Asia," *World Development* 24, no. 12 (1996); Gunningham, Kagan, and Thornton, *Shades of Green, Business Regulation and Environment*; Mainul Huq and David Wheeler, *Pollution Reduction Without Formal Regulation: Evidence from Bangladesh*, World Bank Policy Research Working Paper 1993–39.

is educated and organized enough to initiate action or a nonlocal, independent, and well-organized social organization that is politically and legally able to pressure violators toward compliance. The local community influences the effect of social responsiveness on compliance. In contrast with existing studies claiming that higher social responsiveness leads to greater compliance,[43] Lake Dianchi demonstrates that in contexts in which local communities support norm violation, higher social responsiveness leads to more noncompliance.

Another more theoretical conclusion is that complexity challenges successful law enforcement. Studies from other countries have found that successful law enforcement needs to be flexible, combining accommodative approaches in which cooperation is sought with the regulated actor with more stringent deterrent measures against bad apples.[44] In order to operate successfully with such flexibility, and make the right choices and find the right methods to accommodate to or deter the regulated actor, enforcement agents need to understand why regulated actors comply with or violate the law. The study of Lake Dianchi has demonstrated how complex compliance behavior is and that it is highly case-based, depending on a set of internal and external variables not easily understood. In such a context of complexity, the lack of enforcement resources precludes solid empirical knowledge. This obstructs enforcement agents' understanding of the behavior of regulated actors, necessary to find the balance needed for good law enforcement. Even if regulated actors can be understood, it is difficult to translate such knowledge into successful enforcement strategies because of the dilemma that adaptation to widely differing circumstances of regulated ac-

---

43 van de Bunt, *Organizational Crime*; Braithwaite, *Crime, Shame and Reintegration*.

44 Robert A. Kagan, "Regulatory Enforcement," in *Handbook of Regulation and Administrative Law*, eds. David H. Rosenbloom and Richard D. Schwartz (New York: Marcel Dekker, 1994), 387; John Braithwaite, "Rewards and Regulation," *Journal of Law and Society* 29, no. 1 (2002); Ian Ayres and John Braithwaite, *Responsive Regulation* (New York: Oxford University Press, 1992).

tors requires such a high level of discretion that it may lead to corruptive or co-opted law enforcement. Apart from the complexity of understanding the behavior and the interests of the regulated actor, there is the complexity of conflicting interests between those of the law and those of regulated actors and the local state and communities that depend on them. Such conflict of interests undermined law enforcement at Lake Dianchi. Adapting enforcement to such conflicting interests is difficult as either the goals of the law are followed, leading to unreasonable and thus unsustainable law enforcement that lacks local support, as happened in the campaigns, or law enforcement is locally acceptable but too weak to initiate the behavioral change sought by the law.

One can of course wonder why a balance is not struck between accommodative and deterrent enforcement, and why in Lake Dianchi's practice there has been an oscillation of enforcement styles from extreme accomodation during regular enforcement to extreme deterrence in campaigns. The answer is that regulatory law enforcement may often have a political rationality as a result of political reactions to incidents or shifts in power, which precludes acknowledging the full complexity of the situation at hand. From the mid-1990s onward, China's natural-resource protection law enforcement suddenly changed several times, from weak, vague, cooperative, and nonstringent to strict, specific, and stringent. These changes made the law and its enforcement more oriented toward limited goals and less oriented on the full complexity of the regulated issue at hand. Changes seemed to result from shifts in what powerful central leadership deemed important. In addition, changes occurred to some extent as a reaction to incidents, and in a manner widely publicized. Political leaders seemed to want to show their commitment to deal with incidents in a strong manner. The changes witnessed at Lake Dianchi thus had a political rationale.[45] Comparison with other countries teaches that such a political ratio-

---

45 For this term see Ich Snellen, *Boeiend geboeid* [Captivated captured]. Inaugural Lecture, University of Tilburg, 1987.

nale may often inform law enforcement and can explain rapid changes in enforcement strategies following disasters, enforcement scandals, economic crises and electoral changes, or other shifts in power. In these cases, instead of a rationale in which the full complexity of the issue at hand would be analyzed and addressed, a simplified political rationale to show willingness to deal with the incident at hand or react to the shift in power was dominant. [46] Such simplified political rationale may help to soothe the public fear or anxiety related to the incident at hand, but may not help to enhance compliance. Following incidents and shifts in power, one enforcement strategy change may follow another, leading to regulatory conjunctures of different enforcement styles.

Meanwhile, natural-resource loss continues at Lake Dianchi. Our analysis above may seem to indicate that enforcement remains powerless to stop the ongoing construction on arable land and the pollution of air and water at places like Lake Dianchi. Is there hope for amelioration in the future? We believe there is, especially for pollution. For pollution, if China's economic growth continues and especially if the already expanding service sector grows more important and if the local economy diversifies, the local economic interests will change. First, there will be more nonpolluting sources of income. This makes more stringent action against heavily polluting enterprises more acceptable. Second, the diversified economy will also decrease the influence of dominant employers, especially if rather remote regions such as the western side of Lake Dianchi are connected to Kunming through the planned highways. As a result more social pressure to clean up, similar to the Ningshi case, can be expected. Third, the ongoing professionalization, especially the recruitment of environmentalist enforcement agents, will lead to

---

46 Stone and Edelman have detailed how such simplification takes place and what role elements of symbolic politics have in such a political rational, especially of a populist nature. See Deborah Stone, *Policy Paradox, The Art of Political Decision Making* (New York: Norton & Company, 1997) and Edelman, "The Construction and Uses of Social Problems."

more resistance to local protectionism within the enforcement bureaus. Fourth, this will be especially so when the then richer periurban dwellers around the lake realize that their raised economic standard of living is affected by a polluted environment. Fifth, and finally, increased enforcement and protest from local communities that thus results may in the end lead to a situation in which most comply with the law and the costs of compliance are no longer an exception but a rule also recognized by the markets that control the regulated firms. For arable land regulation, unfortunately, we cannot be as hopeful. We expect that China's urbanization and industrialization will continue, and the goals of the law will remain opposed to the interests of most living in periurban areas, who will less and less depend on agriculture as a source of income.

Acknowledgments

Benjamin van Rooij is Professor of Law, at Amsterdam Law School, Amsterdam University and director of the Netherlands China Law Centre, b.vanrooij@uva.nl. This chapter is based on research made possible by generous grants from the Dutch Ministry of Education, Culture and Sciences and the Leiden University Fund. This chapter is an adapted version of the introduction and conclusion of van Rooij's Ph.D. dissertation: B. Van Rooij, *Regulating Land and Pollution in China, Lawmaking, Compliance, and Enforcement; Theory and Cases* (Leiden: Leiden University Press, 2006). The author would like to thank members of his committee, including Jan Michiel Otto, Jianfu Chen, Peter Ho, Robert A. Kagan, Wim Huisman, Wim Voermans, and Adriaan Bedner, for comments on earlier versions of this paper.

Bibliography

Alford, William P. and Yuanyuan. Shen, "Limits of the Law in Addressing China's Environmental Dilemma." In *Energizing China, Reconciling Envi-*

ronmental Protection and Economic Growth, edited by Michael B. McElroy, Chris P. Nielsen, and Peter Lydon (Cambridge: Harvard University Press, 1998)
Ayres, Ian, and John Braithwaite. *Responsive Regulation.* New York: Oxford University Press, 1992.
Braithwaite, John. *Crime, Shame and Reintegration.* Cambridge: Cambridge University Press, 1989.
———. "Rewards and Regulation," *Journal of Law and Society* 29, no. 1 (2002): 12–26.
Brown, Lester R. "Who Will Feed China?" *World Watch,* September/October (1994): 10–19.
CCTV. "Jinri Shuofa" Fushi de Beihou ["Talking of law today," corrosion's background]. CCTV, http://202.108.249.200/news/society/20040317/100967.shtml.
Chen, Jianfu. *Chinese Law, Towards an Understanding of Chinese Law, Its Nature and Development.* The Hague: Kluwer Law International, 1999.
Edelman, Murray. *Constructing the Political Spectacle.* Chicago: University of Chicago Press, 1988.
———. "The Construction and Uses of Social Problems, *University of Miami Law Review* 42, no. September (1987): 7–28.
Feng, Zhimin, Yanzhao Yang, Yaoqi Zhang, Pengtao Zhang, and Yiqing Li. "Grain-for-Green and Its Impacts on Grain Supply in West China," *Land Use Policy* 22 (2005): 301–312.
Fryxell, Gerald E., and Carlos W. H. Lo. "Organizational Membership and Environmental Ethics: A Comparison of Managers in State-owned Firms, Collectives Private Firms and Joint Ventures in China," *World Development* 29, no. 11 (2001): 1941–1956.
Gunningham, Neil, Robert A. Kagan, and Dorothy Thornton. *Shades of Green, Business Regulation and Environment.* Stanford: Stanford University Press, 2003.
Hettige, Hemamala, Mainul Huq, Sheoli Pargal, and David Wheeler. "Determinants of Pollution Abatement in Developing Countries: Evidence from South and Southeast Asia," *World Development* 24, no. 12 (1996): 1891–1904.
Huq, Mainul, and David Wheeler. "Pollution Reduction Without Formal Regulation: Evidence From Bangladesh," *World Bank Policy Research Working Paper* 1993-1939 (1993).

Jing, Jun "Environmental Protests in China." In *Chinese Society: Change, Conflict and Resistance* edited by Elizabeth J. Perry and Mark Selden, 143–161. London: Routledge Curzon, 2004.

Kagan, Robert A. "Regulatory Enforcement." In *Handbook of Regulation and Administrative Law*, edited by David H. Rosenbloom and Richard D. Schwartz, 383–421. New York: Marcel Dekker, 1994.

Keith Ronald C. *China's Struggle for the Rule of Law*. Basingstoke: Macmillan Press LTD, 1994.

Keith, Ronald C., and Zhiqiu Lin. *Law and Justice in China's New Marketplace*. New York: Palgrave, 2001.

Kleinfeld, Rachel. Competing Definitions of the Rule of Law." In *Promoting the Rule of Law Abroad, In Search of Knowledge*, edited by Thomas Carothers, 31–75. Washington D.C.: Carnegie Endowment for International Peace, 2006.

Ma, Xiaoying, and Leonard Ortolano. *Environmental Regulation in China*. Lanham: Rowman & Littlefield Publishing Group, 2000.

Orts, Eric W. "Environmental Law With Chinese Characteristics," *William and Mary Bill of Rights Journal* 11 (2003): 545–565.

Peerenboom, R. *China's Long March toward the Rule of Law*. Cambridge: Cambridge University Press, 2002.

Qin, Zhongda. "Guanyu Zhonghua renmin gongheguo shui wuran fangzhi fa xiuzheng an (caoan) de shuo ming [Explanation on the PRC proposed (draft) amendment to the Water Pollution Prevention and Control Law]." *NPC SC Gazette* 1996: 355–358.

Rothman, Andy. "Thirsty China, Its Key Resource Constraint Is Water," *CLSA Asia Pacific Markets*, no. Summer (2006): 2–39.

Sargeson, Sally. "Subduing "The Rural House-building Craze": Attitudes Towards Housing Construction and Use Controls in Four Zhejiang Villages," *China Quarterly* 172, December (2002): 927–955.

Snellen, Ich *Boeiend geboeid* [Captivated captured]. Inaugural Lecture, University of Tilburg, 1987.

State Council. "State Council Decision on Several Problems concerning Environmental Protection [Guowuyuan guanyu huanjing baohu ruogan wenti de jueding]." *Environmental Work News Report*, no. 8 (1996): 10–13.

Stone, Deborah. *Policy Paradox: The Art of Political Decision Making*. New York: Norton & Company, 1997.

Sun, Homer "Controlling the Environmental Consequences of Power Development in the PRC," *Michigan Journal of International Law* 17, no. 4 (1996): 1015–1049.

Tamanaha, Brian Z. *On the Rule of Law History, Politics, Theory.* Cambridge: Cambridge University Press, 2004.

Van de Bunt, Henk G. *Organisatiecriminaliteit* [Organizational crime]. Arnhem: Gouda Quint, 1992.

Van Rooij, Benjamin "China's War on Graft: Politico-Legal Campaigns Against Corruption in China and Their Similarities to the Legal Reactions to Crisis in the U.S.," *Pacific Rim Law and Policy Journal* 14, no. 2 (2005): 289–336.

———. *Regulating Land and Pollution in China, Lawmaking, Compliance, and Enforcement; Theory and Cases.* Leiden: Leiden University Press, 2006.

———. "The Return of the Landlord, Chinese Land Acquisition Conflicts and Tenure Security illustrated by Peri-Urban Kunming," *Journal of Legal Pluralism* (2007).

Watts, Jonathan. "Satellite Data Revels Beijing as Air Pollution Capital of World," *The Guardian*, October 31, 2005.

World Bank. *Greening Industry, New Roles for Communities, Markets and Governments.* Oxford: Oxford University Press, 2000.

Contributors

OSCAR ALMÉN is a researcher at the Department of Government, Uppsala University whose dissertation was a study of the political role of local people's congresses. His recent publications include "Local Elections in China," *Politologiske Studier* 6, no. 2 (September 2003) and "China's Local People's Congresses, Interest Groups and the Development of Rule of Law," Department of Euroasia Studies Working Paper No. 117, October 2008.

MATTIAS BURELL is assistant professor at the Department of Political Science, Uppsala University. His dissertation examined the role of law in China's labor market reforms. His most recent publication is "China's Housing Provident Fund: Its Success and Limitations," *Housing Finance International* (March 2006). His current research focuses on public opinion change and citizen's trust in government in China.

JONAS GRIMHEDEN, associate professor, Faculty of Law, Lund University, is a program manager for legal research at the European Union Agency for Fundamental Rights. He is coeditor and contributor of two books in the field of international human rights law, both with Brill Academic Publishers: *Human Rights Law: From Dissemination to Application* (2006) and *International Human Rights Monitoring Mechanisms* (2001, 1st edition).

HÅKAN HYDÉN is professor and chair in Sociology of Law, associate professor in Civil Law, holder of the Samuel Pufendorf Professorship at Lund University, as well as a fellow of the World Academy of Arts and Sciences. His primary research is on using and developing the concept of norms as an overriding concept and interdisciplinary tool within socio-legal science.

JOHAN LAGERKVIST is senior research fellow at the Swedish Institute of International Affairs. Recent chapter publications appear in *Youth Engaging With the World. Media, Communication and Social Change* (Nordicom 2009); *Making Online News: the Ethnography of New Media Production* (Peter Lang 2008); and "Global Media for Global Citizenship in India and China," *Peace Review* 21.3 (2009): 367–375.

RANDALL PEERENBOOM is professor of Law, La Trobe University and Associate Fellow at the Centre for Socio-Legal Studies, Oxford University. His edited or single-authored publications include *Judicial Independence in China: Lessons for Global Rule of Law Promotion* (Cambridge 2010); *Regulation in Asia* (Routledge 2009); *China Modernizes: Threat to the West or Model for the Rest?* (Oxford 2007); *Human Rights in Asia* (Routledge 2006); *Asian Discourses of Rule of Law* (Routledge 2004); *China's Long March Toward Rule of Law* (Cambridge 2002).

BENJAMIN VAN ROOIJ is professor of Law at Amsterdam Law School, Amsterdam University, and director of the Netherlands China Law Center. His most recent publications include, "Greening Industry without Enforcement? An Assessment of the World Bank's Pollution Regulation Model for Developing Countries," *Law & Policy* 32, no. 1 (2010): 127–152; "The People Vs. Pollution: Understanding Citizen Action against Pollution in China," *The Journal of Contemporary China* 19, no. 63 (2010); (together with Carlos H. W. Lo.) "A Fragile Convergence, Understanding Variation in the Enforcement of China's Industrial Pollution Law," *Law & Policy* 32, no. 1 (2010): 14–37; and (together with Carlos W. H. Lo and Gerald E. Fryxell) "Changes in Regulatory Enforcement Styles among Environmental Enforcement Officials in China," *Environment and Planning A* 41 (2009): 2706–2723.

FLORA SAPIO is a lecturer at the Istituto Universitario Orientale, Napoli. Her most recent publication is *Sovereign Power and the Law* in China: Zones of Exception in the Criminal Justice System (Brill Academic Publishers, 2010).

MARINA SVENSSON is Associate Professor at the Centre for East and South-East Asian Studies, Lund University. Her recent publications include *The Chinese Human Rights Reader* (M.E. Sharpe, 2001); *Debating Human Rights in China: A Conceptual History* (Rowman and Littlefield, 2002); *Gender Equality, Citizenship and Human Rights: Controversies and Challenges in China and the Nordic Countries* (Routledge 2010).

HATLA THELLE is a senior researcher and head of China Unit at the Danish Institute for Human Rights, Copenhagen. Her research has been on social policies and human rights in China. Her publications include *Better to Rely on Ourselves. Changing Social Rights in Urban China since 1979* (NIAS Press, 2004); "The Need for Evidence-Based Human Rights Research" in *Methods of Human Rights Research* (Intersentia, 2009); and "Who Infringes Their Rights? Discrimination of Chinese Peasant-workers," *International Journal of Human Rights* (May 2010).

Index

Page numbers in *italic* indicate tables

Adjudicative committees, 108, 114
Administrative authorities, 15–16
Administrative law, 16, 36, 55, 70, 86–87, 244
Air Pollution Prevention Control Law, 148
Alford, William, 84
Almén, Oscar, 9n17, 15, 17, 19, 20, 25, 26, 134n89, 143–181, 280
Ambiguity-conflict model of implementation, 126–130, *127*, 133
Anecdotal evidence, 39–40, 46, 48
Anticorruption law
  areas of, 303–304
  in Beijing, 307–312, 316–318, 320–321, 322–323
  Communist Party control of, 297–299, 324–325
  and corruption networks, 312, 320–321
  forms of corruption, 300–302, 311–312, 318–320
  implementing agencies, 302–303, 305–306, 313–317
  information sources on, 325–328
  policy priorities/tools, 304–310, 311, 314, 317
  prosecutions under, 319, 320–322, 323, 324, 325
Anti-Monopoly Law, 53
Appraisal method, 151–152
Aubert, Vilhelm, 79

Bakken, Borge, 42n15
Bardach, Eugene, 130–132, 136
Beijing Cultural Heritage Protection Center, 259
Berkowitz, Daniel, 59n49
Braithwaite, John, 62
Bribery, 300–301, 318–319
Burell, Mattias, 9, 12, 14, 19, 20, 21, 22, 91, 92n37, 335–364

Cai, Dingjian, 76, 150
Case study methodology, 9–10, 13

Center for Women's Development and Rights, 202
Central Commission for Discipline Inspection (CCDI), 305
Chen, Jianfu, 3, 6, 14
Chen Xitong, 307–308, 312, 316, 317, 320, 321
Chen Zhiquan, 164, 166
Cherry, Stephen, 276
China International Economic and Trade Arbitration Commission (CIETAC), 39
Chinese Communist Party (CCP), 170n79, 180, 270, 273
  anticorruption policy of, 297–299, 324–325
  and court system, 106–107
  party discipline of, 146
  and party discipline regulations, 303–304, 315
  and work report appraisals, 151
Choy, D. W., 64
Citizen committees, 56–57, 91
Civil rights, 54–55
Civil society
  and cultural heritage protection, 227–228, 237, 258–259
  distrust of legal system, 24–26, 27, 42–43, 110–111, 273
  and environmental protection, 156, 159, 160, 161, 163, 174–175, 377, 379–380, 386–387, 396–397
  and internet café regulation, 269, 281–283
  and law implementation, 55–58
  regulation of, 81
Clarke, Don, 42, 45n24
Code of Judicial Ethics, 112–113
Cohn, Margit, 135
Coleman, James, 89
Commissions for Discipline Inspection (CDIs), 301, 304, 308–309, 314–315, 319
Competing institutional interests, 52–53
Contract, as legal instrument, 82–83
Copyright protection, 50n34

409

Corruption, judicial, 15, 20, 174
  incidence of, 44–47
  and judicial reform, 125
  popular reports of, 40–42, 46
  and public trust, 42–43
  supervised cases, 46
Corruption, political
  collective, 312, 320–321, 324
  forms of, 300–302, 318–320
  individual, 320–321, 324
  Yuanhua smuggling case, 311, 321n62
  See also Anticorruption law
Cost cutting, 64
Court system
  constraining factors in, 103, 106–111
  cultural heritage protection cases in, 247–249
  environmental protection cases in, 156–158, 174, 175
  implementation models, 125–132
  independence of, 40, 84, 139
  and local protectionism, 14, 39n10
  procuratorate (prosecutors), 57, 107, 109, 113, 120
  public access to, 40
  public trust in, 24–26, 27, 42–43, 110–111
  reform of, 105, 111–125, 133–135
  studies of, 7–8, 104–105
  See also Corruption, judicial; Judges; Legal aid system
Criminal cases, legal aid in, 210–211
Criminal Law, 52, 53n37, 69–70, 304
Criminal Procedure Law (PCL), 190–191
Cultural Heritage Law (CHL), 80, 226, 227, 230, 232, 247, 251, 257
Cultural heritage protection
  and civil society, 227–228, 237, 258–259
  conflicts of interest in, 252–255
  in courts, 247–249
  Dinghai case, 252–253, 256, 260
  institutional framework, 228–229, 238–243
  international work and cooperation, 233–236
  laws and regulations, 229–230, 244, 247–251
  legal awareness/education campaigns, 261–263
  Linfen case, 246–247, 256
  and media, 237, 246, 253, 260–261
  need for, 225–226
  political leaders' role in, 255–256
  problems of management, 232–233

  supervision and enforcement, 244–247, 256–258, 263–264
  types of sites, 230–231, 237–238
  in Zhejiang, 236–238
  Zhuge village case, 254–255, 256

Dasgupta, Susmita, 174
Data collection, 8–9
Death penalty cases, 117, 118
Defamation laws, 58
Deng Xiaoping, 369
Desertification, 368–369
Development and Reform Commission, 56–57
"Develop Westward Campaign", 118
Diamant, Neil J., 5, 6
Dispute resolution, 36, 209, 221
Dualistic tradition in international law, 75
Dutton, Michael, 64n59

Eckhoff, Tortstein, 79
Economic boom phase, 94
Economic development, 19, 20–21, 27, 93–96, 367–368
Economic factors in implementation, 53–54
Edelman, Murray, 393
Empirical research, 2–4, 35–42
Environmental and City Construction Working Committee, 170
Environmental protection, 54, 77, 143–144, 148, 179
  accommodative approach to, 398
  centrally organized enforcement campaigns, 370–371, 381, 388–394, 395
  citizen/community complaints, 156, 159, 160, 161, 163, 174–175, 377, 379–380, 386–387, 396–397, 400
  compliance behavior, 376–378, 379, 394, 395, 397
  conflict of interest in, 51, 52, 173, 398
  economic context for, 382–383, 396
  future of, 399–400
  Guangdong case, 162–169, 176
  implementing agencies, 169–174
  land regulation, 368, 369, 370, 371, 373–374, 381, 389–390
  litigation, 156–158, 174, 175
  and local protectionism, 172–173, 380–381, 384, 387–388, 395
  media role in, 157, 159, 162, 163, 164, 165, 176–177

Index

natural resource, 369–370, 394–395, 398
Qingpu case, 156–162, 177
regional differences in, 175, 177–178
and social responsiveness, 378–379, 397
studies on, 144, 394
transboundary conflicts in, 167
Tuojiang River disaster, 152–153
violation behavior, 373–376, 378, 382, 394
weak regular enforcement, 150–151, 178, 370, 380, 384–388, 395
Environmental Protection Agency (EPA), 169, 172–173
Examinations, implementation, 149–151
Expert Consultation System, 56–57, 91

Fan Chongyi, 123
Fieldwork, 8
Fishkin, James, 56n
Five-Year Reform Plans (FYRPs), 113–116
Ford Foundation, 203n17
Fu, Hualing, 64

Gallagher, Mary, 206n21
Gaowei chemical plant, 156–162
Global economy, 71, 82–83
Government Decision-making Consultation Committee, 57, 91
Grimheden, Jonas, 7, 10, 11, 12, 14, 19, 103–139
Gunningham, Neil, 395

Han Ying, 166
He Baogang, 56n
He Bing, 279, 282
He Weifang, 123
Hong Lu, 8, 9
Housing Committees, municipal, 91
Housing Provident Funds. *See* Housing reform
Housing reform
enforcement measures for, 349–355, *350, 351, 352, 353,* 363
equity problems in, 337, 338, 359–362, *360, 361, 362,* 363–364
features of, 338–341
local adaptation in, 335–336
policy dilution in, 337, 338, 355–359, *358,* 363
policy evolution of, 345–349
shift in social norms, 336–337, 341–345
Howlett, Michael, 61

Huafei factory, 374–375, 379, 386, 390, 391
Human rights conventions, 78
Human rights treaty, 48–49
Hydén, Håkan, 6, 10, 19, 21, 61, 69–99, 110, 179, 180, 274–275, 277, 342n14

"Implementation game" model, 130–132
Implementation of law
ambiguity-conflict model, 126–130, *127,* 133
and civil society, 55–58, 81
comparative context for, 42–44, 47–48
competing institutional interests in, 52–53
cost cutting techniques, 64
defined, 70–71, 73
economic factors in, 44, 53–54
horizontal dimension of, 72, 80–87, 98
incentives-disincentives model, 126, 130–132, 134–136
information sources on. *See* Information sources
and institutional capacity, 59
and judicial corruption, 42–43, 44–47
levels of implementation, 48–51
and overlapping jurisdictions, 63
policy dilution in, 12, 327, 355–359
political factors in, 54–55
and regulatory theory, 60–63
social/cultural factors in, 59–60, 72–73
time dimension of, 71, 92–96, 98–99
vertical dimension of, 71–72, 73–77, 96–98
and voluntary compliance, 38–39
See also Anticorruption law; Court system; Cultural heritage protection; Environmental protection; Housing reform; Internet café regulation; Legal aid system; People's congresses
Implementation of law studies
actors/institutions in, 15–16, *18*
analytical framework for, 10–13
bottom-up *vs* top-down approach to, 6, 16–17, 60–61
economic considerations in, 19, 20–21, 27
empirical, 2–4, 35–42
future agenda for, 23–26
and local stakeholders, 18–19
methodology and fieldwork in, 8–10
multidisciplinary approach to, 4–6
policy areas for, 7–8
political/institutional framework for, 13–15
regional differences in, 19–20
social/cultural norms in, 21–22

INDEX

Incentives/disincentives model of implementation, 126, 130–132, 134–136
Individual case supervision, 152
Information sources
  anecdotal evidence, 39–42, 46, 48
  official statistics, 34–35
  popular press accounts, 40–42
  surveys, 35–38
Information technology, 96
Institutional capacity, 59
Institutional culture, 59
Intellectual property rights, 50n34, 51, 64
International conventions, 71, 75, 234
International Council of Monuments and Sites (ICOMOS), 234
International Covenant for Civil and Political Rights (ICCPR), 48–49
International law, 71, 75, 82–83
Internet café regulation, 50, 92n38, 267–271
  intellectual rationale for, 283–287
  and Internet companies, 270–271, 287–290
  legal framework, 271–273
  and normative change, 274–281, 290–293
  problems of implementation, 273–274, 276
  and public opinion, 281–283
Intervening rules, 89–92, 95

Jiang Zemin, 120n54, 289n44
Judges
  appointment of, 119
  Code of Judicial Ethics, 112–113
  competing interests of, 52–53
  procuratorate relationship, 109
  ranking of, 107–108
  and reform plans, 116
  requirements for, 109n20, 110, 112, 123, 125
  See also Corruption, judicial; Court system
Judges Law of 1995, 108, 111–113
Judicial reform, 105, 111–125, 133–135

Kahan, Dan M., 132n87
Keane, Michael, 281
Kunming porcelain factory, 375, 390

Labor dispute resolution, 37
Labor law, 90
Lagerkvist, Johan, 9n17, 22, 92n38, 267–293
Land protection system, 368, 369, 370, 371, 373–374, 381, 389–390

Law
  defined, 70
  design of, 76–77
  development trends, 95
  of event, 79
  form of, 136–137
  function of, 69–70, 76
  and global economy, 71, 82–83
  and mixed economy, 88–92
  and politics, 85–86
  rule of, 392n33
  and social norms, 71–72, 75–76, 110
  will component of, 78–79
  See also Implementation of law
Lawyers
  disrespect for, 219
  education of, 20
  in legal aid system, 214–215, 219, 221
  and *pro bono* work, 215, 217
  shortage of, 110
  studies of, 3
Lawyers Law (LL), 190, 191, 217
Legal aid system, 20, 84–85
  assessment of, 207–211, 221–222
  case studies, 204–207
  in city district, 195–196, 199–201
  establishment of, 187–190
  local level, 192–195
  motives for establishing, 215–217
  national level, 190–192
  non-state level, 202–204
  problems in implementation, 211–215, 217–219, 221
  in rural areas, 196–199, 221
Legal norms, 73, 79–80, 179–181, 274–275
Legal system. *See* Court system
Legislatures, 145–147. *See also* People's congresses
Letters-and visits system, 153–155, 156, 160–161, 274
Liang, Bin, 8, 9
Liang Zicheng, 259
Lieberthal, Kenneth, 167
Liebman, Benjamin, 84, 211
Li, Ling, 35n3, 45n25, 47
Liu Mingwei, 232
Liu Xudun, 260
Li, Yuwen, 3, 6
Local protectionism, 14–15, 172–173, 380–381, 387–388, 395

Index

Local stakeholders, 18–19
Lubman, Stanley B., 5, 6, 71–72
Luo Gan, 121

Makkai, Toni, 62
Mao Zhaoxi, 260
Market economy, regulation of, 81–83, 91–92, 95
Matland, Richard E., 11–12, 126–127, 132
Media
  anecdotal evidence from, 40–42
  and cultural heritage protection, 237, 246, 253, 260–261
  and defamation laws, 58
  and environmental protection, 157, 159, 162, 163, 164, 165, 168, 176–177
  and implementation examinations, 150
Mertha, Andrew, 64
Michelson, Ethan, 27, 43
Mixed economy, 72n5, 88–92
Monistic tradition in international law, 75
Multidisciplinary studies, 4–6

National Legal Aid Center (NLAC), 190, 208, 210, 212–213, 221
National People's Congress (NPC), 2, 15, 38, 46, 55, 84, 148, 229, 256–258
Natural-resource loss, 368–369, 399
Natural-resource protection, 369–370, 394–395, 398
New Socialist Countryside policy, 255
New York Times, 40–41n14
NIP factories, 163–166
Norms
  defined, 77
  dimensions of, 77–79, 80, 179, 275
  legal, 73, 79–80, 179–181, 274–275
  See also Social norms
Norwegian Housemaid Law, 79

O'Brien, Kevin J., 5, 6
Organizational Law, 112–113
Otto, Jan-Michael, 3, 6, 73

Party discipline, 146, 303–304, 315
Peerenboom, Randall, 8, 10, 27, 33–64, 71–72, 79, 81, 91, 115n40, 135, 363
Pei, I. M., 249n60
People's congresses (PC), 143–144
  appraisal of performance, 151–152

citizen complaints to, 156, 159, 160
constraints on implementation, 180–181
and cultural heritage protection, 257
deputy-citizen interaction, 175–176
deputy initiated supervision, 155–156, 162–169, 176, 178–179
and environmental protection, 152–153, 156–170, 175–176, 177, 179, 180
implementation examinations, 149–151, 178
influence on implementing organs, 169–172, 173, 177
institutionalized supervision by, 148–153, 178
lawmaking powers of, 147–148
letters-and visits system, 153–155, 156, 160–161, 274
party discipline in, 146
plenary sessions of, 146–147
working committees of, 147
People's Congress Standing Committee Supervision Law, 149
People's Political Consultative Conference (PPCC), 258
Police, 109–110
Policy dilution, 12, 327, 355–359
Political rights, 54–55
Political system
  administrative regulation, 83–87
  bureaucratic conflicts in, 173–174
  citizens' trust in, 24–25
  decentralization of, 25
  and environmental enforcement, 381–382
  fragmented nature of, 13–14, 25
  See also Anticorruption law; Chinese Communist Party; People's congresses
Pollution. *See* Environmental protection
Procuratorate (prosecutors), 57, 107, 109, 113, 120
Public housing, privatization of, 343, 363
Public opinion surveys, 38
Putnam, Robert D., 23, 24–25, 26

Qingpu pollution case, 156–162, 177

Ramesh, M., 61
Raoul Wallenberg Institute, 37n7
Read, Benjamin L., 27
Reflexive law, 91
Regulatory theory, 60–63
Responsive law, 91

Sabatier, Paul, 17
Sapio, Flora, 7, 9n17, 14, 15, 19, 20, 21, 99, 297–328
Seeds Case, 119
Siu, Alice, 56n
Smuggling ring, 311, 321n62
Social change, 93–94
Social cooperation, 24–25
Social groups, 57–58
Social norms
  and housing reform, 335–336, 341–345
  and Internet regulation, 274–281, 290–293
  and law, 21–22, 71–72, 75, 76, 110
Social responsiveness, and compliance behavior, 378–379, 397
Societal development, phases of, 93–96
Soil erosion, 368–369
Song Jie, 319
Song Zhangwen, 319
Sousa Santos, Boaventura de, 95n45
State Environmental Protection Administration (SEPA), 173–174
Statistics, official, 34–35
Summers, Robert, 136–137
Supreme People's Court (SPC), 46, 52–53, 106, 113, 114, 122, 124
Supreme People's Court Work Reports, 45
Survey research, 9n15, 35–38
Svensson, Marina, 1–27, 9n17, 12, 14, 17, 19, 20, 25, 26, 80, 225–264
Sveri, Knut, 79

Tang Bingquan, 164
Tanner, Murray S., 64n59
Tarrow, Sidney, 26
Ten Year Program for Economic and Social Development, 11, 314
Teubner, Gunther, 69
Thelle, Hatla, 7, 14, 20, 79, 187–222
Time dimension of implementation, 71, 92–96, 98–99
Trust in legal system, 24–26, 27, 42–43, 110–111, 273

Tsai, Lily, 23–24n37, 26
Tyler, Tom, 132n86, 137n102

United Nations Education, Scientific, and Cultural Organization (UNESCO), 234
United Nations International Covenant on Civil and Political Rights, 75

van Rooij, Benjamin, 7, 11, 12, 15, 17, 19, 20, 21, 25, 26, 79, 92n38, 134n89, 148, 335, 367–400
Voluntary compliance, 38–39

Wan E'xiang, 117
Wang Baosen, 312, 316, 320
Wang, Qing Jie, 163, 165, 166
Wealth, 44, 53, 94
Wheeler, David, 174
Winter, Soren C., 126n73
Woo, Margaret Y. K., 43
Work report appraisals, 151–152
World Bank, 61n51, 235n22, 368, 395
World Heritage Sites, 230, 234
World Trade Organization, 55

Xia, Ming, 168n74
Xiao Lingnuo, 285
Xiao Yang, 121
Xin Chunying, 136n99

Yang, Dali, 44n23, 61
Yuanhua smuggling case, 311, 321n62
Yunzhi paper company, 376, 382
Yu Zhengsheng, 159

Zhang Jianjun, 26, 27
Zhang Wei, 284
Zhao Jingxin, 247–248
Zhao Peng, 279, 282
Zhu Jingwen, 99, 120, 122
Zhu Rongji, 239, 347
Zhu Senlin, 167
Zhu Suli, 209n27

CORNELL EAST ASIA SERIES

8 Cornelius C. Kubler, *Vocabulary and Notes to Ba Jin's Jia: An Aid for Reading the Novel*
16 Monica Bethe & Karen Brazell, *Nō as Performance: An Analysis of the Kuse Scene of Yamamba*
18 Royall Tyler, tr., *Granny Mountains: A Second Cycle of Nō Plays*
23 Knight Biggerstaff, *Nanking Letters, 1949*
28 Diane E. Perushek, ed., *The Griffis Collection of Japanese Books: An Annotated Bibliography*
37 J. Victor Koschmann, Ōiwa Keibō & Yamashita Shinji, eds., *International Perspectives on Yanagita Kunio and Japanese Folklore Studies*
38 James O'Brien, tr., *Murō Saisei: Three Works*
40 Kubo Sakae, *Land of Volcanic Ash: A Play in Two Parts*, revised edition, tr. David G. Goodman
44 Susan Orpett Long, *Family Change and the Life Course in Japan*
48 Helen Craig McCullough, *Bungo Manual: Selected Reference Materials for Students of Classical Japanese*
49 Susan Blakeley Klein, *Ankoku Butō: The Premodern and Postmodern Influences on the Dance of Utter Darkness*
50 Karen Brazell, ed., *Twelve Plays of the Noh and Kyōgen Theaters*
51 David G. Goodman, ed., *Five Plays by Kishida Kunio*
52 Shirō Hara, *Ode to Stone*, tr. James Morita
53 Peter J. Katzenstein & Yutaka Tsujinaka, *Defending the Japanese State: Structures, Norms and the Political Responses to Terrorism and Violent Social Protest in the 1970s and 1980s*
54 Su Xiaokang & Wang Luxiang, *Deathsong of the River: A Reader's Guide to the Chinese TV Series* Heshang, trs. Richard Bodman & Pin P. Wan
55 Jingyuan Zhang, *Psychoanalysis in China: Literary Transformations, 1919-1949*
56 Jane Kate Leonard & John R. Watt, eds., *To Achieve Security and Wealth: The Qing Imperial State and the Economy, 1644-1911*
57 Andrew F. Jones, *Like a Knife: Ideology and Genre in Contemporary Chinese Popular Music*
58 Peter J. Katzenstein & Nobuo Okawara, *Japan's National Security: Structures, Norms and Policy Responses in a Changing World*
59 Carsten Holz, *The Role of Central Banking in China's Economic Reforms*
60 Chifumi Shimazaki, *Warrior Ghost Plays from the Japanese Noh Theater: Parallel Translations with Running Commentary*
61 Emily Groszos Ooms, *Women and Millenarian Protest in Meiji Japan: Deguchi Nao and Ōmotokyō*
62 Carolyn Anne Morley, *Transformation, Miracles, and Mischief: The Mountain Priest Plays of Kyōgen*
63 David R. McCann & Hyunjae Yee Sallee, tr., *Selected Poems of Kim Namjo*, afterword by Kim Yunsik
64 Hua Qingzhao, *From Yalta to Panmunjom: Truman's Diplomacy and the Four Powers, 1945-1953*
65 Margaret Benton Fukasawa, *Kitahara Hakushū: His Life and Poetry*
66 Kam Louie, ed., *Strange Tales from Strange Lands: Stories by Zheng Wanlong*, with introduction
67 Wang Wen-hsing, *Backed Against the Sea*, tr. Edward Gunn
69 Brian Myers, *Han Sōrya and North Korean Literature: The Failure of Socialist Realism in the DPRK*
70 Thomas P. Lyons & Victor Nee, eds., *The Economic Transformation of South China: Reform and Development in the Post-Mao Era*
71 David G. Goodman, tr., *After Apocalypse: Four Japanese Plays of Hiroshima and Nagasaki*
72 Thomas Lyons, *Poverty and Growth in a South China County: Anxi, Fujian, 1949-1992*
74 Martyn Atkins, *Informal Empire in Crisis: British Diplomacy and the Chinese Customs Succession, 1927-1929*
76 Chifumi Shimazaki, *Restless Spirits from Japanese Noh Plays of the Fourth Group: Parallel Translations with Running Commentary*
77 Brother Anthony of Taizé & Young-Moo Kim, trs., *Back to Heaven: Selected Poems of Ch'ŏn Sang Pyŏng*
78 Kevin O'Rourke, tr., *Singing Like a Cricket, Hooting Like an Owl: Selected Poems by Yi Kyu-bo*
79 Irit Averbuch, *The Gods Come Dancing: A Study of the Japanese Ritual Dance of Yamabushi Kagura*
80 Mark Peterson, *Korean Adoption and Inheritance: Case Studies in the Creation of a Classic Confucian Society*
81 Yenna Wu, tr., *The Lioness Roars: Shrew Stories from Late Imperial China*
82 Thomas Lyons, *The Economic Geography of Fujian: A Sourcebook*, Vol. 1
83 Pak Wan-so, *The Naked Tree*, tr. Yu Young-nan
84 C.T. Hsia, *The Classic Chinese Novel: A Critical Introduction*
85 Cho Chong-Rae, *Playing With Fire*, tr. Chun Kyung-Ja
86 Hayashi Fumiko, *I Saw a Pale Horse and Selections from Diary of a Vagabond*, tr. Janice Brown
87 Motoori Norinaga, *Kojiki-den, Book 1*, tr. Ann Wehmeyer
88 Chang Soo Ko, tr., *Sending the Ship Out to the Stars: Poems of Park Je-chun*
89 Thomas Lyons, *The Economic Geography of Fujian: A Sourcebook*, Vol. 2
90 Brother Anthony of Taizé, tr., *Midang: Early Lyrics of So Chong-Ju*
92 Janice Matsumura, *More Than a Momentary Nightmare: The Yokohama Incident and Wartime Japan*
93 Kim Jong-Gil tr., *The Snow Falling on Chagall's Village: Selected Poems of Kim Ch'un-Su*
94 Wolhee Choe & Peter Fusco, trs., *Day-Shine: Poetry by Hyon-jong Chong*
95 Chifumi Shimazaki, *Troubled Souls from Japanese Noh Plays of the Fourth Group*
96 Hagiwara Sakutarō, *Principles of Poetry (Shi no Genri)*, tr. Chester Wang
97 Mae J. Smethurst, *Dramatic Representations of Filial Piety: Five Noh in Translation*
98 Ross King, ed., *Description and Explanation in Korean Linguistics*
99 William Wilson, *Hōgen Monogatari: Tale of the Disorder in Hōgen*
100 Yasushi Yamanouchi, J. Victor Koschmann and Ryūichi Narita, eds., *Total War and 'Modernization'*

103 Sherman Cochran, ed., *Inventing Nanjing Road: Commercial Culture in Shanghai, 1900–1945*
104 Harold M. Tanner, *Strike Hard! Anti-Crime Campaigns and Chinese Criminal Justice, 1979–1985*
105 Brother Anthony of Taizé & Young-Moo Kim, trs., *Farmers' Dance: Poems by Shin Kyŏng-nim*
106 Susan Orpett Long, ed., *Lives in Motion: Composing Circles of Self and Community in Japan*
107 Peter J. Katzenstein, Natasha Hamilton-Hart, Kozo Kato, & Ming Yue, *Asian Regionalism*
108 Kenneth Alan Grossberg, *Japan's Renaissance: The Politics of the Muromachi Bakufu*
109 John W. Hall & Toyoda Takeshi, eds., *Japan in the Muromachi Age*
110 Kim Su-Young, Shin Kyong-Nim & Lee Si-Young: *Variations: Three Korean Poets*; trs. Brother Anthony of Taizé & Young Moo Kim
111 Samuel Leiter, *Frozen Moments: Writings on Kabuki, 1966–2001*
112 Pilwun Shih Wang & Sarah Wang, *Early One Spring: A Learning Guide to Accompany the Film Video* February
113 Thomas Conlan, *In Little Need of Divine Intervention: Scrolls of the Mongol Invasions of Japan*
114 Jane Kate Leonard & Robert Antony, eds., *Dragons, Tigers, and Dogs: Qing Crisis Management and the Boundaries of State Power in Late Imperial China*
115 Shu-ning Sciban & Fred Edwards, eds., *Dragonflies: Fiction by Chinese Women in the Twentieth Century*
116 David G. Goodman, ed., *The Return of the Gods: Japanese Drama and Culture in the 1960s*
117 Yang Hi Choe-Wall, *Vision of a Phoenix: The Poems of Hŏ Nansŏrhŏn*
118 Mae J. Smethurst & Christina Laffin, eds., *The Noh Ominameshi: A Flower Viewed from Many Directions*
119 Joseph A. Murphy, *Metaphorical Circuit: Negotiations Between Literature and Science in Twentieth-Century Japan*
120 Richard F. Calichman, *Takeuchi Yoshimi: Displacing the West*
121 Fan Pen Li Chen, *Visions for the Masses: Chinese Shadow Plays from Shaanxi and Shanxi*
122 S. Yumiko Hulvey, *Sacred Rites in Moonlight: Ben no Naishi Nikki*
123 Tetsuo Najita & J. Victor Koschmann, *Conflict in Modern Japanese History: The Neglected Tradition*
124 Naoki Sakai, Brett de Bary & Iyotani Toshio, eds., *Deconstructing Nationality*
125 Judith N. Rabinovitch & Timothy R. Bradstock, *Dance of the Butterflies: Chinese Poetry from the Japanese Court Tradition*
126 Yang Gui-ja, *Contradictions*, trs. Stephen Epstein and Kim Mi-Young
127 Ann Sung-hi Lee, *Yi Kwang-su and Modern Korean Literature:* Mujŏng
128 Pang Kie-chung & Michael D. Shin, eds., *Landlords, Peasants, & Intellectuals in Modern Korea*
129 Joan R. Piggott, ed., *Capital and Countryside in Japan, 300–1180: Japanese Historians Interpreted in English*
130 Kyoko Selden & Jolisa Gracewood, eds., *Annotated Japanese Literary Gems: Stories by Tawada Yōko, Nakagami Kenji, and Hayashi Kyōko* (Vol. 1)
131 Michael G. Murdock, *Disarming the Allies of Imperialism: The State, Agitation, and Manipulation during China's Nationalist Revolution, 1922–1929*
132 Noel J. Pinnington, *Traces in the Way: Michi and the Writings of Komparu Zenchiku*
133 Charlotte von Verschuer, *Across the Perilous Sea: Japanese Trade with China and Korea from the Seventh to the Sixteenth Centuries*, Kristen Lee Hunter, tr.
134 John Timothy Wixted, *A Handbook to Classical Japanese*
135 Kyoko Selden & Jolisa Gracewood, with Lili Selden, eds., *Annotated Japanese Literary Gems: Stories by Natsume Sōseki, Tomioka Taeko, and Inoue Yasushi* (Vol. 2)
136 Yi Tae-Jin, *The Dynamics of Confucianism and Modernization in Korean History*
137 Jennifer Rudolph, *Negotiated Power in Late Imperial China: The Zongli Yamen and the Politics of Reform*
138 Thomas D. Loooser, *Visioning Eternity: Aesthetics, Politics, and History in the Early Modern Noh Theater*
139 Gustav Heldt, *The Pursuit of Harmony: Poetry and Power in Late Heian Japan*
140 Joan R. Piggott & Yoshida Sanae, *Teishinkōki: The Year 939 in the Journal of Regent Fujiwara no Tadahira*
141 Robert Bagley, *Max Loehr and the Study of Chinese Bronzes: Style and Classification in the History of Art*
142 Edwin A. Cranston, *The Secret Island and the Enticing Flame: Worlds of Memory, Discovery, and Loss in Japanese Poetry*
143 Hugh de Ferranti, *The Last Biwa Singer: A Blind Musician in History, Imagination and Performance*
144 Roger Des Forges, Gao Minglu, Liu Chiao-mei, Haun Saussy, with Thomas Burkman, eds., *Chinese Walls in Time and Space: A Multidisciplinary Perspective*
145 George Sidney & Hye-jin Juhn Sidney, trs., *I Heard Life Calling Me: Poems of Yi Sŏng-bok*
146 Sherman Cochran & Paul G. Pickowicz, eds., *China on the Margins*
147 Wang Lingzhen & Mary Ann O'Donnell, trs., *Years of Sadness: Autobiographical Writings of Wang Anyi*
148 John Holstein, trans. *A Moment's Grace: Stories from Korea in Transition*
149 Sunyoung Park with Jefferson J.A. Gatrall, *On the Eve of the Uprising and Other Stories from Colonial Korea*
150 Brother Anthony of Taizé & Lee Hyung-Jin, *Walking on a Washing Line: Poems of Kim Seung-Hee*
151 Matthew Fraleigh, *New Chronicles of Yanagibashi and Diary of A Journey to the West: Narushima Ryūhoku Reports from Home and Abroad*
152 Pei Huang, *Reorienting the Manchus: A Study of Sinicization, 1583–1795*
153 Karen Gernant & Chen Zeping, trs., *White Poppies and Other Stories by Zhang Kangkang*
154 Mattias Burell & Marina Svensson, eds., *Making Law Work: Chinese Laws in Context*

DVD Monica Bethe & Karen Brazell: "Yamanba: The Old Woman of the Mountains" to accompany CEAS volume no. 16 *Noh As Performance*

CORNELL
East Asia Series

Order online at www.einaudi.cornell.edu/eastasia/publications

www.ingramcontent.com/pod-product-compliance
Lightning Source LLC
Chambersburg PA
CBHW022007300426
44117CB00005B/65